Basic Quantitative Research Methods for Urban Planners

In most planning practice and research, planners work with quantitative data. By summarizing, analyzing, and presenting data, planners create stories and narratives that explain various planning issues. Particularly, in the era of big data and data mining, there is a stronger demand in planning practice and research to increase capacity for data-driven storytelling.

Basic Quantitative Research Methods for Urban Planners provides readers with comprehensive knowledge and hands-on techniques for a variety of quantitative research studies, from descriptive statistics to commonly used inferential statistics. It covers statistical methods from chi-square through logistic regression and also quasi-experimental studies. At the same time, the book provides fundamental knowledge about research in general, such as planning data sources and uses, conceptual frameworks, and technical writing. The book presents relatively complex material in the simplest and clearest way possible, and through the use of real world planning examples, makes the theoretical and abstract content of each chapter as tangible as possible.

It will be invaluable to students and novice researchers from planning programs, intermediate researchers who want to branch out methodologically, practicing planners who need to conduct basic analyses with planning data, and anyone who consumes the research of others and needs to judge its validity and reliability.

Reid Ewing, Ph.D., is Distinguished Professor of City and Metropolitan Planning at the University of Utah, associate editor of the *Journal of the American Planning Association* and *Cities*, and columnist for *Planning* magazine, writing the column *Research You Can Use*. He directs the Metropolitan Research Center at the University of Utah. He holds master's degrees in Engineering and City Planning from Harvard University and a Ph.D. in Urban Planning and Transportation Systems from the Massachusetts Institute of Technology. A recent citation analysis found that Ewing, with 24,000 citations, is the 6th most highly cited among 1,100 planning academic planners in North America.

Keunhyun Park, Ph.D., is an Assistant Professor in the Department of Landscape Architecture and Environmental Planning at Utah State University. He holds master's degrees in Landscape Architecture from Seoul National University and a Ph.D. in Metropolitan Planning, Policy, Design from the University of Utah. His research interests include technology-driven behavioral research (e.g., drone, VR/AR, sensor, etc.), behavioral outcomes of smart growth, and active living.

APA Planning Essentials

APA Planning Essentials books provide introductory background information aligned to planning curricula, with textbooks meant for graduate students to be used in urban planning courses, and continuing education purposes by professional planners.

Titles in the Series

Basic Quantitative Research Methods for Urban Planners
Edited by Reid Ewing and Keunhyun Park

Basic Quantitative Research Methods for Urban Planners

Edited by
Reid Ewing and Keunhyun Park

First published 2020
by Routledge
52 Vanderbilt Avenue, New York, NY 10017

and by Routledge
2 Park Square, Milton Park, Abingdon, Oxon, OX14 4RN

Routledge is an imprint of the Taylor & Francis Group, an informa business

© 2020 selection and editorial matter, Reid Ewing and Keunhyun Park; individual chapters, the contributors

The right of Reid Ewing and Keunhyun Park to be identified as the authors of the editorial material, and of the authors for their individual chapters, has been asserted in accordance with sections 77 and 78 of the Copyright, Designs and Patents Act 1988.

All rights reserved. No part of this book may be reprinted or reproduced or utilised in any form or by any electronic, mechanical, or other means, now known or hereafter invented, including photocopying and recording, or in any information storage or retrieval system, without permission in writing from the publishers.

Trademark notice: Product or corporate names may be trademarks or registered trademarks, and are used only for identification and explanation without intent to infringe.

Library of Congress Cataloging-in-Publication Data
Names: Ewing, Reid H., editor. | Park, Keunhyun, editor.
Title: Basic quantitative research methods for urban planners /
   edited by Reid Ewing and Keunhyun Park.
Identifiers: LCCN 2019043708 (print) | LCCN 2019043709 (ebook) |
   ISBN 9780367343255 (hbk) | ISBN 9780367343248 (pbk) |
   ISBN 9780429325021 (ebk)
Subjects: LCSH: City planning. | Quantitative research—Methodology.
Classification: LCC HT166 .B386535 2020 (print) | LCC HT166 (ebook) |
   DDC 307.1/16—dc23
LC record available at https://lccn.loc.gov/2019043708
LC ebook record available at https://lccn.loc.gov/2019043709

ISBN: 978-0-367-34325-5 (hbk)
ISBN: 978-0-367-34324-8 (pbk)
ISBN: 978-0-429-32502-1 (ebk)

Typeset in Baskerville
by Apex CoVantage, LLC
Visit the eResources: www.routledge.com/9780367343248

Contents

List of Figures		vii
List of Tables		xii

1 Introduction   1
KEUNHYUN PARK AND REID EWING

2 Technical Writing   18
ROBIN ROTHFEDER AND REID EWING

3 Types of Research   46
ROBERT A. YOUNG AND REID EWING

4 Planning Data and Analysis   61
THOMAS W. SANCHEZ, SADEGH SABOURI, KEUNHYUN PARK, AND JUNSIK KIM

5 Conceptual Frameworks   76
KEUNHYUN PARK, JAMES B. GRACE, AND REID EWING

6 Validity and Reliability   88
CARL DUKE, SHIMA HAMIDI, AND REID EWING

7 Descriptive Statistics and Visualizing Data   107
DONG-AH CHOI, PRATITI TAGORE, FARIBA SIDDIQ, KEUNHYUN PARK,
AND REID EWING

8 Chi-Square   133
CARL DUKE, KEUNHYUN PARK, AND REID EWING

9 Correlation   150
GUANG TIAN, ANUSHA MUSUNURU, AND REID EWING

10 Difference of Means Tests (*T*-Tests)   174
DAVID PROFFITT

vi *Contents*

11 Analysis of Variance (ANOVA) 197
PHILIP STOKER, GUANG TIAN, AND JA YOUNG KIM

12 Linear Regression 220
KEUNHYUN PARK, ROBIN ROTHFEDER, SUSAN PETHERAM, FLORENCE BUAKU, REID EWING, AND WILLIAM H. GREENE

13 Logistic Regression 270
SADEGH SABOURI, AMIR HAJRASOULIHA, YU SONG, AND WILLIAM H. GREENE

14 Quasi-Experimental Research 305
KEUNHYUN PARK, KATHERINE KITTRELL, AND REID EWING

List of Contributors 319
Index 321

Figures

1.1	The Number of Scholarly Articles That Use Each Software Package in 2018	15
2.0	*Research You Can Use*	25
2.1	Popular Graphic of Induced Demand and Induced Investment	34
2.2	Technical Graphic of Induced Demand and Induced Investment	34
2.3	Contrasting Floor Plans	41
2.4	Average Annual Percent of Persons Selling Homes in Each Age Group	42
3.1	Short-Term Response to Added Highway Capacity	49
3.2	Long-Term Response to Added Highway Capacity	49
3.3	Qualitative Research Family Tree	53
3.4	Three Ways of Mixing Quantitative and Qualitative Data	56
4.1	Rational Planning Model	62
4.2	Flat File and Relational Database Structure	64
4.3	Spatial Feature Types	65
4.4	Census Hierarchy at the Local Scale	68
5.1	The Simple Conceptual Framework of Garrick (2005)	77
5.2	Adding Confounders	77
5.3	Reversing Causality	78
5.4	A Complex Conceptual Framework	78
5.5	Examples of Conceptual Frameworks	81
5.6	Three Types of the Third Variables: Mediator, Confounder, and Moderator	82
5.7	A Conceptual Framework Example Using Mediators and Moderators	83
5.8	Model of Community Attractiveness	84
5.9	A Conceptual Framework Consisting of Both Abstract Constructs and Operational Variables	85
6.1	Precision Versus Accuracy	89
6.2	High-Rated Video Clip in All Five Dimensions	90
6.3	Low-Rated Video Clip in All Five Dimensions	90
6.4	Use of Google Street View, Bing, and Everyscape Imagery (from top to bottom) to Establish Equivalency Reliability (East 19th Street, New York, NY)	93
6.5	Endless Medium Density of Los Angeles County	96
6.6	Centered Development of Arlington County, Virginia	96
6.7	Most Sprawling County According to the Six-Variable Index (Jackson County, Kansas)	98

viii *Figures*

6.8	Most Sprawling County According to the Four-Factor Index (Oglethorpe County, Georgia)	99
6.9	Security Index Criteria	102
6.10	Percentage Difference in Vehicle Emissions in 2050 Under a Compact Growth Scenario Compared to a Business as Usual Scenario	104
7.1	Pie Chart Example: Land Use and Land Cover Types	116
7.2	Bar Graph Example: MPO Designation Over Time	116
7.3	Line Graph Example: Per Capita GDP and VMT in the United States	117
7.4	Histogram Example: Inaccuracy of Cost Estimates in Transportation Projects	117
7.5	Find Frequency Window	118
7.6	Frequency Window	119
7.7	Frequencies Window	120
7.8	Various Measures of Descriptive Statistics From "Frequencies: Statistics" Window	121
7.9	Cross Tabulation Window	122
7.10	Cell Display Option in Cross Tabulation Window	123
7.11	Available Graph Types in SPSS	124
7.12	Histogram Window in SPSS	125
7.13	A Histogram of Household Size	126
7.14	Reading SPSS Data and Making a Frequency Table: R Script and Outputs	127
7.15	Calculating Central Tendency and Dispersion: R Script and Outputs	128
7.16	A Cross Tabulation and a Histogram: R Script and Outputs	129
7.17	Motives for Nature and Emotions Experienced	130
8.0	Chi-Square	133
8.1	Chi-Square Distributions for Different Degrees of Freedom	138
8.2	Accessing Crosstabs in SPSS	140
8.3	Crosstabs Selection Menu	141
8.4	Crosstabs Statistics Selection Menu	142
8.5	Crosstabs Cell Display Menu	143
8.6	Reading SPSS Data and Running a Chi-Square Test: R Script and Outputs	145
8.7	Symmetric Measures for the Chi-Square Test: R Script and Outputs	146
9.1	Scatterplots and Pearson Correlation Coefficients	153
9.2	Rater 2 Always Rates the Same as Rater 1	155
9.3	Rater 2 Always Rates 4 Points Higher Than Rater 1	155
9.4	Rater 2 Always Rates 1.5 Times Higher Than Rater 1	156
9.5	Find "Bivariate" Menu in "Correlate"	157
9.6	Bivariate Correlation Window	158
9.7	Partial Correlation Window	160
9.8	Options in Partial Correlation	161
9.9	Bivariate Correlations Window: Spearman Correlation	162
9.10	ICC Main Window	164
9.11	Statistics Window for ICC	164
9.12	Reading SPSS Data and Calculating Pearson Correlation Coefficient: R Script and Outputs	166

Figures ix

9.13 Partial Correlation Coefficient and Spearman Correlation
Coefficient: R Script and Outputs   167
9.14 Intraclass Correlation Coefficient and Cronbach's Alpha: R Script
and Outputs   168
9.15 Spectral-Mixture-Analysis Derived Vegetation Fractional Images for
(a) Montreal, (b) Toronto, and (c) Vancouver   169
10.0 *T*-Test   174
10.1 Two Frequency Distributions: Is the Difference Between Mean
Scores in Two Sample Populations Significant or Due to Chance?   176
10.2 The Means of Individual Samples May Differ From the Overall
Population Mean and From One Another, but the Distribution of
Means From Multiple Samples Tends to Approach a Normal
Distribution   178
10.3 t Distributions and Critical Values for Different Degrees of Freedom   179
10.4 "Select Cases" Under "Data" Menu   182
10.5 "Select cases: If" Window   183
10.6 Select Cases Window   184
10.7 Find Histogram Window From Main Menu   185
10.8 Histogram Window   186
10.9 Histograms of Household VMT by Region (in Logarithm Format)   187
10.10 Find Independent Samples *t*-Test Window From Main Menu   187
10.11 Independent Samples *t*-Test Window   188
10.12 Define Groups Window   188
10.13 The Independent Samples *t*-Test Window Is Ready to Run   189
10.14 Reading SPSS Data, Selecting Two Regions, and Drawing
Histograms: R Script and Outputs   191
10.15 One-Tail and Two-Tail *t*-tests: R Script and Outputs   192
11.0 ANOVA   197
11.1 The F-Distribution for Different Degrees of Freedom   199
11.2 Find Boxplot From the Main Menu   201
11.3 Choose a Plot Type in Boxplot Window   202
11.4 Boxplot Window   203
11.5 The Result of Boxplot   204
11.6 Delete a Case by Right-Clicking the Row ID   204
11.7 Find Histogram From the Main Menu   205
11.8 Histogram Window   206
11.9 The Histogram of *lntpm* (in Logarithm Format)   206
11.10 Find One-Way ANOVA Test From the Main Menu   207
11.11 One-Way ANOVA Window   207
11.12 Post Hoc Window   208
11.13 Option Window   208
11.14 The Means Plots of *lntpm* Variable for Four Region   212
11.15 Reading SPSS Data and Drawing a Box Plot: R Script and Outputs   213
11.16 Detecting and Removing Outliers and Drawing a Histogram:
R Script and Outputs   214
11.17 ANOVA Test and Post-Hoc Test: R Script and Outputs   215
11.18 Land Use Type (top) and Thermal Imaging (bottom) of the
City of Toronto   216

x *Figures*

11.19	Street Networks and Land Use Distributions	218
12.0	Linear Regression	220
12.1	A Simple Regression Line	224
12.2	A Regression Line Between Street Width and Traffic Speed	227
12.3	Probability Distribution Curves for F-Statistic With Different Degrees of Freedom	229
12.4	Probability Distribution Curves for t-Statistic With Different Degrees of Freedom	230
12.5	A Best-Fit Plane of a Regression With Two Independent Variables	232
12.6	Finding "Scatter/Dot" Menu	236
12.7	"Scatter/Dot" Window	236
12.8	"Simple Scatterplot" Window	237
12.9	Scatter Plot Between Total Lane Miles and Total VMT	238
12.10	Scatter Plot Between Total VMT and Total Lane Miles	239
12.11	Scatter Plot Between Population Size and Total VMT	239
12.12	Linear Regression Menu	240
12.13	Adding Two Variables in the Linear Regression Window	241
12.14	Regression Model Summary of VMT Per Capita Regressed on Lane Miles per 1000 Population	242
12.15	Adding More Independent Variables in the Linear Regression Window	243
12.16	Regression Model Summary With Four Additional Independent Variables	244
12.17	Efficiency and Bias in Sample Distributions	245
12.18	Regression Model Summary With an Additional Income Variable	246
12.19	Regression Model Summary After Dropping the Population Size and Transit Passenger Mile Variables	247
12.20	Regression Model Summary After Replacing *popden* With *compact* Variable	248
12.21	Simple Scatterplot Window	249
12.22	Scatterplot Between Lane Miles per 1000 Population and VMT Per Capita	250
12.23	Scatterplot Between Population in 1000s and VMT Per Capita	251
12.24	Finding "Compute Variable" Option	252
12.25	Log-Transformation of VMT Per Capita Variable	253
12.26	Scatterplot Between Log-Transformed Population Size and Log-Transformed VMT Per Capita	254
12.27	Regression Model Summary With Log-Transformed Variables	255
12.28	Checking "Collinearity diagnostics" in "Linear Regression: Statistics" Window	256
12.29	Regression Model Summary With Collinearity Statistics	257
12.30	"Durbin-Watson" Test Option for Autocorrelation Diagnostics	258
12.31	Model Summary Table With Durbin-Watson Autocorrelation Diagnostics	259
12.32	Adding a Scatterplot of Residuals for Heteroscedasticity Diagnostics	259
12.33	Two Graphs of Model Residuals for Heteroscedasticity Diagnostics	260
12.34	Reading SPSS Data and Drawing a Scatterplot: R Script and Outputs	262
12.35	Running a Linear Regression: R Script and Outputs	263
12.36	Durbin-Watson Test and Residual Plots: R Script and Outputs	264

Figures xi

12.37	Regression Results	266
13.0	Logistic Regression	270
13.1	Shape of Logistic Probability Function (Depends on b_0 and b_1)	271
13.2	Linear Probability Versus Logistic Model	272
13.3	Frequency Distribution of *lnvmt* Variable (Excluding Zero Values of VMT)	274
13.4	Frequency Distribution of *anyvmt* Variable	275
13.5	Logistic Regression Window in SPSS-Dependent Variable Is *anyvmt*	279
13.6	Saving Predicted Values, Residuals, and Influence	280
13.7	Classification Table—Block 0	280
13.8	Classification Table—Block 1	281
13.9	Model Summary Statistics	281
13.10	Logistic Regression Model Result	282
13.11	Select Cases From Top Menu	283
13.12	Select Cases With If Condition	284
13.13	Multinomial Logistic Regression Menu	285
13.14	Multinomial Logistic Regression Window	286
13.15	Set the First Category as a Reference Category	287
13.16	Multinomial Logistic Regression: Statistics Window	288
13.17	Case Processing Summary Table	289
13.18	Model Fitting Information	289
13.19	Model Fit Outputs	290
13.20	Parameter Estimates Table	290
13.21	Classification Table From the Multinomial Logistic Regression	291
13.22	Importing the Household Dataset to Stata	292
13.23	Converting String Variables to Numeric Variables	293
13.24	Multinomial Logit Regression Output in Stata	294
13.25	Multinomial Logit Regression Output in Stata (Showing Odds Ratio)	295
13.26	Reading SPSS Data and Running a Logistic Regression: R Script and Outputs	296
13.27	Running a Multinomial Logistic Regression: R Script and Outputs	297
13.28	Gross Housing Density and Commuter Mode Share Within the Urban Growth Boundary, 1990–2000	298
13.29	Mode Choice by Residence Block Group (Origin)	299
13.30	Mode Choice by Workplace Tract (Destination)	300
13.31	Multinomial Logistic Regression Models for Mobility Disability Category 2 (Some Disability), 2001–2003	301
13.32	Multinomial Logistic Regression Models for Mobility Disability Category 3 (Severe Disability), 2001–2003	302
14.1	Experiments, Quasi-Experiments, and Non-Experiments	307
14.2	The Relationship Between Observed Effect and Treatment Effect	311
14.3	Program for Neighborhood With 15 Percent or Less Homeownership Rate; No Impacts (Above) and Impacts (Below)	313
14.4	Transit Corridor Versus Three Comparative Highway Corridors	314
14.5	Propensity Score Matched BID and Non-BID Tracts	316

Tables

1.1	Comparison of Research Method Books in Urban Planning Field	3
1.2	Variables in UZA Dataset (FHWA Urbanized Areas in 2010)	10
1.3	Variables in Household Database (Based on Household Travel Surveys From Different Years)	13
1.4	Frequency of Responses by Instructors of Planning Courses to the Question "Which Software Package(s) Do You Utilize in the Methods Course(s) You Teach?" ($n = 44$)	15
7.1a	Quantitative Study With Descriptive Statistics Followed by Inferential Statistics	109
7.1b	Relationship Between Delivered Residential Energy Use in the United States, House Size and Type, and Other Control Variables (With Coefficients, t-Ratios, and Significance Levels)	110
7.2	Data Matrix Example: MSA Characteristics	114
7.3	Frequency Table Example: Educational Backgrounds of Principals in Maker Firms	115
7.4	The Output Table of Frequency	119
7.5	The Output Table of Descriptive Statistics	121
7.6	Statistics Option in Cross Tabulation Window	123
7.7	Descriptive Statistics on Water Use in Phoenix	130
8.1	Contingency Table	136
8.2	Observed Versus Expected Counts	137
8.3	A Contingency Table of Chi-Square About Housing Types and Any Walk Trip	143
8.4	Chi-Square Test Significance About Housing Types and Any Walk Trip	144
8.5	Symmetric Measures for the Chi-Square Test	144
8.6	Chi-Square Analyses of Actions Taken on Sustainability	147
8.7	Perceived Need for Growth Controls in Florida, 1985 and 2001	148
9.1	Pearson Correlation Coefficients Results	159
9.2	Partial Correlation Coefficients	161
9.3	Spearman's Correlation Coefficients Result	163
9.4a	Reliability Statistics and ICC Values	165
9.4b	Intraclass Correlation Coefficient	165
9.5	Inter-Rater Reliability for Rating of Urban Design Qualities	170
9.6	Performance of Urban Design Qualities Relative to Selection Criteria	171
10.1	The Summary Statistics of t-Test	189

10.2	The Result of Independent Samples *t*-test	190
10.3	Difference of Means Test Results for Westside Max Corridor Versus Highway Corridor After LRT Expansion (2011)	194
11.1	The Result of One-Way ANOVA (1)	209
11.2	The Result of One-Way ANOVA (2)	209
11.3	The Result of Bonferroni and Tamhane Post-Hoc Test	211
12.1	Hypothetical Data of Street Width and Traffic Speed	225
12.2	Calculating Deviance	226
12.3	Calculating Error Terms	231
12.4	Hypothetical Data of Street Width, Average Setback, and Traffic Speed	233
12.5	OLS Regression Results: The Relationship Between the Arts and Neighborhood Change	265
13.1	Transformation of Random Numbers Between Probability, Odds, and Log Odds	276

1 Introduction

Keunhyun Park and Reid Ewing

Overview

The distinction between quantitative and qualitative methods primarily lies in the type of data—simply described, numbers versus words. Reid Ewing, the chief editor of this book, has written in *Planning* magazine on the relative strengths of quantitative versus qualitative research. In October 2007, he took the side of qualitative research when the topic or data are inherently subjective. In January 2009, using the example of the transfer of development rights, he took the opposite side, arguing for quantitative research when the variables at play are easily measured. Then, in February 2013, another column addressed three different ways that quantitative and qualitative data can be combined in a mixed-method design.

While acknowledging that it is a spectrum rather than a dichotomy that classifies a variety of research methods, this book series primarily focuses on quantitative methods, from descriptive statistics to inferential statistics, to spatial econometrics, and to meta-analysis and meta-regression. At the same time, this basic quantitative research methods book, and its companion advanced research methods book, provide some fundamental knowledge about research in general, such as planning data sources and uses, research topics and journals in the planning field, conceptual frameworks, and technical writing.

As Tracy (2013, p. 36) notes, "quantitative methods use measurement and statistics to transform empirical data into numbers and to develop mathematical models that quantify behavior." Many statistical analysis methods emerged as researchers sought more precise mechanisms to establish valid models. The objective of this book is to provide readers with comprehensive knowledge and hands-on techniques for a variety of quantitative research studies. The related objective is to present relatively complex material in the simplest and clearest way possible, and, through the use of planning examples, to make the theoretical and abstract content of each chapter as tangible as possible.

Quantitative Methods in Planning

Target readers include students and novice researchers from planning programs, intermediate researchers who want to branch out methodologically, practicing planners who need to conduct basic analyses with planning data, and anyone who consumes the research of others and needs to judge its validity and reliability. We dare to hope that this book, due to its ease of understanding and breadth of material, will

2 Keunhyun Park and Reid Ewing

be used not only by planners but also by those in fields related to planning, such as geography and public policy.

At present, there is a lack of textbooks on quantitative *planning* research methods. This might be because planning research has its roots in other disciplines. Quantitative research in planning emerges from methodologies used in medicine, public health, business, education, and other disciplines. While this condition requires (and enables) multidisciplinary learning, novice researchers need a core book of diverse methods more directly addressing how the methods are applied to planning issues.

Quantitative research methods are essential elements in planning program curricula. In the United States and Canada, there are 91 accredited planning programs (75 master's and 16 bachelor's) at 79 universities, as of December 2019 (www.planning-accreditationboard.org). Among them, about 20 schools have doctoral programs. The Planning Accreditation Board (PAB), founded in 1984, requires planning programs to teach a set of planning skills to be accredited. Relevant to the current book, those necessary skills include "Research: tools for assembling and analyzing ideas and information from prior practice and scholarship, and from primary and secondary sources" and "Quantitative and Qualitative Methods: data collection, analysis and modeling tools for forecasting, policy analysis, and design of projects and plans" (p. 10), which overlap with the main objectives of this book.

An early study (Contant & Forkenbrock, 1986) found evidence of growth in the demand for quantitative methods and a congruence between the supply and demand for such knowledge. In a more recent study, Dawkins (2016) finds that since the mid-1980s, the supply of and demand for quantitative analysis skills have been stable. While communication skills are usually seen as highly important by both planning practitioners and educators (Greenlee, Edwards, & Anthony, 2015), years of experience can improve those kinds of skills (Guzzetta & Bollens, 2003). On the other hand, technical and quantitative skills do not vary substantially with a planner's years of experience, pointing out the importance of school education in the development of those skills (Guzzetta & Bollens, 2003).

A 2011 study of top planning programs found that 29 out of 30 master's programs included Methods: Statistics among their core curricula (Edwards & Bates, 2011). These courses focus mainly on inferential statistics. There is no standard text.

What's Different?

Our survey of 44 responding programs produced a list of 128 different texts used by professors of planning methods courses. No text is used in more than four courses. Among texts used in three or more courses, only two—Klosterman's *Community Analysis and Planning Techniques* and Dandekar's *The Planner's Use of Information*—are specific to planning. Dandekar's volume touches only briefly on analytical methods, and Klosterman's is now nearly 30 years old. Though *Community Analysis and Planning Techniques* was well received and has been relatively popular, important developments in quantitative analysis, such as meta-regression analysis, are not accounted for in Klosterman's work.

Two of the oldest books were written by Dickey and Watts (1978) and Willemain (1980). Both are textbooks of statistical methods for planning students who have no prior knowledge of statistics. Many advanced methods such as multilevel modeling and spatial econometrics were unknown when these books were written, at least in the planning field (see Table 1.1).

Table 1.1 Comparison of Research Method Books in Urban Planning Field

These books			Dickey & Watts (1978)	Willemain (1980)	Bracken (1981)	Gaber & Gaber (2007)	Patton et al. (2013)	Silva et al. (2015)
Vol.1 Basic	2	Technical Writing						
	3	Types of Research				▨		■
	4	Planning Data and Analysis				▨		
	5	Conceptual Frameworks	▨		▨			
	6	Validity and Reliability		■		■	▨	
	7	Descriptive Statistics and Visualizing Data	▨	■			▨	
	8	Chi-square	■	■				
	9	Correlations	■	▨			▨	
	10	Difference of Means (*t*-test)	■	■				
	11	Analysis of Variance (ANOVA)						
	12	Linear Regression	■		▨			■
	13	Logistic Regression	▨					
	14	Quasi-Experimental Research		■	▨		■	
Vol.2 Advanced	2	Technical Writing						
	3	Planning Journals and Topics						▨
	4	Poisson and Negative Binomial Regression		■				
	5	Factor Analysis						
	6	Cluster Analysis	▨					
	7	Multi-Level Modeling						
	8	Structural Equation Modeling						
	9	Spatial Econometrics						■
	10	Meta-Analyses and Meta-Regression				▨		
	11	Mixed Methods Research				■		

Note: Dark gray means that a book covers the method entirely while light gray means partial inclusion. This table omits the first chapter of each book, "Introduction."

Bracken (1981) aims to set out a range of methods relevant to the practice of urban planning. Rather than planning research, the focus of the book is on how to develop more systematized approaches to urban planning and policy making. As a result, this 36-year-old book covers only basic concepts and theories in urban research, such as research design, validity and reliability, sampling, and basic statistical models, most of which need to be updated.

Gaber and Gaber (2007) write about qualitative research methods for planners, students, researchers, and policy makers in planning. This book covers not only the overall qualitative research process but also five specific methods: field research, photographic research, focus group, content analysis, and meta-analysis. By including two actual case studies with each method, the authors aim to show how readers can use a particular technique to analyze an urban problem. In spite of its practicality in qualitative planning research, this book has virtually no connection with quantitative research methods.

Patton, Sawicki, and Clark (2013) present basic methods for analyzing and resolving planning and policy issues. Quantitative and qualitative methods are introduced to address such policy concerns. Besides methods, the book presents the rationale and process of policy analysis as well as policy application cases. The book only deals with basic research methods in the policy analysis and planning process. The authors purposely omit most quantitative methods.

Silva et al. (2015) provide a handbook of various planning research methods, including both qualitative and quantitative approaches. Pointing out the applied and practical nature of much planning research, their book is designed to bridge the gap between the wider research methods literature in various fields and the specifics of planning research. However, as stated in the book, they don't provide a *recipe* for how to do a research study but instead focus on the theory and application examples (usually conducted by the chapter authors).

What differentiates the current books from their predecessors is not only their currency but also their practicality and applicability to planning—each chapter has a step-by-step recipe and two planning examples. Furthermore, the current books cover a variety of quantitative research methods that are not covered in earlier texts (Table 1.1).

Definitions and Concepts You Should Know

When reading a research paper, a reader might find it hard to understand, mainly because of jargon. For the same reason, a student might be frustrated with a steep learning curve to master a specific research method. Like any other skills or knowledge, however, current research methods have been established based on fundamental, underlying concepts. So, the best starting point is to review these key concepts.

Data and Measurements

Empirical research depends on empirical evidence, or observable **data**, to formulate and test theories and come to conclusions. Data used in research can be described in many ways. First, if you collect the data yourself, it is called **primary data**. It can come from a survey or an interview you create and conduct, from direct observation of human behavior, or from measurement of the environment, such as sidewalk widths or the number of street trees. If you use data that someone else has collected, you are using **secondary data**. EPA's Air Quality Index is a good example.

Data can be either aggregate or disaggregate. **Disaggregate data** simply means looking at individuals' characteristics, such as race, income, or education level, plus individuals' behavior, such as fruit and vegetable consumption or minutes of moderate exercise. **Aggregate data** is a summary of disaggregate data, meaning that information of individuals is compiled and aggregated. Examples are average household income, percentage of non-white population, and average vehicle miles traveled within a given spatial boundary. Usually, in planning research, disaggregate data is considered as having higher quality, but it is harder to gather due to privacy or cost. Aggregate data raise issues of aggregation bias and the ecological fallacy, but may be appropriate if you are interested in differences from place to place (Ewing et al., 2017).

Related to the distinction between aggregate and disaggregate data, an important concept is the **unit of analysis**. The unit of analysis is the entity that is being analyzed in a study. In social science research, typical units of analysis include individuals, groups, geographical units (e.g., town, census tract, state), and social organizations. The level of data and the unit of analysis are closely associated with each other: Disaggregate data enables you to conduct an analysis at the individual level, and an individual-level analysis requires you to collect disaggregate data.

The **unit of observation** should not be confused with the unit of analysis. For example, a study may have a unit of observation at the individual level but may have the unit of analysis at the neighborhood level, drawing conclusions about neighborhood characteristics from data collected from individuals.

Data can be either cross-sectional or longitudinal according to the temporal dimension. **Cross-sectional data** is collected at a single point in time. Regardless of the time interval or period (e.g., minutes, days, years), the contemporaneous measurements occur within the same period for all variables and for all cases. In 2015, the Wasatch Front Regional Council (WFRC, 2015) in Utah put extensive efforts into measuring urban design qualities (including pedestrian counts) for over 1,200 blocks throughout the region. This is an example of cross-sectional and aggregate data.

Longitudinal data is collected over time—you have at least two waves of measurement. An example is the Public Transportation Ridership Report quarterly published by the American Public Transportation Association (APTA). The ridership report contains what is sometimes called **time series data**, implying many waves of measurement over time.

A further distinction is made among several types of longitudinal data. **Repeated cross-sectional data** is collected on the same set of variables for multiple time periods but with different cases in each period. For transportation planners, an example is the National Household Travel Survey (NHTS) by the U.S. Department of Transportation (DOT), data on travel and socio-demographic characteristics of the American public. Surveys under the current name were conducted in 2001, 2009, and 2017 with almost identical questions, but for different survey participants.

Another type of longitudinal data is **panel data**. In panel data, both the cases and variables remain the same over time. As an example, the National Crime Victimization Survey (NCVS), administered by the Bureau of Justice Statistics, is a national survey of about 90,000 households on the frequency, characteristics, and consequences of criminal victimization in the United States. The selected households are interviewed seven times (at six-month intervals) over three years. Panel data represents the gold standard for planning research, since the repeated observation of the same cases (individuals or groups) inherently controls for individual and group differences that cannot be measured but can be assumed invariant over time.

6   *Keunhyun Park and Reid Ewing*

Lastly, data can be classified by scale of measurement. There are four scales of measurement. First, **nominal** scale categorizes cases with no numerical equivalent (e.g., male/female, introvert/extrovert, city/suburb). Second, **ordinal** measurement can rank-order the cases, but the distances between attributes have no meaning. For example, five-star hotels are supposed to be *better* than lower-ranked hotels in terms of accommodations and services. However, we do not know if the distance from 5-star to 4-star is the same as 4-star to 3-star. A better example for planners is the categorization of people as low income, medium income, or high income. Thirdly, in **interval** measurement, we can assume equal intervals between values. Typical examples include temperature and IQ. When we measure temperature (in Fahrenheit), the distance from 30 to 40 is the same as the distance from 70 to 80. Note, however, that in interval measurement, ratios don't make any sense and there is no true zero (0 degree Celsius does not mean no temperature). Sprawl metrics developed by Ewing and Hamidi (2014) are measured in terms of standard deviations above and below the mean, but there is no true zero when it comes to compactness or sprawl. Lastly, **ratio** measurement always has a meaningful absolute zero, i.e., zero indicates the absence of variable measured. Weight, age, and frequency of behaviors are examples. It is called ratio scale because you can construct a meaningful fraction or ratio with its values: someone can weigh twice as much as another, or can walk twice as frequently as another. In contrast to sprawl measures, density is a ratio scale variable.

Variables with nominal or ordinal measurement are called **categorical**, whereas those with interval or ratio measurement are called **continuous**. Knowing the level of measurement helps you interpret the data and decide on an appropriate analysis method.

Conceptual Framework

What is of interest to planners is causality. For example, a research question could be, will more highway construction induce more traffic?

A **theory** is an explanation of why things occur. In the preceding research question, a theory could be "if highway capacity increases, people will drive more" ("induced demand theory"). Derived from theory, a statement that is testable is called a **hypothesis**. A hypothesis that follows from the preceding theory is: as highway lane miles increase, vehicle miles traveled (VMT) will increase. When confirmed by many tests of related hypotheses, a theory can be deemed a **law** (e.g., the "universal law of traffic congestion" isn't a real law but was incorrectly labeled a law by Anthony Downs in a famous article about highway induced traffic—highway expansion doesn't always lead to increased driving if there is already free flowing traffic).

Readers might recognize the different words used in theory and hypothesis, such as capacity versus lane-miles, and travel versus VMT. In general, a theory consists of **constructs** or abstract concepts and how they are related to one another. Highway capacity, travel, growth, and sprawl are examples. On the other hand, a hypothesis is phrased in terms of **variables**, quantities that vary, are measurable, and partially capture constructs. VMT, highway lane-miles, population growth, and residential density are examples, respectively, corresponding to the preceding constructs (see Chapter 5). They, too, are ordinarily described by relationships to one another.

A theory or hypothesis, or multiple theories or hypotheses, can be verbally or visually represented by a **conceptual framework** (or conceptual model, causal path diagram).

A conceptual framework consists of logical relations among concepts or variables that guide your research. Despite the importance of adopting conceptual frameworks, researchers in the planning field have not devoted earnest attention to them (see Chapter 5). A survey of planning articles showed that it is rare for planners to articulate conceptual frameworks, and even rarer for them to schematically diagram them.

Two types of variables are defined in most studies. They are **independent** (or predictor, explanatory, or X) variables and **dependent** (or response, outcome, or Y) variables. Dependent variables represent outcomes or consequences that you try to understand. Independent variables are those hypothesized to influence or predict the values of the dependent variables. In causal models, an independent variable represents a cause, and a dependent variable represents an effect.

Correlation refers to a statistical index that describes how strongly variables are related to one another. It simply means that two things happen together: For example, more highway construction is accompanied by more traffic, but we don't know which one is the cause and which one is the effect, or whether there is a third variable that is causing both, such as population growth. Please remember that correlation does not imply **causation** (see Chapters 5 and 9).

Statistics

In a quantitative study, a conceptual framework can be represented as a mathematical model. A **mathematical model** uses mathematical language to describe the behavior of a system. It is composed of mathematical equations representing the functional relationships among variables. Mathematical models can take many forms, including statistical models.

The value of mathematical models may not be evident to many planners. At the core of these statistical approaches is the idea that patterns can be ascertained from our data. For example, without a model, thousands of household travel surveys themselves do not tell us anything about the association between the neighborhood environment and household travel behavior. A **model** allows us to explore relationships that might not be immediately evident from the raw observations themselves (Tolmie, Muijs, & McAteer, 2011).

There are basically two types of statistics in quantitative planning research: descriptive and inferential. **Descriptive statistics** describe a collection of data from a sample or population. They form the basis of virtually every quantitative analysis and are also used in many qualitative studies for the purpose of describing cases. Examples of descriptive statistics are mean or average, median, variance, and standard deviation values (see Chapter 7).

After describing the data, you will usually want to make a decision about the statistical and practical significance of relationships among the variables. **Inferential statistics** involve statistical methods that draw conclusions from data, which reach beyond the data itself. Inferential statistics may also be defined as a process of drawing inferences about a population from a sample. Here, a **population** means the full set of people or things with a characteristic one wishes to understand, whereas a **sample** is a subset of individuals from a larger population. Because there is very rarely enough time or money to gather information from everyone or information about everything in a population, the goal becomes finding a representative sample of that population.

Please note that inferential statistics do not prove something to be *true*. It can only give a measure of how confident or certain we are that it is true. Also, it is often easier to consider whether we should accept or reject that nothing happened (**null hypothesis**) than it is to *prove* that something did happen (**alternative hypothesis**). That's why we reject the null hypothesis and accept the alternative hypothesis when the probability that the null hypothesis is true is low (conventionally, when the probability is less than 1 in 20, or 5 percent).

A **null model** is a model where coefficients (slopes) for all independent variables are set equal of zero and only the constant term (intercept) is allowed to vary. You can interpret the null model as saying that under the null hypothesis there is no relationship between independent and dependent variables and the best estimate of a new observation is the mean of the dependent variable (i.e., the intercept in a regression equation).

A **best-fit model**, or **fitted model**, has just the right number of predictors needed to explain the data well. Fitting a model is a trade-off between parsimony and explanatory power (i.e., goodness of fit), because high parsimony models (i.e., models with few parameters) tend to produce a worse fit to the data than low parsimony models. Occam's Razor, or "the law of briefness," states that you should use no more variables than necessary. This means that we want to reduce our model to the simplest form that still does a good job of predicting outcomes. A model that is missing significant variables is called **under-specified** and will likely produce biased coefficient estimates. A model that has excess variables that are not significant is called **over-specified** and will likely produce inefficient (high standard error) coefficient estimates. A **saturated** model is one in which there are as many estimated parameters as data points. By definition, this will lead to a perfect fit, but will be of little use statistically, as you have no data left to estimate variance.

Structure of the Book

As a comprehensive book of quantitative research methods for novice researchers, this book starts with key definitions and concepts in general social science research (Chapter 1). As writing is the essential communication tool for both planning practitioners and scholars, Chapter 2 presents writing skills and techniques. Three fundamental approaches to research—qualitative, quantitative, and mixed inquiries—are introduced in Chapter 3. Chapter 4 introduces various types of planning data and sources. The following chapters deal with basic concepts in quantitative research—conceptual frameworks (Chapter 5) and validity and reliability (Chapter 6).

One of two types of statistics—descriptive statistics—is presented in Chapter 7, in addition to some data visualization examples. Chapters 8 to 13 are about inferential statistics, from the simplest to the more complex. This is the core of the book. Chapter 14 presents the rationale and mechanics of quasi-experimental research.

Chapter Structure

Most chapters have a recurring structure to help readers understand each of the methods more easily, albeit varied among chapters. Each section answers specific questions.

- **Overview**: What is the essence of the method? What do we need to know before applying the method?
- **Purpose**: How is this method used and what is it used for?
- **History**: When was it developed? Who developed the method?
- **Mechanics**: What are the components of the method? What assumptions must be met, or under what conditions would you use this method? What are the limitations of the method?
- **Interpreting results**: How can we understand the results? How can we know if the results are valid and reliable?
- **Step by step**: How can we utilize the method using SPSS or R (or another appropriate software package)? How can we apply the method to real planning data?
- **Planning examples**: What are two interesting studies from the planning literature that use the method?
- **Conclusion**: How can we summarize the method and assess its usefulness.

Actual examples from peer-reviewed journal articles are provided to show how planning scholars have used the particular method to analyze a real planning problem(s). This part makes our books distinguishable from other textbooks in other fields, by connecting the methods to our readers.

Datasets

Step-by-step is another section that makes our books different from earlier planning texts. These books provide not only theoretical understanding but also seek to foster understanding of how to apply each method using real planning data. Both datasets are available online through the publisher's website.

UZA Dataset

One dataset used in this book, the urbanized area (UZA) dataset, allows us to test the theory of induced travel demand (highways generate their own demand) and also test theories about how the built environment is related to highway demand. The highway data come from the Federal Highway Administration's (FHWA) *Highway Statistics*. Our transit data come from the National Transit Database. Other data come from other sources. For spatial units, we used FHWA's urbanized area boundaries. We limited our sample to large urbanized areas with populations of 200,000 or more for which all variables in Table 1.2 could be estimated. Of the 173 urbanized areas meeting the population criterion, some cases were lost for lack of other data (e.g., compactness metrics, transit data, or fuel price data). Our final sample consists of 157 urbanized areas.

The variables in our models are defined in Table 1.2. They are as follows:

- Our dependent variables: daily VMT per capita and annual traffic delay per capita.
- Our independent variables: The independent variables of primary interest are lane miles of highway capacity and population density and other measures of compactness. Control variables include population size, per capita income, and metropolitan average fuel price.

Table 1.2 Variables in UZA Dataset (FHWA Urbanized Areas in 2010)

Variable	Definition	Source	Mean	Sta. Dev.
ua_id	Urbanized area ID	US Census 2010	–	–
urbanarea	Urbanized area name	US Census 2010	–	–
region	Census region (1 = Northeast, 2 = Midwest, 3 = South, 4 = West)	US Census 2010	–	–
pop000	population (in thousands)	US Census 2010	1124.7	2072.3
inc000	income per capita (in thousands)	American Community Survey	26.9	5.2
hhsize	average household size	US Census 2010	2.6	0.3
veh	average vehicle ownership per capita	American Community Survey	0.4	0.04
area	land area in square miles	US Census 2010	514.3	597.5
popden	gross population density in persons per square mile	US Census 2010	1877.6	897.3
lm	road lane mile per 1000 population	FHWA Highway Statistics NAVTEQ	3.1	0.8
flm	freeway lane miles per 1000 population	FHWA Highway Statistics	0.7	0.3
olm	other lane miles per 1000 population	FHWA Highway Statistics NAVTEQ	2.4	0.7
rtden	transit route density per square mile	National Transit Database	2.4	2.3
tfreq	transit service frequency	National Transit Database	6717.0	3396.9
hrt	directional route miles of heavy-rail lines per 100,000 population*	National Transit Database	9.7	53.1
lrt	directional route miles of light-rail lines per 100,000 population*	National Transit Database	9.2	26.8
tpm	annual transit passenger miles per capita	National Transit Database	98.9	138.0
fuel	average metropolitan fuel price	Oil Price Information Service	2.8	0.2
vmt	daily vehicle miles traveled (VMT) per capita	FHWA Highway Statistics	23.9	5.3
empden	gross employment density in employees per square mile	LEHD 2010	863.1	414.0
pct1500	percentage of the population living at low suburban densities (less than 1500 persons per square mile)	US Census 2010	23.1	12.9
pct12500	percentage of the population living at medium to high urban densities (greater than 12,500 persons per square mile)	US Census 2010	4.8	8.5
urbden	net population density of urban lands	US Census 2010; NLCD	3287.7	1046.8
denfac	density factor	multiple sources – see Ewing and Hamidi (2014)	100.0	25.0
mixfac	mix factor	multiple sources – see Ewing and Hamidi (2014)	100.0	25.0

(*Continued*)

Table 1.2 (Continued)

Variable	Definition	Source	Mean	Sta. Dev.
cenfac	centering factor	multiple sources – see Ewing and Hamidi (2014)	100.0	25.0
strfac	street factor	multiple sources – see Ewing and Hamidi (2014)	100.0	25.0
compact	compactness index	multiple sources – see Ewing and Hamidi (2014)	100.0	24.9
delay	annual delay per capita in hours	INRIX/TTI congestion data	27.7	9.8
tti	travel time index	INRIX/TTI congestion data	1.2	0.1
jobpopwgtwgt[1]	job-population balance	multiple sources – see Ewing and Hamidi (2014)	0.6	0.04
entropywgt[2]	degree of job mixing (entropy)	multiple sources – see Ewing and Hamidi (2014)	0.4	0.05
varpop	coefficient of variation in census block group population densities	multiple sources – see Ewing and Hamidi (2014)	0.7	0.2
varemp	coefficient of variation in census block group employment densities	multiple sources – see Ewing and Hamidi (2014)	2.2	0.9
pctempcen	percentage of MSA employment in CBD or subcenters	multiple sources – see Ewing and Hamidi (2014)	15.2	7.5
pctpopcen	percentage of MSA population in CBD or subcenters	multiple sources – see Ewing and Hamidi (2014)	2.0	1.5
avgblk	average block size (square mile)	multiple sources – see Ewing and Hamidi (2014)	0.03	0.01
pctsmlblk	percentage of small urban blocks that are less than 1/100 square mile	multiple sources – see Ewing and Hamidi (2014)	61.0	8.6
Intden	intersection density (per square mile)	TomTom 2007	51.8	16.9
pct4way	percentage of four-or-more-way intersections	TomTom 2007	25.4	6.4

Note: When you open the dataset, you will notice that there are some variables starting with "ln." It represents log-transformed variables.

1 The job–population index measures balance between employment and resident population within a buffer. Index ranges from 0, where only jobs or residents are present within a buffer, not both, to 1, where the ratio of jobs to residents is optimal from the standpoint of trip generation. Values are intermediate when buffers have both jobs and residents, but one predominates. jobpop = 1 – [ABS(employment – 0.2*population)/(employment + 0.2*population)]. ABS is the absolute value of the expression in parentheses. The value 0.2, representing a balance of employment and population, was found through trial and error to maximize the explanatory power of the variable.

2 The entropy index measures balance between three different land uses. The index ranges from 0, where all land is in a single use, to 1 where land is evenly divided among the three uses. Values are intermediate when buffers have more than one use but one use predominates. The entropy calculation is: entropy = – [residential share*ln(residential share) + commercial share*ln(commercial share) + public share*ln(public share)]/ln(3), where ln is the natural logarithm of the value in parentheses and the shares are measured in terms of total parcel land areas.

12 *Keunhyun Park and Reid Ewing*

All variables are presented both in linear and logged forms (the latter transformed by taking natural logarithms). The use of logarithms has two advantages (see Chapter 12). First, it makes relationships among our variables more nearly linear and reduces the influence of outliers (such as New York and Los Angeles). Second, it allows us to interpret parameter estimates as elasticities (the ratio of the percentage change in a dependent variable associated with the percentage change in an independent variable), which summarize relationships in an understandable and transferable form.

This database has been used in three published articles (Ewing et al., 2014, 2017, 2018) which relate daily VMT per capita or annual delay per capita for urbanized areas to regional compactness, highway capacity, transit service, average fuel price, and other covariates. More studies using this database are coming.

Household Dataset

The other dataset used in this book is the household travel dataset, which allows us to test how the built environment is associated with people's travel choices. We have been collecting household travel survey data from metropolitan planning organizations (MPOs) in the United States for many years. Additional GIS data (land use parcels, street network, transit stops, travel time skims, etc.) were also collected from state, county, and local governments. The unit of analysis is the individual household. The spatial unit is the half-mile road network buffer around the household's address.

The full dataset consists of 931,479 trips made by 94,620 households in 34 regions of the United States. For this book, we make available data for a subset of 14,212 households from ten regions: Seattle, WA; Kansas City, MO; Eugene, OR; San Antonio, TX; Detroit, MI; Richmond, VA; Charleston, SC; Winston-Salem, NC; Syracuse, NY; and Madison, WI. Precise XY coordinates for households, often provided to us under strict confidentiality requirements, have been replaced with census block group geocodes.

The variables in this dataset are defined in Table 1.3. They are as follows:

- Household related variables: any VMT (a dummy variable for households with any VMT versus those with no VMT), household VMT (for those with VMT), number of auto trips, any walk (again, a dummy variable), number of walk trips (for those with any walk trips), any bike, number of bike trips, any transit, number of transit trips, number of vehicles, household size, number of workers, household income, housing type
- Built environment variables within a half mile of household location: activity density, job-population balance, land use entropy, intersection density, percentage of four-way intersections, transit stop density, percentage of regional employment that can be reached within 10, 20, and 30 minutes by auto and 30 minutes by transit
- Regional variables: population size, regional average fuel price, compactness indices

Most variables are presented in linear form. Some variables are logged (transformed by taking natural logarithms). The reason for using logarithms is the same as mentioned previously for the UZA dataset.

The household travel dataset has been used in three published articles (Ewing et al., 2010, 2015; Tian et al., 2015). More studies using this database are coming. The

Table 1.3 Variables in Household Database (Based on Household Travel Surveys From Different Years)

Variable	Definition	N	Mean	Sta. Dev.
rhhnum	household ID	*14,212*	–	–
region	region ID	*14,212*	–	–
geoid	Census block group FIPS code (only for Seattle region)	*3,904*	–	–
dependent variables				
anyvmt	any household VMT (1 = yes, 0 = no)	14,199	0.94	0.25
lnvmt	natural log of household VMT (for households with any VMT), adjusted by average vehicle occupancy rate	13,285	3.07	1.02
autotrips	household car trips	14,212	8.49	7.23
anywalk	any household walk trips (1 = yes, 0 = no)	14,212	0.21	0.41
walktrips	household walk trips (for households with any walk trips)	2,960	3.41	2.94
anybike	any household bike trips (1 = yes, 0 = no)	14,212	0.03	0.18
biketrips	household bike trips (for households with any bike trips)	450	3.22	2.69
anytransit	any household transit trips (1 = yes, 0 = no)	14,212	0.07	0.26
transittrips	household transit trips (for households with any transit trips)	1,004	2.68	2.27
Independent variables – household				
veh	number of vehicles	14,212	1.90	1.03
hhsize	household size	14,212	2.38	1.26
hhworker	number of employed household members	14,212	1.16	0.87
htype	housing type (0 = other, 1 = single-family-detached, 2 = single-family-attached, 3 = multi-family) (no data in Detroit)	13,249	–	–
sf	housing type (1 = single-family, 0 = other)	13,273	0.81	0.40
hhincome	real household income (in 1000s of 2012 dollars)	13,355	69.10	41.73
income_cat	household income grouped by three income brackets (1 = less than $35K, 2 = between $35K and $75K, 3 = over $75K)	13,355	2.13	0.76
Independent variables – a half-mile buffer				
actden	activity density within one-half mile (population plus employment per square mile in 1000s)	14,179	5.24	8.69
jobpop[1]	job-population balance within one-half mile	14,151	0.60	0.25
entropy[2]	land use entropy within one-half mile	14,146	0.34	0.27
intden	intersection density (per square mile) within one-half mile	14,179	140.22	123.78
pct4way	percentage 4-way intersections within one-half mile	14,153	29.26	22.29
stopden	transit stop density within one-half mile	14,179	23.55	36.77
emp10a	percentage of regional employment within 10 min by auto	14,212	14.70	17.57
emp20a	percentage of regional employment within 20 min by auto	14,212	45.15	31.34
emp30a	percentage of regional employment within 30 min by auto	14,212	66.63	30.76
emp30t	percentage of regional employment within 30 min by transit	14,212	20.78	20.77

(*Continued*)

14 *Keunhyun Park and Reid Ewing*

Table 1.3 (Continued)

Variable	Definition	N	Mean	Sta. Dev.
Region variables (HTS.region.10regions.sav, only used in the Advanced book)				
region	region ID	10	–	–
date	year of the household travel survey	10	–	–
regname	region name	10	–	–
regpop	population within the region in 1000s	10	1529.39	1524.59
fuel	average regional fuel price	10	2.87	.14
compact	measure of regional compactness developed by Ewing and Hamidi (2014); higher values of the index correspond to more compact development, lower values to more sprawling development.	10	104.68	31.59

Note: Variables starting with "ln" represents that the original variable is log-transformed.

1 The job–population index measures balance between employment and resident population within a buffer. Index ranges from 0, where only jobs or residents are present within a buffer, not both, to 1 where the ratio of jobs to residents is optimal from the standpoint of trip generation. Values are intermediate when buffers have both jobs and residents, but one predominates. jobpop = 1 – [ABS(employment – 0.2*population)/(employment + 0.2*population)]. ABS is the absolute value of the expression in parentheses. The value 0.2, representing a balance of employment and population, was found through trial and error to maximize the explanatory power of the variable.

2 The entropy index measures balance between three different land uses. The index ranges from 0, where all land is in a single use, to 1 where land is evenly divided among the three uses. Values are intermediate when buffers have more than one use but one use predominates. The entropy calculation is: entropy = – [residential share*ln(residential share) + commercial share*ln(commercial share) + public share*ln(public share)] / ln(3), where ln is the natural logarithm of the value in parentheses and the shares are measured in terms of total parcel land areas.

published studies relate the built environment to travel behavior, at the household level or at the trip level.

Computer Software Used in This Book

The statistical software packages used in the step-by-step sections of Chapters 7 through 13 were chosen for ease of use. In all chapters, the software of choice is SPSS and R. SPSS is available on a trial basis and R is a free software.

Released in 1968, SPSS is a classic, leading software package for quantitative research in the social sciences. Thanks to its user-friendly interface and easy-to-use drop-down menus, it is a useful tool for non-statisticians as well. One of the advantages in terms of learning is its similarities to Excel, software that many students are already familiar with. Other benefits include official support and extensive documentation. Thus, SPSS is by far the most common software used in academic research generally and in planning programs.

In 2018, Robert Muenchen analyzed Google Scholar, a scholarly literature search engine, to see the trend of data analysis software in scholarly use (http://r4stats.com/articles/popularity). The most popular software package in scholarly publications was SPSS, more than twice the second most widely used package, R (Figure 1.1). He attributed this result to the balance between power and ease-of-use of SPSS.

A survey of planning programs in the United States showed SPSS is very popular for use in the classroom. At both the graduate and undergraduate levels, professors reported using SPSS nearly three times as often as the next most popular software package, Stata. The similarity between SPSS and Excel was cited as a major reason for using the IBM-produced software. (Indeed, most professors reported using SPSS alongside Excel in the classroom.)

Results, shown in Table 1.4, are based on a survey of Association of Collegiate Schools of Planning (ACSP) full member accredited schools. Forty-one of the 107 programs responded, a response rate of 38 percent. Additionally, one affiliate member school and two corresponding member schools responded to a request for information.

Of course, SPSS is not without limitations—it is commercial (i.e., not free) and may be slower in handling large datasets than other software. It cannot estimate all types of models. For instance, its multinomial logistic regression model is constrained. Emerging open-source, free software such as R or Python can be an alternative to SPSS for urban researchers. While this book sticks to menu-driven software—SPSS, we also provide R codes for all step-by-step sections.

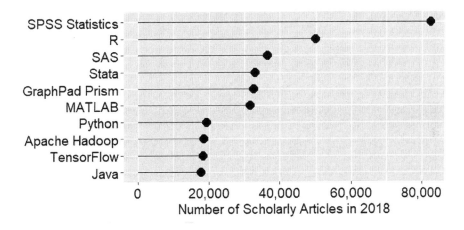

Figure 1.1 The Number of Scholarly Articles That Use Each Software Package in 2018

Source: adjusted from http://r4stats.com/articles/popularity/

Table 1.4 Frequency of Responses by Instructors of Planning Courses to the Question "Which Software Package(s) Do You Utilize in the Methods Course(s) You Teach?" ($n = 44$)

Software	Frequency of Use
SPSS	52%
Stata	20%
SAS	7%
R	4%
All others	17%

Works Cited

American Public Transportation Association. (2017). *Public transportation ridership report.* Retrieved from www.apta.com/resources/statistics/Pages/ridershipreport.aspx

Bracken, I. (1981). *Urban planning methods: Research and policy analysis.* London: Methuen Publishing.

Contant, C. K., & Forkenbrock, D. J. (1986). Planning methods: An analysis of supply and demand. *Journal of Planning Education and Research, 6*(1), 10–21. https://doi.org/10.1177/0739456X8600600104

Dickey, J. W., & Watts, T. M. (1978). *Analytic techniques in urban and regional planning.* New York, NY: McGraw-Hill.

Edwards, M. M., & Bates, L. K. (2011). Planning's core curriculum: Knowledge, practice, and implementation. *Journal of Planning Education and Research, 31*(2), 172–183. https://doi.org/10.1177/0739456X11398043

Ewing, R., Greenwald, M., Zhang, M., Walters, J., Feldman, M., Cervero, R., & Thomas, J. (2010). Traffic generated by mixed-use developments: Six-region study using consistent built environmental measures. *Journal of Urban Planning and Development, 137*(3), 248–261. https://doi.org/10.1061/(ASCE)UP.1943-5444.0000068

Ewing, R., & Hamidi, S. (2014). *Measuring urban sprawl and validating sprawl measures.* Washington, DC: National Institutes of Health and Smart Growth America.

Ewing, R., Hamidi, S., Gallivan, F., Nelson, A. C., & Grace, J. B. (2014). Structural equation models of VMT growth in US urbanised areas. *Urban Studies, 51*(14), 3079–3096. https://doi.org/10.1177/0042098013516521

Ewing, R., Hamidi, S., Tian, G., Proffitt, D., Tonin, S., & Fregolent, L. (2017). Testing Newman and Kenworthy's theory of density and automobile dependence. *Journal of Planning Education and Research.* https://doi.org/10.1177/0739456X16688767

Ewing, R., Tian, G., Goates, J. P., Zhang, M., Greenwald, M. J., Joyce, A., . . . Greene, W. (2015). Varying influences of the built environment on household travel in 15 diverse regions of the United States. *Urban Studies, 52*(13), 2330–2348. https://doi.org/10.1177/0042098014560991

Ewing, R., Tian, G., Lyons, T., & Terzano, K. (2018). Does compact development increase or reduce traffic congestion? *Cities, 72,* 94–101.

Dawkins, C. J. (2016). Preparing planners: The role of graduate planning education. *Journal of Planning Education and Research, 36*(4), 414–426.

Gaber, J., & Gaber, S. (2007). *Qualitative analysis for planning & policy: Beyond the numbers.* Chicago, IL: American Planning Association.

Greenlee, A. J., Edwards, M., & Anthony, J. (2015). Planning skills: An examination of supply and local government demand. *Journal of Planning Education and Research, 35*(2), 161–173. https://doi.org/10.1177/0739456X15570321

Guzzetta, J. D., & Bollens, S. A. (2003). Urban planners' skills and competencies: Are we different from other professions? Does context matter? Do we evolve? *Journal of Planning Education and Research, 23*(1), 96–106. https://doi.org/10.1177/0739456X03255426

Muenchen, R. A. (2015). *The popularity of data science software.* Retrieved from http://r4stats.com/articles/popularity/

Patton, C. V., Sawicki, D. S., & Clark, J. J. (2013). *Basic methods of policy analysis and planning* (3rd ed.). Upper Salle River, NJ: Pearson Education, Inc.

Planning Accreditation Board. (2017). *PAB accreditation standards and criteria.* Retrieved November 19, 2019, from https://www.planningaccreditationboard.org/

Silva, E. A., Healey, P., Harris, N., & Van den Broeck, P. (Eds.). (2015). *The Routledge handbook of planning research methods.* London: Routledge.

Tian, G., Ewing, R., White, A., Hamidi, S., Walters, J., Goates, J. P., & Joyce, A. (2015). Traffic generated by mixed-use developments: Thirteen-region study using consistent measures of built environment. *Transportation Research Record, 2500,* 116–124. https://doi.org/10.3141/2500-14

Tolmie, A., Muijs, D., & McAteer, E. (2011). *Quantitative methods in educational and social research using SPSS*. London: McGraw-Hill Education.

Tracy, S. J. (2012). *Qualitative research methods: Collecting evidence, crafting analysis, communicating impact*. Hoboken, NJ: John Wiley & Sons.

U.S. Bureau of Justice Statistics. (2016). *National crime victimization survey*. Retrieved from www.bjs.gov/index.cfm?ty=dcdetail&iid=245

U.S. Census Bureau. (2018). Retrieved from www.census.gov/data.html

U.S. Department of Transportation. (2017). *National household travel survey*. Retrieved from http://nhts.ornl.gov/

U.S. Environmental Protection Agency. (2016). *Air quality index*. Retrieved from https://airnow.gov/index.cfm?action=aqibasics.aqi

U.S. Federal Highway Administration. (2016). *Highway statistics*. Retrieved from www.fhwa.dot.gov/policyinformation/statistics.cfm

Wasatch Front Regional Council. (2015). *Walkability and measuring urban street design*. Retrieved from https://wfrcgis.maps.arcgis.com/apps/MapSeries/index.html?appid=7d1b1df5686c41b593d1e5ff5539d01a

Willemain, T. R. (1980). *Statistical methods for planners*. Cambridge, MA: The MIT Press.

2 Technical Writing

Robin Rothfeder and Reid Ewing

Overview

Writing is an essential communication tool for planners. Practitioners use writing to produce plans, ordinances, staff reports, legal documents, consulting reports, and other deliverables. Scholars use writing to situate their research within existing literature, to describe their research methods, to explain their research results, and to apply those results in a practical setting. Whether professional or academic, most final planning products take the form of written communication. Planners, in short, write for a living.

If you read the dry pages of journals and reports, you might be tempted to conclude that great writing by planners is a lost art. We believe otherwise. Classic planning works—Mumford, Jacobs, Appleyard, Whyte, and many others—contain brilliantly insightful and artistic writing. In the following quotation, for instance, Whyte uses just a few simple sentences to highlight an essential planning problem, to provide a specific example of the problem, and to suggest within that example the seed of a solution. In so doing, he indicates many of the essential characteristics of current planning trends, such as Smart Growth and New Urbanism, decades before their time.

> In almost all U.S. cities the bulk of the right-of-way is given to the roadway for vehicles, the least to the sidewalk for pedestrians. New York's Lexington Avenue is a prime example, in particular the four block stretch between Fifty-seventh and Sixty-first streets. It is the reductio ad absurdum of the U.S. city street—and by its very excesses it provides clues for its redemption.
>
> —William H. Whyte, 1988, p. 69

Most of us may never write as elegantly as William H. Whyte. But today's planners can and should be able to write prose that is informative and well-composed. This chapter presents many of the basic skills and techniques needed to write well. The chapter will:

1. Provide an overview of why planners write
2. Describe key features of the early writing process, including objectives, scope, and audience

Technical Writing 19

3. Review the mechanics of writing, from individual word choices to the organization of whole documents
4. Offer guidance for rewriting and editing
5. Discuss in detail the standard structure of academic research papers
6. Present two very different articles written by planners that exemplify the craft of writing

Each section of the chapter uses planning examples to highlight important concepts. The emphasis is on technical writing for academic planners. Nevertheless, many of the tools and strategies described herein apply to any writing project, from a poem to a magazine article to a staff report. In the end, clear thinking, good writing, and enjoyable reading all go hand-in-hand (Gopen & Swan, 1990).

> Writing well requires more than putting words on paper. Writing is best when it is concise, meaningful, and easily understood.
> —Victor C. Pellegrino, 2003, p. 9

Purpose

Planners write for a living. But many planners also have more personal and more fundamental motivations for writing. We want to influence and inspire people. We want to promote positive social and environmental changes. We want to see core values realized in the world around us: health, livability, sustainability, justice, etc. Good writing is one of our most important tools for making these goals a reality.

In terms of substantive content, planners may write for any number of reasons. Here, we consider two broad categories: writing intended primarily for technical or specialized consumption, and writing intended primarily for non-technical or public consumption.

Technical Writing

Writing for technical or specialized communication includes both professional planning practice and academic planning research. According to the American Planning Association (APA): "Professional planners help create a broad vision for the community. They also research, design, and develop programs; lead public processes; effect social change; perform technical analyses; manage; and educate" (APA, 2013). Associated technical writing products typically include plans, zoning and subdivision ordinances, staff reports, legal deliberations, and consulting agency reports.

Plans take stock of a local municipality and craft a future vision for that place (e.g., City of Portland Comprehensive Plan, 2011). Zoning and subdivision ordinances establish regulations for land use, density, building envelope, site development, public infrastructure, and other planning issues (e.g., Salt Lake City, Utah City Code, 2013). Staff reports make recommendations about project applications and record the details of decision-making processes (e.g., City of Berkeley Planning Commission, Agendas and Minutes, 2014). Consulting agency reports may have a variety of purposes, including informing decision-makers, educating the public, arguing for or against planning activities, solving planning problems, translating planning research results for non-technical audiences, and/or synthesizing the results of a public engagement process (e.g., Blueprint Jordan River, 2008).

Academic planning researchers may share many of the same motivations as practicing professional planners. In addition, according to the *Journal of the American Planning Association* (JAPA, 2019), planning scholars typically "do at least one of the following:

- Contribute to the theoretical and conceptual foundation of planning;
- Improve the link between planning and successful policy implementation;
- Advance the methods used in planning practice and planning research;
- Explain empirical relationships important to planning;
- Interpret noteworthy physical, economic, and social phenomena that have spatial dimensions; or
- Analyze significant consequences of planning approaches, processes, and contexts

Myers and Ryu exemplify many of these goals in their award-winning 2009 JAPA article, *Aging Baby Boomers and the Generational Housing Bubble*. This article is an excellent example of clear, important research coupled with clear, effective writing. The authors explain their work with succinct but entertaining prose:

> We aim to identify the point at which boomers will begin to offer more homes for sale than they buy. . . . We project when this will occur in all 50 states . . . (and) we discuss the planning implications of these possible futures.
> —Myers & Ryu, 2008, p. 18

Along with such peer-reviewed journal articles, other scholarly writing products for technical or specialized communication include books, conference papers, and chapters in edited volumes. This book contains dozens of relevant examples.

Public Scholarship

Some planners participate in research and practice simultaneously, through processes of public scholarship. One example is Bent Flyvbjerg, who developed and employed the phronetic research method to explain transportation planning in Denmark, and to promote political, institutional, and environmental changes. Flyvbjerg's work in Denmark led to peer-reviewed articles (Flyvbjerg, Holm, & Buhl, 2002; Flyvbjerg, Skamris Holm, & Buhl, 2004), chapters in edited volumes (Burchell, Mandelbaum, & Mazza, 1996; Allmendinger & Tewdwr-Jones, 2002; Campbell & Fainstein, 2003), and complete books (Flyvbjerg, 1998, 2001). Eventually, his writing extended to multimedia communication, including radio, print, and television. Ultimately, Flyvbjerg's public scholarship led to substantive changes in local planning documents and public engagement processes.

When we read work by Bent Flyvbjerg, we can understand why he has had such a profound impact. His writing is incisive and evocative. Consider these lines, from his 2002 JPER article "Bringing Power to Planning Research":

> First, I would choose to work with problems that are considered problems not only in the academy but also in the rest of society. Second, I would deliberately and actively feed the results of my research back into the political, administrative, and social processes that I studied.
>
> —Bent Flyvbjerg, 2002, p. 362

In this chapter, we will return to Bent Flvybjerg as we highlight key writing concepts and strategies.

Technical Versus Non-Technical Writing

As you might assume, the difference between technical and non-technical writing is more of a spectrum, or sliding scale, than a black-and-white distinction. For instance, while the preceding quotation comes from a highly regarded and rigorously peer-reviewed journal, some academic planners may find the language overly personal or subjective. Indeed, public scholarship like Flyvbjerg's frequently falls into the gray area between technical and non-technical writing.

One very common strategy that blurs the line between technical and non-technical writing is storytelling. Stories play a variety of roles in planning research and practice (Sandercock, 2003; Throgmorton, 2003). Even in quantitative empirical work, stories are important for engaging the reader and for leading them through a sea of complicated information (Bem, 2002). Flyvbjerg demonstrates how storytelling can set the stage for decades of research and practice. In the following quote, he begins the story of the now infamous Aalborg Project. The details of this very first meeting remain relevant throughout all of the articles, books, interviews, and public policies that Flyvbjerg ultimately produced:

> In Aalborg, Denmark, on an autumn day in the late 1970s, a group of high-level city officials gather for a meeting. Only one item is on the agenda: initiation of what will eventually become an award-winning project recommended by the OECD for international adoption, on how to integrate environmental and social concerns in city politics and planning, including how to deal with the car in the city. From the very outset the stakes are high. Making the car adapt to the city in the scale now envisioned is something never before tried in Denmark.
>
> —Bent Flyvbjerg, 1998, p. 9

While the line between technical and non-technical writing can be blurry, it is nevertheless useful to make certain distinctions. One difference concerns the logic and chronology of the narrative structure. Non-technical writing may employ a complex chronology or obscure logic, but technical writing never will. As Daryl Bem explains in *Writing the Empirical Journal Article*: "It is not a novel with subplots, flashbacks, and literary allusions, but a short story with a single linear narrative line" (2002, p. 4).

Another difference concerns tone. Non-technical writing may employ colorful imagery and emotionally charged language. On the other hand, even if the author is a strong advocate of certain ideals, technical writing "aims to be clean, clear, and unemotional" (Katz, 2009, p. 3). Flyvbjerg may be an advocate for change, but he advances his position through rigorous research and through his willingness to engage potentially confrontational dialogues without aggression—not through allusion or through emotional appeal.

A third difference concerns evidentiary standards. Peer-reviewed journal articles, in particular, must show extensive evidence in support of their arguments (Katz, 2009). Non-technical writing, on the other hand, does not have set standards for what constitutes appropriate evidence. This does not mean, however, that non-technical writing is incapable of presenting rigorous evidence.

Finally, good technical writing involves layers of expertise. Bem states that a person who is "intelligent . . . (but) with no expertise . . . should be able to comprehend the broad outlines" of technical writing (2002, p. 4). At the same time, "specialized audiences who share a common background" should be able to gain a much deeper understanding of the same project. Non-technical writing, on the other end, is generally intended to inform and inspire a non-expert audience (Bern, 2002).

With these considerations in mind, we can see that some written products, including peer-reviewed articles, ordinances, and legal documents, require mostly technical writing. Other written products, such as poetry and fiction, require mostly non-technical writing. Still other written products—such as plans, reports, and newspaper or magazine articles—may involve a mix of technical and non-technical writing.

Public scholar Nan Ellin employs this mixed approach to writing. She translates complex ideas for a lay audience, seeking to give her work a broader reach and a wider impact than it would have strictly within the academy. Consider this passage from Ellin's book *Good Urbanism*. Here, she draws the reader in with a simple and accessible metaphor, which at the same time captures a subtle and insightful observation about cities. In this way, Ellin uses colorful, non-technical writing to set the stage for the more technical case studies that follow.

A house I once lived in came with a potted grape ivy. I watered the plant regularly but oddly, it never grew. It didn't die, but during the two years I lived there, it never changed shape nor sprouted a leaf. Leaving this grape ivy behind for the next inhabitants, it became emblematic for me of so many places that, while they may be surviving, are clearly not thriving.

—Nan Ellin, 2013, p. 1

Planning and JAPA

In considering technical and non-technical writing for planners, it is interesting to compare the writing guidelines provided by *Planning* magazine with the instructions for authors provided by the scholarly *Journal of the American Planning Association*. Both are products of the American Planning Association.

Planning is intended for popular consumption by "professionals and interested laypeople" (Tait, 2012). *Planning*'s guidelines are brief, requesting "a straightforward, nontechnical style" with "a minimum of elaboration." JAPA is a leading academic planning journal (Goldstein & Maier, 2010), although it is also targeted at a professional audience. JAPA's guidelines are extensive, with several pages of requirements and instructions for authors. The journal wants "vivid and direct writing in the active voice," with as much detail and elaboration as needed to establish "significant research news."

These guidelines differ substantially. *Planning* magazine prefers brevity and overall clarity to rigorous specificity—a non-technical writing style. JAPA also wants clarity, but at a much higher level of detail and for a much more specialized audience—a more technical writing style. Both publications seek to provide lessons for practicing planners, but lessons are central to *Planning* magazine while they provide a conclusion to JAPA articles. Unlike many academic journals, to remain accessible to readers, the most technically challenging sections of JAPA articles are relegated to appendices.

Research You Can Use

The two styles of writing come together in a bi-monthly column written for *Planning* magazine by the second author of this chapter, titled *Research You Can Use*. The column has been appearing since 2006, and has covered at one time or another almost every type of research method in language intended to be accessible to the practicing planner (see Chapter 3, Planning Journals and Topics, in *Advanced Quantitative Research Methods for Urban Planners*). A few simple writing principles underlie these columns:

1. Tell readers something they don't already know in almost every paragraph, only occasionally state the obvious, and never dwell on the obvious.
2. Strive to make technically challenging material seem simple and familiar (creating a series of ah-ha moments).
3. Write in terms of concepts and examples, always describing the forest (a concept) before exploring the trees (examples). People don't learn well with one or the other, but not both.
4. Wherever possible, add graphic illustrations to clarify text, break up text, and create interest. It is the reason why planning reports and books are almost always illustrated.
5. Whenever possible, present the material as a story. People like stories. It is the reason newspaper articles often start with a human-interest story, politicians often tell stories to illustrate their larger points, and many of us read stories for entertainment.
6. Circle back to earlier ideas, particularly at the very end, as familiarity is the key to understanding.

24   *Robin Rothfeder and Reid Ewing*

7.   Remember that more (volume of writing) is usually less, and less is usually more. The columns were initially a single page, but have spilled over to a second page in recent years. They are seldom much more than 1,000 words.

One of the columns is presented in Figure 2.0; it illustrates the preceding concepts with concrete examples (following all seven rules). The column is a story of discovery. It is short and contains a high density of information. It has one big concept and several examples. It simplifies complex technical information to the extent possible. It contains a graphic illustration. It circles back to the lead sentence at the end. These concepts are evident in all the *Research You Can Use* columns, which now number more than 70. See mrc.cap.utah.edu/publications/research-you-can-use.

This column originally ran in *Planning* magazine, and permission has been granted by the American Planning Association to reprint here.

Preliminaries

Understanding why you are writing helps you determine for whom to write, what to write, and what your specific goals for writing should be. Budinski suggests that, after identifying your underlying reasons for writing, your initial plan of action should include three basic elements: identify your audience, determine the scope of your document, and specify your particular objectives (2001, p. 56). We would add a fourth: learn everything practical about your subject before you start writing.

Audience

Planners must write to meet the needs and expectations of their audience. These will vary from situation to situation. If you are writing a general plan, your audience will be the residents, politicians, and other planners who will work with the general plan. If you are preparing a traffic impact analysis, your audience may include traffic engineers, a developer, and a planning commission. If you are writing a grant for a research or design project, your audience will be the sponsoring agency's selection committee. If you are writing for scholarly publication, your initial audience will be a journal editor and a panel of reviewers, and your eventual audience may include the journal's entire readership.

Whatever the context, it is crucial to clearly identify the person, group, or organization that you are writing for. Your audience will determine the style, tone, and structural format of your document, including word choices, length and complexity of sentences and paragraphs, and overall organization (Katz, 2009).

Scope

Scope refers to boundaries on the technical depth, the level of detail, and the number of ideas/cases/subjects in your written document (Budinski, 2001, p. 60). How much time do you have to complete the project? Is the project relevant to just one place, or will it be applicable on a larger scale? Does your audience expect a succinct summary or an extensive, detailed analysis?

Answering these questions will help you identify what needs to be included in your document, and what does not. Both the writer and the reader will benefit when the scope of the writing is focused and refined.

DEPARTMENTS

■ RESEARCH YOU CAN USE

A "New" (250-Year-Old) Way of Thinking about Statistics

My last column (October) was critical of a recent *JAPA* article by Echenique et al., which, in my view, neglected mountains of evidence in order to make the case that changes in urban form would have little effect on regional sustainability. This month, I will pivot to two more publication-worthy articles coming up in *JAPA* and *JPER*, and promise never again to return to the offending study. But first I want to make one more point.

When I wrote the October column, I was unaware that I was arguing for a Bayesian approach to planning research. Bayesian theory and its inventor are the subjects of a best-selling book by Nate Silver called *The Signal and the Noise: Why So Many Predictions Fail—but Some Don't*. The book describes the work of a statistician named Thomas Bayes, who lived in 18th century England and who came up with a dramatically new way of thinking about probability. After hearing Silver on NPR and the *Daily Show* talking about the odds of victory for the two candidates in last month's presidential election, I ran out and bought the book. But it wasn't until I read it that I realized that there is an alternative to the conventional way of testing research hypotheses.

Bayes's theory is concerned with conditional probability—the probability that a hypothesis is still true even after an event has taken place that provides evidence to the contrary. In short, a single event isn't likely to dramatically change the odds because the probability after the event depends not only on the event but on prior probabilities, or "priors."

Another characteristic of Bayesian statistics is that predictions are constantly being refined as new events occur, new data become available, and prior probabilities change. In our times, presidential election odds change with new polls, new economic news, and new debate performances. Thus, Silver had to repeatedly revise his priors and his election predictions.

Now check out typical quantitative studies published today. The only nod to prior research—or to any sort of context—is found in an article's literature review or, occasionally, in its conclusion. In the table above, I have applied Bayes's theorem to the urban form question. The prior probability that urban form matters is very high. Considering more than 200 land-use travel studies and 100 regional scenario studies, I set the prior probability at 95 percent. Then along came a simulation and a *JAPA* article that concluded the opposite.

Under reasonable assumptions, Bayes's theorem tells us that, even after the simulation, there is still a 79 percent chance that urban form matters. This kind of probabilistic thinking is entirely absent from the Echenique article. Instead, its authors make sweeping conclusions about the inconsequence of urban form ("overconfident conclusions," Silver would say).

> Bayes's theory is concerned with conditional probability . . . that a hypothesis is still true even after an event has taken place that provides evidence to the contrary.

Moving on (let it go, Reid), let's look at two recent articles that, while well-constructed and admirable in many ways, illustrate a non-Baysian view of probability. The *JAPA* article, by Bernadette Hanlon, Marie Howland, and Michael McGuire, evaluates Maryland's smart growth program. Using conventional statistics in the manner of R.A. Fisher (another English statistician who was a critic of Bayes), they model farmland conversion under the state's program and then use the model to "predict" conversions. They conclude that "Maryland's incentive-based strategy is not completely effective at preventing sprawl."

The *JPER* article, by Aaron Golub, Subhrajit Guhathakurta, and Bharath Sollapuram, addresses the effects on property values of light-rail transit in Phoenix. Using Fisher's approach, they develop a hedonic price model that also passes a conventional significance test. They then create price profiles and confirm "the value of proximity" to light-rail stations. Mind you, I am not suggesting that these conclusions are wrong. I suspect they are right. I am just saying that they ignore prior probabilities in making statistical inferences.

According to Silver, hypothesis testing without regard to prior research is on the way out. "Some professions," he writes, "have considered banning Fisher's hypothesis test from their journals. In fact, if you read what's been written in the past ten years, it's hard to find anything that does not advocate a Bayesian approach." But you wouldn't know that from reading planning journals. Why are planners the last to know? ■

Reid Ewing

Ewing is a professor of city and metropolitan planning at the University of Utah and an associate editor of *JAPA*. Past columns are available at www.arch.utah.edu/dgi-bin

BAYES'S THEOREM APPLIED TO URBAN FORM

Prior probability that urban form matters		
• Initial estimate of likelihood	x	95%
New simulation concludes that urban form does not matter		
• Probability of simulation result if it matters	y	20%
• Probability of simulation result if it does not matter	z	100%
• Posterior probability that urban form matters		
• Revised estimate of likelihood that urban form matters, $\underline{xy}$ in light of simulation	$xy+z(1-x)$	79%

Reid Ewing

Reprinted with permission from *Planning*, copyright 2012 by the American Planning Association

American Planning Association | 45

Figure 2.0 Research You Can Use

Objectives

Identifying your audience and setting your scope will paint a clear picture of the style, organizational structure, and range of ideas covered in your document. The other crucial component is a list of goals and objectives: the particular outcomes your writing will produce.

As Budinski explains, specific project objectives (outcomes) are different from the overall purpose (intention) for writing (2001, p. 63). If you are writing a plan, as just described, the purpose is to take stock of the community and to craft a future vision. Goals and objectives might be to increase transit-oriented development, to improve access to open space, to reduce water pollution, etc. If you are writing for scholarly publication, your purpose is to complete a research article that adds to a body of disciplinary knowledge. Goals and objectives might be to model the influences on transit ridership, to explain the relationship between open space and mental health, or to test a green infrastructure design for its ability to decontaminate storm water runoff. Along with the scope and audience, your specific objectives will determine the substantive content of your writing—the words you choose, and the way you put them together.

Learn Everything Practical

Read and research your subject thoroughly before starting to write. The authors of this chapter copy and paste significant points from earlier writings on a subject into a Word file. Another approach is taking written notes. A third is highlighting key points on a pdf or hard copy. It is amazing how quickly one can become relatively expert on a subject just by reading widely and conscientiously.

In the experience of the authors of this chapter, when writing on a subject is fuzzy it is usually because thinking on the subject is fuzzy, and the way to clarify is to learn more about the subject. When writing is blocked or sluggish, it is usually because the writer doesn't have enough information about the subject. Go back and learn more and the writing block will likely disappear.

Example

Before moving to the mechanics of writing, let us return to the example of Bent Flyvbjerg, reflecting on audience, scope, and objectives. For the 2002 article, we know that his initial audience was a JPER editor and a panel of reviewers, and that his extended audience eventually included the entire JPER readership. Regarding scope and objectives, Flyvbjerg's article is wonderfully succinct and clear:

> I decided to study how rationality and power shape planning in the town where I live and work, Aalborg, Denmark.
>
> —Bent Flyvbjerg, 2002, p. 355

Flyvbjerg could be certain that his specialized audience would have a complex understanding of the words "rationality" and "power." For a social scientist versed in critical theory, these terms have specific meanings that clearly express the author's objectives. This is an article about the underlying, structural elements of public policy. What reasons do planners and politicians use to legitimate or justify their decisions? How do the dynamics of unequal power relationships impact those decisions and related decision-making processes? Specifically, how do these issues come to bear in the town of Aalborg, Denmark? With one simple sentence, Flyvbjerg alerts his expert JPER audience as to exactly what his article's scope and objectives will be. His knowledge of place was unquestionable—wide and deep—since he was a long-time resident and student of Aalborg.

Writing this well is a tall order. Even crafting clear, simple sentences is more difficult than it may seem. But the process is not a mystery. If you understand and practice the basic mechanics of writing, you will learn to write well.

Mechanics

Whether your written document is a general plan, a research article, a grant application, or a staff report, the fundamental tools of writing remain the same. Understanding writing mechanics means knowing how to make structural choices at each scale of your document: words, sentences, paragraphs, and whole document organization. This section focuses on these basic building blocks of writing.

Words

First and foremost are the words we choose. As demonstrated earlier, single words (e.g., rationality, power) can convey large amounts of information, especially in technical writing for a specialized audience. In these circumstances, it is important to avoid ambiguous terms, loaded language, slang, and colloquialisms (Rubens, 2002). In addition, much of scientific and technical writing relies on writers and readers sharing a common language (id.). Therefore, it is important to use familiar terminology for your audience in an accepted and consistent manner (id.). Writers must realize that many technical terms are not known to everybody, even in a specialized audience (Budinski, 2001). A good technical paper should explain terminology in words that are understandable to the reader and should provide definitions if necessary. Acronyms are particularly common in planning, and need to be defined when first used.

No matter the audience, word choices determine and are determined by grammar, including punctuation, number (singular or plural), tense (past, present, or future), and perspective (first, second, or third person) (Kolln & Gray, 2009). In general, it is important to keep a consistent, or parallel, tense and perspective throughout a written document (id., p. 84).

Together, tense and perspective also influence whether your writing is in active voice or passive voice. As the name implies, writing in the active voice connects a clear subject with a clear action. The preceding Flyvbjerg quote—"I decided to study how rationality and power shape planning"—is a good active sentence.

Suppose that Flyvbjerg had wished to obscure his role in the research process. In this case, he might have written, "the influence of rationality and power on planning was the subject studied." In this passive sentence, the active transitive verb phrase (decided to study) has become a past participle combined with the verb "to be" (was studied). The object of the active sentence (how rationality and power shape planning) has

28 *Robin Rothfeder and Reid Ewing*

become the subject of the passive sentence (the influence of rationality and power on planning). And, most importantly, the subject of the active sentence—Bent Flyvbjerg, the person who will actually conduct the study—has disappeared entirely.

Bem explains that, traditionally, technical writers "used the passive voice almost exclusively" (2002, p. 20). The idea was to make research seem perfectly neutral and objective by eliminating any reference to the subjective role of the researcher. However, as Bem asserts, "this practice produces lifeless prose and is no longer the norm" (id.). As noted previously, JAPA now specifically requests writing in the active voice. Most publishers in most contexts, technical and non-technical, now prefer the same.

Ultimately, word choices will constitute the structure of your sentences, paragraphs, and completed documents. Words are the basic components of rhetorical grammar and the building blocks of sophisticated, precise communication. As Kolln and Gray argue, there is a crucial difference between choosing a word that approximately expresses your thoughts versus choosing a word that conveys your exact meaning. That difference often boils down to whether you get what you want—a scholarship, a job, a published article—or not.

Word choices are quite deliberate in the *Research You Can Use* column reproduced in Figure 2.0. From the title ("A **'New' (250-Year-Old)** Way of Thinking about Statistics") to the body ("promise **never again** to return to the **offending** study") to the final sentence ("Why are planners the **last to know**"), the words and phrases are meant to convey drama and controversy.

Sentences

Sentences consist of words, phrases, clauses, and punctuation. A sentence must have a subject (generally a noun or noun phrase) and a predicate (generally a verb or verb phrase) and should follow grammatical conventions, unless there is a particular reason for doing otherwise (Kolln & Gray, 2009, p. 21). *Rhetorical Grammar* is an excellent resource on grammatical conventions, as are Strunk, White, and Kalman (2007) and Zinsser (2001).

A good sentence should state one or two ideas clearly and simply. Here are a few tips for writing strong sentences:

- Use short, simple sentences (Rubens, 2002).
- Ordinarily, place a verb immediately after a grammatical subject. When the subject is separated from the verb, the reader is challenged to understand what the sentence is all about (Gopen & Swan, 1990).
- Use repetition and parallel construction, within and between sentences, to improve flow, cohesion, precision, and understanding (Kolln & Gray, 2009).
- Scrutinize every word. Can you substitute or remove words to make a sentence convey the same meaning more swiftly? (Ross-Larson, 1999). Especially in technical writing, sentences stripped to their "cleanest components" will generally serve you best (Zinsser, 2001, p. 7).

When crafting sentences, sometimes emulation is an efficient strategy. As writer Bruce Ross-Larson (1999) observes:

It was only when I began trying to identify what was unusual about a sentence—a dramatic flourish, an elegant repetition, a conversational injection—that I began

Technical Writing 29

to see the patterns [in sentences]. So to move from the common to the stunning, begin to look for patterns in good writing that you can emulate.

(p. 18)

This is good advice. Let us look to a great planning author for inspiration.

Kevin Lynch is a highly esteemed planning scholar and writer. In his classic 1984 book, *Good City Form,* he demonstrates a wide variety of sentence styles and structures. Here is a short, **declarative** statement: "When values lie unexamined, they are dangerous" (1984, p. 1). This is an important premise for Lynch's entire book. Planners must examine the underlying values of city form, he says, in order to avoid the dangerous mistakes of the past and plan desirable futures. Such short, declarative sentences can create clear and powerful writing. However, these assertions must be accompanied by strong evidence and insightful analysis. Otherwise, the audience may perceive that the author lacks credibility.

Lynch immediately establishes credibility in *Good City Form* by illustrating how human values have influenced urban form throughout time. He then offers a long **descriptive** sentence, summarizing his observations:

But some general themes are evident, even in the few examples cited: such persistent motives among city builders as symbolic stability and order; the control of others and the expression of power; access and exclusion; efficient economic function; and the ability to control resources.

(1984, p. 36)

This sentence involves sophisticated grammar, punctuation, and structural composition. Lynch establishes a parallel internal phrase scheme—stability *and* order, control *and* expression, access *and* exclusion—before purposefully abandoning that pattern, giving added weight to the final two items on his list. This long descriptive sentence is more complex than the short declarative sentence. It is also more specific and more detailed, improving Lynch's position as an authority on city form.

In addition to declarative and descriptive statements, Lynch also uses **analytical** sentences. Consider this series of insights about the organic metaphor for city form:

The central difficulty is the analogy itself. Cities are not organisms, any more than they are machines, and perhaps even less so. They do not grow or change of themselves, or reproduce or repair themselves. They are not autonomous entities, nor do they run through life cycles, or become infected. They do not have clearly differentiated functional parts, like the organs of animals.

(1984, p. 95)

These sentences analyze the proposition that "a city is a living organism." Lynch (1984) acknowledges that certain elements of this metaphor can be useful, but he takes issue when the model is generalized to all aspects of all cities. He specifically demonstrates how and where the problematic comparison breaks down, concluding that planning actions should be based on reasons "other than 'organic' ones" (p. 95).

These analytical sentences represent a good balance of length and complexity: long enough to form focused arguments, simple enough to enable easy reading. Each sentence is strong and effective in its own right. In addition, considering all of the sentences together, we learn much about the flow between sentences in a cohesive

30   *Robin Rothfeder and Reid Ewing*

paragraph. We will return to this example in the following section. Before doing so, however, let us consider one more sentence style exemplified by Lynch (1984): the **artful summary**.

> Once we can accept that the city is as natural as the farm and as susceptible of conservation and improvement, we work free of those false dichotomies of city and country, artificial and natural, man versus other living things.
>
> (p. 257)

This sentence does more than communicate effectively. The prose is rhythmic. It evokes an emotional response. It inspires the reader to agree with Lynch's conclusion, and with all the ideas that led him there. Such is the power of truly excellent writing.

Paragraphs

Sentences combine to form paragraphs. Paragraphs are the building blocks of insightful ideas and sophisticated arguments. They provide the substance and proof of your claims, theses, and opinions (Sova, 2004). Pellegrino (2003) compares a paragraph to an orange, where "an orange has several distinct sections connected to each other to form a whole fruit" (p. 19). Try to make each paragraph have one main point (the fruit), with each sentence (the orange slices) building the overall argument.

The authors of this chapter try to keep their paragraphs short, typically covering no more than one subject. The first sentence of a paragraph is the topic sentence. The topic sentence states the main point of the paragraph. Writing simple and clear topic sentences is extremely important to good writing, because topic sentences tell the reader what the paragraph is about as well as define the scope and size of the paragraph (Pellegrino, 2003). The rest of the sentences in the paragraph support the topic sentence.

In the preceding example, Kevin Lynch's paragraph has a very clear topic sentence. The second sentence clarifies and expands upon this topic sentence: "The central difficulty is the analogy itself. Cities are not organisms . . ." The next three sentences in the paragraph highlight specific difficulties with the analogy. All three sentences have a parallel structure, with the same subject and nearly identical punctuation and grammar. Additional sentences, not quoted, provide even more specific explanations of why cities are not organisms. The concluding sentence then summarizes the same point as the topic sentence, while also serving as a transition to the topic sentence of the next paragraph.

As with sentences, paragraphs may have a variety of structures and styles. Victor Pellegrino (2003) describes several paragraph types that bear repeating here.

A narrative paragraph: A narrative paragraph tells a story that the reader can relate to. Generally, it is written in chronological sequence and can contain dialogue. A planner may use a narrative paragraph to describe the general vision for a town or city, using a story to establish the goals and values of the residents.

The paragraph by Bent Flyvbjerg quoted earlier (1998, p. 9) is a good example of a narrative paragraph. The story in this paragraph—the genesis of the Aalborg Project—underlies an entire body of work, including large-scale public policies and a fully articulated research paradigm. Notice how Flyvbjerg's writing style is simultaneously entertaining and informative. Narrative paragraphs are very useful for this dual purpose.

A comparison paragraph: This type of paragraph focuses on developing the similarities between subjects. Writing a comparison paragraph is straightforward. Decide which aspects of the subjects to compare, and write down how each of these aspects is similar.

The paragraph by Nan Ellin quoted earlier (2013, p. 1) is a good example of a comparison paragraph. Ellin highlights a fascinating similarity, likening a plant that neither dies nor thrives to cities that suffer the same fate. This unusual comparison helps the reader reflect on the health of urban places from a completely new perspective.

Comparison paragraphs pair nicely with contrast paragraphs. For Ellin, the contrast is obvious: cities that do not die and do not merely survive, but that grow and thrive. In fact, this contrasting idea provides the title of her book, *Good Urbanism*.

A contrast paragraph: As opposed to a comparison paragraph, a contrast paragraph details the difference between two topics. These paragraphs are particularly effective when writing to persuade or to describe. The contrast can help the reader understand that the differences between two subjects are significant and important.

Nan Ellin uses a brief contrast paragraph to summarize the purpose of *Good Urbanism*:

> We have, to some extent, buried our instinctual capacity to create habitats that support us most fully, places where we may thrive. This book asks what exactly has been lost and describes a path for uncovering this buried urban instinct, dusting it off, and updating it to serve us today.
>
> (p. 3)

Good urbanism, then, is all about contrast: what city makers have done before, what they are doing now, and what they might do differently in the future, including strategies both old (buried) and new (updated).

The paragraph by Kevin Lynch quoted earlier (1984, p. 95) is another good example of a contrast paragraph. Here, Lynch contrasts certain characteristics of cities with the properties of living organisms, demonstrating that the organic metaphor is an inadequate model of urban form. This contrasting paragraph supports Lynch's ensuing argument: that the ecosystem is a better model of urban form than the machine or the living organism.

Narrative, comparison, and contrast paragraphs are all useful writing tools. Try using each of these paragraph types to add variety and interest to your writing. For 27 more ways to organize and write effective paragraphs, see Pellegrino's (2003) *A Writer's Guide to Powerful Paragraphs*.

Cohesion Within and Between Paragraphs

Good writing requires cohesion: "the connection of sentences to one another . . . the flow of a text," and the way the individual sentences and paragraphs of that text combine to form "a unified whole" (Kolln & Gray, 2009, p. 84).

Kolln and Gray suggest three key strategies for cohesive writing. First, repeat important words and phrases, so that the reader is frequently reminded of your central subject matter. Second, employ the "known-new" strategy: make sure that each sentence (or paragraph) contains some known information, establishing a logical connection with the preceding sentence (or paragraph), and some new information, keeping the

32 *Robin Rothfeder and Reid Ewing*

writing active and avoiding the mistake of redundancy (Kolln & Gray, 2009, p. 84). Third, use parallelism: "the repetition of structures of the same form for purposes of clarity and emphasis" (id.).

All of the authors quoted here—Flyvbjerg, Ellin, and Lynch—provide excellent examples of cohesion between sentences. Their writing shows clear evidence of repetition, the known-new strategy, and parallelism. Along with this cohesion between sentences, it is also important to create cohesion between the paragraphs of a whole document. Following, we have listed each successive topic sentence from the Introduction section of John Forrester's seminal JAPA article, *Critical Theory and Planning Practice*. Notice how each topic sentence—the main idea of each paragraph—informs and flows into the next topic sentence of the next paragraph.

- This paper introduces *critical theory* for use in planning contexts . . .
- This work is based on eighteen months of regular observation of a metropolitan city planning department's office of environmental review . . .
- In a nutshell, the argument is as follows: critical theory gives us a new way of understanding action, or what a planner does, as attention-shaping (communicative action), rather than more narrowly as a means to a particular end (instrumental action) . . .
- Such a view leads us to ask a more specific set of questions of the planner than the ones we've always asked before about whose ends or interests are being served.

(John Forrester, 1980, p. 275)

Tone and Voice

Good writing conveys the author's unique identity. Just as each person has an individual and recognizable speaking voice, so does our written voice convey a particular persona. In Zinsser's words: "Ultimately the product that any writer has to sell is not the subject being written about, but who he or she is" (2001, p. 5).

Tone expresses the author's relationship with and attitude toward the subject matter: critical or supportive; participant or observer; ignorant or informed. Voice, on the other hand, expresses who the author is. Writing experts stress that the underlying voice of a written document must be authentic: the identity expressed must be consistent with the author's actual mode of communication (Zinsser, 2001; Kolln & Gray, 2009). This still leaves many options available. You have one voice when speaking with family and friends, another when speaking with colleagues, a third when speaking with your boss. All three voices are genuine representations of yourself, but you select different words for each voice to suit the appropriate context.

Writing tone and voice should be determined by your audience and objectives. You want to choose words, sentences, and paragraphs that will express a trustworthy, convincing, and authentic persona. This is the power of mastering written mechanics and rhetorical grammar. With practice, you gain the ability to choose exactly how you communicate, tailoring each writing product to your specific readership and your particular goals. The second author of this chapter uses an entirely different tone and voice when writing the *Research You Can Use* column as opposed to writing a technical paper for a scholarly journal.

Another great example of different tone and voice is the contrast between articles on induced traffic written by Robert Cervero, one for popular consumption in the magazine/journal *Access* and titled "Are Induced Travel Studies Inducing Bad Investments?" the other for professional planners and academics in the *Journal of the American Planning Association* and titled "Road Expansion, Urban Growth, and Induced Travel: A Path Analysis." As a class exercise in our doctoral technical writing course at the University of Utah, we encourage students to compare the two, paragraph by paragraph, section by section.

The popular piece summarizes induced demand results as follows:

> The path analysis showed that for every 100 percent increase in capacity there'd be an eighty percent increase in travel, reflecting increased travel speeds and land use shifts along improved corridors. However, only around half the increases in speed and growth in building permits was due to the added capacity. Factors like employment and income growth accounted for the other half.
>
> (Cervero, 2003a, p. 26)

The technical piece says the same thing differently.

> Overall, the estimated longer-term path model, summarized in Figure 4, performed fairly well in accounting for VMT growth along sampled California freeway segments. Evidence of "induced travel," "induced growth," and "induced investment" was uncovered. Elasticity estimates of induced travel, however, were lower than that found in most previous studies, including those focused on California freeways. An estimated 80% of California's freeway capacity additions were absorbed by traffic spurred by faster speeds and land use shifts; however, less than half (39%) of this absorption can be attributed to lane-mile expansions.
>
> (Cervero, 2003b, p. 158)

Even the graphics used to depict relationships between highway expansion and VMT differ between the two articles (compare Figures 2.1 and 2.2). The technical graphic provides more details but ultimately not a lot more information.

Organization

> Unity is the anchor of good writing . . . it satisfies the readers' subconscious need for order.
>
> —Zinsser, 2001, p. 50

In addition to structuring sentences and paragraphs, it is important to properly organize your whole document. Select the organizational approach that best fits with your audience and objectives. If you are writing a scholarly article, adhere to the guidelines of scholarly writing. The organization is relatively standardized. After the introduction, there is a literature review, then a methods section, a results section, and a discussion/conclusion section. If you are writing a professional report, use examples as models for your writing. Study the organization of articles in professional journals, general plans, and transportation analyses. If you are aware of the structure of your

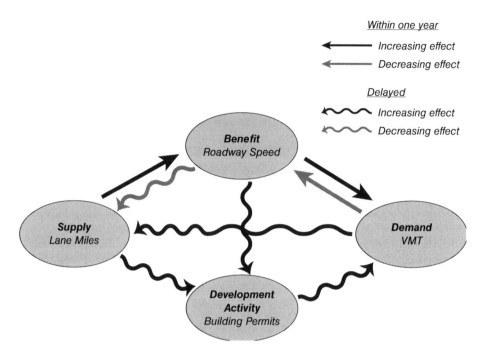

Figure 2.1 Popular Graphic of Induced Demand and Induced Investment
Source: Cervero (2003a)

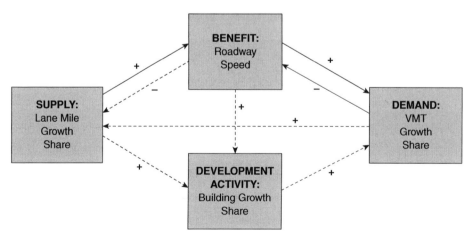

Figure 2.2 Technical Graphic of Induced Demand and Induced Investment
Source: Cervero (2003b)

writing in advance, you can save time and effort writing your manuscript and ensure you meet the expectations of your readers.

The next step is to write your first draft. Get your main points on paper, and reorder those points for logical flow. Use headings and subheadings to help organize information. We cannot stress enough the use of headings and subheadings as an organizing device. Strive for clarity, coherent paragraphs, and logical organization (Zinsser, 2001). It is more important to complete a draft rather than to get stuck struggling over small details. Later on, your work will be revised several times. However, the better your first draft is, the fewer revisions you will need, so strive for a balance between speed and perfection.

Katz (2009) provides several useful suggestions for how to organize a written document, including:

- Use outlines.
- Start by blocking out general ideas, and arrange them in a simple linear order.
- Collect information from outside resources.
- Form rough sentences about the general ideas.
- Arrange the sentences into more specific themes.
- Make your themed lists into rough paragraphs.
- Sculpt the "rough chunks," assembling one specific paragraph for each specific theme.
- Shape a working draft, moving incrementally towards finer levels of detail.
- Only focus on precise wording at the very end.

Katz cautions us to remember that while the writing *product* may be linear, beginning with an introduction and ending with a conclusion, the writing *process* is frequently nonlinear. In a scholarly article, one may often begin by writing a literature review, a description of research methods, and an overview of the results, before constructing parallel introduction and conclusion sections, which frame what has already been written (Bem, 2002).

Rewriting, Editing, and Polishing

> Writing improves in direct ratio to the number of things we can keep out of it that shouldn't be there. . . . Most first drafts can be cut by as much as 50 percent without losing any information or losing the author's voice.
>
> —Zinsser, 2001, p. 17

Write, rewrite, and rewrite again. Good writing is good revising, and it behooves you to conduct several rounds of review before your document is complete. In fact, the process of "rewriting is the essence of writing well" (Zinsser, 2001 p. 84). Just because all the sections of the paper have been composed does not mean that the draft is ready for submission. Almost without exception, the first draft is nowhere near completion. The next essential step is editing and revising. The

36   *Robin Rothfeder and Reid Ewing*

authors of this chapter find that many of their students (not all) rush to finish and submit a first draft, and never spend the necessary time on second and third drafts.

This section presents some useful revision strategies and skills and you will need to develop (Rubens, 2002). The first round of revision should include an analysis of audience, purpose, and organization. Does the paper meet the expectations and organization of the intended audience? Have you clearly stated the purpose of the research? Does the information presented in the paper appear in the correct sections? These questions will help ensure that the paper meets the expectations of the audience, states a clear purpose, and is organized according to accepted conventions. The use of headings and subheadings is important because that will tip you off to when content is misplaced.

As an author, you may be exhausted after producing a draft. So, take a break and come back with fresh eyes. In addition, gain a new perspective by enlisting others as reviewers and editors. Send your first draft to several people for revisions. Pick at least one person who is unfamiliar with the technical specifics of your work—perhaps your spouse or partner—and have them read the document. If your document is written clearly and concisely, even an uninitiated reader should comprehend what you are trying to say. The readers who are familiar with your topic will provide the necessary technical revisions.

Incorporate these revisions into your draft. Manage negative feedback with grace and without defensiveness, and thank your reviewers for their time (Rudenstam & Newton, 2007). In our responses to review comments, any positive comment elicits a thank you. If you think a reviewer is incorrect (they certainly can be), use evidence and persuasion rather than emotion to make your point. A good review is invaluable and they are doing you a favor. The authors of this chapter have always marveled at the value of peer reviews, provided at no cost, simply by submitting an academic paper to a peer-reviewed journal.

As you review, it is most important to ensure that the whole manuscript tells a story or makes a tight-knit argument. Then check the flow of logic from one paragraph to the next. You will almost always find that reordering of paragraphs leads to a more logical flow. Finally check that each sentence relates to the one before and after (Gopen & Swan, 1990).

After you've reviewed the style and organization of your paragraphs and sentences, you should double check that you've cited all your sources correctly. An in-text citation, or *author-date citation*, acknowledges a reference immediately after it appears. Place the citation in parentheses and a period after the parenthesis (Rubens, 2002). Then, ensure all your works cited in text appear in your works cited section and vice versa. Knowing where to find your sources is important for your readers.

Sometimes it is possible that a writer can know too much about a certain topic to write about it clearly (Rubens, 2002). If this is the case, the writer makes inappropriate assumptions about audience knowledge, unless he or she can remember the needs of the intended audience (Rubens, 2002). To avoid this mistake, have a non-expert friend or family member read your work aloud. And, read your work out loud to yourself, to gain a better sense of how the writing flows.

Your document will improve during the process of revision and rewriting. Sometimes it will take several rounds of revisions until the final product emerges. Keep in mind, however, the importance of completing a work on time (Budinski, 2001).

Reports should be completed when action is needed; proposals for funding must obviously meet any submission deadline.

The trick is to find the balance between taking enough time to put your work through several rounds of revision and submission. Academics are notorious for getting things in late. Consultants get things in on time but may sacrifice rigor or completeness. One leading planning academic (who will remain nameless) was known for submitting great reports a year or even two late, and it eventually cost him in competitions for grants and contracts. Another academic planner (who will also remain nameless) is well-known for both quality and timeliness and has had a successful consulting career, as well as a very successful academic career.

Katz suggests a succinct, step-by-step process for rewriting, editing, and polishing. Try to follow his advice as you refine your written documents (2009, pp. 25–28):

- Rework the entire draft, paragraph by paragraph. Create cohesion and flow within and between paragraphs.
- Then, cut, trim, and simplify, sentence by sentence. Fix specific types of problems—"Don't read for overall meaning. Don't pay attention to the global features. Instead, concentrate on sentences and words, and pick a single task each time you sit down" (p. 25).
- Replace passive verbs with active verbs.
- Replace vague descriptions with precise adjectives.
- Stop writing when you come to the end of your ability, and seek outside help.

Literature Reviews

We now focus on one critical section of all academic products and many practice documents. Planning academics and practitioners have one research practice in common: conducting literature reviews. You may think of this as an inherently academic exercise (all academic articles include a literature review right after the introduction or as part of the introduction identifying gaps in the literature). But we would wager that most technical memos written by planners begin with Google searches aimed at finding relevant literature. This section is meant to help both academics and practitioners conduct literature reviews. As a template, we will refer to the publication criteria used by the *Journal of Planning Literature*, and as an example of a solid literature review, we will draw on the JPL article, "Urban Form and Residential Energy Use: A Review of Design Principles and Research Findings," by Yekang Ko of the University of Texas at Arlington.

Style

Is the paper well written, in the active voice? Does it have a cogent statement of purpose? Is it clear, convincingly argued, and logically organized? It's the last of these—the lack of organization—that bothers me most in reviewing academic papers. Thoughts do not flow logically, and extraneous or tangential matters find their way into sections where they don't belong.

Headings and subheadings can help. They serve as signposts for readers and instill discipline in authors, who are less likely to stray from their topic when it is neatly labeled. Ko's review organizes the relevant literature under four headings (housing

38 *Robin Rothfeder and Reid Ewing*

type and size, density, community layout, and planting and surface coverage) with three subheadings under each (statistical studies, simulation studies, and experiments). The review doesn't stray from the topic at hand.

Scope

Does the article cover the literature on the topic comprehensively, focusing on the most important work and citing additional material? The trick to ensuring that a literature review is "systematic" (to use the term of art) is to search bibliographic databases. Academics have access to many excellent databases through their universities, but everyone can make use of Google Scholar. As a test, type in the keywords "residential energy" and "urban planning." Google Scholar comes up with a whopping 1,160 choices and tells you just how often the source article has been cited. How can you possibly be "comprehensive" when faced with so many articles? There are three tricks. First, relegate lesser studies to tables. Ko summarizes 17 articles in one efficient table. Second, limit narrative summaries of individual articles to the most important and synthesize the rest—e.g., "Several authors agree on. . . ." Finally, limit the scope of the review. Ko lists both the topics that will be covered in her review and those that will not be.

Accuracy

Does the author describe and interpret the literature accurately and explain technical items at an appropriate level of detail? Authors tend to present other scholars' findings through the lens of their own thesis. In another paper the second author of this chapter reviewed for JPL, the authors summed up five articles by saying that the authors "all concluded that people living in low-density suburbs are more likely to be overweight, use an automobile more often and for shorter trips, ride bikes and walk less, and have a higher risk of obesity-related illnesses than their more urban counterparts." Not even close to true.

The main findings of articles are usually contained in the abstract, the conclusion, or the results section. When it comes to quantitative studies, we recommend that you also look at the tables. They tell the whole story.

Analysis

Two other JPL review criteria, in our experience, are problematic. To save space, we offer one cautionary note for each. The first is analysis: Articles should be more than a simple presentation of what has been published, avoiding the tendency to uncritically report what Smith or Jones says. We reviewed a paper on sprawl recently for the journal *Sustainability*, which, in the first two drafts, recounted the findings of the now infamous Echenique article without acknowledging the controversy surrounding it (see *Research You Can Use*, October 2012).

Connection to Planning

This is another tricky criterion: The question here is whether the discussion is useful for the planning profession and the practice of planning. Literature reviews and research studies often overreach, going beyond the available evidence to draw broader conclusions that support the author's biases. A paper the second author of this chapter reviewed for *Environment and Planning* recommended streetscape improvements based on a project's Walk Score. But Walk Score does not measure streetscape quality.

Planning Examples

For this section, we have selected award-winning papers in prominent planning journals to use as our case studies of excellent writing.

JPER Winner

Professor Donald Shoup was awarded the Chester Rapkin Award for the Best Paper in the *Journal of Planning Education and Research* in 2009. The award is named after Professor Rapkin who was a distinguished educator, who mentored 70 doctoral and numerous master students at the University of Pennsylvania, Columbia, and Princeton. According to the awards committee, Shoup's article "presents a potentially very important innovation in zoning, which could have significant application in practice." Beyond its practical utility, the "paper is a model for how to write an academic paper within a professional domain" and "it is persuasive, elegant, and economical" (UCLA, 2012).

The premise of Shoup's (2008) article is that it is difficult to assemble sites that are large enough to redevelop at high densities, especially in city centers. As a result, regeneration in city centers is impeded and suburban sprawl spreads onto large sites already in single ownership. He suggests a new planning strategy to encourage voluntary land assembly and graduated density zoning. This strategy can increase the incentive for landowners to cooperate and participate in land assembly so that they can obtain a valuable economic opportunity, rather than hold out and miss the opportunity to combine contiguous properties to trigger higher-density economic benefits.

Shoup demonstrates how to craft an effective introduction. The introduction begins by detailing the traditional approach that cities have used to keep private landowners from holding out in land assemblage. He illustrates the controversy surrounding eminent domain by using examples of cities taking land from private landowners. These examples are strengthened by powerful quotations: "No one should be forced to sell just because a city says a neighborhood isn't rich enough to stay" (Huffstutter, 2006, cited in Shoup 2008, p. 162). By the time the readers reach the end of the introduction, Shoup has clearly demonstrated that eminent domain is a problem and something new is needed. Stating why the research is needed is one of the primary purposes of the introduction.

Also included in the introduction are his research questions, which appear directly after the point is made that this is an important research topic. Shoup asks, "can cities assemble land for infill development without resorting to eminent domain?" Following this research question, Shoup suggests his hypothesis, that graduated density zoning may be a promising strategy, and then he outlines how the rest of the paper will proceed. This is a very good example of an effective introduction.

Shoup uses informative headings to organize his information within the paper. While, he does not explicitly label his sections as methods or results, the information flows logically and is presented in the standard structure of scholarly articles.

40 Robin Rothfeder and Reid Ewing

An effective technique that Shoup uses liberally is pairing concepts with examples. For example, he uses concepts and examples to guide a reader through a complex section describing Graduated Density Zoning. This concept will not be familiar to all readers, but after his description of the concept and use of an example, readers should have a very clear understanding of how it works.

He writes about an example of a city and a rail transit line. The city wants to increase density around the stations, and that transit-oriented development would require sites larger than the existing parcels. The existing properties are small and in poor condition, but many owners either oppose higher density or are holding out for higher prices. Eminent domain is not an attractive option for the city either. Again, Shoup sets the stage to describe the concept of graduated density zoning and the example is made real to the reader.

The awards committee commented that Shoup uses "ingenious figures to make its message clear." These ingenious figures illustrate his concepts and research questions. For example, in order to demonstrate that large single lots gain more square footage than two single lots, Shoup shows the contrasting floor plans (Figure 2.3). Clearly the single lot gains more square footage by reclaiming the setback between the buildings. Furthermore, as Shoup explains, a land assembly of larger lots leads to better urban design, cost savings, and an increase in density.

Overall, Shoup's article demonstrates effective writing. It is clear, concise, and meaningful. One of the *Research You Can Use* columns takes issue with Shoup's methodology, but not with his writing (Ewing, August–September 2008).

JAPA Winner

Another award-winning article that demonstrates a significant original contribution to the field of planning and serves as a model to be emulated by other researchers is Dowell Myers and SungHo Ryu's 2008 article, "Aging Baby Boomers and the Generational Housing Bubble: Foresight and Mitigation of an Epic Transition." Each year, the *Journal of the American Planning Association* honors the authors of excellent JAPA articles with the Best Article award. According to the selection criteria, the award goes to an article that communicates its content in a clear, logical, and comprehensible manner that appeals to a wide audience. This article does just that and received the award in 2008.

Myers and Ryu investigated the impact that the 78 million baby boomers will have on the housing market when they sell off their high-priced homes to relatively less advantaged generations who are fewer in number. Using a long-run projection of annual home buying and selling by age groups in the 50 states, the authors consider implications for communities of the anticipated downturn in demand.

Let us take a look at how the two authors have crafted an introduction that grabs the reader, as well as clearly indicating their contribution to the field:

> The giant baby boom generation born between 1946 and 1964 has been a dominant force in the housing market for decades. This group has always provided the largest age cohorts, and has created a surge in demand as it passed through each stage of the life cycle. As its members entered into home buying in the 1970s, gentrification in cities and construction of starter homes in suburbs increased.

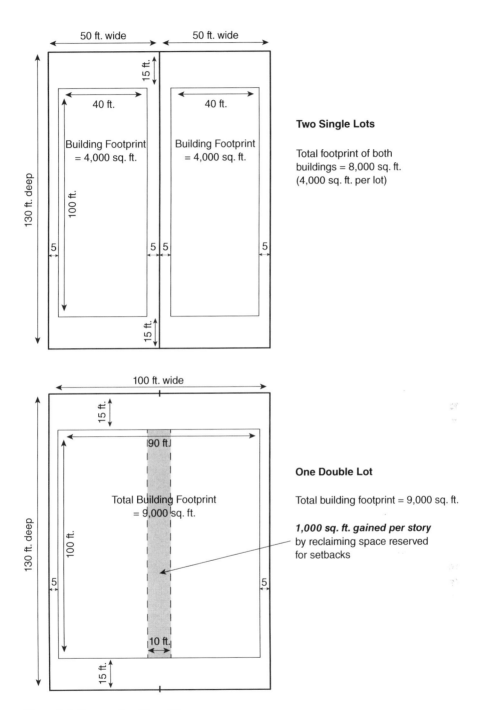

Figure 2.3 Contrasting Floor Plans
Source: Shoup (2008)

> Their subsequent march into middle age was accompanied by rising earnings and larger expenditures for move-up housing. Looking ahead to the coming decade, the boomers will retire, relocate, and eventually withdraw from the housing market. Given the potential effects of so many of these changes happening in a limited period of time, communities should consider how best to plan this transition.

This single paragraph is focused, interesting, and leads the reader directly to why this research is important. Great paragraph.

Following their introduction, the authors review the literature on baby boomers, demographic changes, and changes in the housing market. The literature review is well researched: more than 30 articles are cited. Despite the wealth of research, the authors clearly indicate that their research is filling a gap, the raison d'etre of a literature review:

> What have not been recognized to date are the grave impacts of the growing age imbalance in the housing market.

The methods section of this paper is complete and easy to follow. The authors describe their databases, the size of the sample, and what measures they will use. The steps in their statistical analysis are also detailed. All in all, this is what a methods section should look like.

Their results section is not an exception either: It clearly presents the results. The use of illustrative figures helps tell the story (see Figure 2.4).

They conclude their paper with implications for local planning and open doors to future research.

> Planners must adjust their thinking for a new era that reverses many longstanding assumptions. Though planners in many urban areas have been struggling against gentrification, they may now need to stave off urban decline. Whereas decline once occurred in the central city, it may now be concentrated in suburbs with

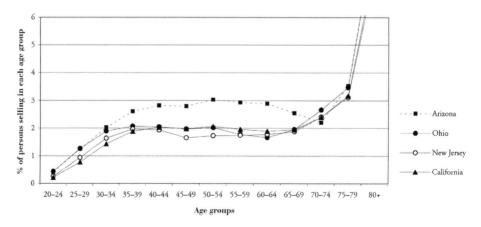

Figure 2.4 Average Annual Percent of Persons Selling Homes in Each Age Group
Source: Myers & Ryu (2008)

surpluses of large-lot single-family housing. Whereas residential development once focused on single-family homes, many states may swing toward denser developments clustered near amenities. Whereas the major housing problem was once affordability, it could now be homeowners' dashed expectations after lifelong investment in home equity. The new challenge may be how to sustain municipal services in the face of declining property values. All of these reversals result from the aging of the baby boomers. By using foresight, planners have a better chance of leading their communities through the difficult transition ahead.

Conclusion

This chapter offers guidance for technical writing, including the purpose of writing in planning, key features of the writing process, its mechanics from individual word choices to the organization of whole documents, guidance for rewriting and editing, and two noteworthy academic papers in top planning journals. In sum, technical writing, applicable to most documents that planners produce, should have a story with a clear, logical narrative line (i.e., argument); be supported by evidence; and involve layers of expertise.

Like any advanced skill, writing must be developed through systematic instruction and practice. However, writing is hard and frustrating for everyone. "If you find that writing is hard," wrote William Zinsser (2001, p. 12), "it's because it is hard." Interestingly, books about writing suggest that the only cure is writing itself. Simply allotting (not finding) time to write and sticking to the schedule should make you a productive writer (Boice, 1990; Silvia, 2007; Zinsser, 2001). We look forward to reading more well-written papers and reports on planning. There are many "good things still to be written" (Saroyan, 1952, p. 2).

Works Cited

Allmendinger, P., & Tewdwr-Jones, M. (Eds.). (2002). *Planning futures: New directions for planning theory.* New York, NY: Routledge.

American Planning Association. (2013). *What is planning?* Retrieved from www.planning.org/aboutplanning/

Appleyard, D. (1981). *Livable streets.* Berkeley, CA: University of California Press.

Bem, D. J. (2002). Writing the empirical journal article. In J. M. Darley, M. P. Zanna, & H. L. Roediger III (Eds.), *The complete academic: A career guide.* Washington, DC: American Psychological Association.

Blueprint Jordan River. (2008). Blueprint Jordan River. Retrieved from http://jordanriver commission.com/wp-content/uploads/BlueprintJordanRiver_LowRes3.pdf (accessed on December 5, 2019).

Boice, R. (1990). *Professors as writers: A self-help guide to productive writing.* Stillwater, OK: New Forums Press.

Budinski, K. G. (2001). *Engineers' guide to technical writing.* Materials Park, OH: ASM International.

Burchell, R. W., Mandelbaum, S. J., & Mazza, L. (Eds.). (1996). *Explorations in planning theory.* Piscataway, NJ: Transaction Publishers.

Campbell, S., & Fainstein, S. S. (2003). *Readings in planning theory.* Studies in Urban & Social Change, Malden, MA: Wiley & Sons, Ltd.

Cargill, M., & O'Conner, P. (2009). *Writing scientific research articles: Strategy and steps.* West Sussex: Wiley Blackwell.

Cervero, R. (2002). Induced travel demand: Research design, empirical evidence, and normative policies. *Journal of Planning Literature, 17*(1), 3–20. https://doi.org/10.1177/088122017001001

Cervero, R. (2003a). Are induced travel studies inducing bad investments? *Access, 22*, 22–27.

Cervero, R. (2003b). Road expansion, urban growth, and induced travel: A path analysis. *Journal of the American Planning Association, 69*(2), 145–163.

City of Berkeley. (2019). *2019 agendas and minutes.* Retrieved from https://www.cityofberkeley.info/Clerk/Commissions/Commissions__Planning_Commission_Homepage.aspx (accessed on December 5, 2019).

City of Portland. (2011). *Comprehensive plan goals and policies.* Retrieved from https://www.portlandonline.com/bps/Comp_Plan_Nov2011.pdf (accessed on December 5, 2019).

Ellin, N. (2013). *Good urbanism: Six steps to creating prosperous places.* Washington, DC: Island Press.

Ewing, R. (2008, August–September). Graduated density zoning—The danger of generalizing from a sample of one. *Planning,* 62.

Ewing, R. & Park, K. (eds.) (2020). *Advanced quantitative research methods for urban planners.* New York, NY: Routledge.

Flyvbjerg, B. (1998). *Rationality and power: Democracy in practice.* Chicago, IL: University of Chicago Press.

Flyvbjerg, B. (2001). *Making social science matter: Why social inquiry fails and how it can succeed again.* Cambridge: Cambridge University Press.

Flyvbjerg, B. (2002). Bringing power to planning research: One researcher's praxis story. *Journal of Planning Education and Research, 21*(4), 353–366.

Flyvbjerg, B., Holm, M. S., & Buhl, S. (2002). Underestimating costs in public works projects: Error or lie? *Journal of the American Planning Association, 68*(3), 279–295.

Flyvbjerg, B., Skamris Holm, M. K., & Buhl, S. L. (2004). What causes cost overrun in transport infrastructure projects? *Transport Reviews, 24*(1), 3–18.

Forester, J. (1980). Critical theory and planning practice. *Journal of the American Planning Association, 46*(3), 275–286.

Goldstein, H., & Maier, G. (2010). The use and valuation of journals in planning scholarship: Peer assessment versus impact factors. *Journal of Planning Education and Research, 30*(1), 66–75.

Gopen, G. D., & Swan, J. (1990). *The science of scientific writing.* Retrieved from https://cseweb.ucsd.edu/~swanson/papers/science-of-writing.pdf

Holtzclaw, J. (2000). Smart growth—As seen from the air: Convenient neighborhood, skip the car. *Sierra Club.* Retrieved from http://vault.sierraclub.org/sprawl/transportation/holtzclaw-awma.pdf

Huffstutter, P. J. (2006, July 27). Ohio landowners win eminent domain case. *Los Angeles Times.* https://www.latimes.com/archives/la-xpm-2006-jul-27-na-eminent27-story.html

Jayaprakash, S. (2008). *Technical writing.* Mumbai: Global Media.

Journal of the American Planning Association (JAPA). (2019). *Aims and scope.* Retrieved from https://www.tandfonline.com/action/journalInformation?show=aimsScope&journalCode=rjpa20 (accessed on December 5, 2019).

Katz, M. J. (2009). *From research to manuscript: A guide to scientific writing.* Cleveland, OH: Springer Science & Business Media.

Kolln, M., & Gray, L. S. (2009). *Rhetorical grammar.* Harlow: Longman.

Lebrun, J. (2007). *Scientific writing: A reader and writer's guide.* River Edge, NJ: World Scientific.

Lester, T., Kaza, N., & Kirk, S. (2014). Making room for manufacturing: Understanding industrial land conversion in cities. *Journal of the American Planning Association, 79*(4), 295–313. https://doi.org/10.1080/01944363.2014.915369

Lindsay, D. (2010). *Scientific writing: Thinking in words.* Collingwood, VIC: CSIRO Publishing.

Lynch, K. (1984). *Good city form.* Cambridge, MA: MIT Press.

Myers, D., & Ryu, S. (2008). Aging baby boomers and the generational housing bubble: Foresight and mitigation of an epic transition. *Journal of the American Planning Association, 74*(1), 17–33. https://doi.org/10.1080/01944360701802006

Nelson, A. C. (2006). Leadership in a new era: Comment on planning leadership in a new era. *Journal of the American Planning Association, 72*(4), 393–409. https://doi.org/10.1080/01944360608976762

Pellegrino, V. C. (2003). *A writer's guide to powerful paragraphs.* Wailuku, HI: Maui ar Thoughts Company.

Pitt, D., & Bassett, E. (2014). Collaborative planning for clean energy initiatives in small to mid-sized cities. *Journal of the American Planning Association, 79*(4), 280–294. https://doi.org/10.1080/01944363.2014.914846

Ross-Larson, B. C. (1999). *Effective writing.* New York, NY: W W Norton & Company.

Rubens, P. (2002). *Science & technical writing.* New York, NY: Routledge.

Rudenstam, K. E., & Newton, R. R. (2007). *Surviving your dissertation* (3rd ed.). Thousand Oaks, CA: Sage Publications.

Ryberg-Webster, S. (2014). Preserving downtown America: Federal rehabilitation tax credits and the transformation of U.S. cities. *Journal of the American Planning Association, 79*(4), 266–279. https://doi.org/10.1080/01944363.2014.903749

Salt Lake City. (2019). *Salt Lake City, Utah City Code.* Retrieved from https://www.sterlingcodifiers.com/codebook/index.php?book_id=672 (accessed on December 5, 2019).

Sandercock, L. (2003). Out of the closet: The importance of stories and storytelling in planning practice. *Planning Theory & Practice, 4*(1), 11–28.

Saroyan, W. (1952). *The bicycle rider in Beverly Hills.* New York, NY: Charles Scribner's Sons.

Shoup, D. (2008). Graduated density zoning. *Journal of Planning Education and Research, 28*(2), 161–179. https://doi.org/10.1177/0739456X08321734

Silvia, P. J. (2007). *How to write a lot: A practical guide to productive academic writing.* Washington, DC: American Psychological Association.

Sova, D. B. (2004). *Writing clearly: A self-teaching guide.* Hoboken, NJ: John Wiley & Sons.

Strunk, W., White, E. B., & Kalman, M. (2007). *The elements of style (illustrated).* London: Penguin.

Tait, M. (2012). Building trust in planning professionals: Understanding the contested legitimacy of a planning decision. *Town Planning Review, 83*(5), 597–618.

Throgmorton, J. A. (2003). Planning as persuasive storytelling in a global-scale web of relationships. *Planning Theory, 2*(2), 125–151.

UCLA. (2012). *Shoup receives his second Rapkin award for best article in JPER.* Retrieved from http://publicaffairs.ucla.edu/news/transportation/shoup-receives-his-second-rapkin-award-best-article-jper

Whyte, W. H. (1988). *City: Rediscovering the center.* New York, NY: Doubleday.

Zinsser, W. (2001). *On writing well: 25th anniversary edition.* New York, NY: HarperCollins.

3 Types of Research

Robert A. Young and Reid Ewing

Overview

Planners commonly engage in three types of research: qualitative, quantitative, or mixed. All research starts with a research question or questions, and these three fundamental approaches to research provide the means by which you answer the question(s). Qualitative research explores the non-numerical traits (qualities) that describe the subject or context under investigation, whereas quantitative research explores the numerical traits (quantities) that are measured or counted, hence their respective names. Mixed methods research combines qualitative and quantitative research, often triangulating to answers based on evidence from both.

The first section of this chapter describes the history of the different research traditions. The second section describes the general concepts and terminology that form the context of research. The third section provides an overview of each of the three types of research and the methods commonly associated with them. Further detailed descriptions of these methods occur later in this book. This chapter concludes with considerations when you choose your research methodology.

History

Planning research has its roots in other disciplines. Qualitative and quantitative research grew out of the scientific method of observation and analysis. Qualitative research approaches descend directly from methods performed on indigenous populations at the height of European colonization (Denzin & Lincoln, 2005). In the 1920s and 1930s, qualitative methods developed at the University of Chicago along with the contemporaneous work in the anthropology of Boas, Mead, Benedict, Evans-Pritchard, Alfred Radcliffe-Brown, Bronislaw Malinowski, and others formed the foundations for contemporary qualitative research (Denzin & Lincoln, 2005).

Drawing from these earlier methods, such noted planning authors as Jacobs (1961), Lynch (1960, 1972), Whyte (1980, 1988), Jackson (1984), and Gehl (1987) published groundbreaking works based on their qualitative observational methods. Indeed, we would argue that the most influential works in planning are based on qualitative, astute observation. Quantitative research tends to come later and test theories grounded in qualitative research.

Quantitative research in planning emerges from methodologies used in economics, political science, public health, business, and other disciplines. The individual chapters in this book, which deal primarily with quantitative research, provide the relevant history of each method.

Research using both qualitative and quantitative approaches has often been overlooked in academia and existed long before the term *mixed methods* appeared in textbooks and publications (Maxwell, 2016). Early investigators who used mixed methods without explicitly stating so include Charles Booth, Jane Addams, Wilhelm Wundt, and Max Weber. Anthropology, archeology, and linguistics have continuously employed qualitative and quantitative methods for many years, but little has been published on how to integrate the two approaches and types of data (Maxwell, 2016). Even newer approaches like design-based research don't get categorized as mixed methods even though they integrate "both qualitative and quantitative data [to] inform the conclusions . . . and test the interpretation (theory) of what took place" (Maxwell, 2016, p. 19).

General Concepts

As you venture into your research, you need to understand the general concepts that provide the underpinnings of all research. This section presents the concepts of data type, inductive versus deductive logic, timeframe, research design, and triangulation.

Data Type

The types of data that you seek will inform and be informed by the research that you intend to do. Greater reliance on primary data dictates more time and funding to collect it and develop the information that informs the findings. Primary data come directly from the responses to surveys, observations, and other data collected by the researcher. Secondary data come from other researchers (e.g., published reports, journals), existing data archives held by a second party (e.g., databases), archival resources (e.g., libraries), or other sources (e.g., books, journal articles, websites) that were not produced by the researcher. The expected results (e.g., verbal descriptions, mathematical models) of the research are the impetus for data collection. Consideration of the story that you ultimately tell will influence your selection of data collected.

Qualitative data reflect a nuanced understanding of the research context and the subsequent development of findings. Due to the time intensive nature of qualitative data collection, it tends to involve smaller samples that may not equally well represent the larger demographic population commonly modeled in quantitative analysis. The findings are also sensitive to research bias in both the collection and analysis of data (Regents of the University of Minnesota, 2014).

Conversely, quantitative data are numerically specific. When properly analyzed, they are objective and reliable. Due to its numeric orientation, quantitative data can be readily communicated using graphs and charts. Best of all, many large datasets already exist. Quantitative data may not accurately describe complex situations as subtleties are distilled into broader singular categories or go missing entirely. Lastly, the use of some of the more sophisticated quantitative analysis methods requires specific expertise that may not be commonly available (Regents of the University of Minnesota, 2014). The authors of this chapter are strong advocates for the use of statistical consultants, and, indeed, have enlisted Bill Greene, Jim Grace, Mark Stevens, Simon Brewer, John Kircher, and others as co-authors of chapters in this book or its advanced-version companion (Ewing & Park, 2020).

We are providing two quantitative datasets with this book on quantitative methods. Both are examples of secondary data, collected in one case by the federal government

48   *Robert A. Young and Reid Ewing*

and processed by us, and in the other case collected by local agencies and processed by us. Chapter 1 provides a description of and data dictionary for each dataset.

Deductive Versus Inductive Logic

Two types of logic are used in research: deductive and inductive. Deductive logic relies on a top-down approach that starts with the more general and moves to the more specific. You first develop a theory on your topic based on your research question(s). To test that theory, you then develop one or more hypotheses. The hypotheses simply present the theory in an operational, testable form.

Through data collection that addresses these hypotheses, you can narrow the focus even further by testing each hypothesis. Through this hypothesis testing, you can confirm or disprove your original theory.

The main theory underlying our first dataset, the UZA dataset, is the theory of highway induced traffic and highway induced development. The theory states that additions to highway capacity generate additional traffic and sprawl development (Ewing, 2008; Ewing, Hamidi, Gallivan, Nelson, & Grace, 2014). Highway building precedes growth. The alternative theory is that of induced highway investment, that is, that departments of transportation are simply responding to growth that has already occurred. Highway building follows growth. Each theory has its proponents.

The main theory underlying our second dataset, the Household Dataset, is that the built environment, or specifically, the D variables mentioned in Chapter 1, affect individual travel behavior. This is sometimes referred to as environmental determinism (Ewing & Cervero, 2010; Ewing, Hamidi, & Grace, 2016). The alternative theory is that of residential self-selection, that is, that people chose to live in places that support their preexisting lifestyle preferences. These people would drive more, or use alternative transport modes more, wherever they lived.

All of these theories lead to testable hypotheses, such as that households living in compact areas produce less vehicle miles traveled (VMT) than those living in sprawling areas, measured in terms of density or compactness indices. Of course, based on a correlation between the two variables, you cannot distinguish between the two theories—environmental determinism and residential self-selection. That requires longitudinal data (Ewing & Cervero, 2010). The deductive process is probably the main process at work in quantitative research.

In contrast to deductive logic, inductive logic involves a bottom-up approach. In inductive reasoning, you begin with specific observations, detect patterns, formulate hypotheses that you can confirm from your observations, and finish by drafting a general theory (Trochim, 2006). The inductive process creates a grounded theory and is probably the main process at work in qualitative research. The theory of environmental determinism, which is tested over and over in the planning literature, ultimately harkens back to the great works referenced previously (Jacobs, 1961, etc.). Qualitative research is beyond the scope of this book.

Timeframe

Within the research design itself, there are two basic timeframes: cross-sectional and longitudinal. A cross-section occurs at a single point in time, whereas a longitudinal study analyzes data over several discrete periods. A cross-sectional study provides insights on what occurred at a particular time, whereas a longitudinal study reveals trends and is more definitive if the research goal is to infer causality.

Let us explain. Everyone has heard the expression "Correlation doesn't equal or imply causation." In Chapter 9, on Correlation, we set forth four conditions for causal inference. One condition for causal interference is theoretical plausibility. The theoretical basis for induced travel is economic. Additional highway capacity reduces the generalized cost (price) of travel in the short-term by reducing travel time. More travel is "consumed." In the longer term, improved accessibility near the highway facility attracts additional highway-oriented development, which increases VMT on the facility and in the corridor (see Figures 3.1 and 3.2).

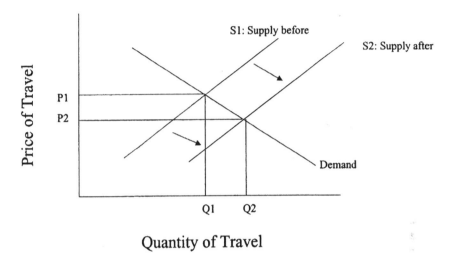

Figure 3.1 Short-Term Response to Added Highway Capacity

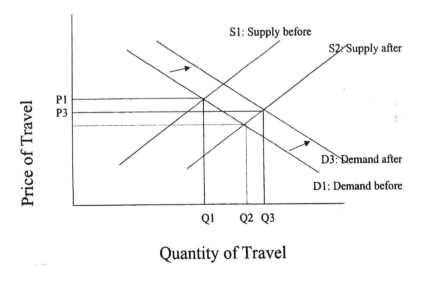

Figure 3.2 Long-Term Response to Added Highway Capacity

Another condition for causal inference is a strong association between variables. That can be established with cross-sectional data. We can and will, later in the book, show a strong association between lane miles of highway capacity and VMT.

The third condition for causal inference is the elimination of rival explanations for a given relationship. This can be partially accomplished with cross-sectional data by controlling statistically for confounding variables. The problem, of course, is that one can never measure and control for every possible influence on an outcome. The fact that Portland has lower VMT per capita than Atlanta may be due in part to less highway capacity, but may also be due to immeasurable and uncontrollable influences such as a different political culture, which may confound the relationship between highway capacity and VMT in a cross-sectional study. The beauty of longitudinal data is that these immeasurables may be relatively constant over time, and hence cancel out when one model changes in VMT over time.

The fourth condition for causal inference is a time sequence, with the cause always preceding the effect. We can say nothing about the time sequence from cross-sectional data since they are collected at a single point in time. Even structural equation modeling, which explores causal pathways, cannot establish a time sequence. SEM is described in Chapter 8 of *Advanced Quantitative Research Methods for Urban Planners*.

Only with longitudinal data can we be sure that the cause precedes the effect. Using the example of induced traffic and induced development, there have been studies that monitored traffic and development levels in highway corridors after highway widenings (Cervero, 2002). By comparing traffic in a corridor just before the widening, to traffic immediately after the widening, and in later years, researchers can estimate the short, medium, and long-term effects of the widening. To account for general trends in traffic growth, such studies often pair treated corridors with untreated control corridors. The time sequence is established by the fact that the treatment, that is, the widening, occurs between the before and after observations.

Research Design

There are four experimental research design types (Edmonds & Kennedy, 2013; Shadish, Cook, & Campbell, 2002): randomized experiments, quasi-experiments, natural experiments, and non-experiments.

Random experiments (Shadish et al., 2002, pp. 12–13) occur when subjects are randomly assigned to treatment and control groups. With random assignment, study participants have the same chance of being assigned to the treatment group or the control group. Random assignment, therefore, ensures that the groups are roughly equivalent before the treatment, so any significant differences after the treatment can be attributed to the treatment itself.

True experiments are commonplace in other fields, such as clinical trials in medicine, but they are very rare indeed in planning (for one example, see Guo, Agrawal, & Dill, 2011). The closest planners ordinarily come to true experiments are stated choice experiments, where special surveys are used to offer different hypothetical options to respondents, and their choices tell you something about their preferences (see, for example, Tian et al., 2015).

The Household Dataset links neighborhood characteristics to household travel behavior. Households have self-selected into neighborhoods. In contrast, a true experiment would require that households be randomly assigned to neighborhoods. If those randomly assigned to compact neighborhoods traveled less by car than those randomly assigned to sprawling neighborhoods, we could then (and only then) be fairly certain that neighborhood design caused differences in household travel—lots of luck conducting such an experiment in a free market economy.

Quasi-experiments (Shadish et al., 2002, pp. 13–17; Ewing, 2012) test hypotheses about causes and include a control group and, frequently, pretest measurements that are compared with posttest responses after the treatment. Quasi-experimental designs in planning have compared modes of travel in a transit corridor before and after a light rail line was constructed, using an otherwise comparable corridor as a control (Ewing & Hamidi, 2014), and have compared traffic crash rates before and after certain streets were traffic calmed, using otherwise comparable streets as controls (Ewing, Chen, & Chen, 2013). The experimental *treatment* in the first case was the installation of the light rail line; the experimental *treatment* in the second case was the installation of speed humps. Time sequence was established in these studies because the before measurement preceded the treatment, and the after measurement followed the treatment. Quasi-experimental designs are described in detail in Chapter 14.

A natural experiment is very closely related to a quasi-experiment, as just defined and illustrated. The individuals (or clusters of individuals) exposed to the experimental and control conditions are determined by nature or by other factors outside the control of the investigator, but the process governing the exposures arguably resembles random assignment. One could argue that the two preceding examples, light rail and traffic calming quasi-experiments, were actually natural experiments because *assignment* to treatment and control groups was outside the control of the investigator, but arguably the households and streets in the two groups were otherwise comparable. If the investigator, or the transportation department, had randomly assigned streets to the treatment and control groups, the latter study would qualify as a true experiment.

Lastly, a non-experiment lacks the random assignment found in true experiments and lacks the pretest observations and control groups found in quasi-experiments. The regression methods in subsequent chapters, whether applied to different urbanized areas that have more or less highway capacity, or to households living in more or less compact neighborhoods, all seek to control for other differences statistically and thus isolate the effects of highway capacity on vehicle miles traveled using the UZA dataset, and the effects of compact neighborhood design on household travel behavior using the household dataset.

Triangulation

Triangulation combines data drawn from different sources and methods, often at different times in different places and from different people. The point of triangulation is to determine if similar findings will emerge from additional methodological approaches and thus confirm or disprove the original findings. For example, a researcher can begin with a single qualitative or quantitative study to develop the initial findings. To triangulate, the researcher then uses additional, but different,

52   *Robert A. Young and Reid Ewing*

sources to confirm or disprove the findings from the original study. As Rudestam and Newton (2007, pp. 214–215) state: "The different sources may include additional participants, other methodologies, or previously conducted studies."

The multiple methods may include structured and unstructured interviews, sample surveys, focus groups, content analyses of documents, participant observation, and examination of archival records. These are all qualitative approaches. And qualitative and quantitative approaches can, of course, be combined.

Meta-analysis and meta-regression, the subjects of Chapter 10 in *Advanced Quantitative Research Methods for Urban Planners*, involve triangulation of quantitative study results to produce weighted averages or pooled coefficient values. The meta-analysis by Ewing and Cervero (2010) is a classic example related to the household dataset, in which the findings of many built environment-travel studies were combined to produce one set of elasticities relating the built environment to household travel behavior. Elasticities were computed for VMT, walk trips, and transit trips with respect to all the D variables. The household dataset, in a sense, is an exercise in triangulation as it pools data from multiple regions. When analyzed with multilevel modeling, the resulting regression models take information from all of these regions and arrive at a common set of regression coefficients.

If we looked to the UZA dataset, which also includes data on VMT and the built environment, to confirm relationships from the household dataset, that would also be an exercise in triangulation. In this case, an aggregate dataset might be used to validate the elasticity of VMT with respect to density from a disaggregate dataset, or vice versa. In fact, we made this comparison in a recent article and found that the aggregate elasticity has the same sign but is greater (in absolute value) than the disaggregate elasticity (Ewing et al., 2017). The reasons are spelled out in the article. But both datasets lend credence to the basic finding—that VMT falls with rising density.

How might qualitative research be combined with the kind of quantitative research made possible with these two datasets? We have already raised the theory of residential self-selection as an alternative explanation for the correlation between neighborhood built environmental characteristics (the D variables) and household travel behavior (VMT, walk trips, and transit trips). One of the qualitative approaches to assessing the strength of self-selection effects is to simply ask people about the factors they considered in choosing a residence. If the walkability of the neighborhood, or if access to transit or highway facilities, are way down the list of location factors, one might conclude that self-selection effects are minor. If they are toward the top of the list, one might conclude the opposite.

As an example, Hollie Lund (2006) surveyed the 605 households that moved to transit-oriented developments (TODs) within the previous five years, finding a wide range of motivations. About one-third of respondents reported access to transit as one of the top three reasons for choosing to live in a TOD. They were equally or more likely to cite lower housing cost or the quality of the neighborhood. Her results tend to bolster results of quantitative studies that show that anywhere from 48 percent to 98 percent of the difference in vehicle miles driven by comparable household living in different neighborhoods is due to direct environmental influences, the balance being due to self-selection (Ewing & Cervero, 2010; Ewing et al., 2016). Thus, we can triangulate to a sound conclusion about the relative importance of environmental determinism versus residential self-selection by combining the results of qualitative and quantitative studies.

Qualitative Methods

The numerous historical approaches to qualitative research are shown in Figure 3.3. There are basically four research traditions: narrative (storytelling), phenomenology (lived experiences), grounded theory (theoretical explanation), and ethnographic (culture-sharing groups) (Groat & Wang, 2002; Lewis-Beck, Bryman, & Futing Liao, 2004; Rudestam & Newton, 2007; Roberts, 2010; Creswell, 2013; Edmonds & Kennedy, 2013).

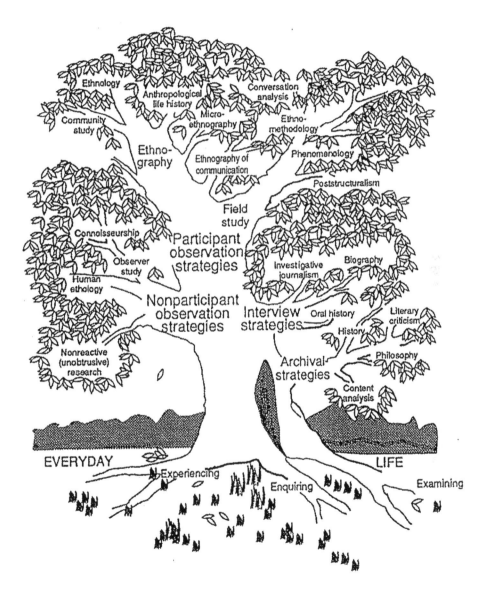

Figure 3.3 Qualitative Research Family Tree
Source: Miles & Huberman (1994, p. 6)

54   *Robert A. Young and Reid Ewing*

In narratives, the researcher seeks out individuals to tell the story of their lives. Phenomenology is similar but with an expanded view of a group that has witnessed or attended a phenomenon. Grounded theorists develop a theory based primarily on observation, with multiple stages of data collection and analysis. Ethnographic researchers study cultural groups in their natural setting over long periods.

Specific qualitative methods used by planners for narrative, phenomenological, grounded theory, and ethnographic research include:

- Case studies (Ewing, August–September 2008)
- Survey research (Ewing, December 2007)
- Observational methods (Ewing, February 2014)
- Interviews and focus groups (Ewing, October 2007)

Draft chapters have already been written on each of the preceding. The next edition of this book will include these chapters.

Quantitative Methods

This is a book about basic quantitative methods used by planners. Individual chapters that follow present all the methods in common use.

- Descriptive statistics
- Chi-square
- Correlation
- Difference of means
- Analysis of variance (ANOVA)
- Linear regression
- Logistic regression
- Quasi-experimental methods

The companion book, *Advanced Quantitative Research Methods for Urban Planners*, covers the following more advanced methods:

- Poisson and negative binomial regression
- Factor analysis
- Cluster analysis
- Multilevel modeling
- Structural equation modeling
- Spatial econometrics
- Meta-analysis and meta-regression

The construction and application of these methods make it impractical to describe them here, and they will instead be described in detail later in this book and in its companion.

Mixed Methods

In February 2013, the second author of this chapter wrote a *Research You Can Use* column for *Planning* magazine on mixed methods research. We borrow from that column now.

The argument for mixed methods goes like this. First, quantitative and qualitative studies answer different, but equally important questions. Qualitative research deals with the why and how of something, whereas quantitative research mostly responds to questions of how much. Second, qualitative research is often the best way to determine causality between variables, not just correlation. Third, quantitative and qualitative studies can provide independent validation of the same phenomenon. Triangulation, or the use of multiple methods to double-check results, was first advocated by Todd Jick of Cornell University, one of the pioneers of mixed method research. In a 1979 article, he wrote, "The convergence or agreement between two methods . . . enhances our belief that the results are valid and not a methodological artifact" (p. 602).

Adam Millard-Ball, an assistant professor of environmental studies at the University of California, Santa Cruz, performed a mixed methods study of climate action planning by California cities. The quantitative portion of the study, published in the *Journal of Urban Economics*, found that cities with climate action plans have more green buildings, spend more on pedestrian and bicycle infrastructure, and implement more programs to divert waste from methane-generating landfills. However, the same study concluded that these actions result not from the climate plans themselves, but rather from the pressure of citizen groups. In short, the correlation between climate action planning and emission-reduction measures does not mean that the former causes the latter, but rather that confounding factors are at work, revealing a classic problem with quantitative studies.

To get at the thorny issue of causation, Millard-Ball conducted a second study, published in the *Journal of Planning Education and Research*. The second study was qualitative. Based on case studies of municipal climate action planning, he found little evidence of causal impacts. Instead, cities use climate plans to codify policies that were likely to happen anyway. This result is not too surprising since climate action planning by local governments in California is strictly voluntary.

The connection between Millard-Ball's quantitative and qualitative studies is two-fold (Figure 3.4). First, and most obviously, the qualitative study validates the findings of the earlier quantitative study. Second, the quantitative study provides a clever method of case study selection. By selecting cases for the qualitative study that outperform expectations in the quantitative study, Millard-Ball could conduct cross-case comparisons of two cities that perform above expectations on environmental indicators (only one with a climate plan) and two cities with climate plans (only one performing above expectations).

Which Method to Use?

Researchers select research methods based on the problem they are studying, how they will use the findings to answer research questions, and the type of data available (Roberts, 2010). The researcher's expertise with a methodology may also dictate the approach selected and whether the research is outsourced to experts like Bill Greene and Jim Grace, both of whom have been called upon for statistical consulting services by the second author of this chapter and are co-authoring chapters of this book in which they have unique expertise.

Above all, research methodology selection depends on funding and time availability. Funding includes the resources available to pay someone to help with the research. Surveys, interviews, and focus groups are more time and capital-intensive than the use of secondary data. Limited funding constrains opportunities to acquire

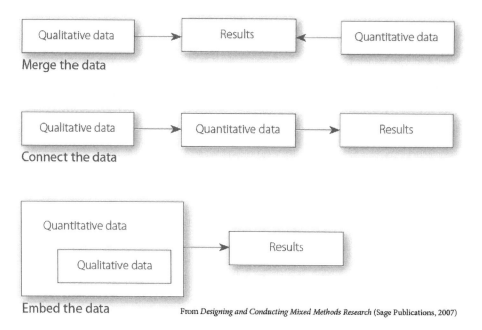

Figure 3.4 Three Ways of Mixing Quantitative and Qualitative Data
Source: Creswell & Clark (2017)

data from proprietary databases or to conduct data collection yourself. Likewise, timeframe plays a role in method selection. A short timeframe may, at the very least, limit sample or case study size in quantitative and qualitative research, respectively.

At this point, we are going to personalize the discussion somewhat based on the second author's experience. We will focus on quantitative methods and the UZA dataset, though the story is just as rich for the household dataset. The story of the first database began with a desire to test the theory of highway induced traffic. All of the previous studies had methodological limitations, and many produced conflicting results.

To test the theory of induced traffic requires VMT data, which are comprehensively available only for FHWA adjusted urbanized areas from *Highway Statistics*. Given this fact, the UZA dataset took more than a year to construct. It was simple enough to extract several variables from *Highway Statistics* and the *National Transit Database*. However, this did not allow us to test the theory of induced traffic because many potential confounders were missing from the databases, such as per capita income and population density. These could be estimated with U.S. Census or American Community Survey data, but we first had to know the boundaries of the FHWA urbanized areas to which *Highway Statistics* applied. These are different from Census urbanized areas. Oddly, FHWA itself didn't have a shapefile of urbanized area boundaries, and instead advised us to contact individual states.

Many months, and hundreds of calls and emails later, we had shapefiles for all 50 states and 443 urbanized areas. We then combined the individual state files into one national shapefile by using the *merge* function in GIS. Many of the urbanized areas cross state boundaries, and in this case, we had more than one polygon for each urbanized area. So, we used the *dissolve* function in GIS to integrate those polygons into one for each urbanized area.

After cleaning the data, we did several spatial joins in GIS to capture data from other sources. For example, we used the *centroid* function to join the 2010 census tracts to FHWA urbanized areas. We then aggregated values of per capita income for census tracts to obtain urbanized area weighted averages (weighted by population).

Other data were proprietary and had to be purchased. Average fuel price will obviously affect VMT, and only statewide averages were available free of charge. So we purchased metropolitan level fuel price data from the Oil Price Information Service.

Once we had a database in hand, we had to decide what statistical method to use to analyze the data. This is not a case for simple linear regression, as there are mediating variables and complex causal pathways. Structural equation modeling was the preferred approach, and Jim Grace, a leading national expert on SEM, was called in as a statistical consultant and co-author of the early studies. SE models were estimated with AMOS, a particularly user-friendly software package specifically for SEM (see Chapter 8 of *Advanced Quantitative Research Methods for Urban Planners*). The original articles arising from this effort dealt with the question of induced traffic (Ewing et al., 2013, 2014), but the focus has since shifted to other research questions that are researchable with the UZA dataset (Ewing et al., 2017; Ewing, Tian, & Lyons, 2018). Perhaps you will find other uses for the dataset as you become familiar with it in the quantitative chapters ahead.

Conclusion

As planning research engages such issues as public health, urban ecology, and social justice, you need to be alert to transcending traditional planning research methods. Methods used outside of planning can help planning address these contemporary problems. Therefore, consider research methodologies that have not been (widely) used in planning research but are in current use elsewhere. As Ewing pointed out in writing about translational research methods used in medicine and how they could be applied to planning research: "I envision a day when progressive MPOs will move beyond average travel speed as the be-all and end-all of transportation planning and begin to deal with the larger issues of public health" (2010, 40).

Works Cited

Baltagi, B. H. (2008). *A companion to theoretical econometrics*. Hoboken, NJ: John Wiley & Sons.

Boslaugh, S., & Waters, P. A. (2008). *Statistics in a nutshell: A quick reference guide*. Beijing: O'Reilly.

Cervero, R. (2002). Built environments and mode choice: Toward a normative framework. *Transportation Research Part D: Transport and Environment, 7*(4), 265–284.

Columbia CNMTL. *Two sample t-test*. Retrieved from http://ccnmtl.columbia.edu/projects/qmss/home.html

Creswell, J. W. (2009). *Research design: Qualitative, quantitative, and mixed methods approaches* (3rd ed.). Thousand Oaks, CA: Sage Publications.

Creswell, J. W. (2013). *Qualitative inquiry and research design* (3rd ed.). Thousand Oaks, CA: Sage Publications.

Creswell, J. W., & Clark, V. L. P. (2017). *Designing and conducting mixed methods research* (3rd ed.). Thousand Oaks, CA: Sage publications.

Denzin, N. K. (1970). *The research act as sociology*. Chicago, IL: Aldine.

Denzin, N. K., & Lincoln, Y. S. (Eds.). (2005). *The Sage handbook of qualitative research* (3rd ed.). Thousand Oaks, CA: Sage Publications.

Edmonds, W. A., & Kennedy, T. D. (2013). *An applied reference guide to research designs*. Thousand Oaks, CA: Sage Publications.

Ellett, W. (2007). *The case study handbook: How to read, discuss, and write persuasively about cases*. Boston, MA: Harvard Business Press.

Ewing, R. (2007, October). When qualitative research trumps quantitative—Cultural economy and smart growth. *Planning, 52*.

Ewing, R. (2007, December). The demand for smart growth: What survey research tells us. *Planning, 52*.

Ewing, R. (2008). Highway-induced development: Research results for metropolitan areas. *Transportation Research Record, 2067*(1), 101–109.

Ewing, R. (2008, August-September). Graduated density zoning—The danger of generalizing from a sample of one. *Planning, 62*.

Ewing, R. (2009, January). When quantitative research trumps qualitative—What makes transfer of development rights work? *Planning, 49*.

Ewing, R. (2010, October). Translational research: The next new thing. *Planning, 40*.

Ewing, R. (2012, February). Experiments and quasi-experiments: Two great new studies. *Planning, 44*.

Ewing, R. (2013, February). Mixing methods for clearer results. *Planning, 46*.

Ewing, R. (2014, February). Observation as a research method (and the importance of public seating). *Planning, 47–48*.

Ewing, R., & Cervero, R. (2010). Travel and the built environment: A meta-analysis. *Journal of the American Planning Association, 76*(3), 265–294.

Ewing, R., Chen, L., & Chen, C. (2013). Quasi-experimental study of traffic calming measures in New York City. *Transportation Research Record: Journal of the Transportation Research Board*, (2364), 29–35.

Ewing, R., & Hamidi, S. (2014). Longitudinal analysis of transit's land use multiplier in Portland (OR). *Journal of the American Planning Association, 80*(2), 123–137.

Ewing, R., Hamidi, S., Gallivan, F., Nelson, A. C., & Grace, J. B. (2013). Combined effects of compact development, transportation investments, and road user pricing on vehicle miles traveled in urbanized areas. *Transportation Research Record: Journal of the Transportation Research Board*, (2397), 117–124.

Ewing, R., Hamidi, S., Gallivan, F., Nelson, A. C., & Grace, J. B. (2014). Structural equation models of VMT growth in US urbanised areas. *Urban Studies, 51*(14), 3079–3096.

Ewing, R., Hamidi, S., & Grace, J. B. (2016). Compact development and VMT: Environmental determinism, self-selection, or some of both? *Environment and Planning B: Planning and Design, 43*(4), 737–755. https://doi.org/10.1177/0265813515594811

Ewing, R., Hamidi, S., Tian, G., Proffitt, D., Tonin, S., & Fregolent, L. (2017). Testing Newman and Kenworthy's theory of density and automobile dependence. *Journal of Planning Education and Research*. https://doi.org/10.1177/0739456X16688767

Ewing, R., Tian, G., & Lyons, T. (2018). Does compact development increase or reduce traffic congestion? *Cities, 72*, 94–101.

Gaber, J., & Gaber, S. (2007). *Qualitative analysis for planning & policy: Beyond the numbers*. Chicago, IL: American Planning Association.

Gardner, W., Mulvey, E. P., & Shaw, E. C. (1995). Regression analyses of counts and rates: Poisson, overdispersed poisson, and negative binomial models. *Psychological Bulletin, 118*(3), 392–404. http://dx.doi.org/10.1037/0033-2909.118.3.392

Gehl, J. (1987). *Life between buildings: Using public space*. New York, NY: Van Nostrand Reinhold.

Gehl, J., & Svarre, B. (2013). *How to study public life*. Washington, DC: Island Press.

Given, L. (Ed.). (2008). *The Sage encyclopedia of qualitative research methods: Volumes 1 and 2*. Thousand Oaks, CA: Sage Publications.

Grace, J. B. (2006). *Structural equation modeling and natural systems.* Cambridge: Cambridge University Press.

Groat, L., & Wang, D. (2002). *Architectural research methods.* New York, NY: John Wiley & Sons.

Guo, Z., Agrawal, A. W., & Dill, J. (2011). Are land use planning and congestion pricing mutually supportive? Evidence from a pilot mileage fee program in Portland, OR. *Journal of the American Planning Association, 77*(3), 232–250. https://doi.org/10.1080/01944363.2011.592129

Jackson, J. B. (1984). *Discovering the vernacular landscape.* New Haven, CT: Yale University Press.

Jacobs, J. (1961). *The death and life of great American cities.* New York, NY: Random House.

Jick, T. D. (1979). Mixing qualitative and quantitative methods: Triangulation in action. *Administrative science quarterly, 24*(4), 602–611.

Kelbaugh, D. (1997). *Common place: Toward neighborhood and regional design.* Seattle: University of Washington Press.

Lewis-Beck, M., Bryman, A., & Futing Liao, T. (Eds.). (2004). *The Sage encyclopedia of social science research methods.* Thousand Oaks, CA: Sage Publications.

Lund, H. (2006). Reasons for living in a transit-oriented development, and associated transit use. *Journal of the American Planning Association, 72*(3), 357–366. https://doi.org/10.1080/01944360608976757

Lynch, K. (1960). *The image of the city.* Cambridge, MA: MIT Press.

Lynch, K. (1972). *What time is this place?* Cambridge, MA: MIT Press.

Maxwell, J. A. (2016). Expanding the history and range of mixed methods research. *Journal of Mixed Methods Research, 10*(1), 12–27.

Merriam-Webster. *Bayesian.* Retrieved from www.merriam-webster.com/dictionary/bayesian

Miles, M., & Huberman, A. M. (1994). *Qualitative data analysis* (2nd ed.). Thousand Oaks, CA: Sage Publications.

Morrish, W. R., & Brown, C. W. (1994). *Planning to stay: Learning to see the physical features of your neighborhood.* Minneapolis, MN: Milkweed Editions.

Plowright, D. (2011). *Using mixed methods: Frameworks for an integrated methodology.* Thousand Oaks, CA: Sage Publications.

Raudenbush, S. W., & Bryk, A. S. (2002). *Hierarchical linear models* (2nd ed.). Thousand Oaks, CA: Sage Publications.

Regents of the University of Minnesota. (2014). *Qualitative or quantitative data?* Retrieved from https://cyfernetsearch.org/ilm_6_3

Roberts, C. (2010). *The dissertation journey* (2nd ed.). Thousand Oaks, CA: Corwin.

Rudestam, K. E., & Newton, R. R. (2007). *Surviving your dissertation: A complete guide to content and process* (3rd ed.). Thousand Oaks, CA: Sage Publications.

Salkind, N. J. (2011). *Statistics for people who (think they) hate statistics* (4th ed.). Thousand Oaks, CA: Sage Publications.

Sanoff, H. (1991). *Visual research methods in design.* New York, NY: Van Nostrand Reinhold.

Sanoff, H. (2000). *Community participation methods in design and planning.* New York, NY: John Wiley & Sons.

Scenic America. (1999). *O say can you see: A visual awareness toolkit for communities.* Washington, DC: Scenic America.

Shadish, W. R., Cook, T. D., & Campbell, D. T. (2002). *Experimental and quasi-experimental designs for causal inference.* Boston, MA: Houghton Mifflin.

Stake, R. (1995). *The art of case study research.* Thousand Oaks, CA: Sage Publications.

Stake, R. (2006). *Multiple case study analysis.* New York, NY: The Guilford Press.

Stake, R. (2010). *Qualitative research: Studying how things work.* New York, NY: The Guilford Press.

Stat Trek. (2014). *Experimental designs in statistics.* Retrieved from http://stattrek.com/experiments/experimental-design.aspx

Tian, G., Ewing, R., & Greene, W. (2015). Desire for smart growth: A survey of residential preferences in the Salt Lake region of Utah. *Housing Policy Debate, 25*(3), 446–462.

Tracy, S. J. (2013). *Qualitative research methods: Collecting evidence, crafting analysis, communicating impact.* Hoboken, NJ: Wiley Blackwell.

60 *Robert A. Young and Reid Ewing*

Trochim, W. M. (2006). *Deduction and induction: The research methods knowledge base.* Retrieved from www.socialresearchmethods.net/kb/dedind.php

University of Strathclyde. (2014). *What is logistic regression.* Retrieved from www.strath.ac.uk/aer/materials/5furtherquantitativeresearchdesignandanalysis/unit6/whatislogisticregression/

Urban Design Associates. (2003). *The urban design handbook: Techniques and working methods.* New York, NY: W W Norton & Company.

Walters, D. (2007). *Designing community: Charrettes, master plans and form-based codes.* Amsterdam: Architectural Press.

Whyte, W. H. (1980). *The social life of small urban spaces.* New York, NY: Project for Public Places.

Whyte, W. H. (1988). *City: Rediscovering the center.* New York, NY: Doubleday.

Young, R. A. (2014). *Economic resiliency of property values in historic districts* (Doctoral dissertation). University of Utah College of Architecture + Planning.

4 Planning Data and Analysis

Thomas W. Sanchez, Sadegh Sabouri,
Keunhyun Park, and Junsik Kim

Overview

Urban planning is information-driven decision-making. Cities and regions are "systems of systems"; their characteristics are many, including the dimensions of time and space. There is much information about the history and characteristics of cities and regions as well as information generated by cities and regions. Plan-making, it can be argued, is a data hungry process as suggested by the rational planning model. As seen in the model (Figure 4.1), identifying the relevant goals and objectives is the first step, which itself requires information from a range of sources and stakeholders. Planners are trained to ask questions, matching them with appropriate data. This chapter focuses on planning data as an important element in planning analysis and research.

Planning questions and issues are often framed as *problems*, including, for instance, traffic congestion, lack of affordable housing, and land use conflicts. Planning questions can also take the form of opportunities. Economic development, open space and parks planning, and community involvement represent situations where alternative actions can lead to increased efficiency, increased satisfaction, and new ideas— while not being specifically rooted in discreet, identifiable problems. Therefore, in addition to identifying deficiencies and challenges, a planner's role includes drawing upon experience and evidence to create or enhance change. Again, this relies on the ability to match appropriate information with the question at hand, as efficiently as possible. Whether a *problem* or an *opportunity*, quantitative and qualitative evidence is used to support decisions and actions as part of the plan-making process. The following discusses planning data types, structures, and formats that are common to planning research and analysis. An understanding of data capacities and limitations is an important part of research design.

Planning Data Types and Structures/Formats

Planners are expected to be fluent in several data types and formats given the wide range of what they observe and measure. These include, but are not limited to, economic, demographic, physical, and environmental conditions over time and space (Ma, Lam, & Leung, 2018). These data may also be aggregated, depending on the type of analysis, the unit of analysis, and the methods of data collection. The data collection step is important not only for acquiring information for analysis, but also because it dictates the kinds of questions that can be answered. This includes dimensions of who, what, where, when, and why. Sufficient time and forethought is needed

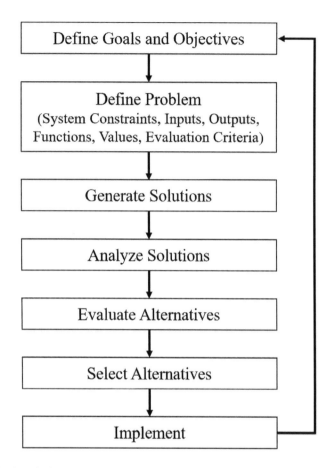

Figure 4.1 Rational Planning Model

to clarify how the data will be used and the types of statements and results that will be communicated (Wang & Hofe, 2008). Answering these questions first will better inform the data collection strategy and overall analysis.

Data are collected from either *primary* or *secondary* sources. Primary data collection occurs when data are obtained firsthand, directly from a source. Examples include surveys, interviews, field observation, or sensed data. For instance, surveys are commonly used by planners to obtain feedback from residents for community involvement activities to gauge satisfaction and to inventory needs and preferences. Such surveys can result in different data types, structured or unstructured, which involve particular data management and analysis approaches (discussed later). This includes open and closed-ended questions depending on question types.

Primary data collection is often expensive because it involves the effort of identifying, contacting, and directly observing individual sources, along with coding, cleaning, and verifying the data. On the other hand, secondary data have been acquired by another (primary) source, which in many cases, has processed, cleaned, and verified

Planning Data and Analysis   63

the data. A very common source of secondary data for urban planners is the U.S. Census. While secondary data can save time and effort, it is essential to understand the methods and purposes of the original data collection to determine appropriateness. This information should be included as part of the meta-data, which documents the origins and reliability of the data.

Sampling and Bias

During either primary or secondary data collection it is important to understand the sampling method employed and how it may introduce bias or error in the data. Sampling usually occurs when it is not feasible or efficient to collect information from every case in a study population. Collecting information about every individual observation in a large population can be expensive and time consuming. In addition, it is often true that the variability of characteristics in a population can be captured with less than a 100 percent sample. At a certain point the increment of new information (or variation) learned by an additional observation begins to decline. This depends on the overall size and variation within a population. Understanding the potential for bias within a dataset has direct implications for the reliability of resulting analyses (see Chapter 6).

Bias in relation to data sampling refers to the misrepresentation of population characteristics. Biased sampling leads to the selection of observations that are not in proportion to the distribution of values in the study population. Analyses using biased data can produce biased or unreliable results. For example, a study of the general public that had only male survey respondents will only represent the characteristics of males, and not that of the whole population as was intended. This can result from faulty sampling methods or poor study design.

Tabular Data

There are a few accepted ways to organize data for storage, manipulation, and analysis. Observations that share the same fields or characteristics can be stored in a table format, represented by rows (observations) and columns (fields). Ideally all of the same types of information are collected for each observation so that direct comparisons can be made and patterns detected across multiple variables. For example, a table of housing characteristics may include the number of bedrooms, number of bathrooms, interior square footage, and lot size. In this case a row of information represents one housing unit, and each column represents the four attributes mentioned. Tabular data is commonly rectangular in shape, with the same number of columns (fields) for each row (observations). Also referred to as a flat file, tabular data is a simple structure, although the number of rows and columns can be quite large.

Relational data structures join together or *relate* multiple flat files when each row or observation in a flat file may have multiple associated records in an external data file. An example is property tax payments associated with a single house address (Figure 4.2). The primary tabular data identifies individual houses by address with an accompanying table of annual tax statements (or transactions) that relate to each other by address, parcel identification number, or other identifier. This can be a more efficient structure for managing the different types of data, such as ownership information (single records) and associated transactions (multiple records), rather than including a significant amount of redundant information in a single file.

Address	Bdrms	Baths	Sq.Ft.	Lot Size
123 Main Street	3	2	1,300	5,000
234 Main Street	4	2	1,500	6,000
345 Main Street	3	1	1,200	5,000
456 Main Street	4	2	1,550	6,250

Address	Date	Amount
123 Main Street	06/01/2019	$3,750
123 Main Street	06/01/2018	$3,250
123 Main Street	06/01/2017	$3,100

Figure 4.2 Flat File and Relational Database Structure

Qualitative Data

Qualitative data represent characteristics that are not easily measured or quantified. There may be a degree of subjectivity involved without having a precise scale or dimensionality. Housing characteristics, like the number of bedrooms or the number of bathrooms and square footage, have quantitative values, but house condition (e.g., excellent, good, fair, poor) or resident satisfaction (e.g., high, medium, low) do not have accepted measurement scales or criteria. Self-reported, qualitative data like condition or satisfaction may also be inconsistent because they are based on personal opinion rather than uniform criteria. Qualitative data can be useful when underlying variables or values are unknown, however, analysts should be careful that these data are collected and interpreted in ways that meet the intended purpose of the study and can be analyzed with appropriate methods (Dandekar, 2003). This is especially true in cases where qualitative and quantitative data are combined within a particular analysis, such as from a survey or interviews.

Structured and Unstructured Data

Data can also be characterized as being *structured* or *unstructured*. Previous examples, such as tabular data with rows, columns, and fields of information are traditional, structured formats. Unstructured data such as text from interviews, emails, and other text-based social media are different and distinct. The methods for accessing and analyzing structured versus unstructured data are quite different. Statistical methods are used for both, with predetermined fields or variables used for structured data. Unstructured data is processed to identify latent variables and underlying patterns due to the lack of distinct variables. This includes the use of machine learning (ML) methods such as natural language processing (NLP). Text-based data from public comments may be of particular use to planners during the community involvement phases of a project.

Spatial Data

Spatial data store locational characteristics along with geographic references (i.e., X and Y coordinates) in either vector or raster formats (Figure 4.3). Vector features can be zero to three-dimensional, where a single X,Y pair indicates a specific point location (no width, depth, or height—therefore, 0-dimensional), a pair of X,Y coordinates identifies a line segment (or edge), several X,Y pairs (in 2-dimensions) identifies an enclosed area, and several X,Y, and Z coordinate sets (3-dimensions) identify a volume or mass. Querying and analyzing these data include both locational and attribute criteria, to answer questions that combine both *what* and *where*. Patterns can be detected when locations also correlate with particular feature characteristics. Clusters are one example of patterns that can be detected using spatial statistics and indices. The scale of observation plays an important role because a grouping or cluster may only be distinguishable from a certain distance or range. Spatial data can represent a wide range of physical and non-physical features such as the location of a landmark (point data), road networks (line data), or jurisdictional boundaries (polygon data).

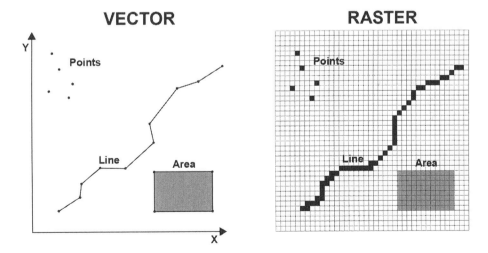

Figure 4.3 Spatial Feature Types

66   *Thomas W. Sanchez et al.*

Raster data are significantly different from vector geographic/spatial features. A raster stores data in a matrix format composed of rows and columns. The *cells* or pixels are geographically referenced and can vary in size depending on the resolution or granularity of the data. Aerial photographs and satellite imagery are common sources of raster data, where cell colors or values represent locational characteristics. While objects such as roads, buildings, and water bodies are visible in a raster, they cannot be identified as such because raster lack the topology of vector data. Additional processing, however, can convert data from raster to vector and vice versa.

Data Processing and Management

Data analysis usually involves a significant amount of time to prepare or *clean* data prior to actual analysis. The amounts of time and effort depend on the methods and sources of data collection, and the amount of error in a dataset. Common examples include missing data, data entry errors, and duplicate entries. It is useful to have error-checking strategies to avoid these problems during data collection and entry. The quality and reliability of the data have direct impacts on the quality and reliability of the analysis results. Missing values are relatively easy to detect with descriptive statistics. Once detected, the question becomes how or whether to code *missing* as unavailable or an incorrect data point. Checking data assumes that the actual ranges of values are known. Data entry errors (manual or automatic) can be examined by reviewing frequencies of values for each field, and identifying extreme or inappropriate values (i.e., outliers). Again, this assumes knowledge of minimum and maximum values, as well as valid individual measurements or values. And depending on the size, complexity, and types of data being collected, duplicate values may or may not be valid. Usually observations or records should not be exactly the same, but differentiated by the time or place of collection. The structure of the data should control for this.

Besides correcting errors, other types of data preparation may involve transforming variables from one form to another. This is commonly referred to as recoding and involves generating different types of variables from valid data, such as creating binary (0,1) variables from continuous, ordinal, or categorical data. Instead of using actual age in years for a person, perhaps indicting whether they are an adult or not may be significant. In this case ages >18 can be recoded into a new field as a 1 if the criteria (age) is met or 0 if it is not met. Continuous variables can also be recoded into multiple ranges where <18 = 1, >18 and <65 = 2, and >65 = 3. Transforming and recoding data is a common practice and depends on how the results need to be communicated. It is easily accomplished with SPSS and other statistical software packages.

Planning Data Sources

Urban planning is multidisciplinary with several diverse subareas. Planners and planning researchers use data from fields that include demographics, economics, housing, transportation, health, and environment, to name a few. As might be expected, these are distinct types of data from each of these fields. The following is a brief description of some data sources frequently used by planners.

Demographic Data

Demographic data are the basis for understanding the composition and changes to urban populations. In the United States, the Census Bureau conducts multiple censuses and surveys, including the Decennial Census, American Community Survey, American Housing Survey, Consumer Expenditure Survey, County Business Patterns, and the U.S. Economic Census. The Decennial Census, dating back to 1790, asks ten questions of all households in the United States and Island Area related to name, gender, age, race/ethnicity, relationship, and home ownership. First released in 2006, the American Community Survey (ACS) takes the place of the long-form census and is a nationwide *sample* survey on social, economic, housing, and demographic characteristics of the U.S. population every year.

One comprehensive and easily accessible source of census data is American FactFinder (https://factfinder.census.gov/). For mapping or spatial analysis of the census data, NHGIS (www.nhgis.org/) provides GIS-compatible versions as well as GIS boundary files for all census geographies. Census data is provided at different spatial levels of aggregation (e.g., state, county, census tract, block group). For the hierarchy of local census geographic entities frequently used by planners, see Figure 4.4.

Economic Data

Along with the Census Bureau, the Bureau of Economic Analysis (BEA) and the Bureau of Labor Statistics (BLS) are important federal data sources for planners. BEA (www.bea.gov/data) provides official macroeconomic and industry statistics, such as the gross domestic product (GDP), employment, and personal income for various units—nation, states, metropolitan areas, and counties. BLS (www.bls.gov/) is a unit of the U.S. Department of Labor and provides labor economics and statistics, such as consumer price index, employment and unemployment, wages, and workplace injuries. There are differences between BEA, BLS, and Census Bureau regarding employment and wage data, which should be reviewed before use in analyses. Their respective websites provide related meta-data. Longitudinal Employer-Household Dynamics (LEHD; https://lehd.ces.census.gov/) is a unique source of employment data because of its granularity (i.e., census blocks). Data is provided for both place of work (how many workers are employed here?) and place of residence (how many workers live here?) and the LEHD has its own mapping tool, OnTheMap (https://onthemap.ces.census.gov/).

Housing Data

Housing data can be obtained from the census (American Community Survey and American Housing Survey) or U.S. Department of Housing and Urban Development (HUD). HUD User datasets (www.huduser.gov/) include data on fair market rents, housing affordability, housing-related program participation (e.g., Low-Income Housing Tax Credit), vacancy data, etc. In general, the AHS is better suited to larger geographic aggregations, such as metropolitan areas, compared to the ACS or decennial census. The appropriateness of each will depend upon the type of study being undertaken.

68 *Thomas W. Sanchez et al.*

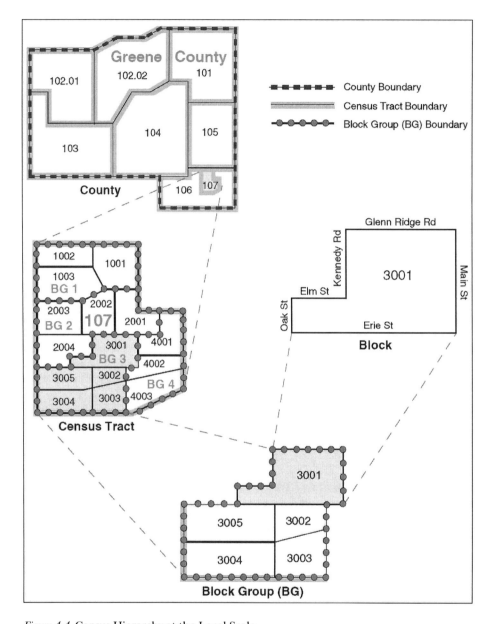

Figure 4.4 Census Hierarchy at the Local Scale

Transportation Data

There is a wide variety of transportation data available. This includes, for example, transit ridership from American Public Transportation Association (APTA; www.apta.com/); transit routes, stops, and frequencies from TransitFeeds (https://transitfeeds.com/); station area data from the National TOD database (https://toddata.cnt.org/); and walkability data from WalkScore® (www.walkscore.com/), to name a few. National Household Travel Survey (https://nhts.ornl.gov/) conducted by the Federal Highway Administration (FHWA) is the source of the travel behavior data for the American public.

Public Health Data

For planning researchers interested in public health, there are three popular national health databases in the United States: the Behavioral Risk Factor Surveillance System (BRFSS; www.cdc.gov/brfss/), the National Health and Nutrition Examination Survey (NHANES; www.cdc.gov/nchs/nhanes/index.htm), and the National Health Interview Survey (NHIS; www.cdc.gov/nchs/nhis/index.htm). As the world's largest telephone survey of over 400,000 adult participants each year, BRFSS collects information on changes in health conditions and risk factors (e.g., health-related risk behaviors, physical activities, chronic health conditions, and use of preventive services). BRFSS provides estimates at the levels of the state, metropolitan and micropolitan areas, and selected counties. The NHANES collects information on health and nutritional data of U.S. children and adults from about 5,000 individuals annually. The survey is unique in that it combines interviews and physical examinations. Lastly, starting in 1957 (the oldest among the three databases), the NHIS is a large-scale cross-sectional household interview survey, collected from about 35,000 to 40,000 households with 75,000 to 100,000 persons of all ages.

Environmental Data

Planning researchers also incorporate environmental data for air, water, land, and ecosystems into their analyses. For a one-stop source of environmental data, the U.S. Environmental Protection Agency (EPA) built a platform called Envirofacts (https://www3.epa.gov/enviro/). Users can search data on topics such as air, water, waste, facility, land, toxics, and radiation. In addition, the EPA's EnviroAtlas (www.epa.gov/enviroatlas) allows users to access data and maps related to ecosystem services. As of December 2019, the EnviroAtlas is available for 30 U.S. regions (more than 1200 municipalities) at the census block group level.

Other than the sources just mentioned, there is a significant amount of secondary data that planning researchers can access. Governments at different levels build platforms for open data (for example, www.data.gov/ at the federal level). Also, many organizations create and publish their own databases (for example, the livability index by the AARP Public Policy Institute; https://livabilityindex.aarp.org/). Thus, when you collect data, online searches should be your starting point.

The example data sources mentioned here are frequently used by planners. While there are many other sources, it is important to note that there are distinctive characteristics among datasets, and time is needed to understand how they can be used in the context of specific planning-related analyses.

The Emergence of Big Data

Today, large amounts of complex and heterogeneous digital data are generated daily. By some estimates, in a single day, 2.5 quintillion bytes (i.e., $2.5*10^{18}$ bytes) of data are produced. This is likely to increase as the number of devices capturing data and digital activities continue to increase. The estimated size of the digital universe—the amount of data created and copied each year—by 2020 is almost 44 zettabytes (i.e., $44*10^{21}$ bytes).[1] While we may associate the availability of more data with more detailed analyses, it is also true that new skills are needed to organize, process, and analyze data that are orders of magnitude greater in size than was previously the case (Kitchin, 2013).

Definitions of big data vary. One definition, provided by Batty (2013) is that big data are related to quantities that do not fit into an Excel sheet (approximately 1 million). In 2012, a survey conducted by IBM revealed that most of the respondents consider data bigger than one terabyte as big data (Schroeck et al., 2012). Eric Scharnhorst, a data scientist at Redfin, believes that data is big if it cannot be stored on a single hard drive (Barkham et al., 2018). It should be noted, however, that storage capacities of several terabytes are quite common today on laptops as well as desktop computers.

Regarding the type of the data, in the big data discourse, two datasets of the same size might require different techniques of data mining and data management technologies. For instance, the size of one minute of ultra-high-definition (Ultra-HD) video might be the same as millions of the comments people post on Facebook and Twitter. Hence, these factors make it impractical to define a universal threshold for big data.

Planning organizations and academic researchers may categorize the main sources of big data differently. In planning, one of the best classifications is presented by Thakuriah, Tilahun, and Zellner in 2017. They divide the primary sources of urban big data into six categories: (1) sensor systems, (2) user-generated content, (3) administrative data in both open (e.g., data on transactions, taxes, and revenue) and confidential micro-data (e.g., data on employment, health, education) formats, (4) private sector transactions data (customer transactions data from store cards and business records), (5) data from arts and human collections (e.g., repositories of text, images, sound recordings, linguistic data, film, art, and material culture), and (6) hybrid data sources (e.g., linked survey-sensor data and census-administrative records). These types provide an illustration of the wide-ranging categories of data that will be increasingly available to planners.

Sensors are an important source of data in planning that can be embedded in both inanimate objects (e.g., building structure, infrastructure) and animate objects and agents (e.g., cars, people, animals). In general, data generated from sensors will help planners get real-time situational awareness and do modifications and adjustments accordingly.

For instance, sensors in parking lots or on-street parking can expedite the process of finding a parking space and, as a result, reduce vehicle emissions. Real-time interaction between sensors shows the empty spaces, and the end user can access this data using applications developed for this purpose, like Parker, SpotHero and ParkMe. Smart street lamps in the city of Glasgow, Scotland, can adjust their brightness according to the number of people in the area. Internet-connected sensors in the trash containers in Barcelona, Spain, can detect how full the bins are and inform the trash truck drivers to only collect the ones that are full. Sensors are also an example of the emerging Internet of Things (IoT), where data collection devices will stream data within urban areas.

Challenges in Using Big Data

Big data's benefits to planning and planners are not yet clear. In addition, there are a number of challenges associated with the use of it. These challenges include data preparation and data quality, data analytics, data confidentiality and security, data access, and privacy. All of these challenges will need attention to address both the technical and policy aspects involved.

Open Data

The Internet vastly increased our capacity to share data. And as governments began to generate more and more digital data, calls for transparency and *openness* also increased (Tauberer, 2014). "Open government" and "open data" initiatives have created opportunities for civic access and analysis of government information. Data sharing from private organizations has also created opportunities for innovation and commercialization (Thakuriah et al., 2017). For instance, data generated from ride-sourcing services (e.g., Uber, Lyft) at the granular level can be incorporated into travel demand modeling conducted by metropolitan planning organizations. While the U.S. Census has been releasing digital data for many years in the form of count data and GIS (Tiger/Line) files, open government and open data have been more focused on information related to organizational operations, decision-making, and oversight. This includes data from budgeting, citizen complaints, and internal performance metrics. One hope is that citizen activists can perform their own analyses that are more specific to their own interests, and also save governments costs associated with labor for data handling and analysis.

Machine Learning and Data Mining

Analyses of large datasets (i.e., big data) are benefitting from advances in data mining, artificial intelligence, and machine learning. These techniques provide sophisticated ways to explore millions or billions of observations, including through learning ability, deduction ability, perception ability, and natural language ability. In other words, these techniques are attempting to imitate human intelligence. In particular, machine learning (ML) is a subfield of artificial intelligence and a way for computers to better recognize patterns through data analysis and self-study process. With these advances, computers can make decisions based on information that has not been provided. Similar to the human learning process, computers are able to generate and accumulate new information and inference to be used in iterative learning processes, thus improving their capabilities.

For example, suppose you want to distinguish whether a new article in JAPA (*Journal of the American Planning Association*) is about *public transportation* or not. The examples that the system uses to learn are called the training set. Each training example is called a training instance (or sample). In this case, task T is to distinguish whether an article is about *public transportation* or not, experience E is the training data, and performance measure P is the probability of accurate categorization, which is called accuracy. In other words, it is a measure of how well the article was classified.

Use of Machine Learning in Urban Planning

In the previous example, if we want to find articles on public transportation, we have to search for a few words such as *transit, subway,* or *bus* in the titles or bodies of previous publications. However, as time passes, new words will emerge relating to

72   *Thomas W. Sanchez et al.*

public transportation such as *mode split, transit equity,* and *transit-oriented development.* It becomes more difficult to classify them accurately using traditional approaches, as classification rules become more complex. Machine learning analysis automatically recognizes frequent occurrence of these terms in an article the user has designated as about public transportation, and the machine can classify these as public transportation articles.

Through a machine learning algorithm, humans can also learn. For example, if the algorithm has been trained sufficiently to classify public transportation articles, a human can identify the best combination of words to correctly predict this. This is called data mining.

As an example of data mining, suppose we analyze words that have appeared in urban planning journals from the past to the present. First, we will have to instruct the machine learning algorithm to remove unnecessary words such as *the, a,* and *this.* Also, similar words such as *public transportation* and *transit, impact* and *effect,* and *environment* and *environmental* should be learned as the same words. Then, check the appearance and disappearance of the words. Through this process, we can identify words that have appeared in the past, have disappeared, and have appeared recently. In addition, correlation and hierarchy of planning words can be grasped. This allows us to understand the trends in changing patterns of concepts in urban planning (see Planning Example later in the chapter).

Types of Machine Learning

Machine learning techniques can be classified into three basic categories: (1) whether the computer is trained under a human supervisor (supervised, unsupervised, semi-supervised, and reinforcement learning), (2) whether the computer is trained incrementally in real time (online learning, batch learning), or (3) whether the computer compares the data points you have with the new data points, to create a predictive model through finding a pattern in a training dataset (instance-based learning, model-based learning).

First, supervised learning is performed by injecting the algorithm with the desired answer, or *label,* into the training data. Classification and regression are typical supervised learning methods. Other examples of supervised learning include K-nearest neighbors, linear regression, logistic regression, Support Vector Machines (SVM), decision tree, random forest, and neural networks. These methods are used to recognize similarities across multiple dimensions to better detect patterns and, therefore, prediction.

Unsupervised learning does not have preassigned labels through training activities. In these cases, algorithms rely on inferential techniques to identify patterns. Examples of unsupervised learning include clustering (K-means, Hierarchical Cluster Analysis (HCA), Expectation Maximization), visualization and dimensionality reduction (Principal Component Analysis (PCA), Kernel PCA, Locally-Linear Embedding (LLE), t-distributed Stochastic Neighbor Embedding (t-SNE)), and association rule learning (Apriori, Eclat). These methods are especially useful for extremely large datasets that may be too costly to more directly train or label observations.

Semi-supervised learning is mainly used for data with only a few labels. In this case, this process is conducted by a combination of supervised and unsupervised learning.

Reinforcement learning applies when an *agent* performs an *action* through observing the environment. As a result, the *agent* repeats the process of receiving a reward or a penalty. This allows the *agent* to learn the *policy* to get the most compensation. DeepMind's AlphaGo program is one of the well-known examples of reinforcement learning.

Second, offline learning is not a gradual learning process but a method that applies to the system after being trained through all the data they have. On the other hand, online learning is a method of injecting data in mini-batch units into a program and training the system and enabling learning as soon as data arrives.

Third, instance-based learning is a method that a system learns by remembering cases. If we perform classification, this process classifies by measuring the similarity of existing ones. For example, if you designate a paper about public transportation, and there are many similar words with the previous public transportation paper in new papers, the new paper is classified as a public transportation paper. Model-based learning is a method of selecting models such as linear regression and logistic regression and creates a model and uses it for predicting the value.

In addition, cautionary points in machine learning process are as follows: poor quality data, insufficient quantity of data, irrelevant features, nonrepresentative training data, and overfitting (underfitting) of the training data. Also, to understand how well the model is generalized to the sample, it is essential to test generalization error by actually applying it to the new samples. In general, the generalization error is tested by a training set and test set. In order to prove this, cross-validation is conducted to efficiently use training data without setting the separate validation set.

Planning Example

If you are a planning scholar or student, you probably have, at least once in your career, felt helpless when faced with an ever-growing pile of literature on your desk. With the advancement of technology, Assistant Professor Kerry Fang at Florida State University and Professor Reid Ewing of the University of Utah have a solution for you, and for the field of urban planning to track its progressive footsteps. In a recent paper "Tracking Our Footsteps: Thirty Years of Publication in JAPA, JPER, and JPL" (available from the authors), they have adopted a data/text mining technique to let the computer efficiently read through all the publications since 1990 in the *Journal of the American Planning Association, Journal of Planning Education and Research,* and *Journal of Planning Literature.* The final text file includes 1,463 research articles and 13 million words, too much for human reading.

Using VOSviewer, a visualization software package with a built-in text-mining technique, and a static topic model in R statistical package to conduct a complete topic analysis, they identified 14 major research themes in these publications. They are, by order of importance, planning process, planning method, plan implementation, community planning, public finance, economic development, sustainability, neighborhood planning, land use, growth management, urban design, housing, planning education, and transportation. Among these themes, some overlap with each other, i.e., frequently occur in the same article and/or share vocabulary, such as planning process and growth management, community and land use, and public finance and economic development. Others are isolated, such as planning method and planning education.

74 *Thomas W. Sanchez et al.*

They also tracked the dynamics of research themes over time. Some themes have always remained important, such as planning process, planning method, and land use/growth management. Others were once prominent, but lost their status over time. Examples are planning theory and planning education. Planning ethics, food, and historic preservation surfaced in the most recent five years as emerging themes in planning publications.

Their paper demonstrates a text mining method to effectively grasp a large number of publications and track our footsteps in the study of urban planning. Their paper can be easily replicated for other journals, and updated every decade in the future to help track research progress, and identify research gaps, emerging trends and future directions.

Summary

This chapter briefly discussed several basic topics related to urban planning data and analysis. In many cases, these topics are not unique to planning but are relevant across many applications of data science. While analysis methods and techniques often receive the most attention, it is important to understand the data being used, why they were collected, how they were collected, and when they were collected relative to the task at hand, topics to be explored, and questions to be answered.

Note

1. www.emc.com/leadership/digital-universe/2014iview/executive-summary.htm

Works Cited

Barkham, R., Bokhari, S., & Saiz, A. (2018). Urban big data: City management and real estate markets. *GovLab Digest*, New York.

Batty, M. (2013). Big data, smart cities and city planning. *Dialogues in Human Geography, 3*(3), 274–279.

Dandekar, H. C. (Ed.). (2003). *The planner's use of information.* Chicago, IL, USA: American Planning Association Planners Press.

Géron, A. (2017). *Hands-on machine learning with Scikit-Learn and TensorFlow: Concepts, tools, and techniques to build intelligent systems.* Sebastopol, CA, USA: O'Reilly Media, Inc.

Kitchin, R. (2013). Big data and human geography: Opportunities, challenges and risks. *Dialogues in Human Geography, 3*(3), 262–267.

Ma, R., Lam, P. T. I., & Leung, C. K. (2018). Big data in urban planning practices: Shaping our cities with data. In K. Chau, I. Chan, W. Lu, & C. Webster (Eds.), *Proceedings of the 21st international symposium on advancement of construction management and real estate.* Singapore: Springer.

Mitchell, T. M. (1997). Does machine learning really work? *AI Magazine, 18*(3), 11.

Samuel, A. J. (1959). *U.S. patent no. 2,904,229.* Washington, DC: U.S. Patent and Trademark Office.

Schroeck, M., Shockley, R., Smart, J., Romero-Morales, D., & Tufano, P. (2012). Analytics: The real-world use of big data. *IBM Institute for Business Value report*, 1–20.

Tauberer, J. (2014). *Open government data: The book.* Lulu. Morrisville, NC, USA. Retrieved March 03, 2019, from https://opengovdata.io/

Thakuriah, P., Tilahun, N., & Zellner, M. (2017). Big data and urban Informatics: innovations and challenges to urban planning and knowledge discovery. In: Thakuriah, P., Tilahun, N. and Zellner, M. (eds.) *Seeing Cities Through Big Data: Research Methods and Applications in Urban Informatics.* Springer: New York, pp. 11–45. ISBN 9783319409009 (doi:10.1007/978-3-319-40902-3_2).

Wang, X., & Hofe, R. (2008). *Research methods in urban and regional planning.* Co-published by Tsinghua University Press, Beijing, China and Springer-Verlag GmbH Berlin Heidelberg, Germany.

5 Conceptual Frameworks

Keunhyun Park, James B. Grace, and Reid Ewing

Overview

Miles and Huberman (1994, p. 33) define a conceptual framework as "the current version of the researcher's map of the territory being investigated." Such a framework is also referred to as a *theoretical framework* or a *conceptual model.*

A research study without a conceptual framework seems unfocused. It has an ad hoc quality to it. The term *data mining* is often applied to such a study. For authors, a well-articulated conceptual framework can provide theoretical clarification of the issues they are investigating while clarifying for readers the purpose of the research (King, Keohane, & Verba, 1994).

Despite the proven utility of conceptual frameworks, we feel that researchers in the planning field do not utilize them as much as they might. In 2013, a review of four issues of *Journal of the American Planning Association* (JAPA) revealed that only 6 of 19 articles (32 percent) outlined clear conceptual frameworks, and none of those six articles diagrammed the conceptual framework. In contrast, a review of the *Annual Review of Public Health* for 2013 found that 14 of 23 articles (61 percent) contained conceptual frameworks and nine of these were diagrammed.

The utility of making conceptual frameworks explicit can be easily illustrated. Consider an example from a *Research You Can Use* column in *Planning* magazine published back in May 2007. Norman Garrick of the University of Connecticut had presented a provocative paper on bicycling in Davis, California, at the Transportation Research Board Annual Meeting in 2005. A *Planning* magazine column was based on a review of this work (Ewing, 2007).

Garrick laid out three sets of facts about bicycling in Davis, a university town 15 miles west of Sacramento:

- Davis has a uniquely high bicycle mode share, about 15 percent of all trips to work. This is two and one-half times the bicycle mode share of Palo Alto, the California runner-up peer city, and 35 times the U.S. average. It is the only city on the peer list with no pedestrian or bicycle fatalities for a five-year period, and an extraordinarily low rate of pedestrian and bicycle injuries.
- Davis is compact. It has a strong downtown for a city its size (65,000, 10,000 of whom are students at the University of California, Davis), and it has almost no urban sprawl beyond the 10-square mile city limit. Davis pioneered bike lanes (which until the late 1960s were prohibited by California traffic codes) and bike-activated traffic signals (reputed to be the first in the nation). The city boasts bike lanes or bike paths on 90 percent of its arterials and collectors.

Conceptual Frameworks 77

- Davis adopted a general plan in 1973 that made growth control its guiding principle, only the second California city to do so. Through various amendments, this plan has always favored the downtown by focusing growth inwards. Its mobility section called for bicycle lanes on all arterials and collectors, and also shared-use paths along arterials where feasible.

Where Garrick's paper raised academic and other eyebrows was in asserting that these three sets of facts are linked causally—that bike-friendly planning is the cause of bike-friendly physical form, which in turn is the cause of unmatched bike usage.

Davis's success, Garrick boldly asserted, "is due in no small part to the fact that, from a planning and design perspective, Davis has worked to integrate bicycle use as a fundamental element of its mobility program and its land use planning."

Garrick didn't provide a conceptual framework, but if he had, it would have looked something like Figure 5.1. The arrows indicate causal relationships (causal pathways).

With this conceptual framework making Garrick's thesis explicit, potential problems become apparent. First, confounding influences are missing from the conceptual framework. Many factors, beyond planning and design, may encourage bicycle use in Davis, including the presence of a large university, gentle terrain, comparatively mild weather, and a progressive political culture. These suggest a more complex conceptual framework (Figure 5.2). The double-headed arrow indicates a correlation.

Figure 5.1 The Simple Conceptual Framework of Garrick (2005)

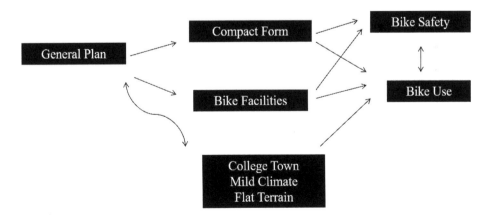

Figure 5.2 Adding Confounders

There is also some question about the direction of causality. Couldn't Davis's great bike network be an effect, rather than a cause, of heavy use of bikes? Or couldn't its heavy bike use have led to General Plan amendments favoring compact development and bicycle facilities? Might an equally plausible conceptual framework look like Figure 5.3?

Finally, there are non-planning policies at work. The city and surrounding Yolo County have a revenue-sharing program (the Davis-Yolo Pass Through Agreement). The county receives a share of the city's property tax revenue only so long as it does not approve residential development outside the city. The school district does not bus students, which means most school-age children walk or ride their bikes to school. So a more complete conceptual framework might look something like Figure 5.4.

This elaboration of logic suggests a very different regression model, with many more variables than Garrick's original model. Actually, it probably requires a structural equation model (SEM) rather than a simply linear regression model to capture its complexity, its inclusion of mediating variables, and its inclusion of bi-directional relationships (see Chapter 8 of *Advanced Quantitative Research Methods for Urban*

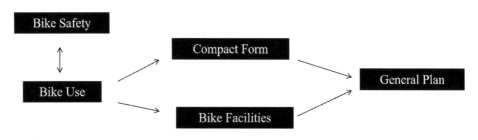

Figure 5.3 Reversing Causality

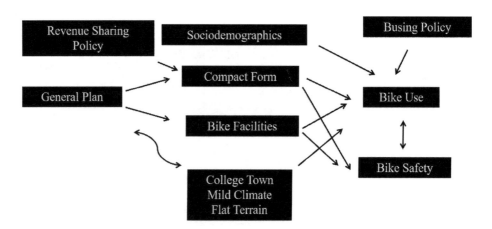

Figure 5.4 A Complex Conceptual Framework

Planners). We would argue that all of these constructs could be operationalized; it would simply be a matter of gathering the requisite data for a sample, let's say, of medium-sized California cities and towns and then estimating a model.

College Town could be represented by a dummy variable, 1 for towns with universities and 0 otherwise. Or it could be represented by college student enrollment relative to total resident population. General Plan might be operationalized with number of references to bike facilities and compact form in the general plan, or more specifically, by the number of actual policy requirements promulgated through the general plan. Bike Safety could be operationalized by the number or rate of accidents involving bicyclists. And so on. You get the idea.

Or data permitting, one might acquire longitudinal data for Davis at various points in time and estimate a model with bike mode share as the dependent variable, and population density, proportion of arterial mileage with bike lanes, college student enrollment, share of employment downtown, and one or two dummy variables related to the general plan as independent variables. Some of the variables in the cross-sectional model, such as flat topography, could be dropped from the longitudinal model since the topography of Davis isn't changing. This, too, might be a simple linear regression model or something more complex.

Or most ambitiously, one might combine cross-sectional and longitudinal data for a sample of medium-sized cities and towns in California to create what are called panel data. There is a well-established body of methods for handling the more complex nature of panel data that would assure appropriate inferences about bike shares in Davis.

This chapter will explain the main characteristics of a conceptual framework and then discuss in more detail the mechanics of constructing a conceptual framework. Finally, it will present two studies from the field of planning that illustrate the application of conceptual frameworks to quantitative research.

Purpose

As a tool for guiding your research, a conceptual framework has three main characteristics. First, it may be constructed from multiple sources, not only academic journals and books but also newspapers, essays, interviews, and even personal knowledge. Unlike a literature review, usually confined in the traditionally defined field of your study, a well-articulated conceptual framework can be built upon multidisciplinary sources even including expert opinion and people's experiential knowledge.

The variables in the Davis bicycling example came from an interview with Katherine Hess, Davis's Community Development Director, who at the time of our interview had 16 years with the city, commuted by bicycle herself, and belonged to the Davis Bike Club. She ranked the many interrelated factors that may contribute to Davis's high bike mode share in descending order of importance:

- University town
- Flat topography
- Progressive political culture
- Mild weather
- Strong downtown
- Almost no sprawl beyond city limit
- Shopping centers with rear entrances from neighborhoods

- Miles of bike lanes on arterials
- Miles of shared use paths
- Low travel speeds
- Pro-bike language of general plan

Note that some of these factors are missing even from our more complete conceptual framework.

Second, a conceptual framework consists of conceptual or theoretical components that should not simply be collected, but connected. These connections between concepts are key components of a conceptual framework (see Figure 5.5 for examples). In the more complete Davis conceptual framework, College Town is a confounder. College Town is shown as correlated with the General Plan and as causally related to Bike Use. College towns are likely to have progressive general plans, and are almost certain to have high levels of bike use among students.

Third, a conceptual framework must be responsive to the progress of research and incorporate new insights and findings. In other words, a conceptual framework is not simply a visual or verbal representation of your initial ideas. The conceptual framework can both influence and be influenced by the research process throughout its stages: developing a research question and design, collecting and analyzing data, and presenting results and conclusions (Ravitch & Riggan, 2012). In particular, the causal path diagram may change after you've worked with data and generated your initial results.

A study of bike use in California's medium-sized cities and towns might start with the conceptual framework just outlined, but evolve as results come in. It might be the case, for example, that even after controlling for College Town, we have not fully captured the abstract construct Progressive Political Culture. If so, then other variables might be added to the model. For example, Progressive Political Culture might be operationalized in terms of survey results (percent of citizens with strong environmental values) or voting records (percent of registered voters with one party or the other).

Mechanics

A conceptual framework consists of concepts and their presumed interrelationships. A concept can be defined as "the relationship between the word (or symbol) and an idea or conception" (Cohen, Lawrence, & Morrison, 2000, p. 13). Concepts in a conceptual framework can be either abstract constructs or operational variables. Abstract constructs are different from operational variables, as the latter are directly measurable and the former are not.

All of the conceptual frameworks shown previously involve abstract constructs. We think this is a good place to start. When the second author of this chapter teaches structural equation modeling, he starts with a conceptual framework involving abstract constructs and their relationships to one another, drawn by hand, and then translates to a causal path diagram involving operational variables and their relationships to another, often drawn with an SEM program like AMOS.

Once you have a sound conceptual framework, the next step is to prepare a causal path diagram that operationalizes constructs with appropriate variables, and relates these variables to one another in a way that can be modeled with data. Having an

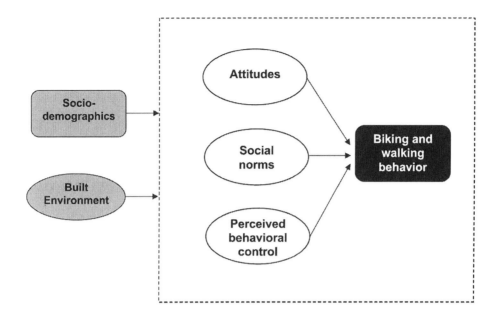

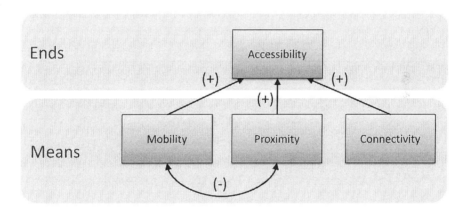

Figure 5.5 Examples of Conceptual Frameworks
Source: top: Dill, Mohr, & Ma (2014), bottom: Levine et al. (2012)

explicit framework makes it easier to spot missing variables and missing relationships. Also, it facilitates consideration of whether the model has construct validity because the variables either appropriately represent the underlying constructs or they do not.

While a model conveys its mathematical logic through a set of equations, an accompanying graph provides an essential guide for researchers to apply causal reasoning. General constructs are often depicted by circles or ovals, measured variables depicted by squares or rectangles, and relationships among the concepts depicted by arrows.

It is typical in causal models that relationships between variables will be unidirectional (e.g., $X \rightarrow Y$). For models where time steps are not explicitly treated, we may hypothesize that causation goes both ways (joint causation or simultaneity). Such relationships should be represented using pairs of arrows to distinguish from simple correlations (e.g., $X \leftrightarrows Y$ versus $X \leftrightarrow Y$). Sometimes there is simply a correlation between two variables. In causal path diagrams, correlations are represented by two-headed arrows. It should be understood that correlations are actually incompletely specified from causal relationships. If two variables are strongly correlated, there is probably some underlying reason. Thus, we should think of the representation $X \leftrightarrow Y$ actually being shorthand for $X \leftarrow Z \rightarrow Y$, which means X and Y are correlated because of joint influences from some latent set of conditions Z.

Conceptual frameworks may include more variables and relationships than the statistical models researchers actually study. Misspecification occurs if variables that operate in the conceptual framework are not accounted for somehow in the research model investigated (Schwab, 2005). The inclusion of irrelevant variables may also lead to specification errors, though these are easier to detect once data is brought to bear.

It is important to distinguish among types of variables, such as mediators, confounders, and moderator variables. These all play different roles in causal models. A mediator or intervening causal variable (M) comes between a predictor variable (A) and a response variable (C) in a causal chain (see Figure 5.6). If a mediator is present, then some or all the influence of the predictor variable can be seen to operate indirectly on the response variable through the mediator. There may be a single

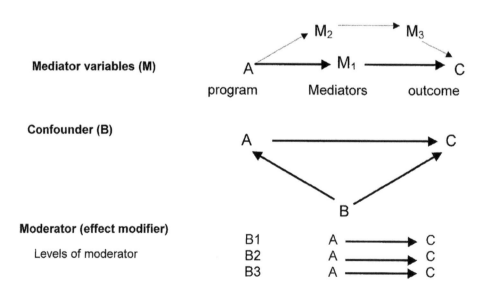

Figure 5.6 Three types of the Third Variables: Mediator, Confounder, and Moderator
Source: Bauman et al. (2002)

mediator (M1) or multiple mediators (M2, M3). During the interpretational analysis of a model, researchers should think about how the intervening components could be reasonably expected to change an outcome (MacKinnon, 2011).

A confounder is a predictor of the response variable that is also correlated with other predictor variables. The confounder will influence the observed association between two variables (e.g., A and C) by creating a *backdoor* association. Failing to control for a confounder will distort estimates of the true magnitude of the effect (Bauman et al., 2002). The direction of the *causal arrows* in Figure 5.6 shows that the proposed confounder should be included as a causal factor for the outcome (B → C) and its predictor (B ↔ A).

A confounder can also be a *moderator* or *effect modifier* if it modifies the sign or strength of another relationship (see Figure 5.6, lowest panel). Moderator effects are also called interactions in the sense that the effect of A → C varies across levels of the moderator B (Bauman et al., 2002). For example, if the effects of an intervention are much greater for men than for women, there is an interaction between gender and the intervention, and gender would be considered a moderator variable. Note that the moderator effect is not part of a causal sequence but qualifies/changes the relation between two variables (MacKinnon, 2011). Effects of moderators are sometimes represented by pointing an arrow from the moderator at the arrow from A to C (instead of at the variables A and C).

Of course, in the real world (as opposed to the model world), there are nearly always understood to be unspecified causal chains behind the direct linkages in our models. An indirect effect in a model operates through a specified mediator variable. In this case, a predictor variable affects the mediator, which in turn influences a response variable. Finally, when you expect that a variable moderates a relationship, you can construct your conceptual framework based on these variables and their relationships to one another (see Figure 5.7).

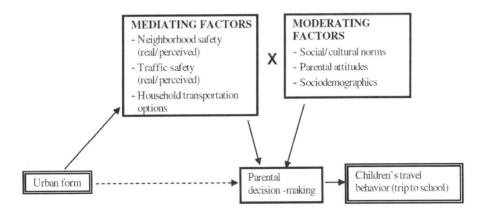

Figure 5.7 A Conceptual Framework Example Using Mediators and Moderators (The X refers to the fact that the moderators have interactive effects on the influences of other variables.)

Source: McMillan (2005)

When constructing a conceptual framework, you must recognize its limitations and how to overcome them. Individual researchers may have unique conceptions of the same phenomenon and may create different conceptual frameworks (Jabareen, 2009). This means that a conceptual framework is subject to the original researcher's perceptual biases. Also, in the ongoing process of your study, the developed conceptual framework may influence the research process and may result in a biased interpretation of findings. You can avoid such limitations by integrating multiple sources of information such as experiential data and topical research into the conceptual framework, and making iterative revisions of the conceptual framework during your research process. It is also important to make assumptions that influence interpretations as explicit as possible.

To illustrate the concepts just laid out, we cite two examples from the peer-reviewed literature. The first is a paper published in the journal *Environment and Behavior* by Lekwa, Rice, and Hibbing (2007). Their conceptual framework is shown in Figure 5.8. Note it relates the construct Community Attractiveness to the constructs Community Form and Community Adornment.

The construct Community Attractiveness was operationalized with an attractiveness score assigned by one author who visited 954 incorporated cities and towns in Iowa, drove around town, and then assigned a Likert score from 1 to 10 to the entire town. The reliance on a single rater potentially impacts the reliability of the response variable measurements (see Chapter 6 for the subject of reliability). Further, the assignment of a single score to towns rather than systematically surveying and rating different parts of town and then combining ratings through some averaging procedure is less than ideal.

Two constructs, Community Form and Community Adornment, are shown as affecting Community Attractiveness. Unfortunately, the two general constructs were never operationalized by the authors. Instead, four other constructs—socio-demographics, economics, attitudes, and a control for the time of year when the town was visited—were

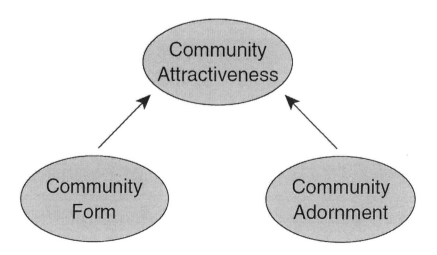

Figure 5.8 Model of Community Attractiveness
Source: Lekwa et al. (2007)

represented by ten operational variables. Some of the variables are clear proxies for the constructs. For others, it is not so obvious. Attitudinal variables measure what the authors referred to as *civic mindedness*. It is unclear whether the additional term *attitudinal* is helpful when civic-mindedness is what is intended. The authors posited that cities and towns with high levels of civic-mindedness would be more attractive than those with low levels, a reasonable proposition. However, civic-mindedness was operationalized with a measure of church attendance (which suggests unstated assumptions, at least as a measure of civic-mindedness) as well as voter turnout.

Another predictor variable, under the heading of socio-demographics, was the distance residents commute to work, which was said to measure the strength of *psychological ties* to the community. Here one can see how insufficient care in selecting terms can lead to ambiguity. With variables in hand, the authors then used multiple regression to explain community attractiveness in terms of these ten independent variables.

We contrast the Lekwa study with a more explicitly explained mixed-methods study by Loukaitou-Sideris and Sideris of children's use of parks, published in *JAPA* (2009). Their conceptual framework is shown in Figure 5.9. This single figure presents both abstract constructs and the variables used to operationalize them. The dependent variable is the average count of children using each park. Counts were done over two months by four graduate students, and tests of inter-rater reliability were performed. The three constructs said to explain park use—user characteristics/behavior, neighborhood characteristics, and park characteristics—were based on a review of the literature on children's use of parks. The three constructs were measured with 21 independent variables, all of which seem reasonably related to them. The authors, as in the previous study, used multiple regression analysis to relate park- and neighborhood-level variables to the numbers of children using the parks. Their conceptual framework contains no mediators or moderators, but still presents a comprehensive understanding of the subject under investigation.

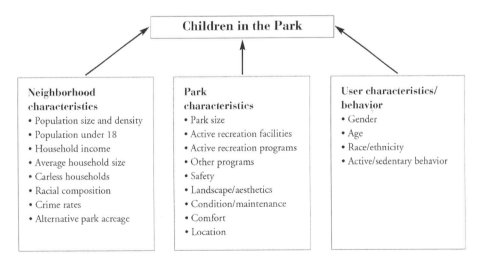

Figure 5.9 A Conceptual Framework Consisting of Both Abstract Constructs and Operational Variables

Source: Loukaitou-Sideris & Sideris (2009)

Step by Step

Step 1. Generate a Set of Concepts

To a large degree, conceptual modeling is an exercise in making linguistic distinctions tangible and unambiguous. Typically, researchers develop a set of concepts from existing theory and research or personal experience. In the absence of direction, a researcher can develop one by employing any of the following strategies:

1. Think about the keywords used when discussing this topic.
2. Refer to a previous study and map the theory that is implicit (or explicit) in it.
3. Select one key concept, idea, or term, brainstorm ideas that relate to it, and then review all of the ideas and select those that appear to be most directly relevant to the study (Maxwell, 2005).

Step 2. Specify the Relations Between Concepts

The arrows represent the proposed relationships among concepts. Apply common sense, theory, and the prior literature in deciding whether concepts are causally related, correlated, or unrelated to one another. When you think about causal relationships between variables, it is important to consider the roles that different variables play, like mediator or moderator, to avoid mis-specifying equations. A confounder is modeled differently than a mediator, and a mediator is modeled differently than a moderator.

Step 3. Write a Narrative for the Conceptual Framework

Even though this step is optional, a written version of the conceptual framework can further articulate how the study is linked to theory. Clear definitions are especially important. This process can reveal that a term being used is simply a "placeholder for the actual concept or relationship" (Maxwell, 2005, p. 63) that is integral to understanding the research. It also paves the way for the interpretation of results.

Step 4. Rethink the Conceptual Framework During the Entire Research Process

One should not expect to generate a final version of the conceptual framework in the first attempt. It is important that one view a conceptual framework not just as an end in itself but also as a tool for developing and honing a theory. Conceptual frameworks require reworking as the understanding of studied material evolves (Maxwell, 2005). As a final point, once actual data are brought to bear, a need for data-concept consistency will enforce discipline on the conceptual modeling process.

Conclusion

Not only qualitative, theoretical researchers but also quantitative researchers should use conceptual frameworks, for "no empirical investigation can be successful without theory to guide its choice of questions" (King et al., 1994, p. 29). Research without such a framework or with a weak framework has an unsound conceptual and theoretical basis for generalization of findings.

Graphically constructed conceptual frameworks can help readers digest the information and structure of the study. To remind our readers, a conceptual framework usually consists of concepts (depicted by circles or squares) and relationships among the concepts (depicted by arrows).

Works Cited

Bauman, A. E., Sallis, J. F., Dzewaltowski, D. A., & Owen, N. (2002). Toward a better understanding of the influences on physical activity: The role of determinants, correlates, causal variables, mediators, moderators, and confounders. *American Journal of Preventive Medicine, 23*(2, s1), 5–14. http://doi.org/10.1016/S0749-3797(02)00469-5

Cohen, L., Lawrence, M., & Morrison, K. (2000). *Research methods in education* (5th ed.). London: Routledge.

Dill, J., Mohr, C., & Ma, L. (2014). How can psychological theory help cities increase walking and bicycling? *Journal of the American Planning Association, 80*(1), 36–51. http://doi.org/10.1080/01944363.2014.934651

Ewing, R. (2007, May). Research you can use: The perils of causal inference bicycling in Davis, California. *Planning*, 51.

Garrick, N. W. (2005, January). *Land use planning and transportation network design in a bicycle friendly American city.* Transportation Research Board 84th Annual Meeting.

Jabareen, Y. (2009). Building a conceptual framework: Philosophy, definitions, and procedure. *International Journal of Qualitative Methods, 8*(4), 49–62.

King, G., Keohane, R. O., & Verba, S. (1994). *Designing social inquiry: Scientific inference in qualitative research.* Princeton, NJ: Princeton University Press.

Lekwa, V. L., Rice, T. W., & Hibbing, M. V. (2007). The correlates of community attractiveness. *Environment and Behavior, 39*(2), 198–216. http://doi.org/10.1177/0013916506288055

Levine, J., Grengs, J., Shen, Q., & Shen, Q. (2012). Does accessibility require density or speed? A comparison of fast versus close in getting where you want to go in US metropolitan regions. *Journal of the American Planning Association, 78*(2), 157–172.

Loukaitou-Sideris, A., & Sideris, A. (2009). What brings children to the park? Analysis and measurement of the variables affecting children's use of parks. *Journal of the American Planning Association, 76*(1), 89–107. http://doi.org/10.1080/01944360903418338

MacKinnon, D. P. (2011). Integrating mediators and moderators in research design. *Research on Social Work Practice, 21*(6), 675–681. http://doi.org/10.1177/1049731511414148

Maxwell, J. A. (2005). *Qualitative research design: An integrative approach* (2nd ed.). Thousand Oaks, CA: Sage Publications.

McMillan, T. E. (2005). Urban form and a child's trip to school: The current literature and a framework for future research. *Journal of Planning Literature, 19*(4), 440–456. http://doi.org/10.1177/0885412204274173

Miles, M. B., & Huberman, M. A. (1994). *Qualitative data analysis: An expanded sourcebook* (2nd ed.). Thousand Oaks, CA: Sage Publications.

Ravitch, S. M., & Riggan, M. (2012). *Reason & rigor: How conceptual frameworks guide research.* Thousand Oaks, CA: Sage Publications.

Schwab, D. P. (2005). *Research methods for organizational studies* (2nd ed.). Mahwah, NJ: Lawrence Erlbaum Associates, Inc.

Young, R. A. (2014). *Economic resiliency of property values in historic districts* (Doctoral dissertation). University of Utah College of Architecture + Planning.

6 Validity and Reliability

Carl Duke, Shima Hamidi, and Reid Ewing

Overview

As planners, we have numerous statistical tools at our fingertips. Many of the chapters of this book will help you determine which tool is appropriate for the job you face or the data you have available. This chapter is unique because it delves into two characteristics of all of the measurements, models, and methods covered in this book: validity and reliability. These qualities apply to all inferential statistical methods and describe how well they do their job.

Reliability is the extent to which an experiment, test, or any measuring procedure yields the same result on repeated trials. Without the agreement of independent observers able to replicate research procedures, or the ability of research tools and procedures to yield consistent measurements, researchers would be unable to satisfactorily draw conclusions, formulate theories, or make claims about the trustworthiness of their research.

An example of a reliable tool would be a thermometer. If a thermometer is deemed to be reliable, it would provide the same temperature reading time after time whether it is measuring the temperature of an infant or the temperature of a latte or the boiling point of water. If you have a reliable thermometer, you know it provides a precise temperature reading every time you use it.

Validity, on the other hand, determines whether the tool, technique, or measurement actually measures what it purports to. Whereas reliability focuses on precision and reproducibility, validity is more concerned with accuracy and lack of bias (see Figure 6.1). A thermometer would be a valid tool when used to measure temperature but would not be valid if it were used to measure blood pressure or pulse. Also, a thermometer would be a valid tool if it, on average, came close to measuring the true temperature of that infant or latte or the boiling point of water, that is, if the thermometer were, on average, accurate.

This chapter first explores reliability in depth. We cover the theory of reliability and discuss precision. From this foundation, we investigate various types of reliability with a focus on those most applicable to planning and inferential statistics. Our discussion of reliability draws upon research on urban design qualities and walkability.

We then explore validity in the context of the research methods this book covers. Our discussion of validity addresses the different kinds of validity, how they are defined, and how they are operationalized. Our discussion of validity draws upon research on urban sprawl and the costs of sprawl.

This chapter, like the others in the book, ends with two peer-reviewed academic articles published in the leading planning research journals. The articles highlighting

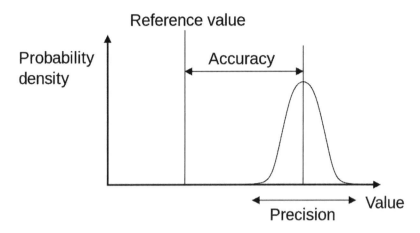

Figure 6.1 Precision Versus Accuracy

Source: by Pekaje at English Wikipedia—transferred from en.wikipedia to Commons., GFDL, https://commons.wikimedia.org/w/index.php?curid=1862863

reliability and validity come from the *Journal of the American Planning Association* and the *Journal of Environmental Management*.

Reliability

Reliability is a concept we use frequently in everyday life. If you drive a reliable car you generally are referring to the degree you can depend on it operating the same way time after time. Said another way, every time you turn the key you get the same response . . . the car starts. This is essentially the same concept in research. A reliable study produces the same outcomes, like the dependable car; every time you observe similar changes in the group of independent variables (you turn the car key) you experience the same response in the dependent variable (the car starts). Similarly, a reliable measurement will provide the same score when a behavior or preference is measured numerous times. The concept of reliability can apply to the overall research approach as well as the measurement or data-gathering tools we use within our research approach.

It is important to keep in mind that our data-gathering tools are not perfect, or without error. For example, if you are conducting a visual preference survey with some residents in your city, they may rank a streetscape more highly one time than the next. This could be because of their mood, whether they ate breakfast or exercised that morning, even the weather they experienced on the way to take the survey. Unfortunately, a visual preference study is not perfectly reliable. There will always be some error in measuring preferences.

Probably a more realistic example comes from Ewing, Handy, Brownson, Clemente, and Winston (2006) and Ewing and Handy (2009). Ten urban design experts rated 48 street scenes for urban design qualities thought to affect walkability and street life. For some of the qualities, such as visual enclosure, expert ratings were consistent, that is, they were reliable. For other qualities, such as legibility, ratings were all over the map. Ultimately, five qualities—imageability, enclosure, human scale, transparency, and complexity—had sufficient inter-rater reliability to be subsequently operationalized and used in studies of pedestrian activity (Ameli, Hamidi, Garfinkel-Castro, & Ewing, 2015; Ewing & Clemente, 2013; Ewing, Hajrasouliha, Neckerman, Purciel-Hill, & Greene, 2016; Hamidi & Moazzeni, 2018; Alasadi, 2016; Ernawati, 2016; Yin, 2017; Maxwell, 2016; Park et al., 2019—see Figures 6.2 and 6.3).

Figure 6.2 High-Rated Video Clip in All Five Dimensions
Source: Ewing & Clemente (2013)

Figure 6.3 Low-Rated Video Clip in All Five Dimensions
Source: Ewing & Clemente (2013)

The same reality applies to the design of our studies and tests. While we would like our models to explain 100 percent of the variance in our dependent variable, there will always be variance that we cannot explain with our set of independent variables. The truth is planning investigates extremely complex and multifaceted problems. Why do some people drive more than others? What causes location preferences for first-time homebuyers? If the independent variables used to model these phenomena are highly correlated to the point of multicollinearity, for example, our estimates of model coefficients will not be highly reliable (see Chapter 12 on Linear Regression).

Going back to Figure 6.1, a reliable or precise measurement tool will provide data upon repeated applications, or repeated sample taking, with a small spread around the mean value. In the language of Chapter 7 on Descriptive Statistics, a reliable tool has small dispersion around the mean.

By contrast, an accurate measurement tool will provide readings wherein the mean from repeated observations, or repeated samples, is close to the true value. In research, we call data gathered from an accurate measurement tool *unbiased*. If the mean of the sample data is near or at the true value, you can consider your dataset unbiased. That doesn't mean that the measurements or samples are highly reliable. There could be a lot of dispersion around the mean. But again, in the language of Chapter 7 on Descriptive Statistics, the central tendency from repeated measurements would be near the true value.

In the preceding examples of driving or home buying, if models exclude important independent variables, our estimates of model coefficients may be precise but will be biased upward or downward from true values (see Chapter 12 on Linear Regression).

Inter-Rater Reliability

As planners, we are constantly in search for data, after all, we celebrate the decennial census because it gives us the latest data to test our assumptions against. Unfortunately, data simply does not exist for much of what we want to study. When you are faced with this problem, you have little choice but to go out and create your own dataset.

However, in the process of gathering data from the world around us, we all look through the various lenses of our individual personalities, backgrounds, educations, and experiences. For instance, if five researchers were to observe kids playing in a park to determine how kids use parks and improvements thereon, each of the five people will observe different subtleties within the same environment. You could understand how a single college-aged male might gather different data from a mother of four.

There are steps that can be taken into account for this variation and make sure that it does not undermine the quality of our data. Inter-rater reliability is simply a measure of whether raters or observers produce similar or consistent observations of the same phenomena. There are two primary ways to address inter-rater reliability, and while they are both fairly rudimentary, it is important to understand both when you feel there could be inter-rater reliability issues.

Joint Probability of Agreement: A number of inter-rater reliability tests are available to the planning professional. When the data being created is nominal in nature, the inter-rater reliability can be tested using a joint probability of agreement test. This test is essentially the times each observation is given the same rating or score by two or more raters, this number is then divided by the number of categories available.

The weakness with this test is that it does not take into account random and chance agreements. If you and I are asked to grade whether a site plan for a proposed development is walkable, we would more likely agree if the choices were between *yes* and *no* than if we had eight different response categories to choose from. The other weakness in this test is that the data is assumed to be nominal.

Cohen's Kappa: Cohen's Kappa takes the joint probability of agreement test and improves it by accounting for the chance agreement that would take place with a limited number of choices available to the raters. This approach, while an improvement from the prior, does not solve the issue with nominal data. If your data is ordinal in nature (e.g., walkability rating on a scale of five), neither of these tests will do an adequate job of measuring inter-rater reliability.

Correlation Coefficients: Correlation is the subject of Chapter 9. If the selections available to your raters are ordinal or continuous in nature, you can use a correlation coefficient to measure the extent to which your raters agree. For ordinal data, a Spearman's rank correlation coefficient can be used to measure the degree to which two raters agree or disagree. For continuous variables, a Pearson's coefficient would be better. When more than two raters or observers are being used, the appropriate correlation coefficient will need to be calculated for every possible combination of raters. The mean coefficient then would be used in explaining how you have measured the degree to which your raters agree.

Perhaps better than either the Spearman or Pearson correlation coefficient for measuring inter-rater reliability is the intraclass correlation coefficient (ICC). Returning to the example of experts rating street scenes, Ewing et al. (2006) and Ewing and Handy (2009) had ten expert panelists rate 48 street scenes with respect to nine urban design qualities. ICCs were computed from their ratings, and then compared to nominal standards of reasonable agreement. From their ICC values, most urban design qualities demonstrated moderate inter-rater reliability among panelists (0.6 > ICCs > 0.4); the exceptions—linkage, coherence, and legibility—showed only fair reliability (0.4 > ICCs > 0.2) (Landis & Koch, 1977). The latter were dropped from further consideration. See Chapter 9 for more on the ICC.

Equivalency Reliability

Another type of reliability considered by researchers is equivalency reliability. This measure of reliability considers the extent to which two variables measure the same construct. This is also known as equivalent form reliability or parallel form reliability.

In considering equivalency reliability, you look at the different measures of a construct and see if your results are similar using different approaches. If they are dissimilar, your test suffers from a lack of equivalency reliability. The challenge with testing equivalency reliability is you are forced to come up with numerous ways to define or test a complicated construct. This is no easy feat.

In the aforementioned study of urban design qualities and pedestrian activity, Ewing and Clemente (2013) wanted to test whether the field pedestrian counts were, in fact, reliable indicators of pedestrian activity. The counts had been taken through two passes up and down a block, rather than standardized counts for an extended period. Four consecutive counts represented a small sample, so they conducted a test of equivalency reliability.

Validity and Reliability 93

They compared field counts for block faces in New York City to pedestrian counts from Google Street View, Bing, and Everyscape for the same block faces (Figure 6.4). To compare field counts to web-based counts, equivalency reliability was judged with Cronbach's alpha. Cronbach's alpha is widely used in the social sciences to see if items—questions, raters, indicators—measure the same thing. If independent counts—four based on field work and three based on street imagery—agreed, they could assume that the field counts were reliable measures of pedestrian activity. Some professionals require a reliability of 0.70 or higher before they will use an instrument. Their alpha values were consistent with these guidelines for two out of three websites (Google Street View and Bing).

Internal Consistency

Internal consistency is similar to the concept of equivalency reliability. Internal consistency is the ability of a test to measure the same concept through different questions or approaches and yet yield consistent data. Said in another way, internal consistency involves measuring two different versions or approaches within the same test and determining the consistency of the responses.

As a researcher, you will want to approach a concept or question from various perspectives because each perspective will provide additional data that will help shape your opinions. However, if you begin to ask questions on the same concept that produce wildly differing responses, you know that your method has a problem.

Generally, the best way to address internal consistency is to divide the test in half and compare the responses from one half to the other half. A high score on the correlation coefficient between the two halves is desirable up to a point. If the test is completely correlated, you have not added any information by asking additional questions.

Figure 6.4 Use of Google Street View, Bing, and Everyscape Imagery (from top to bottom) to Establish Equivalency Reliability (East 19th Street, New York, NY)

Figure 6.4 Continued

There are three common tests to measure internal consistency; split-halves test, Kuder-Richardson test, and Cronbach's alpha test. The split-halves test uses a random approach in splitting up the answers of the test and using a simple correlation to measure consistency. This was a more common technique decades ago, but with the proliferation of statistical software the ease of other methods along with their advantages have made this simple approach less common. The Kuder-Richardson test is a more complex version of the split-halves where a statistical software package will run every possible split-half test possible and gives an average correlation. Cronbach's alpha test is similar to the Kuder-Richardson test and gives the researcher the ability to do a sophisticated split-half test when the questions have different scoring weights.

For instance, if the survey asked, "do you walk to work daily" the possible answers are *yes* and *no* and the appropriate internal consistency test for this type of nominal data would be the Kuder-Richardson test. If the question was "how likely are you to walk to work" with a range of answers, the data would be ordinal and the Cronbach's alpha test would be the best measure of internal consistency.

Validity

As we move from reliability to validity, our focus changes from the tools we use in research to the manner in which we use them. Reliability considers the instruments we use to gather information or data, whereas validity looks at the process we use to draw conclusions from our data.

Validity is the approximate truth of suggestions, inferences, or conclusions. When our work in establishing theories and conducting experiments can be characterized as valid and rigorous, we have done our job. Validity is a difficult concept for many researchers because it is difficult to quantify. There is no threshold or yardstick you can use to determine whether you are conducting a valid study or not.

Validity can be best understood by looking at the four different types of validity and considering how they build upon each other in a sequential manner.

Face Validity

Face validity is the starting point of all research. The question is whether the approach you are taking or the way you are measuring something or the results you are getting, make sense on their face. Do they pass the laugh test?

As a practical example, Ewing and co-authors have been operationalizing urban sprawl and its impacts since the early 2000s (Ewing et al., 2002; Ewing & Hamidi, 2017). Previous sprawl metrics had been based on gross density calculations, and by these metrics, Los Angeles was the least sprawling/most compact region of the country, even less sprawling than New York, San Francisco, Portland, Ann Arbor, and Madison. That certainly isn't the public's perception of Los Angeles, nor the sense you get traveling around Los Angeles's endless medium density. In part for this reason, Ewing et al. developed compactness measures that capture the distribution of density within metropolitan and urbanized areas, plus three other dimensions of compactness— land use mix, population and employment centering, and street connectivity. All of these contribute to accessibility of places to one another, the ultimate definition of compact development. They all provide alternatives to long-distance automobile travel. By these alternative metrics, New York is the most compact metropolitan area (Hamidi, Ewing, Preuss, & Dodds, 2015) and San Francisco the most compact urbanized area (Hamidi & Ewing, 2014). Los Angeles is well down on both lists. This result has face validity (Figures 6.5 and 6.6).

In the work of Ewing et al., compactness/sprawl measures have been the main independent variables, related empirically to many dependent variables (Ewing &

96 *Carl Duke, Shima Hamidi, and Reid Ewing*

Figure 6.5 Endless Medium Density of Los Angeles County
Source: Google

Figure 6.6 Centered Development of Arlington County, Virginia
Source: Google

Hamidi, 2014). In one study, compactness was related to housing costs and separately to transportation costs (Hamidi & Ewing, 2015). Compactness, as they measured it, is positively related to housing costs. This seems reasonable. After all, compact places like New York and San Francisco are known for their exorbitantly high housing costs. At the same time, compactness, as they measured it, is negatively related to transportation costs. Again, this seems reasonable. Compact places like New York and San Francisco are known for their walkability and high-quality transit service, providing alternatives to long-distance travel by automobile. So their findings are intuitively plausible or, stated another way, they have face validity.

Construct Validity

Construct validity is a measure of how well we operationalize our constructs. In Chapter 5 on Conceptual Frameworks, we made much of the distinction between constructs, which are big abstract concepts, and the operational variables we use to imperfectly represent them. What we are trying to do in this step is to show that we have actually measured what we set out to measure, in our example, sprawl or compact development. This is an independent variable in much of Ewing et al.'s research. We also want to properly operationalize our dependent variables when we study the costs of sprawl.

Construct validity is subtly different from face validity. But it is different, as the following examples illustrates. Ewing and colleagues operationalized compactness not only at the metropolitan and urbanized area scales, but additionally at the county scale (Ewing, Meakins, Hamidi, & Nelson, 2014). Two measures of county compactness were calculated, an original index from 2002 based on six variables related to development density and street connectivity, and a refined index from 2014 based on 16 variables related to development density, land use mix, population and employment centering, and street connectivity. The refined index, on its face, would seem to be superior because it captures more dimensions of the construct compactness/sprawl. That is, the refined measure has more face validity. But as it turns out, it also has more construct validity.

The most compact counties are largely the same when measured by the original and refined indices. The top ten include, in both cases, the four boroughs of New York City, San Francisco County, Philadelphia County, the District of Columbia, etc. But the ten most sprawling counties are entirely different for the two indices. Many of the counties rated as most sprawling according to the original index have development patterns that are not what one would expect. They would best be described as small towns surrounded by farmlands. The small towns have moderate densities and gridded streets. The fact they are part of larger census tracts, their units of analysis, depresses their densities and compactness scores. They are not classic examples of suburban or exurban sprawl.

On the other hand, the counties rated as most sprawling according to the new four-factor index have census tracts with very low residential densities, commercial strips, and cul-de-sac street networks. They are classic examples of suburban and exurban sprawl (Ewing & Hamidi, 2017). Put another way, the refined index represents the construct of *sprawl* more accurately than the original index (Figures 6.7 and 6.8).

Construct validity has also been an issue with dependent variables in costs of sprawl studies. Ewing, Hamidi, Grace, and Wei (2016) wanted to relate compactness/sprawl to upward social and economic mobility in the United States. The best available measure of intergenerational mobility was the likelihood that a child born into the bottom fifth of the national income distribution will reach the top fifth by

Figure 6.7 Most Sprawling County According to the Six-Variable Index (Jackson County, Kansas)

Source: Ewing & Hamidi (2017)

age 30. Is this the best metric for representing upward social and economic mobility? Probably not. The obvious problem is this metric's failure to measure smaller gains in social and economic standing, say, from the bottom half to the top half of the income distribution, or from the first quintile to the second quintile of the income distribution. Still, the metric they used is the best available and has enough construct validity to be credible.

Another dependent variable illustrates the idea of construct validity. Ewing and colleagues have long wanted to relate sprawl to traffic congestion, but until recently, the only available measures of congestion were modeled rather than observed (until 2010) and limited to the largest urbanized areas (until 2015). There are now observed measures of congestion from the Texas Transportation Institute for all urbanized areas, and they have enough construct validity to be credible. A recent study relates sprawl, as they have measured it, to traffic congestion, as measured by annual delay per capita from TTI (Ewing et al., 2017). Both measures have construct validity.

Figure 6.8 Most Sprawling County According to the Four-Factor Index (Oglethorpe County, Georgia)

Source: Ewing & Hamidi (2017)

Internal Validity

Internal validity is the next step in the sequential investigation of research validity. Earlier, during our consideration of face validity and construct validity, we suggested that it is reasonable to propose relationships between compactness indices, their main independent variable, and certain dependent variables, such as upward mobility and traffic congestion. Internal validity takes the next step and considers whether the independent variable or variables have causal relationships to these dependent variables.

Internal validity is defined as the extent to which a causal conclusion is warranted from a study, ruling out confounding influences. As we note repeatedly in this book (see, in particular, Chapter 9 on Correlation), correlation does not equal or imply causation. Planners are ultimately interested in causation, not simple correlation. Any research that does not strive for internal validity becomes a simple observational or descriptive study, with limited practical application.

In certain fields, addressing internal validity is simple. You randomly assign individuals to a treatment group and a control group, apply the treatment to the former

100 *Carl Duke, Shima Hamidi, and Reid Ewing*

and not the latter, and see if outcomes differ between the groups to infer causality. Unfortunately, in planning, it is not so simple because planners seldom can randomly assign anyone to anything. You could say this whole book is about inferring causality in the absence of random assignment.

In Chapter 3 on Types of Research, we lay out the four conditions for cause-effect inference, and hence internal validity of study results. One is conceptual plausibility. That is the subject of Chapter 5 on Conceptual Frameworks.

A second condition is a strong association between dependent and independent variables. That can be established with any of the statistical methods highlighted in this book, from Chapter 8 on Chi-Square to Chapter 14 on Quasi-Experimental Research.

A third condition for causal inference is the elimination of rival explanations for a given relationship. This is generally accomplished by controlling statistically for confounding variables. The problem, of course, is that one can never measure and control for every possible influence on an outcome. The general approach, for the statistical methods highlighted in this book, is to account for as many confounding variables as possible.

A fourth condition for causal inference is time sequence, with the cause always preceding the effect. Only with longitudinal data, we can be sure that the cause precedes the effect. The statistical methods highlighted in this book, as well as the quasi-experimental methods in Chapter 14, often deal with longitudinal data and establish time sequence.

Perhaps the most carefully controlled study of sprawl and its impacts was both longitudinal and statistical (Hamidi & Ewing, 2014). Compactness scores for 2000 were compared to the same scores for 2010 to see which UZAs sprawled the most between censuses, and which sprawled the least or actually became more compact. Finally, the study validated the compactness index and its component factors against travel outcomes. Compact areas have higher walk mode shares, higher transit mode shares, and shorter average drive times on the journey to work, after accounting for potential confounders.

External Validity

We have now concluded that measurements of compactness/sprawl are reasonable on their face, that measures of compactness have relationships to travel and other outcomes, and that the relationships are likely to be causal. We must now determine whether these conclusions can be applied to other places. This transferability or generalizability of conclusions to other settings is called external validity. If findings cannot be transferred, studies lack external validity, and if they hold true in additional applications, they can be considered externally valid.

The best way to ensure external validity is to test conclusions in numerous settings. Referring to our preceding example, compactness/sprawl has been related to travel outcomes at three geographic scales—the metropolitan area (Hamidi et al., 2015), the urbanized area (Hamidi & Ewing, 2014), and the county (Ewing, Hamidi, & Grace, 2016). At each scale, samples have included nearly all cases in the population, that is, all metropolitan areas, urbanized areas, and metropolitan counties. All studies have shown that compact areas have higher walk and transit mode shares than sprawling areas.

An entirely different literature, comprised of hundreds of studies, has shown that compactness is also related to travel outcomes at the household/neighborhood scale (Ewing & Cervero, 2010). Households in compact neighborhoods travel less by car and more by walking and transit. Nearly all studies have found *resounding* evidence of statistically significant associations between the built environment and travel behavior, even after accounting for residential self-selection, the most significant threat to causal inference in the study of the built environment and travel (see Chapter 3 on Types of Research).

Meta-analysis and meta-regression, the subjects of Chapter 10 of *Advanced Quantitative Research Methods for Urban Planners*, achieve external validity by analyzing and aggregating results from many different studies. Built environment and travel studies have been subject to both meta-analysis and meta-regression, with similar but not identical conclusions (Stevens, 2017; Ewing & Cervero, 2017). Another approach to external validity is to collect and pool disaggregate data from many different and diverse places. This is the approach to built environment-travel research taken by Ewing and colleagues (Ewing et al., 2015; Tian et al., 2015; Tian, Park, & Ewing, 2018). They now have amassed household travel and neighborhood built environmental data for 34 regions, nearly 100,000 households, and nearly 1,000,000 trips. The conclusion, that compact neighborhoods generate less vehicular travel and more walk and transit trips, continues to hold up.

Planning Examples

Security of Public Spaces

Circa 1990, following in the footsteps of Jane Jacobs, Kevin Lynch, William H. Whyte, and other big thinkers, new urbanists began to argue that the quality of public space is more important than quantity.

New urbanist spaces are relatively small and formal looking, often in the form of village greens, town squares, or urban plazas. They are bordered by buildings (for 24-hour natural surveillance). Local streets converge on these spaces, making them more accessible and more prominent. They are more likely to be used for passive recreation than active, and they are multigenerational rather than being aimed at a particular age group. They are also likely to be linked to other spaces physically and visually, forming a network of public spaces.

Are these good public spaces? Are they better than the spaces in older master planned communities? What, in short, constitutes good public space? And can the qualities that make public space good be measured (in research parlance, can quality be operationalized)?

The answer is *yes*, according to Jeremy Németh and Stephan Schmidt who authored "Toward a Methodology for Measuring the Security of Publicly Accessible Spaces," published in the *Journal of the American Planning Association* in 2007.

The authors do an admirable job of surveying the literature on public space management from different vantage points. They group techniques into hard (or active) control, and soft (or passive) control, and further subdivide the relevant literature into four areas: legal and regulatory restrictions, surveillance and policing, physical design for natural surveillance, and access limitations.

They rely on site visits to dozens of public spaces in New York City to create a security index for public spaces. The index is a composite of 20 features, all defined in

102 *Carl Duke, Shima Hamidi, and Reid Ewing*

the article. To compute the overall score for a particular public space: Subtract the total score for all features that control users from the total score for all features that encourage freedom of use (see Figure 6.9).

The highest possible score is 20 (least controlled). The lowest is −20 (most controlled). The index has been tested and found reliable, in the sense that results from two separate visits arrive at similar scores. What is missing from the article is any validation of the composite index.

Reliability and validity are equally essential properties of measurement. The Németh/Schmidt index could be validated by comparing overall security scores to incident reports, expert judgments, or user perceptions. These two young academics have gotten a start with the JAPA article. After they validate their security index, it could prove a useful planning and design tool.

Urban Sprawl and Air Quality

To model something, you have to be able to measure it. How you measure it can make all the difference, as two studies of urban form and air quality show.

The studies were authored by Brian Stone, of City and Regional Planning at Georgia Tech. His studies take on added importance in light of climate change, our field's looming challenge.

In operationalizing constructs, researchers can get into trouble. No variable or set of variables can perfectly represent a big abstract concept. The variables normally miss certain qualities that are rightfully part of the construct, while encompassing others that are not part. Stone's articles illustrate the challenge.

His 2008 article in the *Journal of Environmental Management* finds statistically significant relationships between four different measures of sprawl and a measure of air quality. These relationships are evident for 45 large metropolitan regions over a

Features encouraging use	Features controlling use
Sign announcing "public space"	Visible sets of rules posted
Public ownership or management	Subjective or judgment rules posted
Restroom available	In a business improvement district (BID)
Diversity of seating types	Security cameras
Various microclimates	Security personnel
Lighting to encourage nighttime use	Secondary security personnel
Small-scale food vendors	Design to imply appropriate use
Art, cultural, or visual enhancement	Presence of sponsor or advertisement
Entrance accessibility	Areas of restricted or conditional use
Orientation accessibility	Constrained hours of operation

Figure 6.9 Security Index Criteria

Source: Németh & Schmidt (2007)

13-year period. The four sprawl measures are combinations of variables representing four commonly accepted dimensions of urban form: density of population and employment, degree of land use mixing, strength of downtowns and other activity centers, and street network connectivity. The air quality measure is the average annual number of ozone standard violations. Accounting for differences in temperature and size, the most sprawling cities are found to experience 60 percent more high ozone days than the most compact cities.

Stone's study is bolstered by the use of sprawl measures that have

1. Construct validity (an undeniable relationship to the construct sprawl) and
2. Internal validity in earlier empirical studies.

A second paper by Stone and others doesn't fare as well, at least in this regard. Published in 2007 in the *Journal of the American Planning Association*, "Is Compact Growth Good for Air Quality?" answers this question in the affirmative. But it is a *yes* followed by a *maybe not*.

Stone et al. estimate the elasticity of vehicle travel with respect to density to be –0.35, meaning that a 10 percent increase in density should result in a 3.5 percent reduction in household vehicle travel and emissions. This is a big number, bigger than any elasticity we have seen in the carefully controlled travel studies of recent years. Ordinarily such a finding would be good news for smart growth advocates. However, this paper goes on to predict that a switch from current growth patterns (read *urban sprawl*) to compact patterns (read *smart growth*) will yield only a 6 percent average reduction in vehicle travel and emissions by 2050 for 11 midwestern metropolitan regions. Even the most diehard *smart growther* would have to ask, why bother?

An anomaly in Stone et al.'s results tips the reader off to a weakness in the way compact development is being operationalized. The Chicago region produces more vehicle travel and emissions with compact development than without (see Figure 6.10). While Chicago is relatively compact by U.S. standards, we know from sprawl research that Chicago has sprawled badly in recent years. How could compact development make things worse than sprawl? The answer lies in Stone et al.'s operational definition of compact development—it is Portland, without Portland's best attributes. By their definition, a compact region is one that experiences the same shares of urban, suburban, and rural growth as Portland. What isn't captured by this operational definition is the density, mix, centering, or street accessibility of Portland's growth.

In this second study, the modest projected benefits of compact development are a simple result of the operational definition chosen to represent it. This definition suffers from a lack of both face and construct validity. Use another definition, like Chicago with a bump up in density, mix, and centering, and you will get a different result. Guaranteed.

As we said at the outset, how you measure something can make all the difference.

Conclusion

In sum, reliability is the consistency and repeatability of measurement or research results, while validity is the correctness or credibility of the measurement or research results. While these two important concepts are distinct and equally important, we may consider that reliability is a necessary but not sufficient condition for validity.

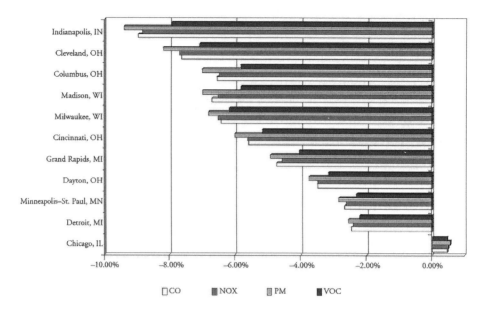

Figure 6.10 Percentage Difference in Vehicle Emissions in 2050 Under a Compact Growth Scenario Compared to a Business as Usual Scenario

Source: Stone, Mednick, Holloway, & Spak (2007)

In other words, in order to be valid, a measurement must be reliable; but reliability does not guarantee validity (Reynolds & Mason, 2009). If a test keeps giving different results (unreliable), it cannot possibly be measuring what you think it is (invalid).

To ensure the quality of research, both reliability and validity should be carefully and separately examined at multiple stages in research. Pertaining to validity, for example, a researcher might focus on construct validity more in the research design stage, the internal validity (i.e., causality) in the research design and interpreting results stages, and the external validity (i.e., generalizability) in drawing conclusions.

Works Cited

Alasadi, R. (2016). *Investigating spatial quality in urban settings: The assessment of walkability in the streets of Doha, Qatar* (Doctoral dissertation). Qatar University, Qatar.

Ameli, S. H., Hamidi, S., Garfinkel-Castro, A., & Ewing, R. (2015). Do better urban design qualities lead to more walking in Salt Lake City, Utah? *Journal of Urban Design, 20*(3), 393–410. http://doi.org/10.1080/13574809.2015.1041894

Ernawati, J. (2016). Dimensions underlying local people's preference of street characteristics for walking. *Procedia-Social and Behavioral Sciences, 234*, 461–469.

Ewing, R. (2007, July). Research you can use: Security of public spaces: New measures are reliable, but are they valid? *Planning*, 54.

Ewing, R., & Cervero, R. (2010). Travel and the built environment: A meta-analysis. *Journal of the American Planning Association, 76*(3), 265–294. http://doi.org/10.1080/01944361003766766

Ewing, R., & Cervero, R. (2017). Does compact development make people drive less? The answer is yes. *Journal of the American Planning Association*, *83*(1), 19–25. http://doi.org/10.10 80/01944363.2016.1245112

Ewing, R., & Clemente, O. (2013). *Measuring urban design: Metrics for livable places.* Washington, DC: Island Press.

Ewing, R., Hajrasouliha, A., Neckerman, K. M., Purciel-Hill, M., & Greene, W. (2016). Streetscape features related to pedestrian activity. *Journal of Planning Education and Research*, *36*(1), 5–15. http://doi.org/10.1177.0739456X15591585

Ewing, R., & Hamidi, S. (2014). *Measuring urban sprawl and validating sprawl measures.* Washington, DC: National Institutes of Health and Smart Growth America.

Ewing, R., & Hamidi, S. (2015). Compactness versus sprawl: A review of recent evidence from the United States. *Journal of Planning Literature*, *30*(4), 413–432. http://doi.org/10.1177/0885412215595439

Ewing, R., & Hamidi, S. (2017). *Costs of sprawl.* Taylor & Francis.

Ewing, R., Hamidi, S., & Grace, J. B. (2016). Urban sprawl as a risk factor in motor vehicle crashes. *Urban Studies*, *53*(2), 247–266. http://doi.org/10.1177/0042098014562331

Ewing, R., Hamidi, S., Grace, J. B., & Wei, Y. D. (2016). Does urban sprawl hold down upward mobility? *Landscape and Urban Planning*, *148*, 80–88. http://doi.org/10.1016/j.landurbplan.2015.11.012

Ewing, R., Hamidi, S., Tian, G., Proffitt, D., Tonin, S., & Fregolent, L. (2017). Testing Newman and Kenworthy's theory of density and automobile dependence. *Journal of Planning Education and Research.* http://doi.org/10.1177/0739456X16688767

Ewing, R., & Handy, S. (2009). Measuring the unmeasurable: Urban design qualities related to walkability. *Journal of Urban Design*, *14*(1), 65–84. http://doi.org/10.1080/13574800802451155

Ewing, R., Handy, S., Brownson, R. C., Clemente, O., & Winston, E. (2006). Identifying and measuring urban design qualities related to walkability. *Journal of Physical Activity and Health*, *3*(s1), S223–S240. http://doi.org/10.1123/jpah.3.s1.s223

Ewing, R., Meakins, G., Hamidi, S., & Nelson, A. C. (2014). Relationship between urban sprawl and physical activity, obesity, and morbidity—Update and refinement. *Health & Place*, *26*, 118–126. http://doi.org/10.1016/j.healthplace.2013.12.008

Ewing, R., Pendall, R., & Chen, D. (2002). *Measuring sprawl and its impact: The character and consequences of metropolitan expansion.* Washington, DC: Smart Growth America.

Ewing, R., Tian, G., Goates, J. P., Zhang, M., Greenwald, M. J., Joyce, A., Kircher, J., & Greene, W. (2015). Varying influences of the built environment on household travel in 15 diverse regions of the United States. *Urban Studies*, *52*(13), 2330–2348. http://doi.org/10.1177/0042098014560991

Ewing, R., Tian, G., & Lyons, T. (2018). Does compact development increase or reduce traffic congestion? *Cities*, *72*, 94–101. http://doi.org/10.1016/j.cities.2017.08.010

Hamidi, S., & Ewing, R. (2014). A longitudinal study of changes in urban sprawl between 2000 and 2010 in the United States. *Landscape and Urban Planning*, *128*, 72–82. http://doi.org/10.1016/j.landurbplan.2014.04.021

Hamidi, S., & Ewing, R. (2015). Is sprawl affordable for Americans? Exploring the association between housing and transportation affordability and urban sprawl. *Transportation Research Record*, *2500*, 75–79. http://doi.org/10.3141/2500-09

Hamidi, S., Ewing, R., Preuss, I., & Dodds, A. (2015). Measuring sprawl and its impacts: An update. *Journal of Planning Education and Research*, *35*(1), 35–50. http://doi.org/10.1177/0739456X14565247

Hamidi, S., & Moazzeni, S. (2018). Examining the impacts of street-level built environmental and urban design qualities on walking behavior in Downtown Dallas, TX, Transportation Research Board 97th Annual Meeting.

Landis, J. R., & Koch, G. G. (1977). The measurement of observer agreement for categorical data. *Biometrics*, *33*(1), 159–174. http://doi.org/10.2307/2529310

Maxwell, J. A. (2016). *Designing for "life between buildings": Modeling the relationship between streetscape qualities and pedestrian activity in Glasgow, Scotland* (Doctoral dissertation). University of Strathclyde.

Németh, J., & Schmidt, S. (2007). Toward a methodology for measuring the security of publicly accessible spaces. *Journal of the American Planning Association, 73*(3), 283–297. http://doi.org/10.1080/01944360708977978

Park, K., Ewing, R., Sabouri, S., & Larsen, J. (2019). Street life and the built environment in an auto-oriented US region. *Cities, 88*, 243–251. https://doi.org/10.1016/j.cities.2018.11.005

Reynolds, C. R., & Mason, B. A. (2009). Measurement and statistical problems in neuropsychological assessment of children. In Cecil R. Reynolds and Elaine Fletcher-Janzen (Eds.), *Handbook of clinical child neuropsychology* (pp. 203–230). New York, NY: Springer.

Stevens, M. R. (2017). Does compact development make people drive less? *Journal of the American Planning Association, 83*(1), 7–18.

Stone, B. (2008). Urban sprawl and air quality in large US cities. *Journal of Environmental Management, 86*(4), 688–698. http://doi.org/10.1016/j.jenvman.2006.12.034

Stone, B., Mednick, A. C., Holloway, T., & Spak, S. N. (2007). Is compact growth good for air quality? *Journal of the American Planning Association, 73*(4), 404–418. http://doi.org/10.1080/01944360708978521

Tian, G., Ewing, R., White, A., Hamidi, S., Walters, J., Goates, J. P., & Joyce, A. (2015). Traffic generated by mixed-use developments: Thirteen-region study using consistent measures of built environment. *Transportation Research Record, 2500*, 116–124. http://doi.org/10.3141/2500-14

Tian, G., Park, K., & Ewing, R. (2018). Trip and parking generation rates for different housing types: Effects of compact development. *Urban Studies, 56*(8), 1554–1575. (No. 18-01484).

Yin, L. (2017). Street level urban design qualities for walkability: Combining 2D and 3D GIS measures. *Computers, Environment and Urban Systems, 64*, 288–296.

7 Descriptive Statistics and Visualizing Data

Dong-ah Choi, Pratiti Tagore, Fariba Siddiq, Keunhyun Park, and Reid Ewing

Overview

Descriptive statistics are the most basic statistical operations to quantitatively describe data. There are two specific branches of statistics—descriptive and inferential.

Descriptive statistics aim at summarizing data for a sample or population, whereas inferential statistics aim at drawing inferences about a population from data for a sample drawn from that population (Trochim, 2006).

This chapter focuses on descriptive statistics. Subsequent chapters delve into different methods of inferential statistics. In practice, peer-reviewed planning articles often start with a section on and table of descriptive statistics and go on to present inferential statistics in subsequent sections and tables. A study comparing the means of two samples may, for example, report the means and standard deviations of the samples first (descriptive statistics) and then use a difference-of-means test (t-test) to see whether the means of the two samples differ significantly from one another (inferential statistics).

This chapter describes the conditions required to use descriptive statistics followed by a demonstration of how to compute several measures using the statistical software package SPSS and R. This chapter also presents two case studies from the field of planning, which use descriptive statistics.

Purpose

There may be many samples collected while performing a research study. Each sample has its own identity, but the research is interested in the collective identity of the entire sample or of large subsamples. Confronted with the complexity of a large number of measurements, the mind cannot readily make a mental image of the overall content of information recorded in the dataset.

Since about 2000, planners have become intensely interested in the connection between planning and public health. Many planning studies have used data from the Centers for Disease Control and Prevention (CDC)'s Behavioral Risk Factor Surveillance System (BRFSS). To obtain the data, CDC on behalf of state health departments surveys hundreds of thousands of adults each year on hundreds of health risk factors and health outcomes. Making sense of so much data without descriptive statistics would be impossible. This is why the data needs to be summarized in a comprehensible way, such that a single number may be representative of the entire sample (e.g., average body mass index) or large subsamples (e.g., average BMI of men versus women, whites versus nonwhites, residents of sprawling counties versus compact counties).

108   *Dong-ah Choi et al.*

Descriptive statistics provide answers to the questions: who, what, where, when, how, but cannot answer the question why. Even inferential statistics have difficulty answering (definitively) the question of why.

While data collection modes vary, descriptive statistics can summarize many types of data, specifically nominal, ordinal, interval, and ratio scale data collected through surveys, censuses, direct observations, interviews, content analyses, and so forth.

Descriptive statistics are most commonly broken down into four types of measures: measures of frequency, measures of central tendency, measures of variability or dispersion, and cross tabulations.

A frequency distribution is the easiest way to represent a single variable by grouping the samples into categories. Graphs allow for data to be analyzed through visual representation. Common types of graphs are bar charts, histograms, pie charts, and boxplots. Of American adults surveyed by BFRSS in 2016, 64.8 percent were overweight or obese (had a Body Mass Index (BMI) of 25 or greater).

Central tendency measures enable researchers to determine the typical score of a group. What is typical may be a mean, median, or mode. While the mean or average is the most common measure of central tendency, and one that plays an outsized role in inferential statistics, the median may be a better measure of what is *typical* for a given sample when the sample is skewed to high or low values.

Descriptive statistics also provide information about variability of data. Variability is the dispersion around the mean or median of a dataset. Variability measures enable researchers to indicate how spread out a group of scores is based on the range, quartile deviation, variance, and standard deviation. Standard deviation and variance play an outsized role in inferential statistics as well.

In the 2016 BRFSS, the mean BMI of U.S. adults was 27.9, while the standard deviation was 6.3. This means that the average U.S. adult was overweight (had a BMI of 25 or more), and that assuming a normal distribution, 95 percent fell within a range of 15.6 and 40.2.

Cross tabulation is a method of summarizing the relationship between two categorical variables, for an overall association of the variables. Correlation is a representation of relationship of two continuous (or numeric) variables, by a single number for a dataset. Cross tabulation and correlation are often treated as a type of inferential statistics to show whether two variables are related or not (see chapters 8 and 9, respectively).

History

Descriptive statistics have an extensive history developed through many disciplines. Basic forms of statistics have been used since the beginning of civilization. Historians posit the ancient use of statistical measures, specifically mean, median, mode. The ancient leaders used these measures to understand their empires in terms of population, geographical area, wealth and taxation, and military power (Kraus, 1994; Jones, 1953; Missiakoulis, 2010).

By the 17th century, *Political Arithmetic* was introduced by William Petty as a way to document all natural, social, and political components of a state with numbers in order to have a sound basis for decisions and, thus, avoid political controversies (1672) (Stochastikon Encyclopedia, 2014). During the same timeframe, John Graunt and Jacob Bernoulli Pascal were studying vital statistics of populations. Graunt had worked with Petty for a few years, and was an accomplished statistician. He was the first statistician to become a member of the Royal Society of London. While Bernoulli's

Descriptive Statistics and Visualizing Data   109

greatest contributions are in calculus, geometry, and algebra, he started his career with demographic analysis. In this timeframe, the first weekly data collections on baptisms, marriages, and deaths were produced in London and France, followed by the first published demographic study on bills of mortality by Jacob Graunt. With centuries of development, descriptive statistics are now widely used across a variety of fields. We would guess that half of the quantitative planning articles include descriptive statistics, often as a precursor to inferential statistics (see Tables 7.1a and 7.1b). Qualitative planning articles also often include summary statistics on their subjects.

Tables 7.1a Quantitative Study With Descriptive Statistics Followed by Inferential Statistics (Ewing & Rong, 2008)

Household Variables	2001 RECS	2000 Census	1998 and 2002 AHS
	Mean (SD)	Mean (SD)	Mean (SD)
Primary energy use per household	95,415	NA	NA
(in thousands of BTUs)	(58,093)		
House size	2,097	NA	1,689
(square feet)	(1,410)		(1,098)
House type			
Single-family detached	60.5%	60.7%	65.5%
Single-family attached	10.4%	7.6%	12.4%
Multi-family	29.1%	31.7%	22.1%
Year built			
1939 or earlier	30.1%	14.3%	10.7%
1940 to 1959	20.7%	23.4%	18.9%
1960 to 1979	23.9%	32.5%	36.4%
1980 to 2000	25.3%	29.7%	34.0%
Household composition			
Number of children	0.51	0.71	0.71
	(0.93)	(1.11)	(1.10)
Number of adults	2.11	1.95	1.92
	(1.07)	(0.91)	(0.83)
Household income			
less than $30,000	38.7%	30.5%	28.4%
$30,000 to $49,999	24.7%	21.5%	20.8%
$50,000 to $74,999	20.7%	19.8%	19.4%
$75,000 or more	15.9%	28.2%	31.4%
Race/Ethnicity of the householder			
White	70.7%	69.0%	71.3%
Black	12.8%	12.7%	10.4%
Hispanic	10.9%	12.3%	11.5%
Asian	3.5%	4.1%	5.2%
Other	2.1%	1.9%	1.6%
Country variables			
County sprawl index	NA	107	110
		(28)	(21)
Residential construction costs	NA	0.982	0.992
		(0.145)	(0.130)
Total population in the MSAs	NA	4,388,905	4,048,688
		(5,696,873)	(4,136,994)

Sources: E1A (2004), Ewing et al. (2003), and U.S. Bureau of the Census (1998, 2002, 2004).

MSA = metropolitan statistical area; NA = not applicable; SD = standard deviation.

110 *Dong-ah Choi et al.*

Table 7.1b Relationship Between Delivered Residential Energy Use in the United States, House Size and Type, and Other Control Variables (With Coefficients, t-Ratios, and Significance Levels)

	Heating		*Cooling*		*Others*	
	Coefficient	p-*Value*	*Coefficient*	p-*Value*	*Coefficient*	p-*Value*
House size (square feet)	0.00015	<0.001	0.00012	<0.001	0.00006	<0.001
House type						
Mobile home	0.086	0.020	0060	0.185	−0.025	0.333
Single family attached	−0.037	0.243	−0.115	0.008	−0.105	<0.001
Multi-family	−0.431	<0.001	−0.230	<0.001	−0.366	<0.001
Year built						
1940 to 1959	−0.194	<0.001	−0.032	0.353	0.033	0.107
1960 to 1979	−0.355	<0.001	−0.025	0.465	0036	0.064
1980 to 2000	−0.456	<0.001	−0.049	0.157	0.044	0.037
Household income						
$30.000 to $49.999	0.017	0.491	0.043	0.147	0.080	<0.001
$50.000 to $74.999	0.021	0.450	0.131	<0.001	0.131	<0.001
	0.142					
$75,000 or more		<0.001	0.169	<0.001	0.233	<0.001
Race/Ethnicity of the householder						
Black	0.283	<0.001	0.166	<0.001	0.117	<0.001
Hispanic	−0.117	0.002	−0.230	<0.001	−0.078	0.001
Asian	−0.162	0.003	−0.350	<0.001	−0.225	<0.001
Other	−0.007	0.918	−0.117	0.161	−0.149	0.001
Household composition						
Number of children	0.016	0.449	0.137	<0.001	0.285	<0.001
Number of adults	−0.002	0.916	0.210	<0.001	0.184	<0 001
ln(energy price)	−1.006	<0.001	−0.571	<0.001	−0.403	<0 001
($ per thousand BTUs)						
HDDs	0 00020	<0.001	NA	NA	NA	NA
CDDs	NA	NA	0.00054	<0.001	NA	NA
R^2	0.7293		0.7072		0.5531	
Number of households	4,666		3,464		4,822	

Source: EIA (2004)

Notes: Dependent variables are the natural logarithms of delivered residential energy use for heating, cooling, and other uses, respectively, per household per year (in thousands of BTUs). Reference dummies included single-family detached housing, houses built before 1940, households with an annual income of less than $30,000, and white householders. Other controls for heating/cooling energy use models were the age of the heating/cooling equipment variable (dummies as less or more than ten years old), the programmability of the thermostat of the heating/cooling equipment variable (dummies as yes or no), and the building insulation variable (dummies as well or poorly insulated), plus whether the cooling equipment was central or not and whether there was someone at home all day on a typical weekday (dummies as yes or no).

In—natural log; NA—not applicable.

Mechanics

This section will break down the mechanics of descriptive statistics by the five measures discussed previously. It will also cover visual representation of data using graphs. While computer programs have curbed the need to be highly familiar with the mathematical steps required to conduct such operations, it is however of utmost

Descriptive Statistics and Visualizing Data 111

importance that one should understand the concepts behind each of these mathematical operations.

Frequency Distribution

A frequency distribution is one of the simplest ways to represent a single variable. It provides a comprehensive overview of a dataset at one glance. For a categorical variable (e.g., seasons) or a small number of numeric cases (e.g., number of cars per household), each possible value may represent a group in a frequency table. When the set of data values are spread out (e.g., housing price), however, it is difficult to set up a frequency table for every possible value. In this case, class intervals are used to group the data. For class intervals, after identifying the maximum and minimum values of a variable, the entire dataset is broken down into a number of subintervals of equal length that covers the range between maximum and minimum values without overlapping. By simply counting the number of observations in each subinterval, we get the 'frequency' of each cell or group. A table of frequencies is drawn up by counting the observations in each group.

For ease of understanding, *relative frequency* may be calculated for each group. Relative frequency for each group is the fraction of observations belonging to that class.

Relative frequency of a group is:

$$R.F. = \frac{Group\ frequency}{Total\ number\ of\ observations}$$

The frequencies can be represented either in a table format or by a relative frequency histogram. A histogram is simply a way of representing the relative frequencies visually (see Figure 7.4 for an example). The class intervals are marked on the horizontal axis of the graph, and for each interval a vertical bar (rectangle) is drawn whose area is equal to the relative frequency of that interval.

Central Tendency

In statistics, a measure of central tendency is an estimate of the center of a distribution of values. This central value can be measured as a mean, median, or mode.

The most commonly used measure is the mean of a dataset, which is the total of all the observed values divided by the number of observations. The formula for the mean is as follows:

$$\bar{x} = \frac{\sum_{i=1}^{n} X_i}{n} = \frac{X_1 + X_2 + X_3 + \cdots + X_n}{n}$$

where
Σ = Summation of all values
X = Refers to individual numerical values
n = Total number of observations
i = A counter, which identifies the first x when $i = 1$, the second x when $i = 2$, and so on to the last, or the nth, when $i = n$

The mean is the only measure of central tendency that can be used in inferential statistics to infer characteristics of a population from which the sample is drawn. The mean can be computed only from interval or ratio scale data. However, the major drawback is that one single observation that is vastly different from the rest of the observations can seriously skew the mean of the entire dataset, giving a faulty estimate of the same. These extreme values are referred to as outliers.

The median of a dataset is the middle value of the observations when they are ordered from lowest to highest in value. When the number of observations is odd, the median is the middle number of the total number of observations. In other words, median is that value of a dataset that divides the dataset in two equal halves. Where there is an even number of observations, the median is considered to be the number halfway between the two middle observations (i.e., mean of the two numbers).

For any given set of data, the median is less sensitive than the mean to extremely low or high values, so it is often used to protect against undue influence by outliers. For a skewed distribution, such as with income, the median is more typical of the sample than is the mean. Due to outlying values of income (the *1 percent* of super-rich individuals), the mean of income will be higher than what is typical for those in the sample.

If the number of samples is quite large, then it is sometimes useful to extend the concept of median and divide the dataset into four equal parts rather than two. Each part is then a quartile. Or samples can be divided into quintiles (five equal parts) or deciles (ten equal parts).

The mode of a dataset is the most frequently occurring observation within the data. The advantage of using mode is that it can be computed with nominal or ordinal data, as well as interval and ratio scale data. While a mode is a good way to tell the most common attribute, there are shortcomings. First, if no value occurs more than once, there can be no mode. Second, if multiple values occur more than once, there can be two or more modes.

Which is the best estimate measure of central tendency to use in planning: the mean, the median, or the mode? The answer is not simple because the choice depends on the purpose. The mode has the disadvantage that it is not influenced at all by the distribution of scores at values other than the mode. The median takes into account more data than does the mode, in that it requires the number of scores to either side of the median to be equal. Yet, the median is not influenced by the size of the scores. In contrast, the mean takes into account every score in the distribution; however, there are cases where using the mean can be misleading (e.g., presence of outliers). One has to cautiously choose a measure of central tendency that describes the data most accurately, noting that sometimes this includes using more than one type of measure.

Dispersion

In addition to locating the center of the data, an important aspect of a descriptive analysis is to numerically measure the extent of variation around the center. Two datasets may exhibit similar positions of the center but may be different with respect to variability. Thus, datasets should also be analyzed for dispersion around the mean. There are three common measures of dispersion: the variance, standard deviation, and range.

Descriptive Statistics and Visualizing Data 113

A small variance indicates that data points tend to be very close to the mean, while a large variance indicates that data points may be very spread out from the mean and from each other. Some of the deviations from the mean—differences between the observed values and the mean—will have positive values (be above the mean), and some will have negative values (be below the mean). If we simply summed them, the negative values would cancel the positive values. So for the purpose of computing a measure of dispersion, we square the deviations from the mean to get rid of the negative signs. The *variance* of a set of data is denoted by s^2 and is defined as the sum of the squared deviations from the mean divided by the number of observations minus one. The formula for the variance is:

$$s^2 = \frac{\sum_{i=1}^{n}(x_i - \bar{x})^2}{n-1}$$

where
$\sum$ = Summation of all values
n = Total number of observations
i = A counter, which identifies the first x when $i = 1$, the second x when $i = 2$, and so on to the last, or the nth, when $i =$ n
$\bar{x}$ = Mean value of observations

For a sample, subtracting one in the denominator gives us an unbiased estimate of the sample variance. For a population rather than a sample, the formula remains the same except the denominator becomes n, rather than $n - 1$.

The variance is one power above, i.e., a *square* value, the unit of the dataset. To have the measure of variation and the observations in the same units, the square root of the variance is more commonly used. This is called the standard deviation of a set of values.

The standard deviation of a set of n observations is denoted by s. The formula for the standard deviation of a sample is:

$$s = \sqrt{s^2} = \sqrt{\sum_{i=1}^{n}\frac{(x_i - \bar{x})^2}{n-1}}$$

where
$\sum$ = Summation of all values
n = Total number of observations
i = A counter, which identifies the first x when $i = 1$, the second x when $i = 2$, and so on to the last, or the nth, when $i =$ n
$\bar{x}$ = Mean value of observations

Again, a low standard deviation shows that data observations tend to be very close to the mean, whereas a high standard deviation indicates that the data observations are spread out around the mean.

Range is the difference between the highest and the lowest value of a dataset. It does not provide much detail about the nature and characteristics of the dataset. For interval and ratio scale data, the range is the difference between the two extreme values,

114   *Dong-ah Choi et al.*

but for ordinal data it is the number of categories used to describe the data. There are few statistical procedures based on the range. It is mostly used as a quick substitute for, or used as an addition to the standard deviation, as a measure of the width of the distribution. It is seldom reported in planning articles.

Data Visualization

Data visualization is a powerful skill that provides readers with insight into information that we have. Among various data visualization methods, four ways are described in this section: data matrix, frequency table, cross tabulation, and informative graphs. Understanding the purpose, advantages, and disadvantages of each visualization method leads researchers to effectively display, summarize, and represent a dataset.

Data Matrix

A data matrix is a matrix that shows observation values arranged by variable and case. Cases are research subjects, variables are the characteristics of cases which researchers want to study. In a data matrix (Table 7.2), cases are displayed in the rows and variables are displayed in the columns. The values presented in the cells are observation scores for which descriptive statistics are often displayed (e.g., mean, median, standard deviation, maximum minimum).

Frequency Table

When handling a large dataset, presenting the complete data matrix would not be feasible or effective. A good way to summarize the data is to estimate frequencies of values of a variable and present them in a table (Table 7.3). The relative frequencies can be represented by percentages.

Table 7.2 Data Matrix Example: MSA Characteristics

Census Bureau Statistical Area Name	*2014 Median Income*	*2014 Population Estimate*	*Median Rent*
Albuquerque, NM MSA	$47,581	904,587	$750
Atlanta-Sandy Springs-Roswell, GA MSA	$56,166	5,614,323	$849
Austin-Round Rock, TX MSA	$63,603	1,943,299	$1,144
Baltimore-Columbia-Towson, MD MSA	$71,501	2,785,874	$1,225
Birmingham-Hoover, AL MSA	$47,046	1,143,772	$849
Boston-Cambridge-Newton, MA-NH MSA	$75,667	4,732,161	$2,400
Buffalo-Cheektowaga-Niagara Falls, NY MSA	$50,074	1,136,360	$810
Charlotte-Concord-Gastonia, NC-SC MSA	$53,549	2,380,314	$926
Chicago-Naperville-Elgin, IL-IN-WI MSA	$61,598	9,554,598	$1,500

Source: Boeing & Waddell (2017)

Descriptive Statistics and Visualizing Data 115

Table 7.3 Frequency Table Example: Educational Backgrounds of Principals in Maker Firms

Bachelor's Degree Type	Count	Share
Art and design	39	41%
Science and engineering	18	19%
Business and law	17	18%
Social science and humanities	11	12%
Other fields	10	11%
Total	95	100%

Source: Wolf-Powers et al. (2017)

Cross Tabulation

The easiest way to examine the relationship between two categorical variables, or any data that is mutually exclusive, is by cross tabulation. It is also known as a contingency table. With this method, the number and percentages of each possible combination of values is calculated, along with the overall association of the variables (see Table 7.6 for an example). This helps one to determine if there is a pattern to the data. If there is, then the data may be further analyzed for statistical significance using various testing methods. Several methods may be used for this, but the most frequently used approach is the chi-square test (see Chapter 8).

Informative Graphs

Graphs represent a dataset in the simplest and most accessible way, that is, visually. Graphs can summarize data at all four scales—nominal, ordinal, interval, and ratio. Planning academics tend to use tables when graphs would communicate as well or better. Graphs have many advantages, the most important of them being ease of understanding by a layman. They also convey a great deal of information in a short period of time.

When variables are nominal or ordinal, pie charts and bar charts are effective. In a pie chart (Figure 7.1), the categories of the variables are expressed by means of slices of a pie and each slice displays the percentage of the frequency distribution. Although pie charts are effective for immediately identifying the proportion of frequency scores without any further calculation, they do not provide the exact numbers in each category.

In this case, a more suitable visualization method may be a bar chart or, synonymously, a bar graph. In a bar chart (Figure 7.2), the categories of the variables are expressed by means of bars and each bar is proportional in length to the frequency it represents. In contrast to a pie chart, when employing a bar chart, it is not easy to immediately identify the proportion of cases in each category. However, it is easy to compare the frequency differences across categories.

When the variables are continuous, pie charts and bar charts don't apply, unless the variable is transformed into groups reasonably (e.g., high-income vs. low-income). Instead, researchers use line graphs (Figure 7.3) or histograms (Figure 7.4). In a histogram, the values of the variable of interest are divided into ranges on the x-axis and the frequency of cases for each range is represented by the height of the bar on the y-axis.

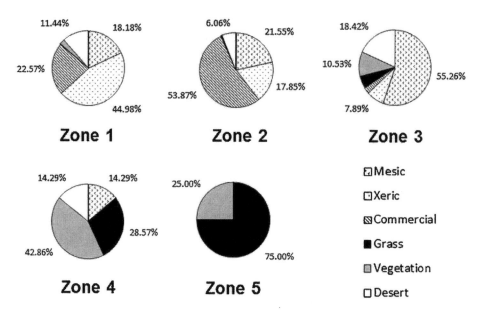

Figure 7.1 Pie Chart Example: Land Use and Land Cover Types
Source: Fan & Myint (2014)

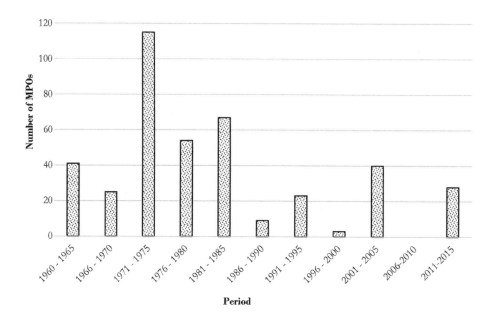

Figure 7.2 Bar Graph Example: MPO Designation Over Time
Source: Sciara (2017)

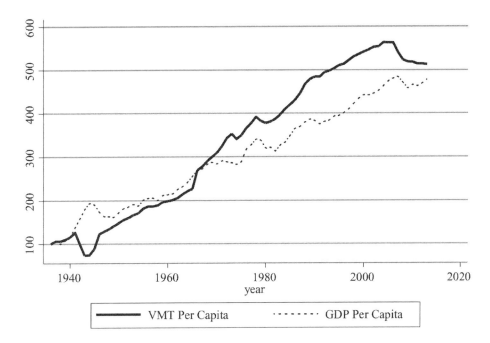

Figure 7.3 Line Graph Example: Per Capita GDP and VMT in the United States
Source: Manville, King, & Smart (2017)

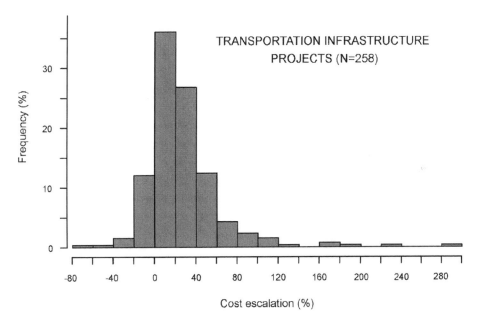

Figure 7.4 Histogram Example: Inaccuracy of Cost Estimates in Transportation Projects
Source: Flyvbjerg et al. (2002)

118 *Dong-ah Choi et al.*

Step by Step

Almost all statistical software packages, including SPSS and R, can easily calculate descriptive statistics such as frequency, central tendency, and dispersion. For the purpose of the exercise, we will use the household travel dataset (HTS.household.10regions.sav).

Frequency Table

Let's start with a frequency table (Figure 7.5) and say we want a quick idea about the household size in those ten regions. In SPSS, click "Analyze" in the main menu. Then "Descriptive Statistics" → "Frequencies."

Once the frequency window is activated (Figure 7.6), select *hhsize* variable (household size) from the variable list on the left. Transfer it to the box labeled "Variable(s)" on the right by clicking on [▶]. Click "OK" to get a result.

Table 7.4 is the result table that we get in the output page. This table presents the number of households with different household sizes, their relative percentages, and their cumulative percentages. You can see that the largest group is a two-person

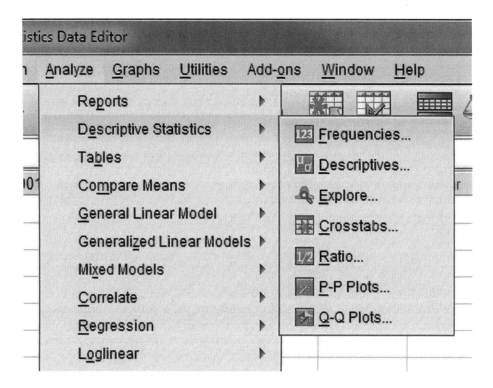

Figure 7.5 Find Frequency Window

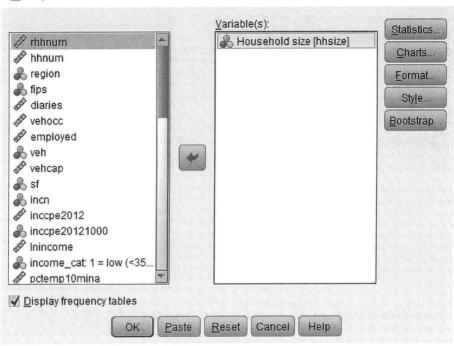

Figure 7.6 Frequency Window

Table 7.4 The Output Table of Frequency

	hhsize			
	Frequency	Percent	Valid Percent	Cumulative Percent
Valid 1	3774	26.6	26.6	26.6
2	5414	38.1	38.1	64.6
3	2203	15.5	15.5	80.2
4	1915	13.5	13.5	93.6
5	637	4.5	4.5	98.1
6	191	1.3	1.3	99.5
7	57	.4	.4	99.9
8	16	.1	.1	100.0
9	2	.0	.0	100.0
10	3	.0	.0	100.0
Total	14212	100.0	100.0	

household (38.1 percent) and 80.2 percent of sample households have three or fewer persons.

Central Tendency and Dispersion

Measures of central tendency and dispersion can be calculated in many ways in SPSS. Let's look at the same dataset and generate mean, median, mode, standard deviation, range, etc.

Go back to "Frequencies" menu ("Analyze" → "Descriptive Statistics" → "Frequencies"). In the Frequencies window (Figure 7.7), add *hhsize* variable to the variable list.

To select which statistics to calculate, click "Statistics" in the menu on the right (Figure 7.8). There are multiple measures for central tendency and dispersion. Check the measures you would like to add and click "Continue." Back to the frequency window and click "OK."

The result table is shown in the output view window. As seen in Table 7.5, the sampled households in the dataset have 2.38 persons on average, with 1.264 of standard deviation and ranging from 1 to 10.

Cross Tabulation

Now we assume that we are interested in if the household income and a probability of car use are related (i.e., more affluent households might be more likely

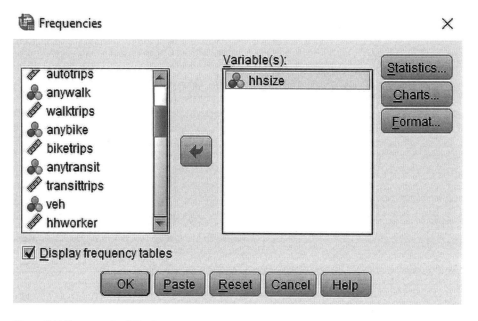

Figure 7.7 Frequencies Window

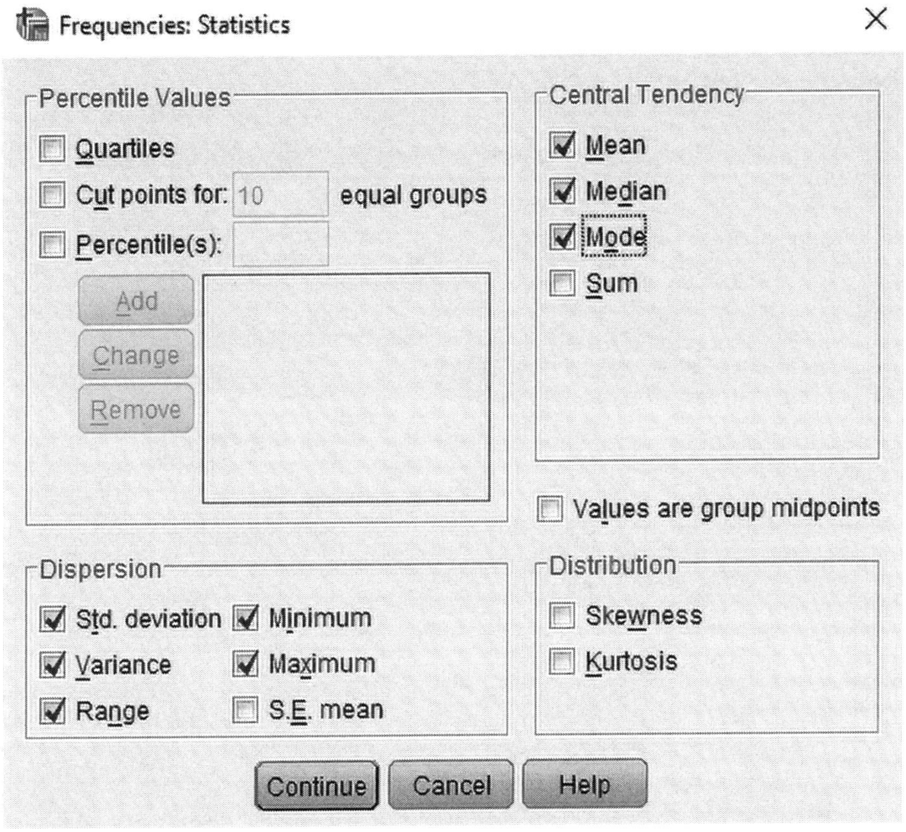

Frequencies: Statistics ✕

Percentile Values
- ☐ Quartiles
- ☐ Cut points for: 10 equal groups
- ☐ Percentile(s):
  - Add
  - Change
  - Remove

Central Tendency
- ☑ Mean
- ☑ Median
- ☑ Mode
- ☐ Sum

☐ Values are group midpoints

Dispersion
- ☑ Std. deviation
- ☑ Variance
- ☑ Range
- ☑ Minimum
- ☑ Maximum
- ☐ S.E. mean

Distribution
- ☐ Skewness
- ☐ Kurtosis

Continue | Cancel | Help

Figure 7.8 Various Measures of Descriptive Statistics From "Frequencies: Statistics" Window

Table 7.5 The Output Table of Descriptive Statistics

Statistics

hhsize

N	Valid	14212
	Missing	0
Mean		2.38
Median		2.00
Mode		2
Std. Deviation		1.264
Variance		1.597
Range		9
Minimum		1
Maximum		10

122 *Dong-ah Choi et al.*

to drive). Go to "Analyze" → "Descriptive Statistics" → "Crosstabs." A Crosstabs window (Figure 7.9) will show up and require at least one variable for "Row(s)" and another one for "Column(s)." We will add *income_cat* (a categorical variable of household income with three income brackets) to the row box and *anyvmt* (a dummy variable of whether a household made any automobile trip or not) to the column box.

Click on "Cells" button, and you can see different options for what you would like to display in the cross tabulation (Figure 7.10). We check "Row" percentages to see what percentage of households in each income bracket (row) made an automobile trip.

From Table 7.6, we can see that the percentage of car use increases with household income bracket (84.9 percent → 95.2 percent → 97.8 percent). To determine statistical significance, see Chapter 8 (Chi-Square test).

Informative Graphs

You would be interested in displaying the data in a form that can be easily understandable for readers. This is where we would need to use graphs.

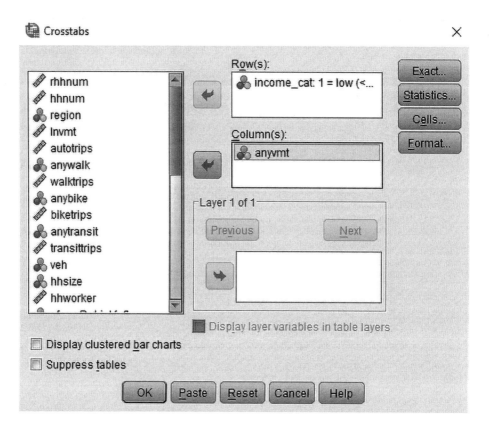

Figure 7.9 Cross Tabulation Window

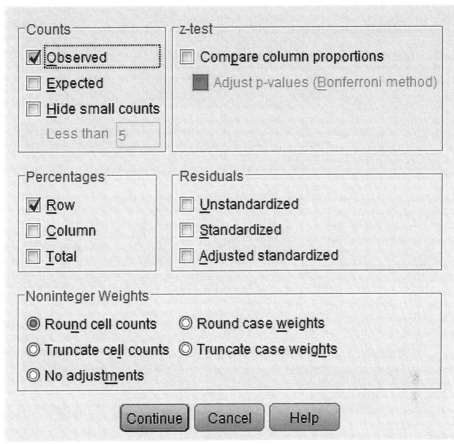

Figure 7.10 Cell Display Option in Cross Tabulation Window

Table 7.6 Statistics Option in Cross Tabulation Window

income_cat anyvmt cross tabulation*

			Anyvmt		Total
			0.00	1.00	
Income_cat: 1 = low (<35K); 2 = middle (35K–75K); 3 = high (>75K)	1.00	Count %	464 15.1%	2,615 84.9%	3,079 100.0%
	2.00	Count %	263 4.8%	5,244 95.2%	5,507 100.0%
	3.00	Count %	106 2.2%	4,650 97.8%	4,756 100.0%
Total		Count %	833 6.2%	12,509 93.8%	13,342 100.0%

124 *Dong-ah Choi et al.*

By clicking on "Graphs" in the main menu and selecting "Legacy Dialogs," we get a variety of graph options (Figure 7.11).

We choose "Histogram" to represent household size (Figure 7.12). Add *hhsize* variable, check "Display normal curve," and click "OK."

From the histogram of household size (Figure 7.13), it is easily discernible that two in household size has the highest frequency, followed by one, three, and four. There are fewer households with more than five members. Such shape of distribution is called positively skewed or right skewed because its tail on the right side is longer than on the left side.

On the top right side of the graph, you can see mean, standard deviation, and the number of cases. This histogram provides a quick overview of the variable of interest.

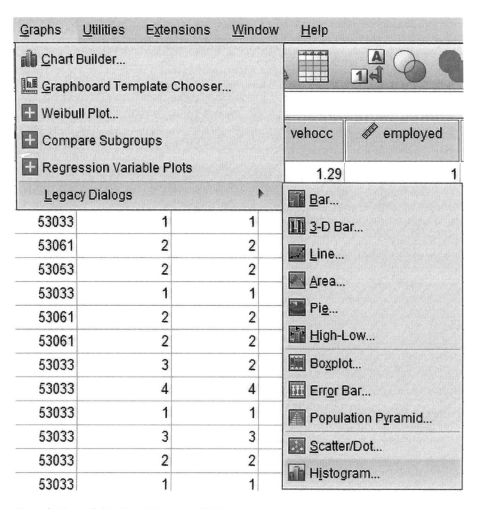

Figure 7.11 Available Graph Types in SPSS

Descriptive Statistics and Visualizing Data 125

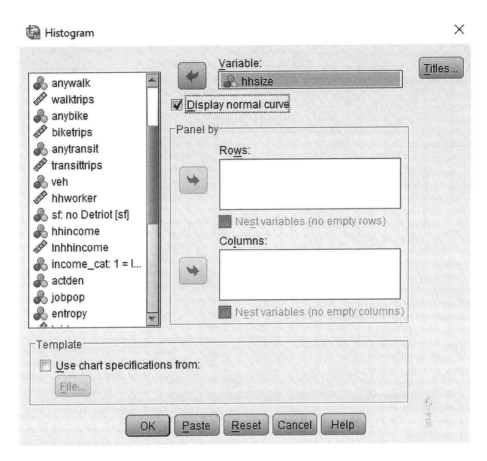

Figure 7.12 Histogram Window in SPSS

In R

Figures 7.14 through 7.16 show how you can compute descriptive statistics and draw a histogram in R. The script starts with reading an SPSS data file through *foreign* package, followed by generating a frequency table, summary statistics, standard deviation, variance, cross-tabulation, and a histogram with a density line. When you use a package for the first time, you need to install it using *install.packages* command (e.g., *install.packages("foreign")*).

Planning Examples

Residential Water Use

In 2007, Subhro Guhathakurta and Patricia Gober published "The Impact of the Phoenix Urban Heat Island on Residential Water Use" in the *Journal of the American Planning Association* using descriptive statistics as an initial step in the analysis.

126 *Dong-ah Choi et al.*

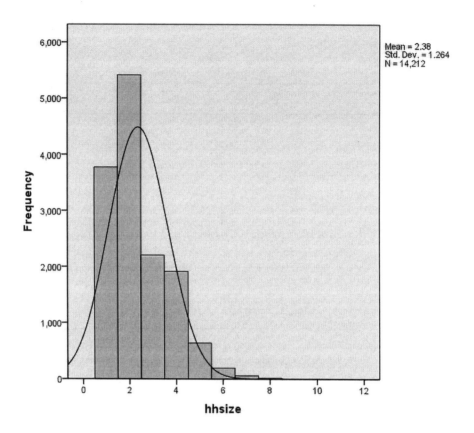

Figure 7.13 A Histogram of Household Size

The study examines whether Phoenix, Arizona's, large and intensifying urban heat island increases the demand for residential water. An urban heat island is an urban landscape that is warmer than the surrounding region. They developed a model to test whether the spatial variation in temperature affects residential water use at the scale of the census tract, after controlling for confounding factors.

Prior to the modeling, the authors provided detailed breakdowns of water use for single-family units for the city of Phoenix. The author's use of descriptive statistics summarizes each census tract's dependent and independent variables by categorizing the data with the minimum and maximum (range), median, and mean (average) to classify important factors that influence water usage in Phoenix (Table 7.7).

With a combination of descriptive and inferential statistics, the study found that the urban heat island affects water use in single-family residences. A 1°F increase in a tract's low temperature increases average water use in single-family units by 1.7 percent, or 290 gallons, for the typical single-family unit per month, holding all else constant (Guhathakurta & Gober, 2007). This study demonstrates that the elevated low temperatures resulting from Phoenix's urban heat island contribute significantly to water use in single-family homes.

Descriptive Statistics and Visualizing Data   127

```
# DESCRIPTIVE STATISTICS AND VISUALIZING DATA
library("foreign")
hts<-read.spss("HTS.household.10regions.sav",to.data.frame=TRU
E)

#frequency table
table<-table(hts$hhsize)              #frequency table
prop.table<-prop.table(table)         #in percentage
ftable<-cbind(table,prop.table(table))
colnames(ftable)<-c("count","percentage")
ftable
```

```
##      count    percentage
## 1     3774 0.2655502392
## 2     5414 0.3809456797
## 3     2203 0.1550098508
## 4     1915 0.1347452857
## 5      637 0.0448212778
## 6      191 0.0134393470
## 7       57 0.0040106952
## 8       16 0.0011258092
## 9        2 0.0001407261
## 10       3 0.0002110892
```

Figure 7.14 Reading SPSS Data and Making a Frequency Table: R Script and Outputs

Urban Parks

In Anna Chiesura's article, "The Role of Urban Parks for the Sustainable City" (2004) published in *Landscape and Urban Planning*, she uses horizontal bar graphs to describe the frequency distribution of the research results.

This article aims at investigating the importance of social services provided in urban parks for city sustainability. Among three sustainability pillars—environmental, economic, and social—the author focuses on social sustainability of urban parks. By surveying visitors of the most popular park of Amsterdam, Vondelpark, the researcher analyzes three issues: motives for nature, emotional dimension perceived benefits, and public satisfaction with the amount of green areas. In total, 467 questionnaires were collected.

In order to describe the motives to visit natural areas and the emotions experienced in urban parks, bar graphs were employed (Figure 7.17). In the first bar graph, "To relax" and "To be in nature" were more frequently cited by the visitors than other

128 *Dong-ah Choi et al.*

```
#central tendency and dispersion
summary(hts$hhsize)
```

```
##      Min. 1st Qu.  Median    Mean 3rd Qu.     Max.
##     1.000   1.000   2.000   2.377   3.000  10.000
```

```
sd(hts$hhsize)                          #standard deviation
```

```
## [1] 1.263886
```

```
var(hts$hhsize)                         #variance
```

```
## [1] 1.597409
```

Figure 7.15 Calculating Central Tendency and Dispersion: R Script and Outputs

motives. In the second graph, more park visitors mention "Freedom" as the feeling evoked for them by nature.

Rather than using a data matrix or a frequency table, the author used bar graphs to effectively illustrate the questionnaire results. From the descriptive statistics, ANOVA test, and qualitative analysis of survey responses, this study confirms that the experience of nature in an urban environment is a source of positive feelings and beneficial services, which fulfill important immaterial and non-consumptive human needs.

Conclusion

Descriptive statistics are almost always necessary. They form the basis for quantitative analysis and also are used in many qualitative studies for the purpose of describing data. The issue is rather which descriptive statistics and visualization techniques to use. In choosing them, researchers should consider how to present the data, what kind of information to keep (and lose), and how much detail needs to be shown. The focus should be on the need to communicate your results clearly and concisely.

Not only for presentation purposes, descriptive statistics can be used for data analysis. As soon as you collect and process the data, you would want to explore them by generating descriptive statistics—a step for exploratory data analysis (EDA)—before conducting any advanced analysis such as inferential statistics. Surely, most researchers go beyond just a description of patterns. After describing the data, you will usually want to draw conclusions from data, which reach beyond the data itself. This is the purpose of inferential statistics, the subject of following chapters in this book.

```
#cross tabulation
xtab<-xtabs(~income_cat+anyvmt,data=hts)
xtab
```

```
##                      anyvmt
## income_cat             0    1
##    low (<35K)         464 2615
##    middle (35K-75K)   263 5244
##    high (>75K)        106 4650
```

```
addmargins(prop.table(xtab,1),2)
```

```
##                      anyvmt
## income_cat                    0          1        Sum
##    low (<35K)         0.15069828 0.84930172 1.00000000
##    middle (35K-75K)   0.04775740 0.95224260 1.00000000
##    high (>75K)        0.02228764 0.97771236 1.00000000
```

```
#informative graphs
hist(hts$hhsize,freq=FALSE)
lines(density(hts$hhsize,adjust=5), col="blue", lty="dotted",
 lwd=1)   #add a density line
```

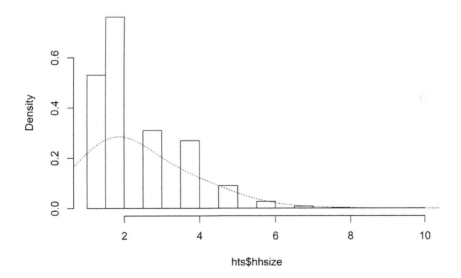

Figure 7.16 A Cross Tabulation and a Histogram: R Script and Outputs

Table 7.7 Descriptive Statistics on Water Use in Phoenix

	Minimum	Maximum	Mean	Deviation
Dependent variable Mean water use per single-family residential unit, June 1998 (gallons)	7,481	80,415	17,025	6,712
Independent variables Median household income ($ in 1999)	9,677	174,840	44,792	22,597
Median persons per unit	2.00	8.40	4.99	1.23
Mean lot size (square feet)	5,259	83,044	10,428	6,934
Mean age of single-family units (years)	1	58	26	12
Percentage of single-family units with pool	0	92%	24%	21%
Mean pool surface area (square feet)	0	832	400	133
Percentage of single family units with evaporative coolers	0	100%	26%	28%
Vegetation index (NDVI)	.44	.62	.50	.03
Percentage of housing units owner occupied	0	100%	63%	25%
Water supply from SRP (0 = no, 1 = yes)	0	1	.44	.50
Mean land parcel price, single-family residences ($)	7,373	217,094	24,779	20,516
Daily low temperature (°F)	64.57	72.77	70.09	1.87
Difference between daily high and low temperatures (°F)	17.08	22.37	18.59	1.21

Source: Guhathakurta & Gober (2007)

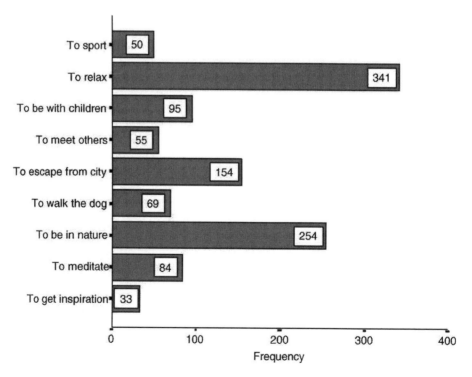

Figure 7.17 Motives for Nature and Emotions Experienced

Source: Chiesura (2004)

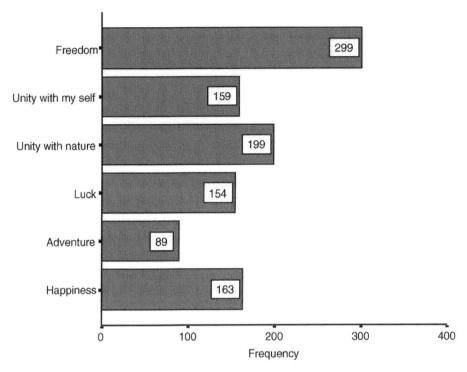

Figure 7.17 Motives for Nature and Emotions Experienced (continued)
Source: Chiesura (2004)

Works Cited

Al-Qāḍī, W. (2008). Population census and land surveys under the Umayyads. *Der Islam, 83*(2), 341–416. http://doi.org/10.1515/ISLAM.2006.015

Bhattacharyya, G. K., & Johnson, R. A. (1977). *Statistical concepts and methods.* Madison, WI: University of Wisconsin Press.

Boeing, G., & Waddell, P. (2017). New insights into rental housing markets across the United States: Web scraping and analyzing Craigslist rental listings. *Journal of Planning Education and Research, 37*(4), 457–476. http://doi.org/10.1177/0739456X16664789

Chiesura, A. (2004). The role of urban parks for the sustainable city. *Landscape and Urban Planning, 68*(1), 129–138. http://doi.org/10.1016/j.landurbplan.2003.08.003

Ewing, R., Hamidi, S., Gallivan, F., Nelson, A. C., & Grace, J. B. (2014). Structural equation models of VMT growth in US urbanised areas. *Urban Studies, 51*(14), 3079–3096. http://doi.org/10.1177/0042098013516521.

Ewing, R., & Rong, F. (2008). The impact of urban form on US residential energy use. *Housing Policy Debate, 19*(1), 1–30. https://www.tandfonline.com/doi/pdf/10.1080/10511482.2008.9521624

Ewing, R., Schmid, T., Killingsworth, R., Zlot, A., & Raudenbush, S. (2003). Relationship between urban sprawl and physical activity, obesity, and morbidity. *American Journal of Health Promotion, 18*(1), 47–57. https://journals.sagepub.com/doi/pdf/10.4278/0890-1171-18.1.47

Fan, C., & Myint, S. (2014). A comparison of spatial autocorrelation indices and landscape metrics in measuring urban landscape fragmentation. *Landscape and Urban Planning, 121*, 117–128. http://doi.org/10.1016/j.landurbplan.2013.10.002

Flyvbjerg, B., Holm, M. S., & Buhl, S. (2002). Underestimating costs in public works projects: Error or lie? *Journal of the American Planning Association, 68*(3), 279–295. http://doi-org.ezproxy.lib.utah.edu/10.1080/01944360208976273

Guhathakurta, S., & Gober, P. (2007). The impact of the Phoenix urban heat island on residential water use. *Journal of the American Planning Association, 73*(3), 317–329. http://doi.org/10.1080/01944360708977980

History of Statistics. (2014). *Stochastikon encyclopedia*. Retrieved from http://132.187.98.10:8080/encyclopedia/en/statisticsHistory.pdf

Jones, A. (1953). Census records of the later Roman Empire. *Journal of Roman Studies, 43*, 49–64. http://doi.org/10.2307/297781

Kraus, C. S. (1994). *Livy ab urbe condita*. Cambridge: Cambridge University Press.

Manville, M., King, D. A., & Smart, M. J. (2017). The driving downturn: A preliminary assessment. *Journal of the American Planning Association, 83*(1), 42–55. http://doi.org/10.1080/01944363.2016.1247653

Missiakoulis, S. (2010). Cecrops, king of Athens: The first (?) recorded population census in history. *International Statistical Review, 78*, 413–418. http://doi.org/10.1111/j.1751-5823.2010.00124.x

Sciara, G. C. (2017). Metropolitan transportation planning: Lessons from the past, institutions for the future. *Journal of the American Planning Association, 83*(3), 262–276. http://doi.org/10.1080/01944363.2017.1322526

Trochim, W. (2006). Descriptive statistics. *Research Method Knowledge Base*. Retrieved from www.socialresearchmethods.net/kb/statdesc.php

U.S. Bureau of the Census. (1998). *American housing survey: Metropolitan data*. Washington, DC. World Wide Web page. Retrieved March 10, 2008, from http://www.census.gov/hhes/www/housing/ahs/metropolitandata.html

U.S. Bureau of the Census. (2002). *American housing survey: Metropolitan data*. Washington, DC. World Wide Web page. Retrieved March 10, 2008, from http://www.census.gov/hhes/www/housing/ahs/metropolitandata.html

U.S. Bureau of the Census. (2003). *2000 Census of Population and Housing, Public Use Microdata Sample, United States: Technical Documentation*. Retrieved from https://www.census.gov/prod/cen2000/doc/pums.pdf

Wolf-Powers, L., Doussard, M., Schrock, G., Heying, C., Eisenburger, M., & Marotta, S. (2017). The maker movement and urban economic development. *Journal of the American Planning Association, 83*(4), 365–376. http://doi.org/10.1080/01944363.2017.13607

8   Chi-Square

Carl Duke, Keunhyun Park, and Reid Ewing

Method	Dependent Variable	Independent Variables	Test Statistics
Chi-Square	Categorical	Categorical	chi-square statistic
Difference of Means	Continuous	Categorical (two categories)	t-statistic
ANOVA	Continuous	Categorical (multiple categories)	F-statistic
Linear Regression	Continuous	Continuous (though can represent categorical)	t-statistic R2 statistic
Logistic Regression	Categorical (Dichtomous)	Continuous (though can represent categorical)	asymptotic t-statistic pseudo-R2 statistic
Poisson/Negative Binomial Regression	Count	Continuous (though can represent categorical)	Wald statistic pseudo-R2 statistic

Figure 8.0 Chi-Square

Overview

As planners, we have the opportunity to work with a wide variety of data. Some data are more nuanced and detailed than others. The first step in knowing which instrument to pull out of our planning toolbox is recognizing what type of data we are working with.

Categorical data is the weakest of all data in the various scales of measurement we see. Categorical data can be broken up into two groups: nominal and ordinal. Of these two, ordinal data is stronger because its attributes can be ordered.

Nominal data is easily recognized, as it is generally expressed with names. If a planner created a survey that asks a *yes or no* question, the data gathered is nominal. A planner can ask whether a respondent lives in a single-family dwelling or in a multi-family dwelling and the response would be considered nominal. There is no inherent order to the two categories. The two are just different. Nominal data, such as race or ethnic origin, can be measured and tested but cannot be ordered.

134 *Carl Duke, Keunhyun Park, and Reid Ewing*

Ordinal data, while still categorical, can be ordered. If a planner ranks MSAs into groups of small, medium, and large the data gathered would be ordinal. Or a planner could ask a citizen how likely they would be to use public transit if a stop was in walking distance from their home. If the choices provided were highly likely, likely, unlikely, or highly unlikely, the data gathered would be considered ordinal because the responses can be ordered.

The chi-square test is useful when we want to explore the association between two categorical variables—for example, housing types (single-family, multi-family, etc.) versus race (white, black, etc.). In the preceding example, we could analyze if specific housing types are statistically associated with specific racial groups, using the chi-square test.

Purpose

Chi-square is the inferential statistics test we use when our dependent variable and our independent variable are both categorical. It is important to remember these tests are reserved for inferential statistics, or those times when we are trying to infer from a sample, attributes of a broader population. This being the case, we need to be cognizant of certain requirements of sample selection. More specifically, we need to ensure our sample is free from bias, i.e., randomly selected from a population.

The chi-square test helps us decide whether sampled differences across categories can be attributed to random chance or are likely due to genuine differences. For example, if the independent variable is high density versus low density of development, and the dependent variable is healthy weight versus overweight status, and individuals are placed into the four categories (high density/healthy weight etc.), chi-square will allow us to infer from a sample of individuals whether differences in weight status are related to differences in density in the broader population.

Because the interest is in the association between two categorical variables, this analysis is also called an **independence test**, or the **analysis of contingency tables**. Although the calculations are similar, readers should not confuse it with a goodness-of-fit test, which is also usually called chi-square test. A goodness-of-fit test helps to determine whether a sample is drawn from a hypothetical distribution or whether two samples come from the same distribution (Davis, 2002). A famous coin example, flipping a coin multiple times (say 100) to see whether a coin is flat or biased, is an example of a goodness-of-fit chi-square test.

History

The chi-square test is denoted by χ^2. *Chi* is a Greek letter pronounced *ki*, as in *kite*. The chi-square test was first developed by Karl Pearson in 1900. Then it became one of the most widely used statistical tests, as a useful tool for interpreting categorical data (Huber-Carol, Balakrishnan, Nikulin, & Mesbah, 2012). As Plackett (1983, p. 70) concludes, "Pearson's 1900 paper on chi squared is one of the great monuments of twentieth century statistics."

A significant modification of Pearson's test was introduced by R. A. Fisher (1922), in which the degree of freedom was decreased by one unit when applied to contingency tables. Another correction made by Fisher (1924) took into account the number of unknown parameters associated with the theoretical distribution, when the parameters are estimated from central moments.

The approximation of the chi-square test becomes inadequate when sample sizes are too small. Pearson's chi-square test is normally acceptable so long as no more than 20 percent of the events have expected frequencies below five. Fisher's exact test (1935) was developed as an alternative to the chi-square test when small cell sizes are present (e.g., expected values less than five). The test is based on the calculation of marginal probabilities.

Alternatively, Yates (1934) showed that a better approximation can be obtained by subtracting the absolute difference between observed and expected frequencies by 0.5 before squaring; this is called Yates's correction for continuity (Yates, 1934). In addition, Mantel and Haenszel (1959) proposed a correction of the chi-square test by dividing its value by $df/(df - 1)$, where df is degrees of freedom. Bolboacă, Jäntschi, Sestraş, Sestraş, and Pamfil (2011) demonstrated that the Fisher exact test proved to be the *golden test* in analyzing the independence, while the Yates and Mantel-Haenszel corrections could be applied as alternative tests.

Mechanics

Applying the chi-square test is quite simple. The following paragraphs outline the process, which when followed, will provide the user a template for practical applications of this statistical method.

Types of Data

The chi-square test is a non-parametric test, also called a distribution free test. Non-parametric tests can be used when any one of the following conditions pertains to the data (McHugh, 2013):

1. The level of measurement of all the variables is nominal or ordinal.
2. The original data were measured at an interval or ratio scale, but violate one of the following assumptions of a parametric test:
   a. The distribution of the data is seriously skewed, violating the assumption that the dependent variable is approximately normally distributed.
   b. The data violate the assumption of equal variance or homoscedasticity.
   c. For any of a number of reasons, the continuous data were collapsed into a small number of categories, and thus the data are no longer interval or ratio. For example, number of vehicles in a household could be used in a chi-square test if you categorize them into groups (e.g., no vehicle or any number of vehicles).

Assumptions

As with any statistic, there are requirements for its appropriate use, which are called *assumptions* of the statistic. The assumptions of the chi-square include:

1. The data in the cells are frequencies, or counts of cases. Categorical data may be displayed in a contingency table. For example, Table 8.1 shows counts of cases regarding two variables—trip modes and housing types.

136 *Carl Duke, Keunhyun Park, and Reid Ewing*

Table 8.1 Contingency Table

Counts of survey respondents		housing type (1-single family detached; 0-others)		Total
		0	1	
mode: 1-walk, 2-bike, 3-transit, 4-auto, 0-others	0	591	3,303	3,894
	1	1,979	6,424	8,403
	2	272	1,470	1,742
	3	963	1,424	2,387
	4	14,087	101,856	115,943
Total		17,892	114,477	132,369

2. The levels (or categories) of the variables are mutually exclusive. That is, a particular subject fits into one and only one level of each of the variables. You can't ride both transit and automobile at the same time. In Table 8.1, if you asked respondents "what is your means of transportation to go to school or work?" and allow them to select multiple modes used in an entire trip (e.g., both walk and transit), you cannot apply the chi-square test for figuring out the statistical differences among different modes.
3. Each subject may contribute data to one and only one cell in the $\chi 2$. If, for example, the same subjects are tested over time such that the comparisons are of the same subjects at Time 1, Time 2, Time 3, etc., then $\chi 2$ may not be used. This kind of data is called paired samples.
4. The expected value of the cell should be five or more in at least 80 percent of the cells, and no cell should have an expected value of less than one (Yates, Moore, & McCabe, 1999). This assumption is most likely to be met if the sample size equals at least the number of cells multiplied by five. You will see what the expected value means later.

Hypothesis in Chi-Square Test

In this step, we will create both a null hypothesis and an alternative hypothesis. The null hypothesis is that there is no difference in the proportion of occurrences in each category. So the variables are unrelated in any way. On the contrary, the alternative hypothesis, or the research hypothesis, is that there is a difference in the proportion of occurrences in each category. If you are interested in the relationship between two variables, you can word the alternative hypothesis that there is a statistically significant relationship between the variables.

Going back to our example, our null hypothesis would be that there is no difference in the proportion of occurrences in each category and so two variables—trip modes and housing types—are not related. Then, our alternative hypothesis is the exact opposite, which is that the relationship between trip modes and housing types is statistically significant. If the p value is lower than 0.05, it indicates that there is less than a 5 percent chance that the values of each category are randomly distributed. In other words, there is a difference in the proportion of occurrences in each category. In this case, the null hypothesis is rejected and the alternative hypothesis is accepted as true.

Calculate the Test Statistic

The chi-square test statistic is obtained by contrasting the observed frequencies with the expected frequencies. The expected frequencies represent the number of observations that would be found in each cell if the null hypothesis were true or, in other words, the categorical variables were unrelated. The chi-square equation is shown here.

$$\chi^2 = \sum \frac{(o-e)^2}{e}$$

In this equation, χ^2 is chi-square. o is the observed frequency of each category and e is the expected frequency, or the number of observations that would be found if the null hypothesis were true.

$$e = \frac{M_R \times M_C}{n}$$

In this equation for the expected value, M_R represents row marginal values, or the sum of each row, and M_C represents column marginal values, or the sum of each column while n is the total sample size. For cell 1 in Table 8.1, the math is as follows: (17,892 * 3,894) / 132,369 = 526.3. Table 8.2 provides the results of this calculation for each cell.

Once the expected values have been calculated, the cell $\chi2$ values are calculated with the formula. Then they are summed to obtain the $\chi2$ statistic for the table.

Why square the difference between observed and expected frequencies? It is to get rid of the minus signs and provide a set of measures whose sum will reflect the aggregate degree of difference that actually exists between the observed and expected patterns of frequencies. So a large value of the χ^2 statistic would not support the null hypothesis and thus lead to its rejection. Otherwise, a small value of the χ^2 statistic

Table 8.2 Observed Versus Expected Counts

			housing type: 1-single-family detached; 0-others		Total
			0	1	
	0	Count	591	3,303	3,894
mode: 1-walk, 2-bike,		Expected Count	526.3	3,367.7	3,894.0
3- transit, 4- auto,	1	Count	1,979	6,424	8,403
0- others		Expected Count	1,135.8	7,267.2	8,403.0
	2	Count	272	1,470	1,742
		Expected Count	235.5	1,506.5	1,742.0
	3	Count	963	1,424	2,387
		Expected Count	322.6	2,064.4	2,387.0
	4	Count	14,087	101,856	115,943
		Expected Count	15,671.7	100,271.3	115,943.0
Total		Count	17,892	114,477	132,369
		Expected Count	17,892.0	114,477.0	132,369.0

indicates a high probability of the result occurring by chance and you can conclude that no association between two variables exists.

In the end, you have computed a chi-square test statistic of a certain value. This test statistic will be compared to a critical value of chi-square to determine a level of statistical significance. Figure 8.1 shows chi-square frequency distributions for different degrees of freedom (df). The area under these curves to the right of each value represents the probability that you might get a value of chi-square this great or greater by random chance. You can see, for example, that for 2 or 3 df, you will almost never get a chi-square value greater than 10 by chance, while for 10 df, you may get a value of chi-square greater than 10 by chance more than 5 percent of the time. For 5 df, it is not obvious how much area is to the right of the critical value of 10, and you would have to consult a chi-square table to determine the level of statistical significance. In fact, the critical value of chi-square at the 0.05 significance level is 11.07. If you computed a chi-square value of 10, you could not reject the null hypothesis since you could get a value this great by chance more than 5 percent of time.

Determine the Degrees of Freedom and a Critical Value

We are getting close to drawing some conclusions; however, we cannot interpret the test statistic without considering the degrees of freedom (df).

The chi-square table requires the df in order to determine the significance level of the statistic. The df for a χ^2 table is calculated with the formula:

(Number of rows −1) × (Number of columns −1).

For the preceding example, the 5 × 2 table has 4 degrees of freedom for (5−1) × (2−1). So degrees of freedom become a multiplied value of two variables' number of categories minus one.

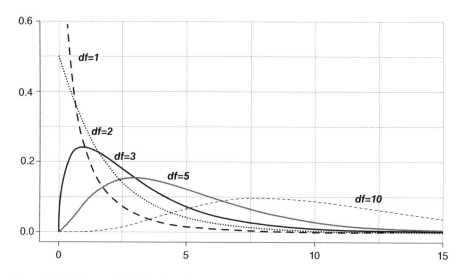

Figure 8.1 Chi-Square Distributions for Different Degrees of Freedom

In this final step of our analysis, we take all of the information we have obtained in earlier steps and begin to pull it together to draw a conclusion. We will assess the test statistic against the critical value at our chosen level of significance (usually 0.05) and either reject or fail to reject our null hypothesis. For Table 8.2, the computed chi-square statistic is 2,394 and we can reject the null hypothesis at the 0.05 level or beyond (way beyond). That is, we can say with 95 percent or greater confidence that travel mode varies by housing type, or equivalently, that the two variables are related to one another.

Strength Test for the Chi-Square

The researcher's work is not quite done yet. Finding a significant difference merely means that there is less than a 5 percent chance that the values of each category are randomly distributed and two variables are not related. But recall that statistical significance is not equivalent to practical significance. Statistical significance depends on both the strength of the relationship between two variables and the number of cases. Because the numerator in the chi-square formula is squared, you will likely get statistically significant values when you have a large sample, even if the association between variables is weak.

For the chi-square, the most commonly used strength tests are phi test and Cramer's V tests. Both depend only on the strength of the relationship between two categorical variables in a contingency table.

Phi is used with 2×2 contingency tables and Cramer's V is used with larger tables. Phi and Cramer's V assume values between 0 and 1. Phi eliminates sample size by dividing chi-square by n (the sample size) and taking the square root. V eliminates sample size by taking the square root of chi-square divided by n and multiplied by m (which is the smaller of [rows – 1] or [columns – 1]). Since phi and V have known distributions, statistical software packages can give us the significance level of the computed phi or V value.

Step by Step

Using our household database (HTS.household.10regions.sav), let's assume that you wonder if there are differences in the probability of walking between different housing types. The household data has a housing type variable (*sf*) having two categories— single family detached house (coded as 1) or not (0). The *anywalk* variable shows whether a given household made any walk trips in the survey day (coded as 1) or not (0). Both variables are categorical, having two groups.

The first step for any inferential statistical test is to ensure you are using the right test. In our example of any walk trip and housing types, we can use the chi-square test because both variables are categorical. Also, the samples could be assumed as randomly selected, the categories don't overlap (i.e., mutually exclusive), and the sample size is large enough across the whole categories.

Our null hypothesis would be that there is no difference in the proportion of occurrences in each category and so two variables—housing types and any walk trip—are not related. Then, our alternative hypothesis is the exact opposite, which is that there *is* a relationship. In other words, the probability that a household makes any walk trips varies by whether the household lives in single-family detached house or not.

140 *Carl Duke, Keunhyun Park, and Reid Ewing*

A planner would expect a negative association: a walk trip probability decreases with single-family detached house residence.

The following paragraphs outline a step-by-step process for chi-square test in SPSS; which when followed, will provide the user a template for practical applications of the chi-square method (Figures 8.2 through 8.5).

1. Go to "Analyze" → "Descriptive Statistics" → "Crosstabs"
2. Add two variables to Row and Column respectively (e.g., *sf* to Row and *anywalk* to Column)
3. Click "Statistics" button and make sure "Chi-square" and "Phi and Cramer's V" test are checked
4. Go to "Cells" button and check "Observed" and "Expected" in Counts box and check "Row" in Percentages box → Click "Continue"
5. Then click "OK." The results will appear.

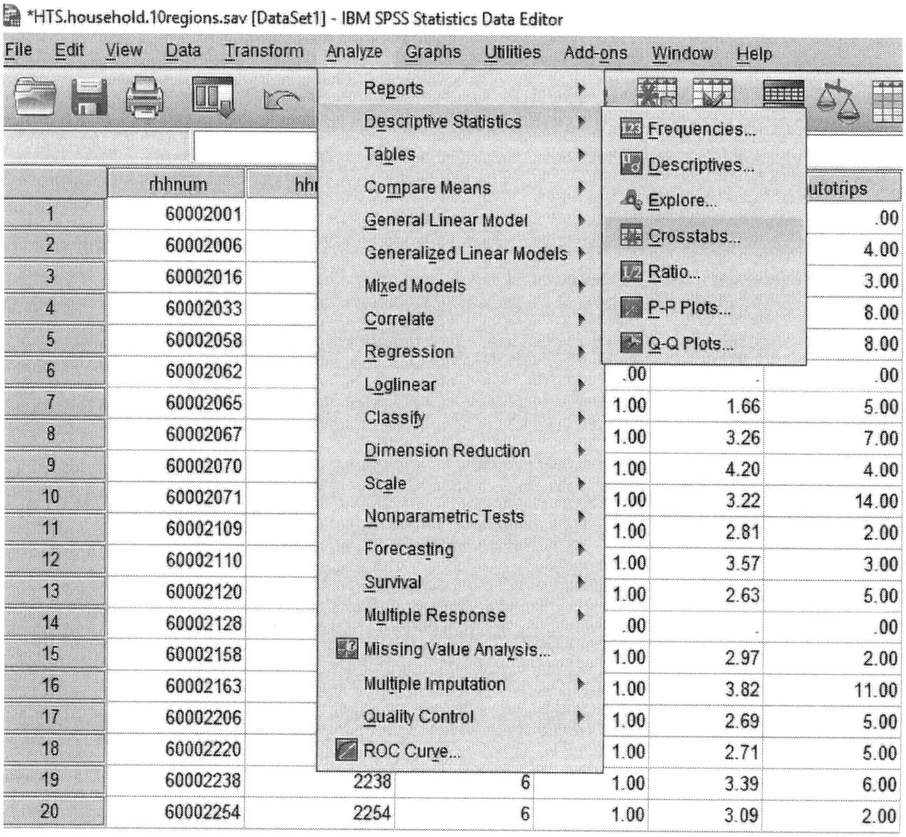

Figure 8.2 Accessing Crosstabs in SPSS

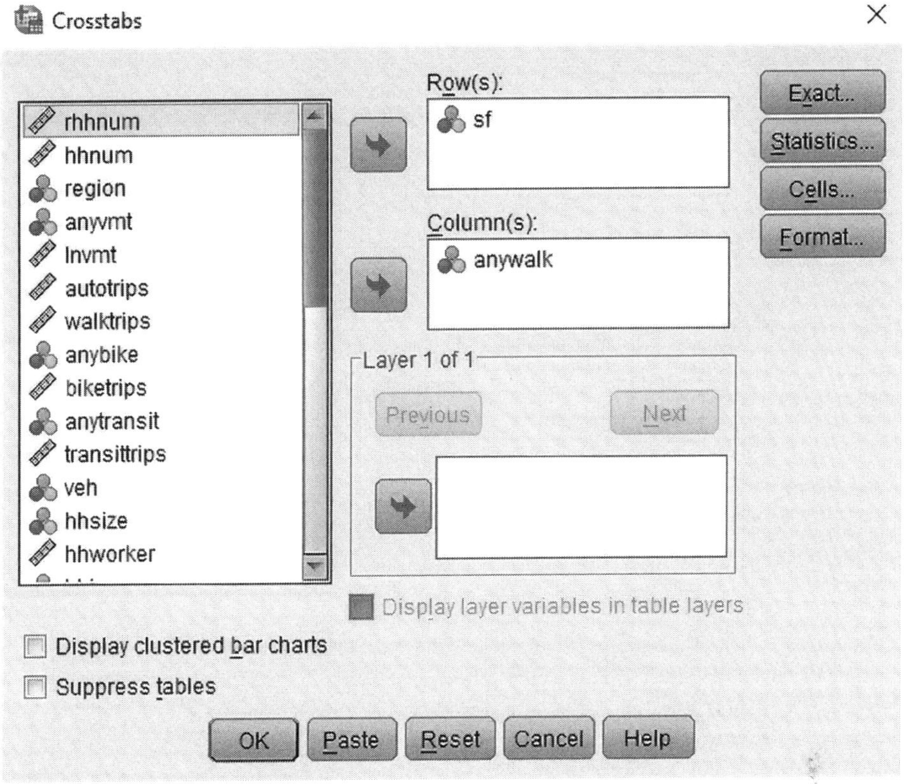

Figure 8.3 Crosstabs Selection Menu

In the cross tabulation, or contingency table, you can see observed and expected values of each cell (Table 8.3). In each cell, the observed count is not much different from the expected count. From the percentages in the table, you can see that lower percentage of households living in single-family detached house (20.0 percent) made any walk trip, compared with those in other types of house did (23.8 percent).

In Table 8.4, you need to see the Pearson Chi-Square row. It presents high chi-square value (18.566) and that it is statistically significant ($p<.001$). At the bottom of the table, a caption "a" tells us that there is no concern of small cell sizes, which would otherwise suggest the Fisher's Exact test.

You can see also the strength test results in Table 8.5. In this example, you would see the phi result because the contingency table is 2×2. For a larger table, you would look at the Cramer's V result. The value is –0.037, which means relative low correlation measures, even for a statistically significant result ($p<.001$).

Now take a look at some specific examples from recent planning literature to see how chi-square has been used in academic research.

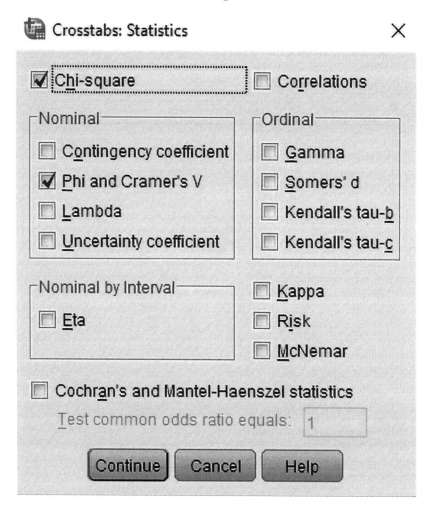

Figure 8.4 Crosstabs Statistics Selection Menu

In R

Figures 8.6 and 8.7 show an example of a chi-square test in R. The script first presents a contingency table of housing types and *anywalk* variable (0 = no walking, 1 = walking) for counts and probabilities, respectively. Then, *chisq.test* function is used to run a test. Note that the *chisq.test* function uses Yates' continuity correction as a default, generating the value of 18.333 in this case. If you want Pearson chi-square, you should add a parameter in your *chisq.test* code, "correct=FALSE," which will give you a value of 18.566 in this example. The *assocstats* function in *vcd* package is then used to check symmetric measures for the chi-square test.

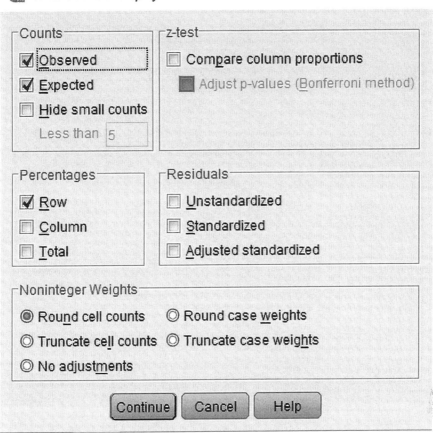

Figure 8.5 Crosstabs Cell Display Menu

Table 8.3 A Contingency Table of Chi-Square About Housing Types and Any Walk Trip

sf * anywalk cross tabulation

			anywalk .00	anywalk 1.00	Total
sf	other	Count	1,951	610	2,561
		Expected Count	2,030.4	530.6	2,561.0
		% within sf	76.2%	23.8%	100.0%
	single family detached	Count	8,572	2,140	10,712
		Expected Count	8,492.6	2,219.4	10,712.0
		% within sf	80.0%	20.0%	100.0%
Total		Count	10,523	2,750	13,273
		Expected Count	10,523.0	2,750.0	13,273.0
		% within sf	79.3%	20.7%	100.0%

144 *Carl Duke, Keunhyun Park, and Reid Ewing*

Table 8.4 Chi-Square Test Significance About Housing Types and Any Walk Trip

	Value	df	Asymp. Sig. (2-sided)	Exact Sig. (2-sided)	Exact Sig. (1-sided)
Pearson chi-square	18.566[a]	1	.000	.000	.000
Continuity correction[b]	18.333	1	.000		
Likelihood ratio	18.088	1	.000		
Fisher's exact test					
Linear-by-linear association	18.565	1	.000		
N of valid cases	13,273				

a 0 cells (.0 percent) have expected count less than five. The minimum expected count is 530.61.
b Computed only for a 2 × 2 table

Table 8.5 Symmetric Measures for the Chi-Square Test

		Value	Approx. Sig.
Nominal by nominal	Phi	−.037	.000
	Cramer's V	.037	.000
N of valid cases		13,273	

Planning Examples

Sustainable Development Policies

In 2001, Edward J. Jepson Jr. sent out a survey to planning departments in 390 municipalities of over 50,000 people. The author's purpose was to find common characteristics among cities that were more aggressive in sustainable initiatives. The author was also interested in identifying the impediments local governments faced as they tried to take actions toward sustainability. The findings of this survey were summarized in the *Journal of Planning Education and Research* (JPER) in March 2004.

The author needed to first answer the question of whether certain cities were more likely to take sustainable actions. He grouped the cities into two groups: those that took sustainable actions and those that did not. Note this is clearly a categorical dependent variable. He then considered the population, educational, and locational characteristics of both groups.

Educational level and population size are both traits that can be expressed by categorical, interval, or even ratio measurements. In the case of this article, the author considered both educational level and population size in relation to the mean of each variable, respectively. In other words, he looked at the city and whether they had a greater or lesser population than the mean population of the all surveyed communities. He did the same for educational level; specifically, the percentage of adults over the age of 25 with a college degree was compared to the mean. This approach yielded categorical independent variables that enabled the author to use the chi-square test.

If the author found that those cities with an educated population were more likely to enact sustainable initiatives, he could suggest the possibility that individual

Chi-Square   145

```
# CHI-SQUARE
library("foreign")
hts<-read.spss("HTS.household.10regions.sav",to.data.frame=TRU
E)

table<-table(hts$sf,hts$anywalk)
table
```

```
##
##                              0    1
##   other                   1951  610
##   single family detached  8572 2140
```

```
addmargins(prop.table(table,1),2)
```

```
##
##                              0         1        Sum
##   other                  0.7618118 0.2381882 1.0000000
##   single family detached 0.8002240 0.1997760 1.0000000
```

```
chisq.test(hts$sf,hts$anywalk) #chi-square test
```

```
##
##   Pearson's Chi-squared test with Yates' continuity correcti
on
##
## data:  hts$sf and hts$anywalk
## X-squared = 18.333, df = 1, p-value = 1.855e-05
```

Figure 8.6 Reading SPSS Data and Running a Chi-Square Test: R Script and Outputs

awareness is important for the adoption of sustainable actions. Similarly, if the data showed that larger cities were more likely to take sustainable actions, this discrepancy could be researched and perhaps related to government capacity. Finally, if the data showed that some regions of the country were more likely to focus on sustainability, further research could be done on what causes this locational variance.

```
library(vcd)
assocstats(table) #symmetric measures for the chi-square test
```

```
##                      X^2 df   P(> X^2)
## Likelihood Ratio 18.088  1 2.1097e-05
## Pearson          18.566  1 1.6413e-05
##
## Phi-Coefficient     : 0.037
## Contingency Coeff.: 0.037
## Cramer's V          : 0.037
```

Figure 8.7 Symmetric Measures for the Chi-Square Test: R Script and Outputs

As Table 8.6 shows, none of the chi-square tests yielded a statistically significant result wherein the author was able to reject his null hypotheses. In fact, the chi-square test statistics are all quite low. No real variation was found across the three characteristics.

It is important to note the author in this study did not solely rely on the chi-square test. This tool was used to answer a small question within his broader area of study. Yet, it was the only appropriate method for this portion of his analysis. The author then went on to look at whether planning office leadership led to greater action taken. For this step, he used linear regression (see Chapter 12), as his data was continuous not categorical, and found a significant positive association between the number of times each local planning office took a leadership role and the number of times action was taken.

Attitudes Toward Growth Management

In 2004, Timothy Chapin and Charles Connerly published an article in the *Journal of the American Planning Association* that considered whether citizens' attitudes toward growth management change over time. Prior to this study, there was a great deal of academic research that looked at how people perceived growth controls, and yet no one had tracked whether these attitudes were static or evolved over time.

Florida, for this study, was the perfect case study. In 1985, the state passed one of the most progressive growth management programs that called for state oversight of local land use decisions. The law also required consistency across jurisdictions along with a mandate that adequate public facilities and services be provided in an area before additional development was approved (so-called concurrency). The 1985 legislation achieved a mixture of success and failure leading to a shift in 2001 that relaxed the requirements for concurrency and placed a greater emphasis on affordability.

Table 8.6 Chi-Square Analyses of Actions Taken on Sustainability

Community Characteristic	Action Taken[a]	No Action Taken[b]	Count
$x^2 = .61$, $V = .09$			
Less than or equal to mean education level[c]	13.3	23.7	58
More than mean education level	16.2	19.8	44
$x^2 = .51$, $V = .08$			
Fewer than or equal to mean population[d]	13.8	22.9	78
More than mean population	16.6	19.7	25
$x^2 = .36$, $V = .07$			
Region 2 (South)[e]	12.1	24.8	35
All	14.5	22.2	103
$x^2 = .03$, $V = .02$			
Region 3 (Midwest)	14.8	20.9	26
All	14.5	22.2	103
$x^2 = .39$, $V = .07$			
Region 4 (West)	17.2	19.6	32
All	14.5	22.2	103

a The average number of times that an action-taken response was given across all 39 policy areas.
b The average number of times that a no-action-taken response was given across all 39 policy areas.
c Educational level is defined in terms of the percentage of residents 25 years or older with a college degree. The mean percentage among the surveyed communities was 26.3.
d The mean population of the surveyed communities was 212,000.
e The regions correspond to the definitions of the U.S. Census Bureau. Region 1 (Northeast) was not included in the analysis because of the small sample size (ten).

The authors gathered data from an annual policy survey conducted by Florida State University Survey Research Lab for both 1985 and 2001 when respondents were questioned about the issue of growth. The results were useful in identifying changes across racial, gender, and socio-economic groups.

The authors used chi-square test for this work because the data the survey gathered was categorical in nature. Respondents typically answered *yes* and *no* questions. Furthermore, respondents were broken up into categorical groups to see if the group's perceptions of growth controls had changed over time. As an illustration see Table 8.7. In this case, the respondents were asked "Do you feel growth in your community should be stopped, limited, or not controlled at all?" If a respondent answered that it should be stopped or limited they were characterized as favoring growth controls.

When 1985 respondents were classified by race (whites versus blacks), the chi-square results showed a significant difference only in 2001. Black respondents supported growth controls at a lower level than white respondents in 2001 at the 0.01 significance level (as shown in *** symbol). There was no significant difference between the two races in 1985.

Then, chi-square was also used to assess whether attitudes within these groups had changed at the same or different rates than the total respondents. Support for growth controls among black respondents fell from 71.9 percent to 57.5 percent, a 14.4 percentage point decline compared to a 4.1 percentage point decline across all respondents. The chi-square test showed that the chances of this happening because of random chance would be less than 1 in 20, or statistically significant at the 0.05 level, as indicated by the ** symbol.

These kinds of tests—with both cross-sectional and longitudinal lenses—were repeated for other demographic, socioeconomic, and political variables. Overall, this

148 *Carl Duke, Keunhyun Park, and Reid Ewing*

Table 8.7 Perceived Need for Growth Controls in Florida, 1985 and 2001 (Chapin & Connerly, 2004)

	Respondents Favoring Growth Controls		Change 1985–2001	DoP
	1985	2001		
All respondents	71.8%	67.7%	–4.1%	**
Demographic variables				
Race				
Whites	71.8%	74.3%	2.5%	
Blacks	71.9%	57.5%	–14.4%	**
X^2		***		
Ethnicity				
Hispanics	67.1%	43.5%	–23.6%	***
X^1		***		
Florida native				
Yes	65.7%	71.1%	5.4%	
No	73.1%	66.6%	–6.5%	***
X^1	*			

study found that while overall support for controlling growth remains high, support for government intervention in growth management has diminished.

Conclusion

The chi-square test is used to explore the association between two categorical variables. Like other statistical tests of hypothesis, however, the chi-square test will just tell us whether our results are statistically significant or not, not whether they are practically important. This point is especially relevant when a researcher runs a chi-square test with large samples. The obtained value of chi-square will increase at the same rate as sample size, possibly resulting in the rejection of the null hypothesis when the actual relationship is trivial (Healey, 2014). To deal with the questions of importance, we may have to apply additional analyses such as logistic regression (see Chapter 13).

Works Cited

Bolboacă, S. D., Jäntschi, L., Sestraş, A. F., Sestraş, R. E., & Pamfil, D. C. (2011). Pearson-Fisher chi-square statistic revisited. *Information*, 2(3), 528–545. http://doi.org/10.1080/01944363.2017.1360787

Chapin, T. S., & Connerly, C. E. (2004). Attitudes towards growth management in Florida: Comparing resident support in 1985 and 2001. *Journal of the American Planning Association*, 70(4), 443–452. http://doi.org/10.1080/01944360408976393

Creswell, J. W. (2008). *Research design: Qualitative, quantitative, and mixed methods approaches* (3rd ed.). Thousand Oaks, CA: Sage Publications.

Davis, J. C. (2002). *Statistics and data analysis in geology* (3rd ed.). New York, NY: John Wiley & Sons.

Fisher, R. A. (1922). On the interpretation of χ2 from contingency tables, and the calculation of P. *Journal of the Royal Statistical Society*, 85(1), 87–94. http://doi.org/10.2307/2340521

Fisher, R. A. (1924). The conditions under which χ^2 measures the discrepancy between observation and hypothesis. *Journal of the Royal Statistical Society, 87*(3), 442–450.

Fisher, R. A. (1935). The logic of inductive inference. *Journal of the Royal Statistical Society, 98*(1), 39–82. http://doi.org/10.2307/2342435

Frankfort-Nachmias, C., & Nachmias, D. (2007). *Study guide for research methods in the social sciences.* Basingstoke: Worth Publishers.

Healey, J. F. (2014). *Statistics: A tool for social research* (10th ed.). Stamford, CT: Cengage Learning.

Huber-Carol, C., Balakrishnan, N., Nikulin, M., & Mesbah, M. (Eds.). (2012). *Goodness-of-fit tests and model validity.* Heidelberg: Springer Science & Business Media.

Jepson, E. J. (2004). The adoption of sustainable development policies and techniques in U.S. cities: How wide, how deep, and what role for planners? *Journal of Planning Education and Research, 23*(3), 229–241. http://doi.org/10.1177/0739456X03258638

Mantel, N., & Haenszel, W. (1959). Statistical aspects of the analysis of data from retrospective studies of disease. *Journal of the National Cancer Institute, 22*(4), 719–748. http://doi.org/10.1093/jnci/22.4.719

McHugh, M. L. (2013). The chi-square test of independence. *Biochemia Medica, 23*(2), 143–149. http://doi.org/10.11613/BM.2013.018

Pearson, K. (1900). X. On the criterion that a given system of deviations from the probable in the case of a correlated system of variables is such that it can be reasonably supposed to have arisen from random sampling. *The London, Edinburgh, and Dublin Philosophical Magazine and Journal of Science, 50*(302), 157–175.

Plackett, R. L. (1983). Karl Pearson and the chi-squared test. *International Statistical Review/ Revue Internationale de Statistique, 51*(1), 59–72. http://doi.org/10.2307/1402731

Rovai, A. P., Baker, J. D., & Ponton, M. K. (2012). *Social science research design and statistics: A practitioner's guide to research methods and SPSS analysis.* Chesapeake, VA: Watertree Press.

Salkind, N. J. (2012). *Statistics for people who (think they) hate statistics: Excel 2010 edition.* Thousand Oaks, CA: Sage Publications.

Wellington, J., & Szczerbinski, M. (2007). *Research methods for the social sciences.* New York, NY: Continuum.

Yates, D., Moore, D., & McCabe, G. (1999). *The practice of statistics* (1st ed.). New York, NY: W. H. Freeman.

Yates, F. (1934). Contingency tables involving small numbers and the χ^2 test. *Supplement to the Journal of the Royal Statistical Society, 1*(2), 217–235. http://doi.org/10.2307/2983604

9 Correlation

Guang Tian, Anusha Musunuru, and Reid Ewing

Overview

Most of the variables of interest to, and used by, urban planners are related to each other. That is to say, they are correlated with one another. It is rare to find two variables with essentially no correlation. A famous example of correlation from outside planning, mentioned in research methods classes as an example of correlation without causation, is the historic relationship between sunspot activity and the business cycle.

Correlation analysis is used to determine:

- Whether the apparent relationship is due to chance or likely is real
- Whether the relationship is positive or negative
- Whether the relationship is strong or weak

The degree of association between two numeric variables is measured by the correlation coefficient, which is usually symbolized as r. The correlation coefficient ranges from -1 to $+1$. $r > 0$ indicates positive relationship and $r < 0$ indicates negative relationship. The mathematical formula and the strength of the relationship are explained in a later section.

Measures of correlation are also used in other statistical analyses and models. For instance, in factor analysis, a correlation matrix is generated to measure the relationships among many variables. In other statistical methods like linear regression, one of the main assumptions is that the independent variables are not too highly correlated with one another, a condition known as multicollinearity.

Purpose

In a variety of scientific disciplines, a common objective is to find the relationship or association between variables in a dataset. In urban planning, correlations have been found between urban form and physical activity (Ewing, Handy, Brownson, Clemente, & Winston, 2006), spatial distribution of vegetation and demographic status (Tooke, Klinkenberg, & Coops, 2010), building frontal area and urban heat island intensity (Wong & Nichol, 2013), functional zoning and land use (Zhang et al., 2012), spatial pattern of forest cover and forest accessibility (De Clercq, De Wulf, & Van Herzele, 2007), and past and present transport and urban planning policies (Pflieger, Kaufmann, Pattaroni, & Jemelin, 2009). As evidenced by these studies, correlations are widely used to quantify relationships in urban planning.

But remember that correlation does not imply causation. Correlation is when two or more events tend to occur at the same time and might be associated with each other, but they aren't necessarily connected by a cause-effect relationship.

Four conditions must be met for causal (cause-effect) inference:

- Conceptual plausibility (a supporting theory)
- Strong association (a strong correlation)
- Time sequence (a cause preceding an effect)
- Elimination of rival explanations (controlling for confounding variables)

For example, consider the variables vehicle miles traveled (VMT) and fuel price. When fuel prices increase, people are found to drive less. Thus, these variables are correlated in the sense that a change in any one variable is likely accompanied by a change in the other variable.

By employing correlation analysis, a negative relationship between VMT per capita and fuel price can be verified (using this book's UZA dataset). The simple bivariate correlation coefficient is –0.36. It is statistically significant at the 0.001 level or beyond, suggesting that the probability that the relationship is due to chance is less than one in a thousand. The partial correlation coefficient (controlling for confounding variables) is –0.17, significant at the 0.002 level. The elasticity of VMT per capita with respect to fuel price (again, controlling for confounding variables) is –0.45 in a cross-sectional model (Ewing, Meakins, Hamidi, & Nelson, 2014). An elasticity is just the percentage change in one variable associated with a 1 percent change in another variable. So an elasticity of –0.45 implies that when fuel price increases by 1 percent, VMT in the long-run declines by 0.45 percent. While inelastic (less than 1 in absolute magnitude), this is still a strong relationship. The short-run elasticity is much smaller.

The consistency with which these two variables have been found to be correlated, the solid economic basis for the relationship, the longitudinal as well as cross-sectional evidence of a relationship, and the presence of a relationship even after confounding variables are controlled, allow us to infer a causal relationship in this case (Ewing et al., 2014)

History

There are several correlation coefficients of interest to, and used by, planners. The most common are the Pearson correlation coefficient (r), the Spearman correlation coefficient (r_s), and the intraclass correlation coefficient (ICC).

Correlation was developed by Karl Pearson from a similar but slightly different idea introduced by Francis Galton in the 1880s. Galton had completed the theory of bivariate normal correlation. Then Pearson developed the mathematical formula to measure correlation—the Pearson correlation coefficient is widely used today (Pearson, 1920; Lee Rodgers & Nicewander, 1988). The Pearson correlation coefficient might be called Galton-Pearson correlation coefficient in regard for Galton's contribution.

The Spearman correlation coefficient or Spearman's rank correlation coefficient, named after Charles Spearman, is a nonparametric (distribution-free) rank statistic that was proposed by Spearman in 1904 as a measure of the strength of the associations

152 *Guang Tian, Anusha Musunuru, and Reid Ewing*

between two variables, without making any assumptions about the frequency distribution of the variables (Spearman, 1904; Lehmann & D'Abrera, 1998).

The ICC was first introduced by Ronald Fisher, based on the modifications of the Pearson correlation coefficient (which is interclass correlation) (Fisher, 1938). Bartko first proposed to assess reliability (see Chapter 6) with the ICC (Bartko, 1966).

Mechanics

Pearson Correlation Coefficient

The mathematical formula for computing the Pearson correlation coefficient r is:

$$r = \frac{n \sum xy - (\sum x)(\sum y)}{\sqrt{n(\sum x^2) - (\sum x)^2} \sqrt{n(\sum y^2) - (\sum y)^2}}$$

where n is the number of pairs of data and x and y are the two variables.
We present a second equivalent formula that is harder to compute but easier to interpret.

$$r = \frac{\sum_i (x_i - \bar{x})(y_i - \bar{y})}{\sqrt{\sum_i (x_i - \bar{x})^2 \sum_i (y_i - \bar{y})^2}}$$

where $\bar{x}$ and $\bar{y}$ are the means of x and y.

> *Positive correlation*: If x and y have a strong positive linear correlation, r will be close to +1. An r value of exactly +1 indicates a perfect positive fit (all points lying on an upward sloping line).
>
> *Negative correlation*: If x and y have a strong negative linear correlation, r will be close to −1. An r value of exactly −1 indicates a perfect negative fit (all points lying on a downward sloping line).
>
> *No correlation*: If there is no linear correlation or a weak linear correlation, r will be close to 0. A value near 0 means that there is a random (or conceivably a nonlinear) relationship between the two variables.

A key mathematical property of the Pearson correlation coefficient is that the value is invariant to changes of location and scale. For instance, when the variable x is linearly transformed to $a + bx$, where a and b are constants, the correlation coefficient with y does not change. This makes sense. If the relationship between two variables exists, the correlation coefficient will pick up the relationship regardless of how the variables are measured.

The Pearson correlation coefficient is only appropriate for examining the relationship between continuous variables (interval and ratio scale variables such as VMT and fuel price), not nominal or ordinal measurements. In addition, both variables should be approximately normally distributed (i.e., a bell-shaped curve in a histogram). Also, the Pearson correlation coefficient only measures linear relationships (Lee Rodgers & Nicewander, 1988). It is possible that while r is close to 0, there is strong nonlinear relationship between the variables (see the third row in Figure 9.1).

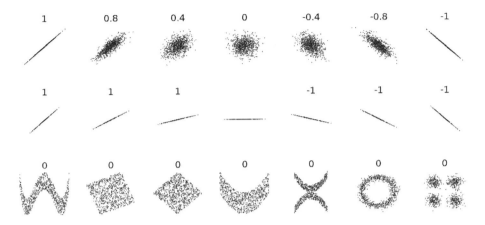

Figure 9.1 Scatterplots and Pearson Correlation Coefficients
Source: https://commons.wikimedia.org/wiki/File:Correlation_examples2.svg

Spearman Correlation Coefficient

In statistics, a rank correlation coefficient measures the degree of similarity between two rankings, and can be used to assess the significance of the relation between them. Continuous variables (interval and ratio scale variables) can be ranked and analyzed this way. Ordinal variables can also be ranked, and hence the relationship can be analyzed this way. For example, urbanized areas can be ranked in terms of VMT per capita and fuel price, and the rankings can be compared. Or cities might be (and often are) ranked in terms of livability and economic performance, and the rankings can be compared.

The Spearman correlation coefficient has a wide range of applications because there is no strict requirement of data condition—neither linear relationship or normal distribution (Philips et al., 2009). Regardless of the distribution and the size of sample, the Spearman correlation can be used as long as the two observations are paired.

The rank correlation statistics are as follows:

- Spearman's correlation coefficient
- Kendall tau correlation coefficient
- Goodman and Kruskal's gamma coefficient

Of the three, the most popular correlation statistic is the Spearman's correlation coefficient (r_s).

The Spearman correlation coefficient is just the Pearson correlation coefficient for data that is rank ordered (Myers, Well, & Lorch, 2010). Two variables x and y are converted to the rankings x and y, and then the formula for the Pearson correlation is applied to them.

Naturally, since the same formula is applied, the Spearman correlation coefficient is like the Pearson correlation in that it falls between +1 and −1. Like in the Pearson correlation, the sign of the Spearman correlation coefficient indicates the direction

154 *Guang Tian, Anusha Musunuru, and Reid Ewing*

of the association between x and y. If y tends to increase with x's increase, r_s is positive. Or, if y tends to decrease with x's increase, r_s is negative. When r_s equals 0, there is no tendency for y to either increase or decrease when x increases.

Intraclass Correlation Coefficient

In statistics, the intraclass correlation coefficient (ICC) is used to measure the correlation of variables representing different measurements of the same phenomena. The ICC is most often used to test the reliability or equivalency of measurements, one rater versus another, one variable versus another (see Chapter 6).

The Pearson correlation coefficient r between rater 1 and rater 2 can be represented as:

$$r = \frac{\sum_i \left(x_{i1} - \overline{x_1}\right)\left(x_{i2} - \overline{x_2}\right)}{(n-1)S_{x1}S_{x2}}$$

Conversely, the ICC is:

$$ICC = \frac{\sum_i \left(x_{i1} - \overline{x}\right)\left(x_{i2} - \overline{x}\right)}{(n-1)S_x^2}$$

where $\overline{x}$ is the mean, x_1 and x_2 represent two raters, and S_x is the standard deviation.

The key difference between ICC and r is, then, the estimation of mean and variance. For the Pearson correlation coefficient, the mean and variance are calculated separately for the two groups. But for ICC, they are the aggregate of the two groups.

The ICC is the preferred measure of inter-rater reliability when cases are rated in terms of some interval variable or interval-like variable, such as a Likert scale measurement (Alexander, Bergman, Hagströmer, & Sjöström, 2006; Ewing et al., 2006). The Pearson correlation coefficient is sensitive only to random error (chance factors), while the ICC is sensitive to both random error and systematic error (statistical bias). If one rater always assigns scores that are x points higher than another rater (systematic error), the Pearson correlation coefficient would indicate complete agreement between them. This follows from the mathematical property that the Pearson correlation coefficient is invariant to changes of location and scale. By contrast, the ICC would more accurately portray the extent of disagreement between them (see Figures 9.2 through 9.4). In these figures, consistency refers to the context of two repeated measures by the same rater. In this case, systematic errors of the rater are canceled, and only the random error is kept; thus, ICC (consistency) is always higher than ICC (absolute agreement).

Like the Pearson correlation, the *ICC* is confined to the interval +1 to −1. As a general guide, many researchers follow the adjectival ratings suggested by Landis and Koch (1977), who considered scores between 0.8 and 1.0 as indicating almost perfect agreement and those between 0.6 and 0.8 as indicating substantial agreement.

Beyond inter-rater reliability, another common application of the ICC to planning is in multilevel analysis. ICC is used to measure the proportion of variance in the dependent variable (at lower level, such as individual) that is explained by the differences between groups (at higher level, such as region). For example, in a study of Kelly-Schwartz, Stockard, Doyle, and Schlossberg (2004), they aimed to examine the influences of urban sprawl on public health. The ICC was used to measure the extent

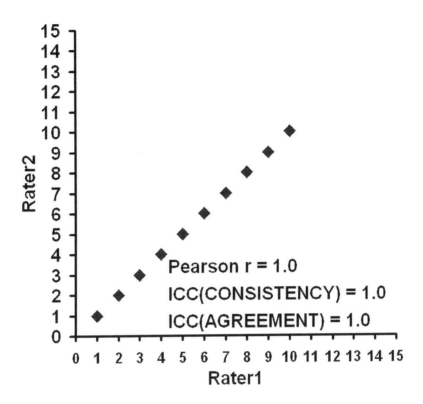

Figure 9.2 Rater 2 Always Rates the Same as Rater 1

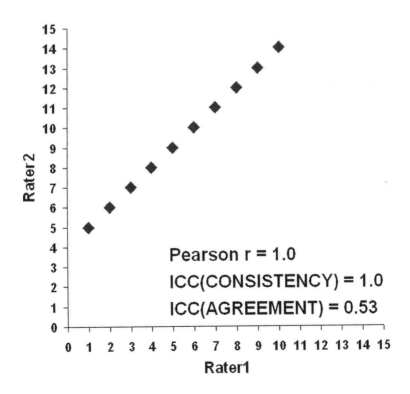

Figure 9.3 Rater 2 Always Rates 4 Points Higher Than Rater 1

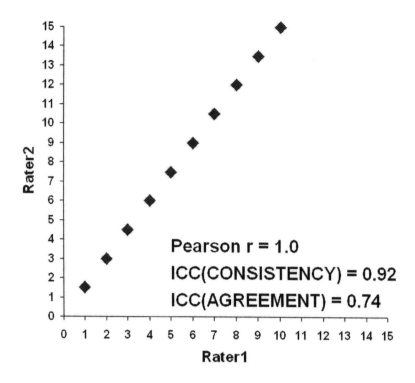

Figure 9.4 Rater 2 Always Rates 1.5 Times Higher Than Rater 1

to which regional sprawl can account for differences in individual health (Kelly-Schwartz et al., 2004).

Step by Step

Now we will learn how to estimate different types of correlation coefficients in SPSS, using the UZA dataset (UZA.sav). The standard steps to test a correlation between two continuous variables are as follows:

1. Propose a null hypothesis (there is no relationship between two variables) and an alternative hypothesis (there *is* a relationship between two variables or there is a *positive/negative* relationship between two variables).
2. Choose and compute an appropriate correlation coefficient.
3. Interpret the results, paying particular attention to the correlation coefficient value and its associated level of significance. Reject the null hypothesis if the coefficient is large, and the *p*-value is lower than the predetermined significance level (e.g., 0.5).

Pearson Correlation Coefficient

Let's assume that you are a planner interested in the relationship between travel and built environment, particularly road capacity and people's driving distance. Road

Correlation 157

capacity is usually measured as "total lane miles per thousand population" and driving distance is measured as "vehicle miles traveled (VMT) per capita."

Our first step is to confirm that the data meets the Pearson correlation coefficient assumptions of interval data and normality. VMT per capita and lane miles per thousand population are both continuous variables and when log transformed, are approximately normally distributed. Thus, we will use *lnvmt* and *lnlm* variables.

Then, we propose the null hypothesis: that there is no relationship between VMT per capita and lane mile per thousand population among the 157 urbanized areas in our sample. The alternative hypothesis is that there is a *positive* relationship between two variables: when lane miles go up, VMT also goes up. This is the theory of highway induced traffic.

To conduct a Pearson *r* in SPSS, select "<u>A</u>nalyze" in the main menu, go to "<u>C</u>orrelate," and select "<u>B</u>ivariate."

Once you open the "Bivariate Correlations" window (Figure 9.6), select two variables—*lnvmt* and *lnlm*—and move them to the "<u>V</u>ariables" list. There are three correlation statistics you can choose. The default setting is Pearson. For this example, we choose Pearson.

The next option is "Test of Significance." There are two options: two-tailed and one-tailed. We will select one-tailed test because we have a directional hypothesis—in this case, a positive relationship between VMT per capita and lane miles per thousand population. You should select two-tailed test (the default) when you cannot assume

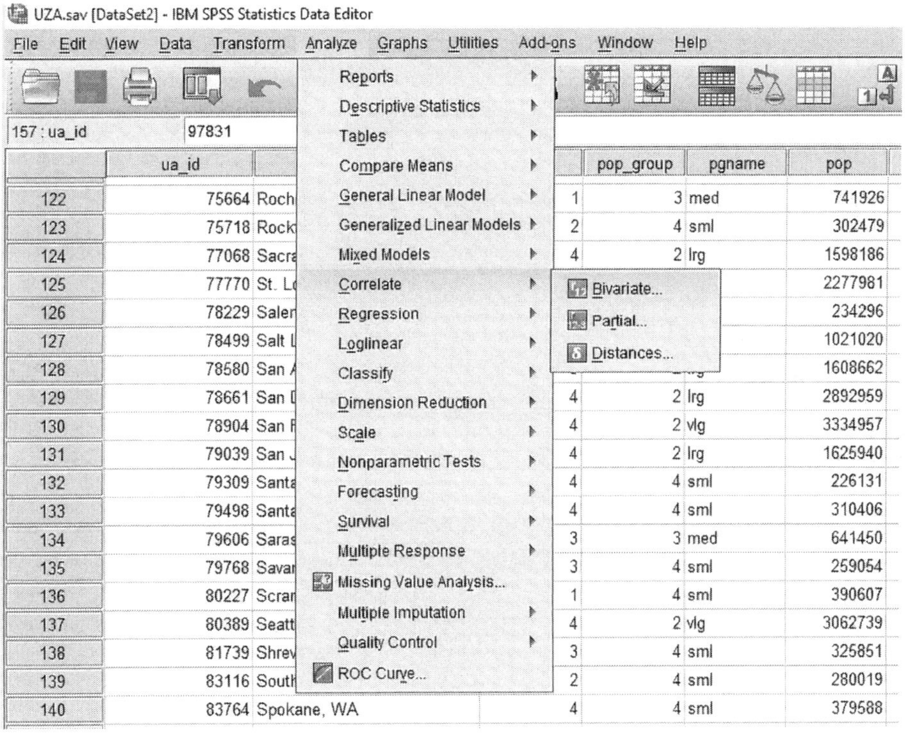

Figure 9.5 Find "<u>B</u>ivariate" Menu in "<u>C</u>orrelate"

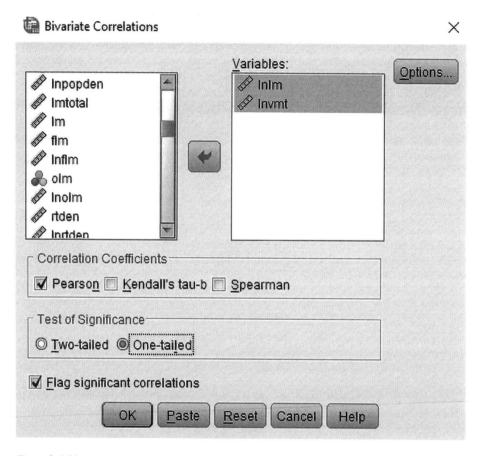

Figure 9.6 Bivariate Correlation Window

the direction of the relationship—whether it is positive or negative. Lastly, click "OK" to get the resulting Pearson correlation coefficient.

In the Output Viewer window, SPSS provides a matrix of the correlation coefficients for the two variables (Table 9.1), the significance level of the correlation, and the sample size. Correlation coefficient (*r* value) indicates the strength and direction (±) of the linear correlation: the higher the absolute value is, the stronger the linear relationship between the two variables is.

"Sig." indicates *p*-value of the one-tailed correlation test, the probability that you would see the resulting *r* value by chance. Here the *p*-value equals 0.000, meaning less than 0.001. "N" is the number of pairs in the sample. From this analysis, we can reject the null hypothesis and conclude that the VMT per capita is positively associated with lane miles per thousand population, supporting the theory of induced traffic.

Partial Correlation Coefficient

The Pearson correlation coefficient told us that there is a strong correlation between road capacity and people's driving distance. The more lane miles a

Correlation 159

Table 9.1 Pearson Correlation Coefficients Results

Correlations

		lnlm	*lnvmt*
lnlm	Pearson Correlation	1	0.496**
	Sig. (1-tailed)		0.000
	N	157	157
lnvmt	Pearson Correlation	0.496**	1
	Sig. (1-tailed)	0.000	
	N	157	157

** Correlation is significant at the 0.01 level (1-tailed).

region has, the more VMT per capita it has. However, there might be some other factors affecting VMT, such as fuel price. Theoretically, a higher fuel price discourages people from driving and leads to less VMT. If fuel price is correlated with lane miles, some of the apparent relationship between lane miles and VMT may be due to fuel price, not lane miles itself. We are wondering whether the strong relationship between VMT and lane miles is still the case after controlling for the effect of fuel price.

We can test that by estimating a partial correlation coefficient. A partial correlation coefficient is a measure of the strength and direction of a linear relationship between two continuous variables while controlling for the effect of one or more other continuous variables, often referred to as confounding variables.

We propose the null hypothesis: that there is no relationship between VMT per capita and lane miles per thousand population among the 157 urbanized areas after controlling for the effect of fuel price. The alternative hypothesis is that there is still a positive relationship after controlling for the fuel price effect.

Go to "Analyze" in the main menu and "Correlate" $\rightarrow$ "Partial" (Figure 9.7).

Select the variables *lnvmt* and *lnlm* from the variable list on the left and move them to the "Variables" box. Select *lnfuel* (log-transformed value of fuel price) and move it to the "Controlling for" box. Check "One-tailed" for the test of significance (because we still assume a positive relationship between VMT and lane miles).

Click "Options" button and check "Zero-order correlation" and click "Continue" (Figure 9.8). The zero-order correlations option gives you the Pearson correlation coefficients between three variables in addition to the partial correlation coefficients.

Back to the main window of partial correlation and click "OK" to run the test.

In the Output table, the first part is the bivariate Pearson correlation coefficients between VMT, lane miles, and fuel price (Table 9.2). VMT is positively correlated with lane miles (as we saw before) and negatively correlated with fuel price (as we expected). Both relationships are statistically significant at $p = 0.001$ level.

We are more interested in the bottom part of the table: the correlation coefficient between VMT and lane miles after controlling for fuel price. The correlation coefficient is slightly smaller (0.389) than the one without controlling for fuel price (0.496), but still statistically significant ($p < .001$). Thus, the null hypothesis is rejected and we can conclude that VMT is positively correlated with lane miles after controlling for the fuel price effect.

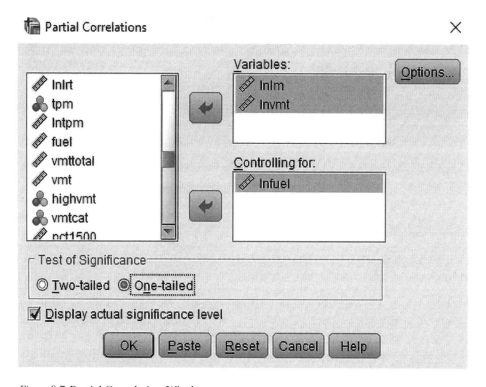

Figure 9.7 Partial Correlation Window

Spearman Correlation Coefficient

Next, we will generate a Spearman correlation coefficient matrix. Its only difference with the Pearson *r* is that the Spearman correlation is generated based on the rank of the original values instead of the actual values. Also, it does not require the variables to be normally distributed.

Let's assume that we are interested in the relationship between VMT per capita and regional population size. Is an urbanized area with more population likely to have more VMT per capita? In larger urban areas, trip productions are likely to be farther away from trip attractions, which may lead to more VMT. At the same time, larger urbanized areas are likely to have better transit systems, which may lead to less VMT. Theoretically, it could go either way. So we need to explore the relationship statistically. First, we propose a null hypothesis: there is no relationship between VMT per capita rank and regional population rank. The alternative hypothesis is that the regional population rank *is* associated with VMT per capita rank. We will use *pop000* and *vmt* in the UZA dataset. Again, we don't need variables with normal distribution for the Spearman correlation.

The steps for conducting a Spearman correlation are the same as for a Pearson correlation except you check "Spearman" for the "Correlation Coefficients" (Figure 9.9).

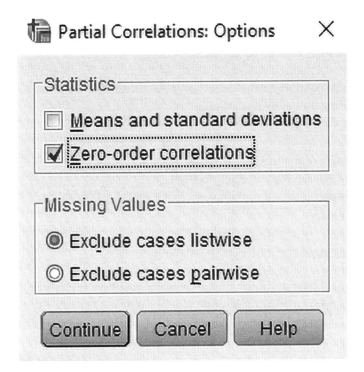

Figure 9.8 Options in Partial Correlation

Table 9.2 Partial Correlation Coefficients

Correlations

Control Variables			lnlm	lnvmt	lnfuel
-none-[a]	lnlm	Correlation	1.000	0.496	−0.504
		Significance (1-tailed)		0.000	0.000
		df	0	155	155
	lnvmt	Correlation	0.496	1.000	−0.365
		Significance (1-tailed)	0.000		0.000
		df	155	0	155
	lnfuel	Correlation	−0.504	−0.365	1.000
		Significance (1-tailed)	0.000	0.000	
		df	155	155	0
lnfuel	lnlm	Correlation	1.000	0.389	
		Significance (1-tailed)		0.000	
		df	0	154	
	lnvmt	Correlation	0.389	1.000	
		Significance (1-tailed)	0.000		
		df	154	0	

a Cells contain zero-order (Pearson) correlations.

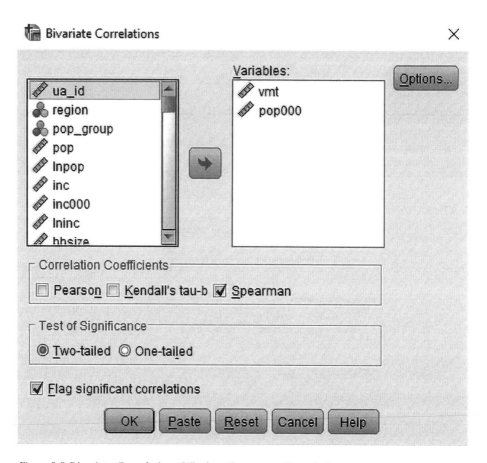

Figure 9.9 Bivariate Correlations Window: Spearman Correlation

The Output window provides a Spearman correlation matrix (Table 9.3). The correlation coefficient between the two variables is 0.078 and the *p*-value of this correlation is 0.330. Thus, the relationship between VMT per capita and population rank is weak and not statistically significant. The null hypothesis cannot be rejected.

Intraclass Correlation Coefficient

In creating sprawl metrics for urbanized areas, Ewing et al. (2014, 2018a, 2018b) use two variables that presumably measure the same attribute, population density. One measure is gross population density, computed by dividing the total population of a FHWA urbanized area by its area. This calculation necessarily excludes rural areas.

The other measure is described as net population density, computed by dividing total population by the urban land area within the FHWA urbanized area, from the U.S. Geological Survey's National Land Cover Database (NLCD). NLCD serves as the definitive Landsat-based, 30-meter resolution, land cover database for the nation. It is

Table 9.3 Spearman's Correlation Coefficients Result

Correlations

			vmt	*pop000*
Spearman's rho	vmt	Correlation Coefficient	1.000	0.078
		Sig. (2-tailed)		0.330
		N	157	157
	pop000	Correlation Coefficient	0.078	1.000
		Sig. (2-tailed)	0.330	
		N	157	157

a raster dataset providing spatial reference for land surface classification (for example, urban, agriculture, forest). It can be geo-processed to any geographic unit. For the current work, the urban land area was generated at the FHWA urbanized area level using NLCD 2006 for the entire United States. The value codes treated as urban were: 21 (developed, open space), 22 (developed, low intensity), 23 (developed, medium intensity), and 24 (developed, high intensity). Note that the net population density (*urbden* variable) is always higher than the gross population density (*popden* variable).

We first establish a null hypothesis: There is no difference between gross population density and net population density, or they measure the same construct. The alternative hypothesis is that gross population density and net population density measure different constructs.

To test the extent to which different variables measure the same underlying construct—in this case, population density, we can conduct a test of equivalence reliability (Ewing and Clemente, 2013). Equivalence reliability is determined by relating values of the different variables to one another to highlight the degree of consistency. The ICC is an appropriate measure of reliability.

To estimate an ICC with SPSS, go to "Analyze" in the main menu, find "Scale," and select "Reliability Analysis" (Figure 9.10).

Select two density variables—*popden* and *urbden*—from the variable list and move them to the "Items" box. Click "Statistics" and check "Intraclass correlation coefficient" box (Figure 9.11). Then, choose "Two-Way Mixed" for "Model." "One-way Random" option is used only when you have inconsistent raters for ratees. If you have consistent raters/ratees (e.g., ten raters each rate ten ratees), and you use a sample of raters, use "Two-Way Random." In our example, two density variables are a fixed factor, which means that you infer about only these specific variables (not all possible *density* variables). Thus, "Two-Way Mixed" is chosen. Then, the "Consistency" in "Type" option assesses how well two variables correlate, rather than how identical their values are (the absolute agreement). As two density variables are not supposed to be identical, we use the "Consistency" option. Click "Continue" to go back to the reliability analysis window and click "OK."

In the Output window (Table 9.4), the "Intraclass Correlation Coefficient" table has two parts: Single Measures and Average Measures. Average measures ICC tells you how reliably a group of measures agree. Single measures ICC tells you how reliable it is for you to use just one measure. In this example, we are interested in single measures. The single measures ICC is 0.879. Based on Landis and Koch's (1977)

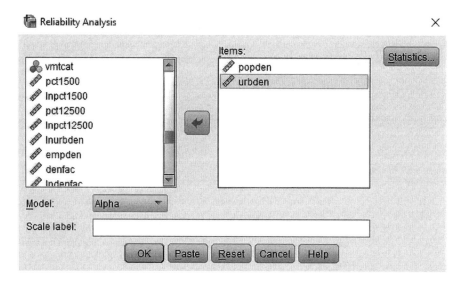

Figure 9.10 ICC Main Window

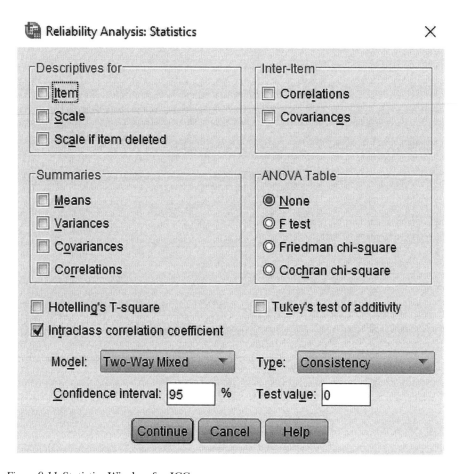

Figure 9.11 Statistics Window for ICC

Correlation 165

Table 9.4a Reliability Statistics and ICC Values

Reliability Statistics	
Cronbach's Alpha	N of Items
.936	2

Table 9.4b Intraclass Correlation Coefficient

Intraclass Correlation Coefficient

	Intraclass Correlation[a]	95% Confidence Interval		F Test With True Value 0			
		Lower Bound	Upper Bound	Value	df1	df2	Sig
Single Measures	0.879[b]	.838	.911	15.585	156	156	.000
Average Measures	0.936[c]	.912	.953	15.585	156	156	.000

Two-way mixed effects model where people effects are random and measures effects are fixed.

a Type C intraclass correlation coefficients using a consistency definition; the between-measure variance is excluded from the denominator variance.

b The estimator is the same, whether the interaction effect is present or not.

c This estimate is computed assuming the interaction effect is absent, because it is not estimable otherwise

suggestion, this value indicates almost perfect agreement. The null hypothesis is not rejected. In other words, gross population density and net population density measure the same construct.

With measuring consistency, note that average measures ICC are always identical to Cronbach's alpha, a typical measure of equivalence reliability.

In R

Figures 9.12 through 9.14 show an example of several correlation computations in R. Figure 9.12 first shows two different functions computing Pearson's correlation coefficient between the two variables—*lnlm* and *lnvmt*. The computed coefficient value, 0.496, is the same between two; but *cor.test* function provides the *p*-value associated with the coefficient. Figure 9.13 presents scripts to calculate the partial correlation coefficient between VMT (*lnvmt*) and lane miles (*lnlm*) after controlling for fuel price (*lnfuel*), the same as the SPSS example. The figure also introduces how to calculate Spearman's rank correlation coefficient between *vmt* and *pop000*. Lastly, Figure 9.14 shows a script using *icc* function in *irr* package to compute a two-way ICC value between two density variables—*popden* and *urbden*. Additionally, the *psych* R package provides a function to calculate a Cronbach's Alpha.

```
#CORRELATION
library(foreign)
uza<-read.spss("UZA.sav",to.data.frame=TRUE)


cor(uza$lnlm,uza$lnvmt) #Pearson correlation coefficient
```

```
## [1] 0.4964325
```

```
cor.test(uza$lnlm,uza$lnvmt) #Pearson correlation coefficient
 and p-value
```

```
##
##  Pearson's product-moment correlation
##
## data:  uza$lnlm and uza$lnvmt
## t = 7.1198, df = 155, p-value = 3.789e-11
## alternative hypothesis: true correlation is not equal to 0
## 95 percent confidence interval:
##   0.3684448 0.6059517
## sample estimates:
##        cor
## 0.4964325
```

Figure 9.12 Reading SPSS Data and Calculating Pearson Correlation Coefficient: R Script and Outputs

Planning Examples

Environment Equity

By analyzing the relationship between socioeconomic status of the population and the spatial distribution of vegetation, Tooke et al. (2010) addressed human-environment interactions in three major Canadian cities—Montreal, Toronto, and Vancouver. Correlation analysis was used to make comparisons of socioeconomic variables and vegetation both between cities and within cities.

There were two datasets used in this study. Socioeconomic data came from the Canadian census and included income, education, family status, and immigrant

```
library(ggm)

uza_par<-uza[,c("lnlm","lnvmt","lnfuel")]
pcor<-pcor(c(1,2,3),cov(uza_par)) #partial correlation coefficient
pcor
```

```
## [1] 0.3885317
```

```
pcor.test(pcor,1,157)
```

```
## $tval
## [1] 5.232653
##
## $df
## [1] 154
##
## $pvalue
## [1] 5.384892e-07
```

```
cor.test(uza$vmt,uza$pop000,method="spearman") #Spearman correlation coeffic
ient
```

```
##
##  Spearman's rank correlation rho
##
## data:  uza$vmt and uza$pop000
## S = 594458, p-value = 0.3293
## alternative hypothesis: true rho is not equal to 0
## sample estimates:
##        rho
## 0.07829681
```

Figure 9.13 Partial Correlation Coefficient and Spearman Correlation Coefficient: R Script and Outputs

status. To obtain vegetation data for each of these cities, the Landsat 7 Enhanced Thematic mapper (ETM+) summer raster image with 30 meters per unit were used. Vegetation fractional images are depicted in Figure 9.15.

At the census tract level, the socioeconomic variables were joined with mean values of vegetated and impervious land-surface cover. The Pearson correlation coefficient was used to quantify the relation between vegetation fraction and socioeconomic variables for the three cities.

```
#ICC
library(irr)
icc(cbind(uza$popden, uza$urbden),model="twoway") #Intraclass
  correlation coefficient
```

```
##  Single Score Intraclass Correlation
##
##     Model: twoway
##     Type : consistency
##
##     Subjects = 157
##       Raters = 2
##     ICC(C,1) = 0.879
##
##  F-Test, H0: r0 = 0 ; H1: r0 > 0
##  F(156,156) = 15.6 , p = 1.88e-52
##
##  95%-Confidence Interval for ICC Population Values:
##     0.838 < ICC < 0.911
```

```
library(psych)
alpha(cbind(uza$popden, uza$urbden))$total$std.alpha #Cronbac
h's Alpha
```

```
## [1] 0.9417304
```

Figure 9.14 Intraclass Correlation Coefficient and Cronbach's Alpha: R Script and Outputs

The highest correlations for all cities belonged to median family income. Results exhibited strong and consistent correlations between median family income and vegetation fraction for Montreal ($r = 0.473$), Toronto ($r = 0.467$), and Vancouver ($r = 0.456$). The coefficients are positive, meaning that wealthier neighborhoods have more vegetation, a sign of environmental inequality. The strongest relationship with education came with the variable "no high school degree," which was negatively correlated with vegetation. Of family status variables, families with no children resulted in a higher positive correlation with vegetation. Finally, immigrant status variables were much more highly correlated with vegetation in Toronto than either Montreal or Vancouver.

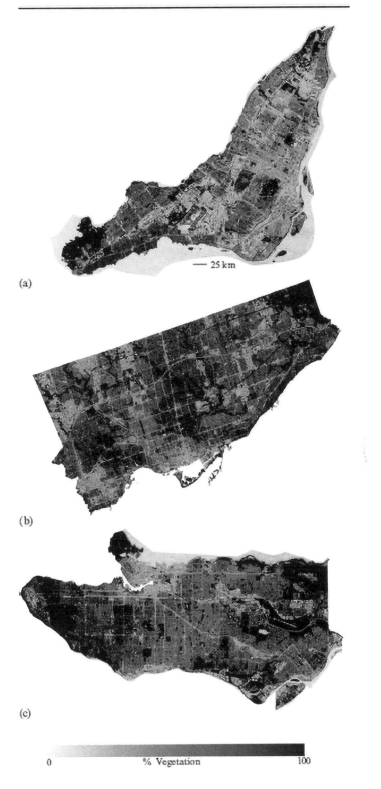

Figure 9.15 Spectral-Mixture-Analysis Derived Vegetation Fractional Images for (a) Montreal, (b) Toronto, and (c) Vancouver

Source: Tooke et al. (2010)

170 *Guang Tian, Anusha Musunuru, and Reid Ewing*

Planners and community organizations can use these results to help guide policies and initiatives to help mitigate recognized inequalities. In addition, cross-city comparisons can help policy analysts examine the successes and failures of urban development processes in these major cities.

Urban Design Qualities

The second case study relates the built environment to walkability. This study is an example of how to employ the ICC to evaluate inter-rater reliability. Ewing et al. (2006) developed operational definitions and measurement protocols for urban design qualities related to walkability.

From numerous perceptual qualities of the urban environment in the literature, this study selected eight of them for subsequent study: imageability, legibility, visual enclosure, human scale, transparency, linkage, complexity, and coherence. To obtain operational definitions, more than 200 video clips were shot for streetscapes with sidewalks and other pedestrian amenities in dozens of cities across the US. Forty-eight video clips were sent to an expert panel, and the panelists rated and assigned a score to each quality on a Likert scale. At the same time, the research team measured the physical features of the streetscapes in this sample.

The authors used ICCs to evaluate inter-rater reliability for both the ratings of urban design qualities by the expert panel and the measures of physical features by the research team. The results for the expert panel are shown in Table 9.5. According to the ICC values, the authors concluded that most urban design qualities demonstrated moderate inter-rater reliability among panelists ($0.6 \geq ICCs \geq 0.4$); the exceptions—linkage, coherence, and legibility—showed only fair reliability ($0.4 \geq ICCs \geq 0.2$).

For the inter-rater reliability test of physical feature measurements, there was almost perfect agreement ($ICCs \geq 0.8$) or substantial agreement ($0.8 \geq ICCs \geq 0.6$) between ratings of most features. Meanwhile, several features had low or even negative ICC values like landscape maintenance.

To decide which urban design qualities could be defined operationally, the authors established five criteria, including two based on inter-rater reliability. As shown in

Table 9.5 Inter-Rater Reliability for Rating of Urban Design Qualities

	Intra-Class Correlation Coefficient	95% Cl of ICC	Cronbach's Alpha
Imageability	0.494	0.385–0.618	0.930
Legibility	0.380	0.276–0.509	0.895
Enclosure	0.584	0.478–0.697	0.945
Human scale	0.508	0.399–0.630	0.928
Transparency	0.499	0.390–0.622	0.926
Linkage	0.344	0.169–0.621	0.896
Complexity	0.508	0.398–0.632	0.926
Coherence	0.374	0.271–0.504	0.880
Tidiness	0.421	0.314–0.550	0.915
N	48		

Source: Ewing et al., 2006

Table 9.6 Performance of Urban Design Qualities Relative to Selection Criteria (Ewing et al., 2006)

	Inter-Rater Reliability of Rating of Quality (ICC)	Portion of Scene Variance/Total Variance Explained by Best-Fit Models	Inter-Rater Reliability of Significant Variables (Number With ICC > 0.4)	Relationship to Walkability in Best-Fit Model (P-value)	Criteria Met
Imageability	0.494	0.72/0.37	7 of 7 (1 missing)	0.000	5 of 5
Legibility	0.380	0.54/0.21	5 of 5 (1 missing)	—	1 of 5
Enclosure	0.584	0.72/0.43	5 of 5	0.016	5 of 5
Human scale	0.508	0.62/0.35	7 of 7	0.000	5 of 5
Transparency	0.499	0.62/0.32	3 of 3	0.023	5 of 5
Linkage	0.344	0.61/0.21	4 of 5	—	1 of 5
Complexity	0.508	0.73/0.38	5 of 6	—	3 of 5
Coherence	0.374	0.67/0.25	3 of 4	—	1 of 5
Tidiness	0.421	0.70/0.30	2 of 3 (1 missing)	0.117	3 of 5

Table 9.6, imageability, enclosure, human scale, transparency, complexity, and tidiness met the first ICC criterion. For the third criterion, the ICCs for each of the physical features significant in the final models of urban design qualities were examined. Finally, adding other criteria, imageability, visual enclosure, human scale, transparency, and complexity were selected as operational urban design qualities related to walkability, and were included in the final field manual for subsequent use in physical activity research. The other urban design qualities were dropped from further consideration.

Conclusion

In sum, a correlation analysis examines the degree to which two variables are related, by calculating a specific type of correlation coefficient. However, they cannot provide us with any notion of whether one variable has any impact on the value of the other variable. Thus, a researcher is advised to use expressions like "associated" or "likely to" rather than "causes" or "influences." In other words, a cause-effect relationship needs to meet further requirements (see the Overview section at the beginning of the chapter), often accomplished by more sophisticated analytic methods, such as structural equation modeling (Chapter 8 of *Advanced Quantitative Research Methods for Urban Planners*) or quasi-experimental research (Chapter 14 of this volume).

Readers should note that correlation can only be used when two variables are continuous (i.e., interval or ratio scale) or ordinal, not nominal. In the case of ordinal variables, Spearman's correlation needs to be used. When both variables are categorical, go back to chi-square test in Chapter 8. When only the independent variable is categorical and thus can be grouped (while the dependent variable is continuous), see the difference of means test (*t*-test) in Chapter 10 for two groups or analysis of variance (ANOVA) test in Chapter 11 for more than two groups. The correlational analysis can expand to regression methods to assess the relationship between an outcome (dependent) variable and one or more predictor (independent) variables, the subjects of later chapters in this book.

172 *Guang Tian, Anusha Musunuru, and Reid Ewing*

Works Cited

Alexander, A., Bergman, P., Hagströmer, M., & Sjöström, M. (2006). IPAQ environmental module; reliability testing. *Journal of Public Health, 14*(2), 76–80.

Bartko, J. J. (1966). The intraclass correlation coefficient as a measure of reliability. *Psychological Reports, 19*, 3–11. http://doi-org.ezproxy.lib.utah.edu/10.2466/pr0.1966.19.1.3

Benesty, J., Chen, J., Huang, Y., & Cohen, I. (2009). Pearson correlation coefficient: Noise reduction in speech processing. *Springer Topics in Signal Processing, 2*, 1–4.

De Clercq, E. M., De Wulf, R., & Van Herzele, A. (2007). Relating spatial pattern of forest cover to accessibility. *Landscape and Urban Planning, 80*(1–2), 4–22. http://doi.org/10.1016/j.landurbplan.2006.04.007

Doyle, S., Kelly-Schwartz, A., Schlossberg, M., & Stockard, J. (2006). Active community environments and health: The relationship of walkable and safe communities to individual health. *Journal of the American Planning Association, 72*(1), 19–31. http://doi.org/10.1080/01944360608976721

Ewing, R., & Clemente, O. (2013). *Measuring urban design: Metrics for liable places.* Washington, DC: Island Press.

Ewing, R., Hamidi, S., Tian, G., Proffitt, D., Tonin, S., & Fregolent, L. (2018a). Testing Newman and Kenworthy's theory of density and automobile dependence. *Journal of Planning Education and Research, 38*(2), 167–182.

Ewing, R., Handy, S., Brownson, R. C., Clemente, O., & Winston, E. (2006). Identifying and measuring urban design qualities related to walkability. *Journal of Physical Activity and Health, 3*(1), 223–240. http://doi.org/10.1123/jpah.3.s1.s223

Ewing, R., Meakins, G., Hamidi, S., & Nelson, A. C. (2014). Relationship between urban sprawl and physical activity, obesity, and morbidity—Update and refinement. *Health & Place, 26*, 118–126.

Ewing, R., Tian, G., & Lyons, T. (2018b). Does compact development increase or reduce traffic congestion?. *Cities, 72*, 94–101.

Fisher, R. A. (1938). *Statistical methods for research workers* (7th ed.). Edinburgh: Oliver and Boyd.

Fleiss, J. L., Levin, B., & Cho Paik, M. (2013). *Statistical methods for rates and proportions.* Hoboken, NJ: John Wiley & Sons.

Kelly-Schwartz, A. C., Stockard, J., Doyle, S., & Schlossberg, M. (2004). Is sprawl unhealthy? A multilevel analysis of the relationship of metropolitan sprawl to the health of individuals. *Journal of Planning Education and Research, 24*(2), 184–196. http://doi.org/10.1177/0739456X04267713

Lee Rodgers, J., & Nicewander, W. A. (1988). Thirteen ways to look at the correlation coefficient. *The American Statistician, 42*(1), 59–66. http://doi.org/10.2307/2685263

Landis, J. R., & Koch, G. G. (1977). The measurement of observer agreement for categorical data. *Biometrics,* 159–174.

Lehmann, E. L., & D'Abrera, H. J. M. (1998). *Nonparametrics: Statistical methods based on ranks.* New York, NY: Springer.

McGraw, K. O., & Wong, S. P. (1996). Forming inferences about some intraclass correlation coefficient. *Psychological Methods, 1*(1), 30–46.

Myers, J. L., Well, A., & Lorch, R. F. (2010). *Research design and statistical analysis.* London: Routledge.

Pearson, K. (1920). Notes on the history of correlation. *Biometrika,* 25–45.

Pflieger, G., Kaufmann, V., Pattaroni, L., & Jemelin, C. (2009). How does urban public transport change cities? Correlations between past and present transport and urban planning policies. *Urban Studies, 46*(7), 1421–1437. http://doi.org/10.1177/0042098009104572

Philips, S. J., Dudik, M., Elith, J., Graham, C. H., Lehmann, A., Leathwick, J., & Ferrier, S. (2009). Sample selection bias and presence-only distribution models: Implications for background and pseudo-absence data. *Ecological Applications, 19*(1), 181–197. http://doi.org/10.1890/07-2153.1

Shrout, P. E., & Fleiss, J. L. (1979). Intraclass correlations: Uses in assessing reliability. *Psychological Bulletin, 86*, 420–428.

Spearman, C. (1904). The proof and measurement of association between two things. *The American Journal of Psychology, 15*(1), 72–101. http://doi.org/10.2307/1412159

Tooke, T. R., Klinkenberg, B., & Coops, N. C. (2010). A geographical approach to identifying vegetation-related environment equity in Canadian cities. *Environment and Planning B: Planning and Design, 37*, 1040–1056. http://doi.org/10.1068/b36044

Wong, M. S., & Nichol, J. E. (2013). Spatial variability of frontal area index and its relationship with urban heat island intensity. *International Journal of Remote Sensing, 34*(3), 885–896.

Zhang, F., Wang, X., Hailong, S., & Yong, Y. (2012). *The influence of functional zoning on land use and travel behavior in Shanghai, China*. 6th International Association for China Planning Conference.

10 Difference of Means Tests (*T*-Tests)

David Proffitt

Method	Dependent Variable	Independent Variables	Test Statistics
Chi-Square	Categorical	Categorical	chi-square statistic
Difference of Means	Continuous	Categorical (two categories)	t-statistic
ANOVA	Continuous	Categorical (multiple categories)	F-statistic
Linear Regression	Continuous	Continuous (though can represent categorical)	t-statistic R2 statistic
Logistic Regression	Categorical (Dichtomous)	Continuous (though can represent categorical)	asymptotic t-statistic pseudo-R2 statistic
Poisson/Negative Binomial Regression	Count	Continuous (though can represent categorical)	Wald statistic pseudo-R2 statistic

Figure 10.0 *T*-Test

Overview

Difference of means tests, or *t*-tests, are inferential statistical methods used to detect whether differences between the means of two samples are statistically significant. Another way of saying this is that they tell us whether the unknown means of two populations are different from each other based on the known means of samples.

Because it is often impractical (or impossible) to gather data for an entire population, planning research follows other social sciences in looking at samples. However, this creates a problem of how to interpret results because, in reality, no sample can be completely representative of the population as a whole. Employing statistically random sampling and other methods designed to reduce bias in sample selection makes it more likely that a given sample will resemble the larger population in most ways, but a certain amount of error is unavoidable. Difference of means tests compare variance within a sample to quantify the likelihood that the mean difference between two samples would be found in the population as a whole or is just due to chance.

This comes in handy when you want to, say, assess residents' satisfaction with a new transit stop in their neighborhood. Brown and Werner (2011) did just this by surveying residents of a neighborhood in Salt Lake City, Utah, about their perceptions of pedestrian safety, traffic, crime, sense of community, and economic factors in their neighborhood both before and after a new light-rail stop opened nearby. The authors used *t*-tests to determine whether differences in the means of before and after answers were statistically significant. In this case, they were significant, indicating that residents' satisfaction with their neighborhood improved following the new transit stop.

Purpose

Difference of means tests are a simple but powerful way to validate hypotheses about the effects of an intervention or phenomenon. They help us decide whether or not to reject the null hypothesis (H_0), which posits that there is no difference between two sample means. If we reject the null hypothesis, we assume that our alternative hypothesis (H_1)—that there is a difference between the means of two samples—is true (or at least the most likely explanation for the observed difference).

A helpful shorthand is to think about them as tests of the difference between *experimental* and *control* groups, or *with* and *without* groups, or *before* and *after* groups. T-tests quantify the likelihood that observed differences between two sample means—that is, the mean (or average) difference between all the values within two samples—is the result of chance or whether it is likely to be found in the corresponding populations as a whole.

Difference of means tests are related to confidence intervals, which describe the range of values that contain the population mean (or any other parameter) with a known probability, e.g., 95 percent (Vogt & Johnson, 2011).

History

The wide applicability of the *t*-test makes it the most common statistical procedure used in the social sciences (Elliott & Woodward, 2007). But it has its origins in a different field entirely: beer brewing. William Sealy Gosset developed the procedure during the first years of the 20th century while working at the Guinness brewery in Dublin. As a chemist responsible for ensuring a perfect pint, he was concerned with the amount of yeast in each batch. Too much yeast gave the beer a bitter taste, while too little led to incomplete fermentation. To make the job even more difficult, Gosset had to rely on small samples to judge the number of yeast colonies in entire vats. The young scientist solved his problem with statistics rather than chemistry, and published the results under the name *Student* because the brewery barred employees from publishing articles (Raju, 2005). Hence the common reference to the test as the "Student's *t*-test."

Mechanics

Two main tests are used to determine whether differences in the means of two samples are statistically significant (see Figure 10.1). The first is the independent samples *t*-test, and the second is the dependent sample (or matched-pairs) *t*-test. Both are

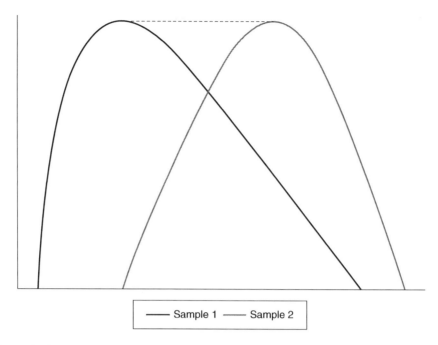

Figure 10.1 Two Frequency Distributions: Is the Difference Between Mean Scores in Two Sample Populations Significant or Due to Chance?

significance tests that quantify the probability of correctly rejecting the null hypothesis, but there are some important differences in when and how to apply them.

Independent Samples T-Test

Let us look at the independent samples *t*-test first. It answers a fairly straightforward question: Do the mean scores of some variable differ significantly from one sample to another? This is the classic *experimental* and *control* group test commonly used in medical trials, behavioral studies, and, of course, planning to compare the effects of policy and design interventions. This test uses two variables: a categorical independent variable (membership in one of two groups; e.g., men and women, movers and nonmovers) and a continuous a dependent, or outcome, variable (the variable of interest, e.g., crash rates, attitudinal scores). The type of outcome variable considered is important because the *t*-test compares means, which limits its applicability to continuous variables. It does not make sense, for instance, to consider the mean value of a categorical variable such as "mode of transportation" even if it has been coded numerically.

The independent samples *t*-test makes three basic assumptions that must be met for it to be accurate.

- The two samples, or comparison groups, are independent. That is, there is no overlap between the groups, and a single subject cannot be a member of both groups.

Difference of Means Tests (T-Tests) 177

- The data are normally distributed. Normality is particularly important for small sample sizes, where skewed distribution or outliers can invalidate the results. For larger samples (n>40), normality can be assumed even if it is not strictly observed.
- The variances can be considered equal (or not). Different versions of the test exist for samples with equal and unequal variances, so it is important to run a test of the variance such as Levene's *F*-test (Elliott & Woodward, 2007).

The statistic that answers our question of whether differences between the samples are due to chance or not is the *p* value. The *p* value is the probability of finding data as extreme as observed assuming the null hypothesis is true. This means that *p* values beyond a predetermined critical point (typically the 0.05 significance level) are necessary to reject the null hypothesis.

The results of the *t*-test do not provide the *p* value directly. Instead, the degrees of freedom and the value of t are used to locate the right *p* value in a t distribution table. Sound confusing? Don't worry. Statistical software packages, including SPSS and R, calculate the *p* value automatically and list it in the "sig."—or significance—column. Just know that mathematically, t is the observed difference between the two sample means divided by the standard error of the difference between the means.

In notation form, the *t* value is determined by:

$$t = \left(\overline{X}_1 - \overline{X}_2 \right) / s_{\bar{x}1-\bar{x}2}$$

where
$\overline{X}_1 - \overline{X}_2$ is the observed difference between two independent-sample means, and
s_{x1-x2} is the standard error of the difference between the sample means.

Standard Error

This section introduces a new concept, standard error. Standard error is the standard deviation of the sampling distribution of some statistic (in this case, the difference of means). The sampling distribution of the mean is a special type of frequency distribution. It is the distribution of the means from many different samples of equal size (see Figure 10.2). Putting these definitions together, we can say that standard error is a measure of how much random variation we would expect from samples of equal size drawn from the same population. The concept is similar to standard deviation, but it always applies to a sampling distribution rather than a population or individual sample.

Mathematically, the standard error of the sample mean is calculated by dividing the sample estimate of the standard deviation, i.e., the standard deviation of the sample, by the square root of the sample size.

In notation form, the standard error of the sample mean is:

$$s_{\bar{x}} = s / \sqrt{n}$$

where
s is the standard deviation of the sample mean, and
n is the sample size.

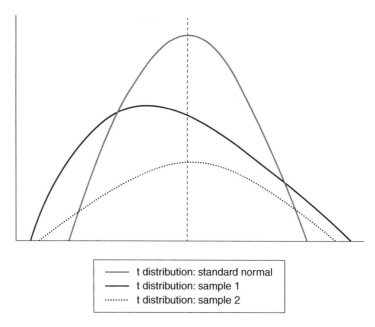

Figure 10.2 The Means of Individual Samples May Differ From the Overall Population Mean and From One Another, but the Distribution of Means From Multiple Samples Tends to Approach a Normal Distribution

Understanding the basic concept of standard error is important, but if you review the equation for determining t, you may notice that it is calculated using the standard error of the difference between the sample means rather than a single sample mean. The concept of standard error is the same whether it is applied to a single sample or the difference between sample means: It is the amount of difference we expect to see between the population mean and a sample mean or, in this case, the difference we would expect to see between the means of two randomly selected samples. However, the way we calculate the standard error of the difference between two sample means is slightly more complicated than for a single sample.

When the samples are roughly equal size, we can calculate the standard error of the difference between the sample means by taking the square root of the sum of the squared standard errors of the sample means. (This is less confusing than it sounds.)

$$s_{\bar{x}1-\bar{x}2} = \sqrt{\left(s_{\bar{x}1}^2 + s_{\bar{x}2}^2\right)}$$

where

$s_{\bar{x}1}$ is the standard error of the mean for the first sample, and
$s_{\bar{x}2}$ is the standard error of the mean for the second sample.

Determining Significance

Once we have a *t* value, it is assessed for significance by consulting a table of probabilities that depend on degrees of freedom and hence sample size (or just looking at what the computer tells you). In either case, it generally is safe to assume that differences are significant at the standard 0.05 significance level.

t distributions are shown in Figure 10.3. They are flatter than the normal distribution (*z* distribution), and hence require larger values for a finding of statistical significance. They become more peaked as the degrees of freedom increase, which means that smaller values can be considered significant. This makes sense, because with large samples we can be more confident in rejecting the null hypothesis. Note that when the sample size and degrees of freedom become infinite, the *t* distribution just becomes the normal distribution.

There is an important caveat to keep in mind when judging significance: Statistical significance does not always equal practical significance. For instance, a mean difference of one pound between two groups in a weight-loss study may be statistically significant, but does it really matter from a health or policy standpoint? Probably not.

The best way to deal with the question of practical (versus statistical) significance is to assign a critical value based on theory. But it also is possible to determine the magnitude of the treatment effect by calculating the effect size. Cohen's *d* statistic is the most commonly used measure of effect size when sample sizes and standard deviations are similar. Cohen's *d* is defined by the difference between two sample means divided by the pooled standard deviation of the two groups.

$$d = (\bar{X}_1 - \bar{X}_2) / SD_{pooled}$$

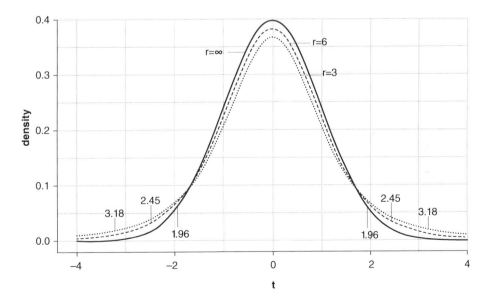

Figure 10.3 t Distributions and Critical Values for Different Degrees of Freedom

180   *David Proffitt*

where
$\bar{X}_1$ is the mean for sample 1,
$\bar{X}_2$ is the mean for sample 2, and
SD_{pooled} is the pooled standard deviation of the two groups.

Note that this is very similar to the equation for the t score, but instead of using the standard error in the denominator, we use the standard deviation.

We can calculate the pooled standard deviation by calculating the root mean square of the two samples' standard deviations:

$$SD_{pooled} = \sqrt{\left[\left(SD_1^2 + SD_2^2\right)/2\right]}$$

where
SD_1 and SD_2 are the standard deviations of the two samples.

Why do we care about effect size? For one thing, statistical significance is highly dependent on sample size. Larger samples are more likely to show statistically significant differences between their mean scores than smaller samples. We can see why this is the case by looking more closely at the equations for calculating the t score and standard error. (It might be helpful to literally look at both equations at this point. Both are spelled out earlier in this chapter.)

First, note that the square root of the sample size forms the denominator of the equation for standard error, which means that a larger sample will always produce a smaller standard error. Next, note that the standard error of the difference between sample means forms the denominator of the t-score equation, which means that a smaller standard error will produce a larger t score. Therefore, a larger sample will always produce a greater likelihood that a t-test will show a statistically significant result. Dividing by the standard deviation rather than the standard error in the effect-size calculation has the effect of stripping the influence of the sample size from our effect size metric.

Judging effect size is not an exact science. The best approach is to use theory to decide the critical values, but when theory does not provide clear direction, there are also some general rules of thumb. Generally, a result of 0.2 or smaller is a *small* effect, 0.5 is *medium*, and 0.8 or above is *large* (Urdan, 2001).

Dependent Samples T-Test

The dependent samples, or matched pairs, t-test is similar to the independent samples t-test in many ways. The key difference is the composition of the two sample groups. Instead of independent samples, the matched pairs t-test compares the means of paired samples. Paired samples refers to two samples that are linked somehow, either because they represent the before and after observations, with and without treatment, or some other form of matching between subjects in the two groups. Paired samples are also referred to as matched samples.

An example may help explain when to use the matched pairs t-test. Ewing, Chen, and Chen (2013) used the matched pairs t-test to evaluate the effectiveness of traffic-calming measures in reducing automobile crashes in New York City. The study tested

Difference of Means Tests (T-Tests) 181

whether the addition of speed tables to city streets reduced crashes on the treated streets—a straightforward before-and-after comparison. The matched pairs in this case were the before-treatment and after-treatment crash rates for each of the 391 streets treated with a speed table. A dependent samples t-test showed a statistically significant drop in pedestrian crashes ($p = .012$) and injury crashes ($p = .045$) but a less-than-statistically significant reduction in overall crashes ($p = .096$) on treated streets. For advocates of traffic calming, this is good news. The bad news is that this result also shows one of the pitfalls of research designs relying on t-tests. This *simple* before and after comparison did not take into account the overall drop in crash rates for New York City as a whole. So the authors relied on an additional (independent-samples) t-test to determine whether the reduction in crashes on treated streets minus the reduction in crashes on comparable untreated streets differed significantly from zero. This time, the results showed that crashes on treated and untreated streets fell at about the same rates, meaning that it was impossible to reject the null hypothesis that the speed tables had no measurable effect on crashes. This is referred to as a "difference in difference" study design. Despite these results, the authors point out that traffic calming tends to raise property values, reduce noise levels, encourage bicycling and walking, and allay residents' concerns about traffic safety, making them "one of the most cost-effective measures available to cities for improving the residential environment" (Ewing et al., 2013, p. 35).

Other than the composition of the samples, the basic structure and interpretation of the paired samples t-test is the same as the independent samples test. However, the math is slightly different. In this case, it is the difference between the paired values that is being divided by the standard error of the difference to see if it is significantly different from zero (Urdan, 2001).

One advantage of using matched pairs is that they make small differences within the samples easier to detect (Elliott & Woodward, 2007). In many cases, variability within a group can mask subtle, but very real, signals of effect. Researchers used this technique to detect differences in the intensity of the urban heat island across Athens (Giannopoulou et al., 2011). By comparing observations at paired locations, the researchers created a test that was more sensitive to small changes.

Step by Step

Now we will perform an independent samples t-test using household travel dataset (HTS.household.10regions.sav). Let's assume that you are interested in the relationship between travel and the built environment, particularly differences in how much people drive in Seattle, Washington, and Kansas City, Missouri. The dependent variable, VMT per capita, is continuous, and the independent variable, regions, is categorical having two groups—Seattle and Kansas City. Thus, we need difference-of-means tests, or t-tests.

We will go through five key steps in an independent samples t-test.

1. Ensure the data meet the assumptions of the t-test.
2. Confirm that the dependent variable is a continuous variable, and there are two categories of the independent variable.
3. Establish a null hypothesis and an alternative hypothesis.

182 *David Proffitt*

4. Conduct an independent samples *t*-test.
5. Interpret the results, paying particular attention to the *t*-statistic and its associated level of significance. Reject the null hypothesis if the *t*-statistic is large, and the *p*-value is lower than the determined significance level.

First, we need to select households only from Seattle and Kansas City. Open "HTS. household.10regions.sav" data, go to "Data" in the menu, and choose "Select cases" (Figure 10.4).

Then select "If condition is satisfied" and click "If" (Figure 10.5). In the new window, enter "region = 6 | region = 7." Click "Continue." Note that Seattle is region number 6 and Kansas City is 7. The symbol " | " is defined as "or," meaning that the formula reads "region number equals to 6 or 7."

Back in the "Select Cases" window, select "Copy selected cases to a new dataset" and enter a dataset name (e.g., HTS_tworegion) to make a copy of the two-region dataset (Figure 10.6). Now only cases from regions 6 (Seattle) and 7 (Kansas City) will be included in the analysis.

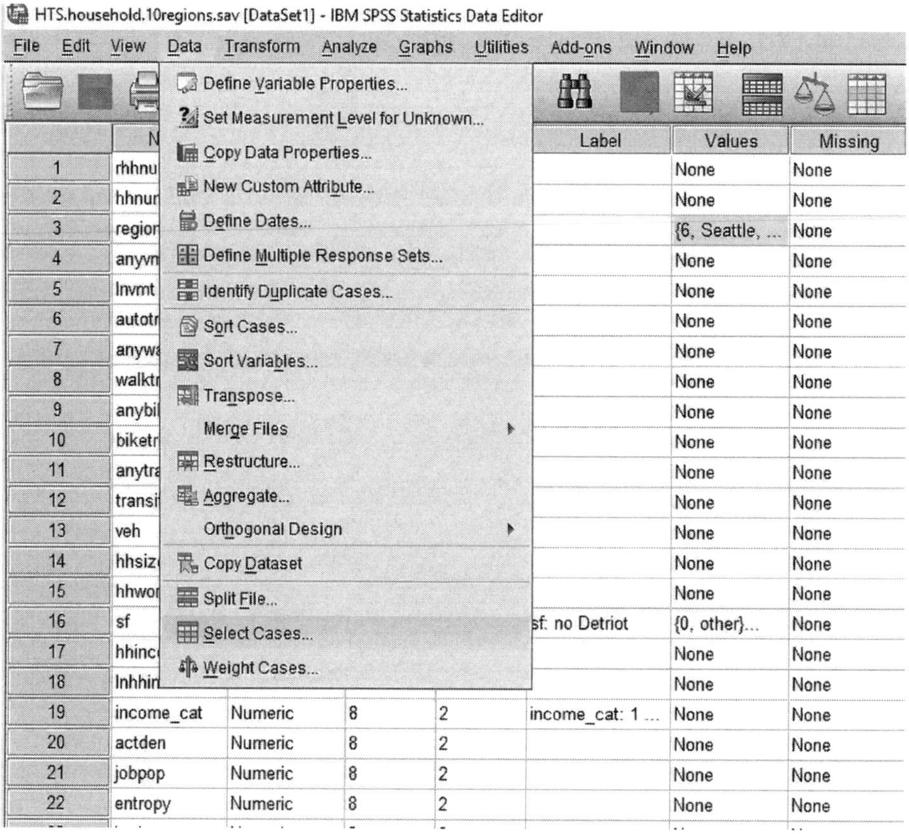

Figure 10.4 "Select Cases" Under "Data" Menu

Difference of Means Tests (T-Tests) 183

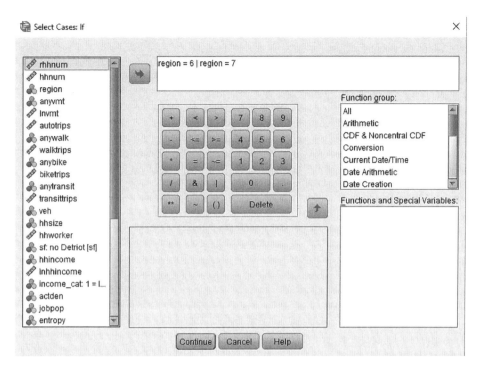

Figure 10.5 "Select cases: If" Window

Check Assumptions

Our first task is to confirm whether the data follow the independent samples *t*-test's assumptions of normality and equal variance.

We will check normality of the data with a histogram. Select "graph" in menu, "Legacy Dialogs," and then "Histogram" (Figure 10.7).

Insert our dependent variable, *lnvmt* (a log-transformed VMT variable), into the "Variable" box, click "Display normal curve." Add the *region* variable into the "Rows" box. The last step helps to draw histograms by region. This is important because the *t*-test assumes a normal distribution of the dependent variable for each category. See Figure 10.8.

The histogram shows that the dependent variable *lnvmt* is approximately normally distributed in both regions, which meets the assumption of *t*-test (Figure 10.9).

The variance of the dependent variable needs to be similar between two groups, which we can evaluate with the *t*-test test result that follows.

It is possible that samples have unequal variance and non-normal distribution. This violates both of the preceding assumptions, but all is not lost. SPSS gives results for samples with both equal and unequal variances. And there are actually two courses of action to deal with data that are not normally distributed.

The first alternative is to ignore the non-normal distribution, but this only works for large samples. The *t*-test is relatively insensitive to skewed or otherwise non-normal

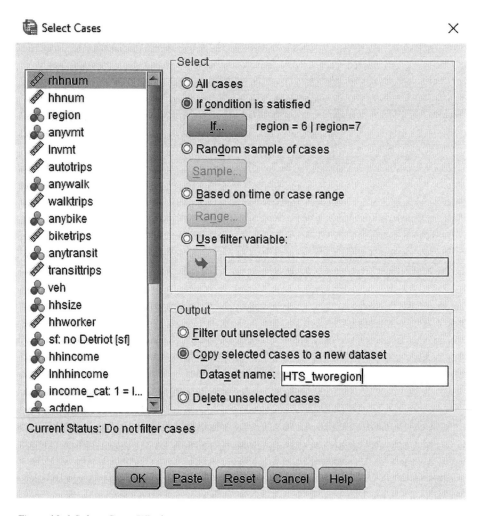

Figure 10.6 Select Cases Window

distribution for sample sizes larger than 40 or 50 (Elliott & Woodward, 2007). With more than 3,000 cases in each region, our data safely meet this benchmark. The second—and probably better—alternative is to conduct a nonparametric test such as the Mann-Whitney *u*-test. It is essentially a Student's *t*-test for nonparametric data— that is, non-normal data.

Null Hypothesis

Our null hypothesis, H_0, is that any observed differences in mean VMT in the two regions are due to chance, rather than regional conditions. The alternative hypothesis, H_1, is that on average, people in Seattle drive more than those in Kansas City, or

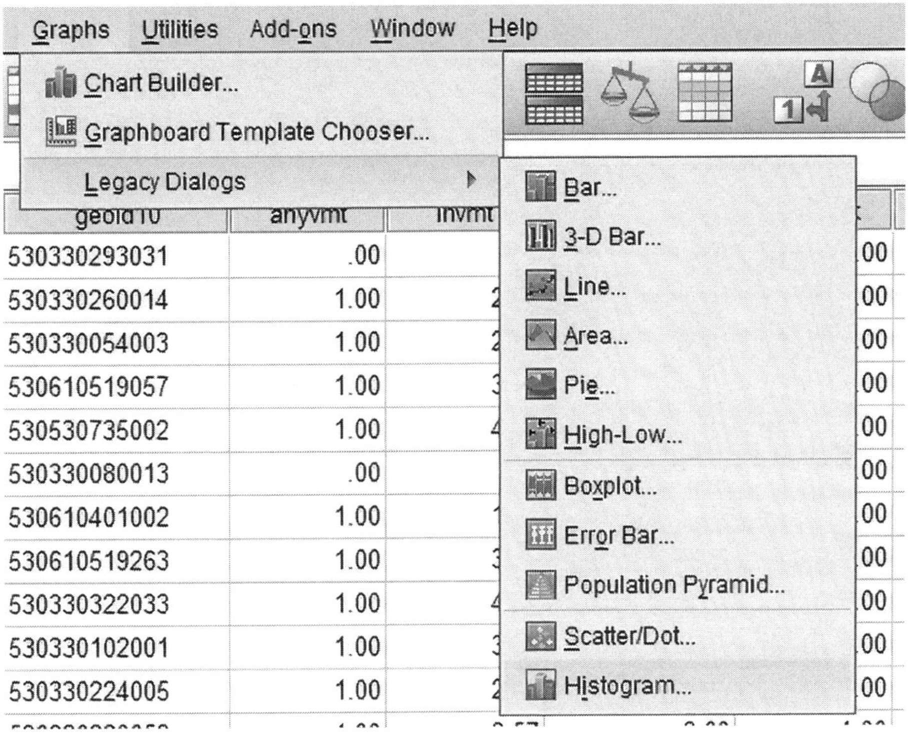

Difference of Means Tests (T-Tests) 185

Figure 10.7 Find Histogram Window From Main Menu

vice versa. The Independent samples *t*-test quantifies the likelihood that differences between the mean VMT are due to chance.

Independent Samples T-Test

To conduct an independent samples *t*-test, first select "Analyze" in the menu, choose "Compare Means," and select "Independent-Samples *T*-Test" (Figure 10.10).

Once the window opens, select the dependent variable *lnvmt*, which is a continuous variable, and add it to "Test Variable(s)" box (Figure 10.11).

Next, we need to select an independent variable. Select *region*, which has two categories, from the variable list and move it to the box labeled "Grouping Variable." When the grouping variable has been selected, the "Define Groups" button will become active. This is the place we enter what numeric codes we assigned to the two groups. We coded Seattle as 6 and Kansas City as 7, so type them into the boxes. If your grouping variable has more than two groups or is continuous, you can specify a cut point in which all cases greater than or equal to that value are assigned to one group and other values below the cut point are assigned to the second group (Figure 10.12).

When you have defined the groups, click on "Continue" to return to the *t*-test window. Then click "OK" to run the *t*-test (Figure 10.13).

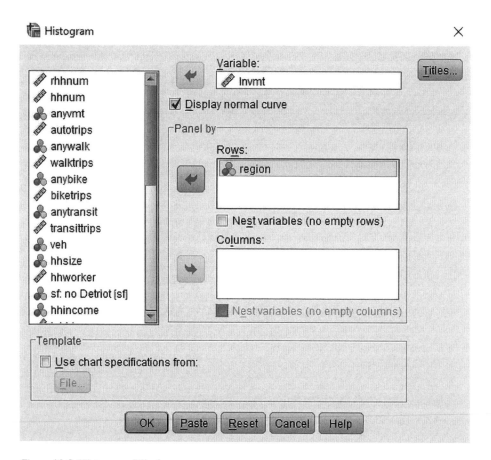

Figure 10.8 Histogram Window

Results

The results of the independent samples *t*-test contain two tables. The first table, Table 10.1, provides summary statistics: sample size, mean, standard deviation, and estimated standard deviation of the sample mean. On average, Seattle residents generated more VMT than Kansas City residents did.

Table 10.2 provides the main test statistics. The first thing to check is whether the variances are equal. Look at the results for "Levene's Test for Equality of Variances" and its *p* value (given in the "Sig." column). The null hypothesis of Levene's test is that the variances of two groups are equal. In our example, the *p* value is less than .05, meaning that the variances between the two samples are not equal. Therefore, the appropriate *t*-test is the one with unequal variance assumed, the second row in the table.

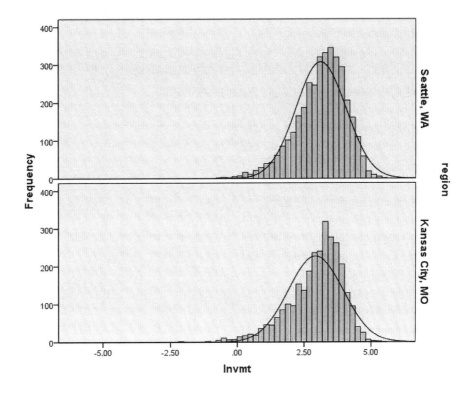

Figure 10.9 Histograms of Household VMT by Region (in Logarithm Format)

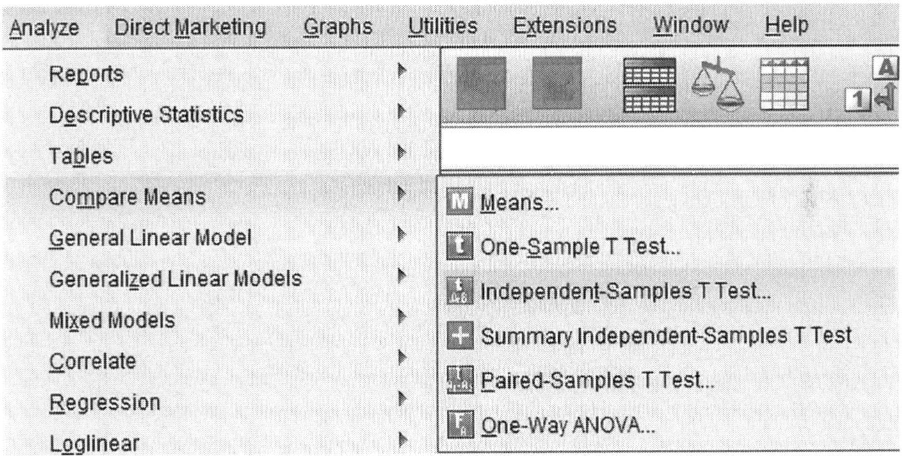

Figure 10.10 Find Independent Samples *t*-Test Window From Main Menu

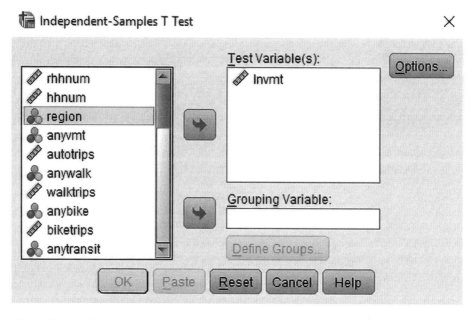

Figure 10.11 Independent Samples *t*-Test Window

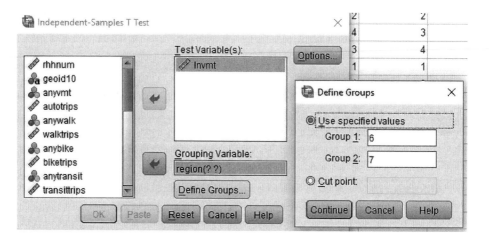

Figure 10.12 Define Groups Window

Then, we are ready to see t-statistic and the *p* value. The *t*-statistic is 7.948 and its *p*-value is less than 0.001. Thus, the null hypothesis is rejected and we can conclude that, on average, people in Seattle drive more than those in Kansas City by 0.19 miles per capita (see the "Mean Difference" section). The 95 percent confidence interval of the mean difference—0.146 to 0.242—also confirms the result. The interval does not

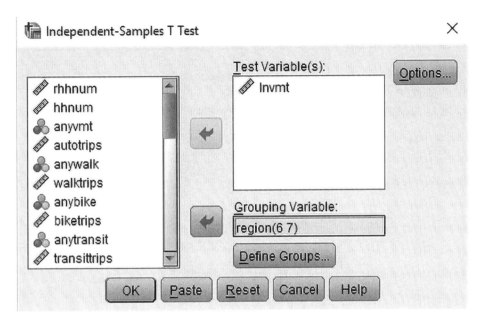

Figure 10.13 The Independent Samples *t*-Test Window Is Ready to Run

Table 10.1 The Summary Statistics of *t*-Test

Group Statistics

	Region	N	Mean	Std. Deviation	Std. Error Mean
lnvmt	Seattle, WA	3,576	3.1254	0.92742	0.01551
	Kansas City, MO	2,897	2.9312	1.01600	0.01888

include zero, so we can say that there is a statistically significant difference in average household VMT per capita between two regions.

One more thing: SPSS provides only the two-tailed significance value; if you want the one-tailed significance (i.e., you hypothesize that one group has a higher mean than the other group's mean), you can just divide the *p* value by 2.

In R

Figures 10.14 and 10.15 show an example of one-tail and two-tail *t*-tests in R. After reading the SPSS data file, we create a subset of the data for two regions—Seattle and Kansas City—to compare VMT (*lnvmt*) between two cities. Two histograms are first drawn, followed by the two-tail *t*-test and one-tail *t*-test, both of which results are statistically significant at $p < .05$ level.

Table 10.2 The Result of Independent Samples *t*-test

Independent Samples Test

Invmt	*Levene's Test for Equality of Variances*		*t-Test for Equality of Means*							
	F	*Sig.*	*T*	*df*	*Sig. (2-tailed)*	*Mean Difference*	*Std. Error Difference*	*95% Confidence Interval of the Difference*		
								Lower	*Upper*
Equal variances assumed	12.143	0.000	8.025	6471	0.000	0.19418	0.02420	0.14675	0.24162
Equal variances not assumed			7.948	5,934.694	0.000	0.19418	0.02443	0.14629	0.24208

```
#DIFFERENCE OF MEANS TESTS (T-TESTS)
library(foreign)
hts<-read.spss("HTS.household.10regions.sav",to.data.frame=TRU
E)
hts_two<-hts[which(hts$region=="Seattle, WA"|hts$region=="Kans
as City, MO"),]
hist(hts_two$lnvmt[which(hts_two$region=="Seattle, WA")])
```

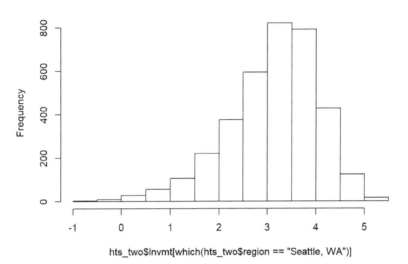

```
hist(hts_two$lnvmt[which(hts_two$region=="Kansas City, MO")])
```

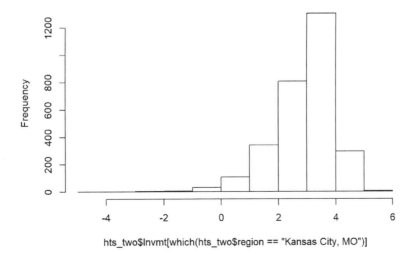

Figure 10.14 Reading SPSS Data, Selecting Two Regions, and Drawing Histograms: R Script and Outputs

```
t.test(hts_two$lnvmt~hts_two$region)  #two-tail t-test
```

```
##
##   Welch Two Sample t-test
##
## data:  hts_two$lnvmt by hts_two$region
## t = 7.9485, df = 5934.7, p-value = 2.243e-15
## alternative hypothesis: true difference in means is not equ
al to 0
## 95 percent confidence interval:
##   0.1462916 0.2420764
## sample estimates:
##      mean in group Seattle, WA mean in group Kansas City, MO
##                       3.125424                      2.931240
```

```
t.test(hts_two$lnvmt~hts_two$region,alternative="greater") #on
e-tail t-test
```

```
##
##   Welch Two Sample t-test
##
## data:  hts_two$lnvmt by hts_two$region
## t = 7.9485, df = 5934.7, p-value = 1.122e-15
## alternative hypothesis: true difference in means is greater
than 0
## 95 percent confidence interval:
##   0.1539933        Inf
## sample estimates:
##      mean in group Seattle, WA mean in group Kansas City, MO
##                       3.125424                      2.931240
```

Figure 10.15 One-Tail and Two-Tail *t*-tests: R Script and Outputs

Difference of Means Tests (T-Tests) 193

Planning Examples

Transit and VMT

The term "transit multiplier" refers to the idea that transit expansions can reduce vehicle miles traveled (VMT) by inducing more walk and bike trips around stations many times over the amount of driving shifted to transit directly. But like so many seemingly straightforward ideas, the devil is in the details, and the exact size of the multiplier is a topic of much debate in planning circles. Ewing and Hamidi (2014) used *t*-tests as part of a quasi-experimental study design to quantify the transit multiplier for an expansion of Portland's Westside Max light-rail line.

One of the interesting aspects of the study is the way the authors used *t*-tests to show causation. They employed a longitudinal, quasi-experimental design that compares household VMT along two different transportation corridors in Portland before and after the light-rail expansion. In this design, the expanded transit corridor functions as the treatment group, i.e., the sample group experiencing the change under study. The highway corridor functions as the control group. Before the light-rail expansion, the two corridors were comparable in terms of their built environments, socioeconomic variables, and levels of household VMT. But after the expansion (i.e., the treatment), the story changes.

Ewing and Hamidi (2014) found that the transit multiplier in this case was 3.04, which means that VMT along the expanded Westside line fell a total of three vehicle miles for every one vehicle-mile drop attributable to transit. The direct reduction due to transit comes from drivers switching modes to transit and associated reductions in VMT. The indirect reductions are primarily due to an increase in walking trips around stations and secondarily to shorter auto trips around stations, both linked to increased densities.

The authors use *t*-tests to confirm that travel behavior, as stated in local household travel diaries, differs significantly in the periods before and after the treatment (in 1994 and 2011, respectively) and that they do not differ between the two transportation corridors during the before period. Differences between the two corridors are indeed negligible in 1994. The only statistically significant difference is in the number of transit trips. (Surprisingly, travel-survey data show that households in the highway corridor actually took more transit trips in 1994 than households in the transit corridor.) But things get interesting following the treatment.

From 1994 to 2011, activity density (actden) within the transit corridor increased by nearly 100 percent thanks to rezoning for TOD and the light-rail expansion. Walk trips (wtrips) and transit trips (ttrips) within the corridor increased by 151 percent and 1,750 percent, respectively. While VMT increased slightly in the transit corridor, the rise was much smaller than in the highway corridor (22 percent versus 62 percent, respectively). Table 10.3 shows the differences between travel behavior in the transit corridor and the highway corridor in 2011 following the light-rail expansion. Note that differences between the two corridors in 2011 are significant at the 0.05 level or beyond when it comes to household employment (employment), the number of vehicles owned by a household (vehicles), activity density within a one-half-mile buffer (actden), household VMT (vmt), work trips (wtrips), transit trips (ttrips), and the number of person trips by automobile (atrips).

194   *David Proffitt*

Table 10.3 Difference of Means Test Results for Westside Max Corridor Versus Highway Corridor After LRT Expansion (2011)

	LRT	Control	t ratio	p value
hhsize	2.12	2.23	−1.11	0.27
employed	1.19	1.42	−3.52	<0.001
income (thousands)	74.30	78.97	−1.25	0.21
vehicles	1.67	1.85	−2.18	0.030
actden (thousands)	8.60	8.53	2.02	0.044
vmt	21.22	29.40	−3.68	<0.001
wtrips	2.16	1.53	2.21	0.018
btrips	0.11	0.24	−1.76	0.079
ttrips	0.85	0.50	2.83	0.005
atrips	6.31	8.09	−3.29	0.001
trips	10.80	10.87	−0.11	0.92
n (varies but max)	311	294		

As the statistical analyses in planning studies grow more and more sophisticated, the elegance of Ewing and Hamidi's study design stands out for its simplicity. The quasi-experimental approach allowed them to use simple, understandable techniques such as the t-test to confirm an important finding about transit multipliers.

Shrinking Cities

Planners' interest in the forces driving *shrinking cities* is relatively new for a field long obsessed with figuring out what makes cities grow. Hollander (2011) contributed to our understanding of shrinking cities by comparing quality of life in growing and shrinking cities. He used an independent samples t-test to answer his research question—how the group of shrinking cities differed from the group of growing cities in terms of perceptions of neighborhood quality.

Hollander compiled data on residents' perceptions of their neighborhood from the American Housing Survey and changes in population and occupied housing stock from the American Community Survey for 38 U.S. cities. The housing data showed which cities are shrinking, while the attitude surveys were used as proxies for *happiness*. The study looked at how these metrics changed from one American Community Survey period to another (1994–1998 and 1997–2007).

Just looking at the satisfaction scores, Hollander found "a broad spectrum of neighborhood quality scores across the cities, with no obvious trends or patterns connecting population decline and neighborhood quality" (p. 136). Therefore, the use of the t-test in this study was the classic application that proves the value of the method.

Hollander prepared the data by splitting neighborhood ratings into two groups, one for shrinking cities (n = 20) and another for growing cities (n = 18). Each of these groups also has two sets of observations, one for the first American Community Survey (ACS) period (1994–1998) and another for the second (1997–2007). Though it would be easy to run a matched pairs t-test in this case, Hollander was more interested in differences between the two groups than differences in one group over time. The independent samples t-test was therefore the method of choice.

The variable of interest to Hollander was the mean difference in neighborhood-satisfaction scores from the first period to the second between growing and shrinking cities. Specifically, he calculated the percent change in each city's satisfaction scores from the first ACS period to the second period, then compared the mean change from the shrinking-cities group to the growing-cities group. The results showed a statistically insignificant difference between them ($p = .503$) despite the statistically significant drops in both population and housing totals for the shrinking cities and wider variation among neighborhood quality scores for shrinking cities.

The lack of a difference in this case validated Hollander's hypothesis that much of the emphasis on negative aspects of shrinking cities is misguided. This study ends with a call for future research to better understand how smart decline might affect neighborhood change.

Conclusions

The difference of means *t*-test is a simple and powerful test of statistical significance. It answers the foundational question of hypothesis testing: Are two samples different enough that we can reject the assumption that variations are due only to chance? Understanding how *t*-tests work will give you greater insight into a number of other statistical tests, as well. ANOVA, most forms of regression, and even hierarchical linear models (all discussed in later chapters of this book and *Advanced Quantitative Research Methods For Urban Planners*) all use the t-statistic to measure significance. However, the elegance of the *t*-test means it is also easy to misuse.

Remembering two rules will help you avoid the common pitfalls of using *t*-tests. First, structure your study like an experiment. It is no accident that drug trials and other medical experiments are the most common use of the *t*-test today. Medical and other experimental investigators typically want to explore the difference between a test group and a control group. Planners often do the same thing, but if your research questions do not lend themselves to an experimental or quasi-experimental design, think long and hard before using difference of means to test your hypotheses. Second, cover your basics. Violating assumptions about minimum samples sizes, normal distribution, and matching paired samples can have serious consequences. Let the law of large numbers be your friend. Even a small amount of *fudging* these basic assumptions can lead to a big problem later on.

Works Cited

Brown, B. B., & Werner, C. M. (2011). The residents' benefits and concerns before and after a new rail stop: Do residents get what they expect? *Environment and Behavior, 43*(6), 789–806. http://doi.org/10.1177/0013916510392030

Elliott, A. C., & Woodward, W. A. (2007). Comparing one or two means using the *T*-test. In M. B. Crouppen (Ed.), *Statistical analysis quick reference guidebook: With SPSS examples* (pp. 47–76). Thousand Oaks, CA: Sage Publications.

Ewing, R., Chen, L., & Chen, C. (2013). Quasi-experimental study of traffic calming measures in New York City. *Transportation Research Record, 2364*(1), 29–35.

Ewing, R., & Hamidi, S. (2014). Longitudinal analysis of transit's land use multiplier in Portland (OR). *Journal of the American Planning Association, 80*(2), 123–137. http://doi.org/10.1080/01944363.2014.949506

Giannopoulou, K., Livada, I., Santamouris, M., Saliari, M., Assimakopoulos, M., & Caouris, Y. G. G. (2011). On the characteristics of the summer urban heat island in Athens, Greece. *Sustainable Cities and Society*, *1*(1), 16–28. http://doi.org/10.1016/j.scs.2010.08.003

Hollander, J. B. (2011). Can a city successfully shrink? Evidence from survey data on neighborhood quality. *Urban Affairs Review*, *47*(1), 129–141.

Raju, T. N. K. (2005). William Sealy Gosset and William A. Silverman: Two "students" of science. *Pediatrics*, *116*(3), 732–735. http://doi.org/10.1542/peds.2005-1134

Urdan, T. C. (2001). *Statistics in plain English*. Mahwah, NJ: Lawrence Erlbaum Associates, Inc.

Vogt, W. P., & Johnson, R. B. (2011). *Dictionary of statistics & methodology: A nontechnical guide for the social sciences* (4th ed.). Thousand Oaks, CA: Sage Publications.

11 Analysis of Variance (ANOVA)

Philip Stoker, Guang Tian, and Ja Young Kim

Method	Dependent Variable	Independent Variables	Test Statistics
Chi-Square	Categorical	Categorical	chi-square statistic
Difference of Means	Continuous	Categorical (two categories)	t-statistic
ANOVA	Continuous	Categorical (multiple categories)	F-statistic
Linear Regression	Continuous	Continuous (though can represent categorical)	t-statistic R2 statistic
Logistic Regression	Categorical (Dichtomous)	Continuous (though can represent categorical)	asymptotic t-statistic pseudo-R2 statistic
Poisson/Negative Binomial Regression	Count	Continuous (though can represent categorical)	Wald statistic pseudo-R2 statistic

Figure 11.0 ANOVA

Overview

Analysis of Variance, or ANOVA, compares the variance among and within many groups at one time. The test is therefore able to determine if the mean of a continuous variable depends on which group (given by the categorical variable) the individual case is in. So whether evaluating the spatial variation of green buildings across the country, or the effects of land use type on urban surface temperatures, ANOVA will help planners identify whether or not significant differences exist among multiple groups.

This chapter describes the conditions required to use ANOVA followed by a demonstration of how to conduct ANOVA. This chapter will also present two very different studies from the field of planning and show how researchers successfully applied ANOVA in a planning context.

Purpose

The ANOVA tests are inferential statistics utilized in hypothesis testing. In ANOVA, the null hypothesis proposes that there is no relationship between dependent and independent variables or, equivalently, no difference among three or more groups with respect to the dependent variable. The null hypothesis assumes that any relationship or difference observed is due to chance. Therefore, the alternative hypothesis is that the observed relationship or difference is real, that is not due to chance.

Several types of ANOVA tests exist, but the simplest is a one-way ANOVA. A one-way ANOVA tests the statistical significance of the difference of means among three or more groups on one continuous variable (Vogt, 2005). More specifically, ANOVA tests are used to find out if the mean of a continuous variable depends on a categorical variable. A continuous variable can be measured on an interval or ratio scale, and a categorical variable is measured on a nominal or ordinal scale, usually called categories or groups. If a categorical variable has only two values, then you can use a two-sample difference-of-means test (see Chapter 10). An ANOVA allows for three or more groups to be tested simultaneously.

When there are three or more groups, why not simply use difference-of-means t-tests for every pair of groups to test the null hypothesis? One reason is logistical. As the number of groups increases, the number of pairs of groups that would need to be tested becomes unwieldy. For example, with just four groups, there are six distinct pairs of groups requiring difference-of-means testing. With five groups, there are 10 pairs. You see the problem.

There is a subtler reason not to use difference-of-means t-tests with multiple groups—that is, an increase in the probability of committing a Type I error; rejecting a true null hypothesis (Devore, 2011). If the probability of committing a Type I error on a t-test is 0.05 and there are seven groups in the independent variable, the probability of making a Type I error is more than a 5 percent even if the null hypothesis is true. This is because consecutive t-tests increases the probability of having a Type I error each time you perform the test. In contrast, ANOVA simultaneously examines the differences among any number of groups while holding the Type 1 error at the chosen significance level (usually 0.05). In fact, ANOVA may be considered an extension of t-test holding Type I error constant (Rutherford, 2001).

History

ANOVA test was originally developed by the statistician Sir Ronald Fisher in the 1920s as he explored the effects of different fertilizers on the yields of crops. Fisher used several different fertilizers on one species of crop, and then observed the different yields. He thought that if there was more variability between yields with different fertilizer treatments than within the yields of the same fertilizer treatment, then that would be evidence against the null hypothesis that the fertilizers had the same effect (Bingham & Fry, 2010). In other words, Fisher was comparing the effects of fertilizers by analyzing the variability of crop yields, hence analysis of variance.

Since its initial application, ANOVA has been widely used in the fields of business and economics (Anderson, Sweeney, & Williams, 2003), social and health research (Argyrous, 2000), engineering (Devore, 2011), as well as planning (Ewing, Haliyur, & Page, 1994; Handy, 1996, Cidell & Beata, 2009; Rinner & Hussain, 2011). Practitioners and researchers in each of these fields have used ANOVA to test and identify the differences among multiple groups.

Mechanics

To determine whether differences in means among groups are significant, ANOVA calculates an F-statistic, which was named after Fisher. A large F-statistic is evidence against the null hypothesis, since it indicates that there is greater difference between groups than within groups (Bingham & Fry, 2010).

The actual calculation of the F-statistic is as follows. The F-statistic is the ratio of between group variance to within group variance.

$$\text{Within Groups Variance} = \Sigma \frac{\Sigma (X_{ij} - \mu_j)^2}{n - k}$$

$$\text{Between Groups Variance} = \Sigma \frac{\Sigma n_j (\mu_j - \mu_t)^2}{k - 1}$$

$$\text{ANOVA F statistic} = \frac{\text{Between Groups Variance}}{\text{Within Groups Variance}}$$

As you can see from Figure 11.1, the probability distributions of the F-statistic are such that you would not expect to get large values strictly by chance, although it depends on the degrees of freedom.

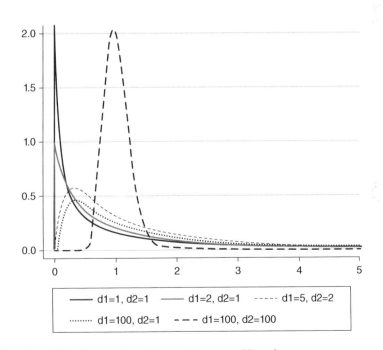

Figure 11.1 The F-Distribution for Different Degrees of Freedom

Assumptions

There are four assumptions that must be met to use the ANOVA test.

First, all observations should be independent of one another. This means that there is no relationship or dependency between the observations within groups or between groups, and the data are from random selection.

Second, there should be no significant outlying values of the dependent variable. The outliers can be detected by using a scatter plot or a box plot.

Third, every group being compared must be approximately normally distributed with respect to the dependent variable. Plotting the data in a histogram is one easy way to determine if the data are approximately normal and will reveal the overall distribution and normality of data. ANOVA tests can handle some non-normality, but if the data are heavily skewed by severe outliers, ANOVA is inappropriate (Devore, 2011). Put simply, ANOVA is a parametric test.

The last assumption that must be met is that the variance of each group in the dependent variable is approximately equal. Therefore, the researcher must calculate the variance for each group first. If variances are approximately equal, then an ANOVA test can proceed, but if the variances are not, a non-parametric test may be more appropriate.

Interpreting Results

When you get results from the one-way ANOVA test, you can first check the F-statistic and the significant level of the p-value to determine whether to accept or reject the null hypothesis.

Once the results of ANOVA determine that differences exist, post-hoc tests identify which group means differ and which do not between or within groups. Post-hoc tests are either range tests or pair-wise multiple comparisons. Range tests identify similar subsets of means that are not different from each other, while pair-wise multiple comparisons test the difference between each pair of means and identify which group means are different compared to each other. When deciding which post-hoc test to use, the variance between groups must either be assumed to be equal or assumed not equal (SPSS Inc, 2011).

Step by Step

Now we will estimate a one-way ANOVA test using the UZA dataset (UZA.sav) in SPSS. The standard steps for a one-way ANOVA test are as follows:

1. Ensure the assumptions of ANOVA.
2. The dependent variable is a continuous variable, and there are three or more categories for the independent variable.
3. Propose the null hypothesis: there is no difference among the groups.
4. Conduct a one-way ANOVA.
5. Interpret the results, paying particular attention to the F-statistic and its associated level of significance. Reject the null hypothesis if the F-statistic is large, and the p-value is lower than the determined confidence level.

Analysis of Variance (ANOVA) 201

6. Conduct post-hoc tests to identify where the differences arise. Choose the post-hoc test based on whether or not variance is equal among groups.

Let's assume that we are investigating transit ridership in urbanized areas in the U.S. and particularly interested in seeing if certain regions (among Northeast, Midwest, South, and West) have more transit passenger miles per capita than others do.

Check Assumptions

We first need to check if the assumptions for using ANOVA are met. Having confirmed that the data represents all urbanized areas with populations over 200,000 in the U.S., there is no selection bias and we regard them as independent for this exercise.

We can check for outliers by using the boxplot graph. Select "Graphs" on the menu, and choose "Legacy Dialogs" and then, select "Boxplot" (Figure 11.2).

The default Boxplot window is shown in Figure 11.3, and you can click "Define."

Then, select the variable *lntpm* from the left list of variables and put it in "Variable" box. *lntpm* is the natural logarithm of the annual transit passenger miles per capita for each urbanized area. We use a log transformation to reduce the effect of outliers and have a normal distribution of the dependent variable.

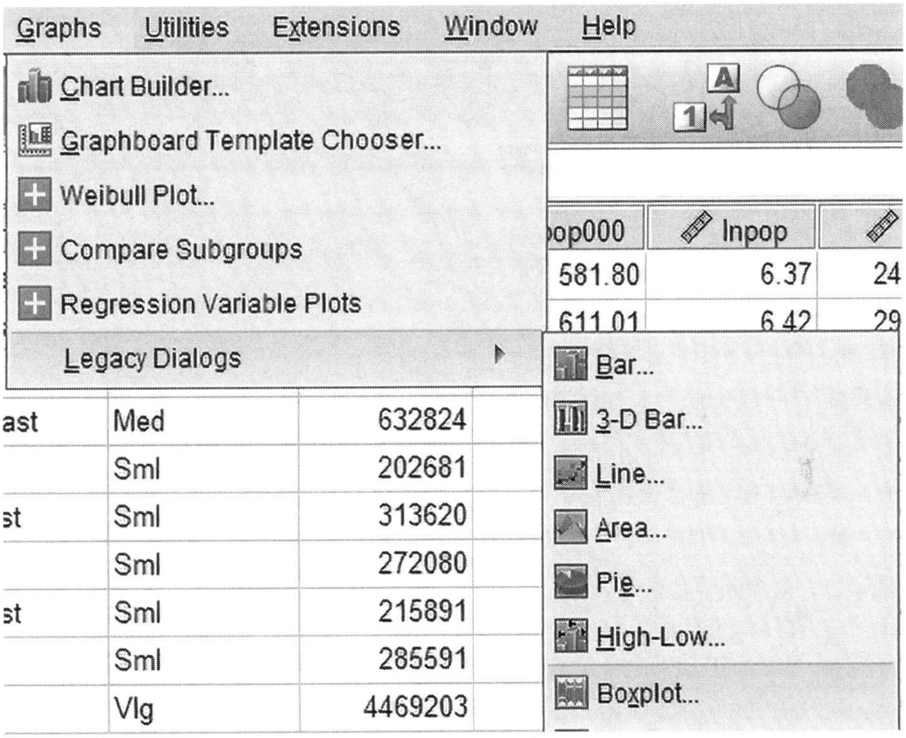

Figure 11.2 Find Boxplot From the Main Menu

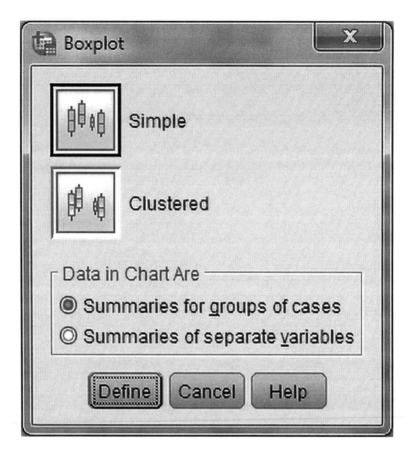

Figure 11.3 Choose a Plot Type in Boxplot Window

Then, put *region* in the Category Axis tab. The *region* is Census Regions having four values—Northeast, Midwest, South, and West. Then click "OK" (Figure 11.4).

The boxplot shows that there are only a few outliers in our data (Figure 11.5). Circles represent mild outliers and stars represent extreme outliers. The three outliers are #28 (Chicago, IL-IN), #84 (Lorain-Elyria, OH), and #88 (McAllen, TX).

We need to be cautious about dealing with outliers. In this exercise, we will drop three outliers. To remove a data case, right-click the row id (in this case, 28—Chicago, IL-IN) and select "Cut" (Figure 11.6). Repeat it for Lorain-Elyria, Ohio, and McAllen, Texas. Note that after you remove #28 Chicago, the row id for #84 (Lorain-Elyria, OH) is changed to #83. An important caveat: Whenever you modify the dataset, always save it as a new file (e.g., UZA_noThreeOutliers.sav). As a result, a total of 157 UZAs comes down to 154.

Now, we will check normality of the data with a histogram. Select "Graphs" in menu, "Legacy Dialogs," and then, "Histogram." See Figure 11.7.

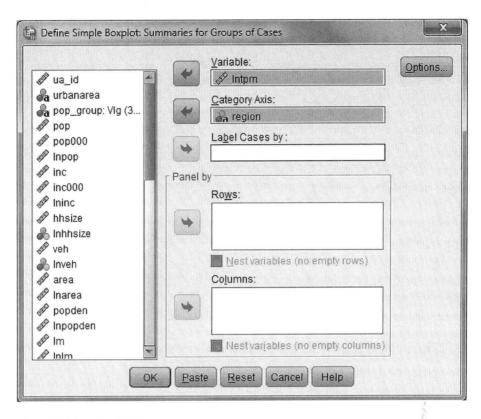

Figure 11.4 Boxplot Window

Insert the variable *lntpm* in the Variable tab, check the box for Display normal curve, and then, click "OK" (Figure 11.8).

The histogram shows that the dependent variable *lntpm* is almost normally distributed, which meets the assumption of ANOVA (Figure 11.9).

The last assumption is homogeneity of variance, that is the variance needs to be same across the groups. We can evaluate this with the one-way ANOVA test result below.

Null Hypothesis

We propose the null hypothesis: that there is no difference in transit passenger miles among the different geographic regions in the United States. An alternative hypothesis will be that transit passenger miles vary across the regions.

One-Way ANOVA Test

To conduct a one-way ANOVA test, first, select "Analyze" in the menu, choose "Compare Means," and select "One-Way ANOVA" (Figure 11.10).

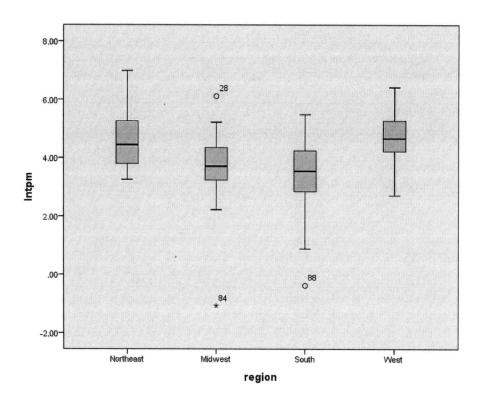

Figure 11.5 The Result of Boxplot

23	13375	Canton, OH	2	4	sml
24	13510	Cape Coral, FL	3	4	sml
25	15508	Charleston-North Ch	3	3	med
26	15670	Charlotte, NC-SC	3	2	lrg
27	15832	Chattanooga, TN-GA	1	4	sml
28		Chicago, IL-IN	2	2	vlg
29	Cut	Cincinnati, OH-KY-I	2	2	lrg
30	Copy	Cleveland, OH	2	2	lrg
31	Paste	Colorado Springs, C	4	3	med
32	Clear	Columbia, SC	3	4	sml
33	Insert Cases	Columbus, GA-AL	3	4	sml
34	19234	Columbus, OH	2	2	lrg
35	19504	Concord, CA	4	3	med
36	20287	Corpus Christi, TX	2	4	sml

Figure 11.6 Delete a Case by Right-Clicking the Row ID

Analysis of Variance (ANOVA) 205

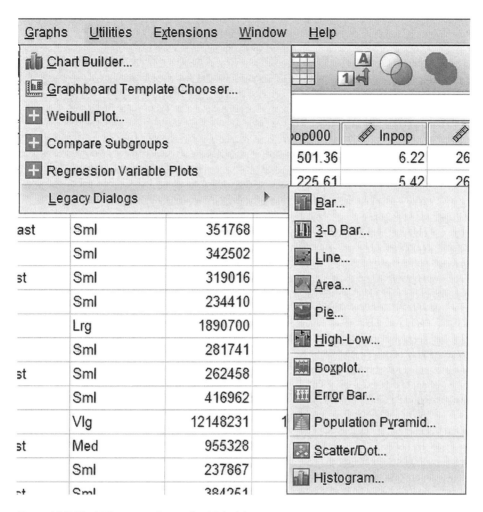

Figure 11.7 Find Histogram From the Main Menu

We need to put *lntpm* (a continuous dependent variable) into the "Dependent List" and insert *region* (a categorical independent variable) into the "Factor" box (Figure 11.11).

Then, select "Post Hoc" box on the right side. In the new window, check the boxes on "Bonferroni" and "Tamhane's T2," and click "Continue" (Figure 11.12).

Now you come back to the ANOVA setting window. Select "Options" box below the "Post Hoc" box you clicked previously. In another new window, check "Descriptive" and "Homogeneity of variance test" in Statistics, and "Means plot." Then, click "Continue" (Figure 11.13).

Lastly, select "Okay" to get the results of ANOVA.

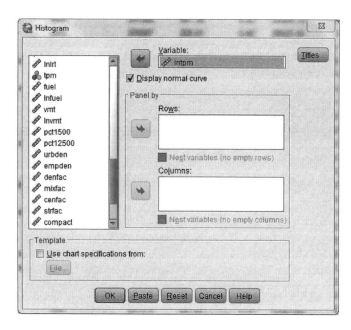

Figure 11.8 Histogram Window

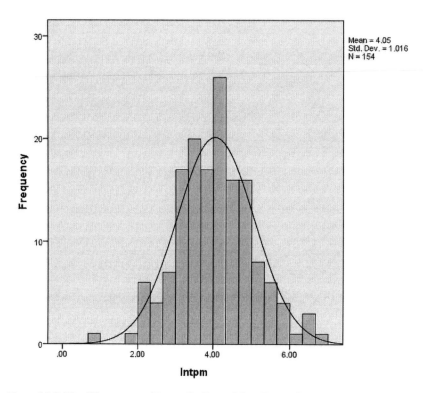

Figure 11.9 The Histogram of *lntpm* (in Logarithm Format)

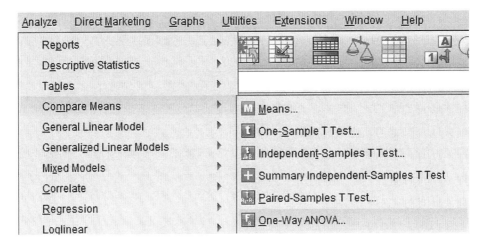

Figure 11.10 Find One-Way ANOVA Test From the Main Menu

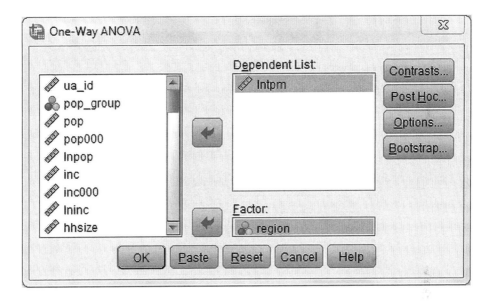

Figure 11.11 One-Way ANOVA Window

Results

The results of the test are presented in the output window. To know whether the equal variance assumption is met or not, we need to look at the "Test of Homogeneity of Variances" in Table 11.1. Similar to the "Levene's Test for Equality of Variances" for *t*-test, the null hypothesis is that the variances of different groups are equal. In

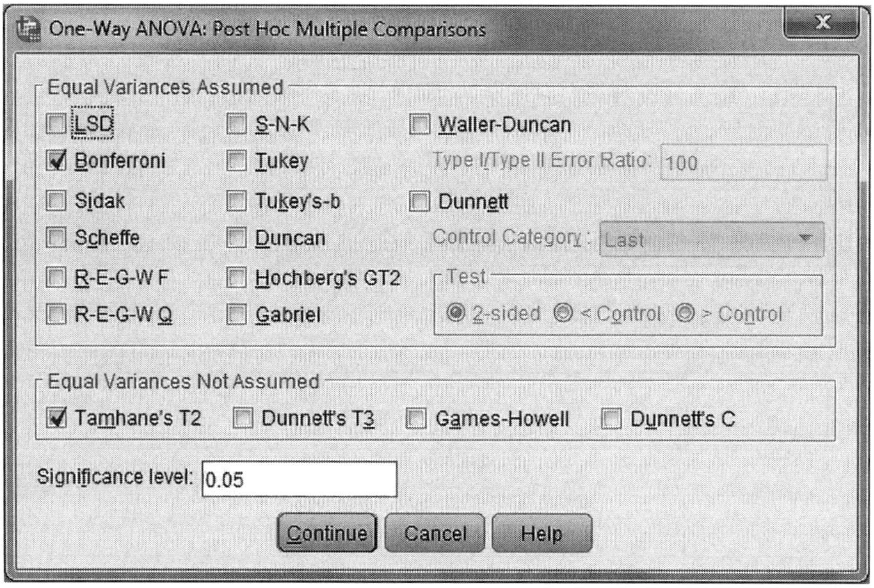

Figure 11.12 Post Hoc Window

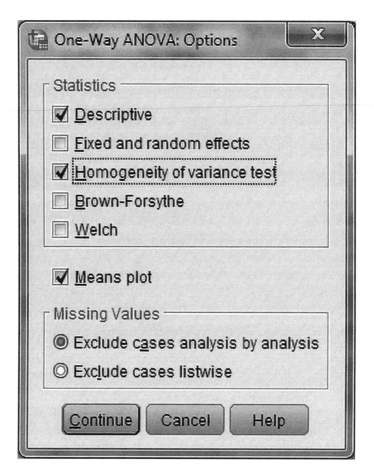

Figure 11.13 Option Window

our example, the p value is higher than .05, meaning that we cannot reject the null hypothesis, and the variances between the four regions are equal.

Now let's look at the ANOVA test result (Table 11.2). The row "Between Groups" shows the measures of variance among the different regions, while the row "Within Groups" shows the measures of variance within each region. The "Sum of Squares" is the result of adding together the squares of the deviation scores. The column "df" represents the degrees of freedom and tells us how much data were used to calculate the particular statistic. The "Mean Square" is the measure of variance, and the "F" statistic is the ratio of between-group variance to the within group variance. Finally, the "Sig." column is the p-value of the F-distribution for the specified degrees of freedom (Vogt, 2005).

The most important values are the F-statistic and the associated level of significance. The F-statistic is high enough, which indicates that the variance between groups is higher than the variance within group. The significance level confirms that the difference among regions is statistically significant at $p < .001$ level. Thus, we can conclude that there is a statistically significant difference in transit passenger miles among four census regions.

Post-Hoc Test

Now that a difference has been established, we are interested in identifying which region or regions are different from which others. The post-hoc tests show the group-wise differences.

The post-hoc test runs multiple comparisons between transit passenger miles for each region compared to the others, one region at a time. Such analysis allows the researcher to identify exactly where the differences in groups arise. The results of post-hoc test include both Bonferroni and Tamhane tests. The Bonferroni post-hoc test is appropriate when equal variances are assumed, whereas the Tamhane is generally appropriate when equal variances are not assumed (see Huck (2008) for a

Table 11.1 The Result of One-Way ANOVA (1)

Test of Homogeneity of Variances

lntpm

Levene Statistic	df1	df2	Sig.
1.446	3	150	0.232

Table 11.2 The Result of One-Way ANOVA (2)

ANOVA

lntpm

	Sum of Squares	df	Mean Square	F	Sig.
Between Groups	38.257	3	12.752	15.975	.000
Within Groups	119.738	150	0.798		
Total	157.995	153			

210 *Philip Stoker, Guang Tian, and Ja Young Kim*

detailed description about the post-hoc tests). In this exercise, we choose the Bonferroni test because of the above-mentioned "Test of Homogeneity of Variances" result.

Interpreting these results is made easy by SPSS, which places an asterisk mark "*" by values where the mean difference between two groups is statistically significant at the $p = .05$ level (Table 11.3). Alternately, the "Sig." column indicates the p values. We can see that the mean differences in transit passenger miles are significant in almost all region pairs except Northeast-West and Midwest-South pairs.

In addition to post-hoc results, the means plots can help us to compare the mean differences between the regions easily and visually. UZAs in the Northeast and West regions have higher transit usage than those in the Midwest and South regions (Figure 11.14).

Now we have statistical evidence that the mean transit passenger miles are significantly different among regions and have identified where those differences exist. You may go further to explore how and why these differences exist in future studies.

In R

Figures 11.15 through 11.17 show an R script to run an ANOVA analysis. We first start by drawing a boxplot to graphically explore the distribution of transit passenger miles (*lntpm*) across four Census regions. Then, three outliers are detected using an outcome value from the *boxplot* function. After removing these outliers, Figure 11.17 shows a script to run ANOVA test (*aov* function), followed by Bartlett test of homogeneity of variance (*bartlett.test* function) and a post-hoc test with pairwise comparisons (*TukeyHSD* function).

Planning Examples

Urban Heat Islands

In a study that explores the relationship between land use and the urban heat island effect, Claus Rinner and Mushtaq Hussain provide an excellent example of how urban planners can utilize ANOVA to identify significant differences among groups.

The urban heat island (UHI) effect refers to the tendency of urban areas to have higher surface temperatures in comparison to their rural surroundings. You can imagine that it would be warmer to stand in a parking lot on a hot summer day than it is to stand in a park. The UHI effect simply expands this observation to the city scale; the surface temperature in an urban environment is higher than in a natural setting.

High temperatures in urban centers have led to serious impacts on human health, including sunburn, heat exhaustion, heat rash, and mortality (Smoyer-Tomic, Kuhn, & Hudson, 2003; Pengelly et al., 2007). Extreme heat waves can be linked to large numbers of deaths in urban environments; the heat wave in Chicago in 1995 killed 500 people over five days, and nearly 70,000 people died of heat-related illnesses in 16 European countries in 2003 (Robine et al., 2008). These past events, coupled with the potential of climate change to increase extreme temperatures, make it important for urban planners to explore the association between different types of urban land uses and surface temperatures.

Table 11.3 The Result of Bonferroni and Tamhane Post-Hoc Test

Multiple Comparisons

Dependent Variable: lntpm

	(I) region	(J) region	Mean Difference (I-J)	Std. Error	Sig.	95% Confidence Interval	
						Lower Bound	Upper Bound
Bonferroni	Northeast	Midwest	0.82955*	0.24662	0.006	0.1702	1.4889
		South	1.08413*	0.22513	0.000	0.4822	1.6861
		West	−0.03637	0.24662	1.000	−0.6958	0.6230
	Midwest	Northeast	−0.82955*	0.24662	0.006	−1.4889	−0.1702
		South	0.25458	0.18836	1.000	−0.2490	0.7582
		West	−0.86592*	0.21358	0.000	−1.4370	−0.2949
	South	Northeast	−1.08413*	0.22513	0.000	−1.6861	−0.4822
		Midwest	−0.25458	0.18836	1.000	−0.7582	0.2490
		West	−1.12050*	0.18836	0.000	−1.6241	−0.6169
	West	Northeast	0.03637	0.24662	1.000	−0.6230	0.6958
		Midwest	0.86592*	0.21358	0.000	0.2949	1.4370
		South	1.12050*	0.18836	0.000	0.6169	1.6241
Tamhane	Northeast	Midwest	0.82955*	0.26287	0.021	0.0905	1.5686
		South	1.08413*	0.26184	0.001	0.3482	1.8201
		West	−0.03637	0.27532	1.000	−0.8035	0.7308
	Midwest	Northeast	−0.82955*	0.26287	0.021	−1.5686	−0.0905
		South	0.25458	0.16849	0.579	−0.1991	0.7082
		West	−0.86592*	0.18877	0.000	−1.3780	−0.3539
	South	Northeast	−1.08413*	0.26184	0.001	−1.8201	−0.3482
		Midwest	−0.25458	0.16849	0.579	−0.7082	0.1991
		West	−1.12050*	0.18733	0.000	−1.6266	−0.6144
	West	Northeast	0.03637	0.27532	1.000	−0.7308	0.8035
		Midwest	0.86592*	0.18877	0.000	0.3539	1.3780
		South	1.12050*	0.18733	0.000	0.6144	1.6266

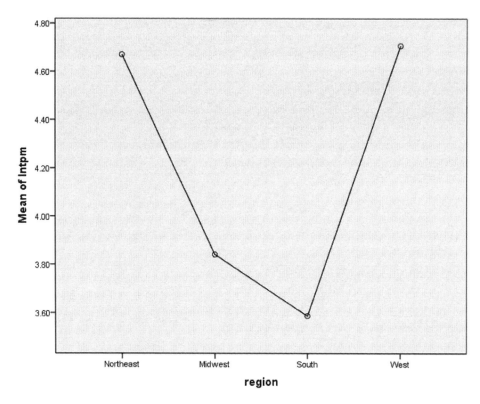

Figure 11.14 The Means Plots of *lntpm* Variable for Four Regions

The UHI effect is primarily caused by the built environment in urban areas, where natural areas are replaced with non-permeable and high-temperature surfaces of concrete and asphalt (Maloley, 2009). Factors such as urban form, thermal properties of buildings, and anthropogenic heat sources also affect the magnitude of the UHI (Taha, Hammer, & Akbari, 2002). Rinner and Hussain hypothesized that the mean temperature for different land uses would be different. To test this, these researchers performed a one-way ANOVA to identify the difference in mean surface temperatures between seven land use types in Toronto, Canada.

The researchers used two main datasets (Figure 11.18). The first was a GIS inventory of the Greater Toronto Area which included land use polygons for seven types of land uses: commercial, government and institutional, open area, parks and recreation, residential, resource and industrial, and water body. The second dataset was a thermal image which measured the surface temperatures with a resolution of 60-m (Figure 11.18).

You can see how an ANOVA test was appropriate; the researchers were working with a continuous dependent variable (surface temperature), and they were interested in the differences between multiple categories of an independent variable (land use type). The dependent variable was normally distributed within land use types, and the variance in the dependent variable among groups was comparable. Therefore a one-way ANOVA was an appropriate test for Rinner and Hussain.

Analysis of Variance (ANOVA) 213

```
#ANALYSIS OF VARIANCE (ANOVA)
library(foreign)
uza<-read.spss("UZA.sav",to.data.frame=TRUE)

boxplot<-boxplot(uza$lntpm~uza$region,main="UZA data",xlab="Re
gion",ylab="Transit passenger miles (log)")
```

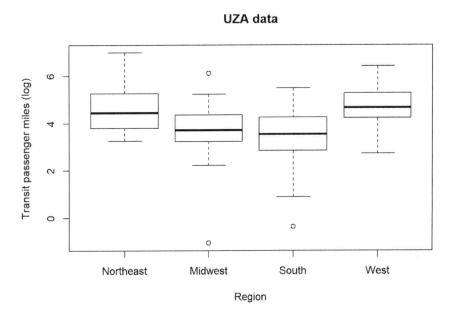

Figure 11.15 Reading SPSS Data and Drawing a Box Plot: R Script and Outputs

ANOVA results showed that the differences between the average temperatures of land use types were statistically significant. The researchers then performed a pairwise post-hoc test to identify where the significant differences existed, and they elected to use a Bonferonni test because variance between groups was equal. The Bonferroni post-hoc test revealed that only two pairs of land uses did not exhibit statistically significant differences: commercial relative to resource/industrial land uses, and residential land use in relation to government/institutional areas. Average temperatures were significantly higher in commercial and resource/industrial land uses, and lower for parks and recreational land uses as well as water bodies. While these findings were not unexpected, several implications for urban planners emerged.

Building codes could require that new industrial or commercial development include green spaces or reflective roofing. Alternate polices could support tree planting programs for residential front and backyards. These and similar policies

```
outliers = boxplot$out
uza[uza$lntpm %in% outliers,c(1,2)]
```

```
##    ua_id         urbanarea
## 28 16264 Chicago, IL-IN
## 84 51364 Lorain-Elyria, OH
## 88 52390 McAllen, TX
```

```
uza2<-uza[-c(28,84,88),]

hist(uza2$lntpm)
```

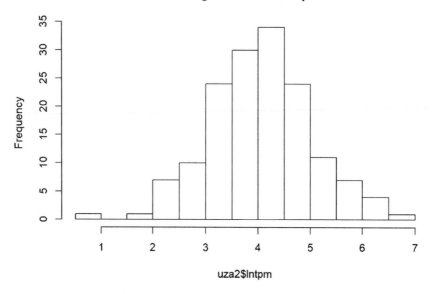

Figure 11.16 Detecting and Removing Outliers and Drawing a Histogram: R Script and Outputs

could promote heat mitigation as urban planners attempt to minimize the UHI effect.

Future research could investigate cities that have implemented policies to reduce the UHI effect, and could use ANOVA to compare average surface temperatures by land use type and by city in order to see if these policies were effective.

```
fit<-aov(uza2$lntpm~uza2$region)
summary(fit)
```

```
##              Df Sum Sq Mean Sq F value   Pr(>F)
## uza2$region   3  38.26  12.752   15.97 4.59e-09 ***
## Residuals   150 119.74   0.798
## ---
## Signif. codes:  0 '***' 0.001 '**' 0.01 '*' 0.05 '.' 0.1 '
' 1
```

```
bartlett.test(lntpm ~ region, data=uza2)
```

```
##
##  Bartlett test of homogeneity of variances
##
## data:  lntpm by region
## Bartlett's K-squared = 4.8494, df = 3, p-value = 0.1832
```

```
plot(TukeyHSD(fit))
```

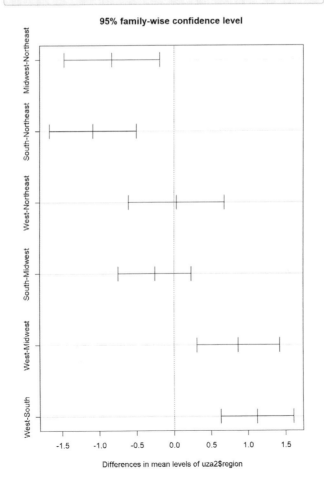

Figure 11.17 ANOVA Test and Post-Hoc Test: R Script and Outputs

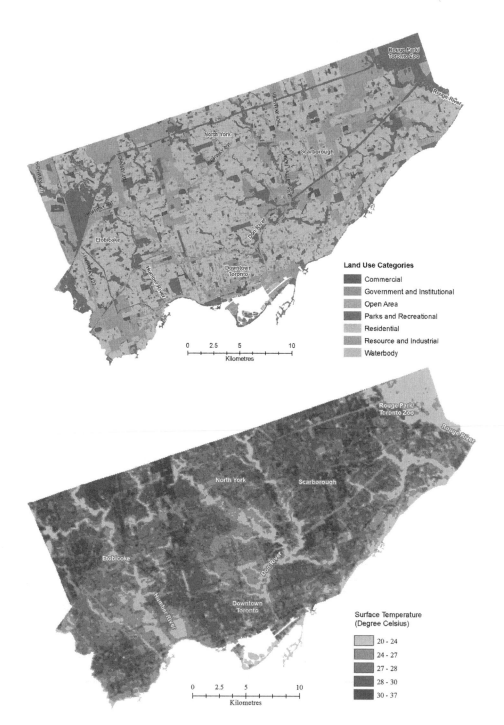

Figure 11.18 Land Use Type (top) and Thermal Imaging (bottom) of the City of Toronto
Source: Rinner & Hussain (2011)

Urban Form and Travel Behavior

In a classic article investigating the relationship between urban form and travel behavior, Susan Handy (1996) provides an example of how planners can use ANOVA to understand the relationship between urban form and travel behavior.

While many studies have attempted to link urban form and travel behavior, Handy hypothesized that high levels of accessibility would be associated with shorter average travel distances, greater variety in destinations, increased trip frequencies, and greater use of non-motorized modes of travel. To test these hypotheses, Handy selected two subregions within the San Francisco Bay Area that contained centers of retail activity: Silicon Valley and Santa Rosa. Within each subregion, she selected one traditional and one modern neighborhood. The traditional neighborhoods are characterized by turn-of-the-century urban form, with rectilinear street patterns, while the modern neighborhoods are characterized by post–World War II urban form, with curvilinear street patterns and numerous cul-de-sacs (Figure 11.19).

These four neighborhoods are the groups that Handy used to compare differences in accessibility and travel behavior. First, she compiled data on the demographics of the neighborhoods, the number and type of commercial establishments, and the type of road network for each neighborhood. Following the physical inventory, she conducted a telephone survey of the 100 residents of each neighborhood that asked residents about their travel choices, destination choices, mode choices, and trip frequencies, giving her continuous dependent variables to compare for her categorical independent variable, the neighborhood in which respondents resided. The data were found to be normally distributed, and variance between the groups was found to be equal. The ANOVA results indicated that there was significantly greater variation between the neighborhoods than within the neighborhoods, for the following multiple survey items: average number of supermarkets within two, five, and ten minutes, minimum time to supermarket, average travel time, percentage of people who walk to usual supermarket, average number of businesses visited last month, and average frequency of trips downtown. Before she could draw conclusions on these results though, she performed a second ANOVA test to ensure that variations in travel behavior were due to the urban form of the different neighborhoods rather than the different demographics in each area.

In the second ANOVA test, she categorized the households in each neighborhood based on the number of adults and children in the house and conducted ANOVA tests to see if the responses on the survey varied according to household type (rather than neighborhood), which they did. However, when she compared F-statistics and associated probabilities, the comparison revealed that for all but two travel behavior variables, neighborhood type had a greater effect on travel than did household type.

The findings of this study revealed not just that accessibility and travel behavior were linked as hypothesized, but different aspects of accessibility affect travel in different ways.

This study shows that ANOVA can be an effective method for investigating the built environment and travel behavior.

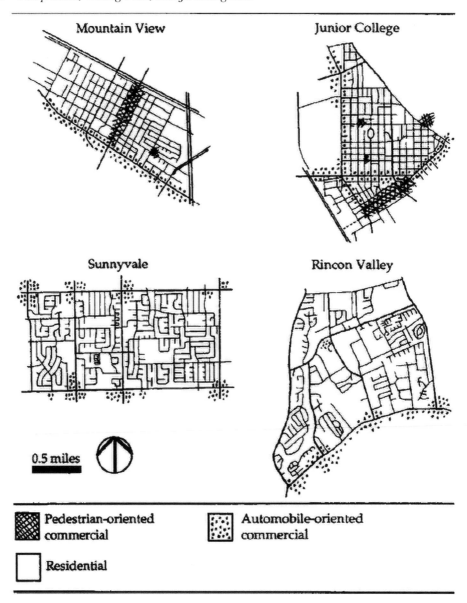

Figure 11.19 Street Networks and Land Use Distributions
Source: Handy (1996)

Conclusion

This chapter focused on ANOVA with its purpose, history, mechanics, and a practical demonstration to perform ANOVA in SPSS and R. Although this chapter is limited to one type of ANOVA, one-way ANOVA, it gives fundamental understandings of the method and allows the readers to go beyond to other types of ANOVA, such as two-way ANOVA where two categorical independent variables are simultaneously related to a continuous dependent variable or analysis of covariance (ANCOVA) where the dependent variable is related to one categorical and one continuous independent variable (Rutherford, 2001).

Works Cited

Anderson, D., Sweeney, D., & Williams, T. (2003). *Essentials of statistics for business and economics.* Mason, OH: Thomson South Western.

Argyrous, G. (2000). *Statistics for social and health research.* London: Sage Publications.

Bingham, N., & Fry, J. (2010). *Regression: Linear models in statistics.* London: Springer Undergraduate Mathematics Series.

Cidell, J., & Beata, A. (2009). Spatial variation among green building certification categories: Does place matter? *Landscape and Urban Planning, 91*(3), 142–151.

Devore, J. (2011). *Probability and statistics for engineering and the sciences.* Boston, MA: Brooks Cole.

Ewing, R., Haliyur, P., & Page, G. W. (1994). Getting around a traditional city, a suburban planned unit development (PUD), and everything in-between. *Transportation Research Record, 1466,* 53–62.

Fisk, W. J. (2002). How IEQ affects health productivity. *Journal-American Society of Heating Refrigerating and Airconditioning Engineer, 44,* 56–60.

Greene, J. (2005). *Learning to use statistical skills in psychology* (3rd ed.). Maidenhead: McGraw-Hill Education.

Handy, S. L. (1996). Understanding the link between urban form and nonwork travel behavior. *Journal of Planning Education and Research, 15*(3), 183–198.

Hansen, W. G. (1959). How accessibility shapes land use. *Journal of the American Planning Institute, 25,* 73–76.

Huck, S. (2008). *Reading statistics and research.* New York, NY: Pearson Publishing.

Maloley, M. (2009). Thermal remote sensing of urban heat island effects: Greater Toronto area. In *Enhancing resilience to climate change program.* Ottawa, ON: Natural Resources Canada.

McGraw Hill Construction. (2010). *Green outlook 2011: Green trends driving growth.* Retrieved from www.ecocosminc.com/img/2011_McGraw_Hill_Green_Outlook.pdf

Pengelly, L., Campbell, M., Chad, F., Fu, C., Gingrich, S., & Macfarlane, R. (2007). Anatomy of heat waves and mortality in Toronto: Lessons for public health protection. *Canadian Journal of Public Health, 98*(5), 364–368.

Rinner, C., & Hussain, M. (2011). Toronto's urban heat island—Exploring the relationship between land use and surface temperature. *Remote Sensing, 3*(6), 265. http://doi.org/10.3390/rs3061251

Robine, J., Cheung, S. K., Le Roy, S., Oyen, H. V., Griffith, C., Michel, J., & Herrmann, F. R. (2008). Death toll exceeded 70,000 in Europe during the Summer of 2003. *Comptes Rendus Biologies, 331*(2), 171–178. http://doi.org/10.1016/j.crvi.2007.12.001

Rutherford, A. (2001). *Introducing ANOVA and ANCOVA: A GLM approach.* London: Sage Publications.

Smoyer-Tomic, K. E., Kuhn, R., & Hudson, A. (2003). Heat wave hazards: An overview of heat wave impacts in Canada. *Natural Hazards, 28*(2–3), 463–485.

Sprinthall, R. (2003). *Basic statistical analysis.* Trenton, NJ: A and B Publishing.

SPSS. (2011). *SPSS base 16.0 for Mac user's guide.* Chicago, IL: SPSS Inc.

Taha, H., Hammer, H., & Akbari, H. (2002). *Meteorological and air quality impacts of increased urban surface albedo and vegetative cover in the greater Toronto area, Canada.* Berkeley, CA: Lawrence Berkeley National Laboratory.

Vogt, P. (2005). *Dictionary of statistics and methodology: A nontechnical guide for the social sciences* (3rd ed.). Thousand Oaks, CA: Sage Publications.

Walford, N. (2011). *Practical statistics for geographers and earth scientists.* Oxford: Wiley Blackwell.

12 Linear Regression

Keunhyun Park, Robin Rothfeder, Susan Petheram, Florence Buaku, Reid Ewing, and William H. Greene

Method	Dependent Variable	Independent Variables	Test Statistics
Chi-Square	Categorical	Categorical	chi-square statistic
Difference of Means	Continuous	Categorical (two categories)	t-statistic
ANOVA	Continuous	Categorical (multiple categories)	F-statistic
Linear Regression	Continuous	Continuous (though can represent categorical)	t-statistic R2 statistic
Logistic Regression	Categorical (Dichtomous)	Continuous (though can represent categorical)	asymptotic t-statistic pseudo-R2 statistic
Poisson/Negative Binomial Regression	Count	Continuous (though can represent categorical)	Wald statistic pseudo-R2 statistic

Figure 12.0 Linear Regression

Overview

From birds and butterflies to street widths and urban sprawl, linear regression explores the details of relationships. Researchers from many disciplines frequently use linear regression, evaluating two or more variables to understand how those variables are related—or, to reveal that no relationship exists.

In earlier chapters you learned how to use descriptive statistics, along with tools such as cross tabulation and correlation, to assess and describe the associations between variables. In this chapter you will learn about more sophisticated tools that can assist practicing planners and academics alike. With a firm understanding of linear regression, you will be able to interpret a great deal of quantitative research and will gain an important technique for your own research. It will also prepare you for subsequent chapters in a companion book, *Advanced Quantitative Research Methods for Urban Planners*, in which more advanced statistical methods are discussed that draw on concepts from linear regression.

Linear regression allows planning researchers to predict the value of one variable—known as the outcome, response, or *dependent variable*—from the value of one (in the case of simple regression) or more (in the case of multiple regression) other variables—known as predictor, explanatory, or *independent variables*. Because it enables a straightforward analysis of relationships between multiple, measurable constructs, linear regression is one of the most commonly used analytical methods in planning research. This chapter includes:

- A brief intellectual history of linear regression
- A general explanation of how and when planners use linear regression
- A detailed description of ordinary least squares (OLS) regression, including how to perform simple and multiple regression, how to evaluate model strength and reliability, and how to interpret model results, all using a simplified hypothetical planning example
- A realistic example of how to perform multiple regression for planning research, including screenshots from SPSS and R
- A discussion of the assumptions behind OLS linear regression, problems that violate these assumptions, ways to diagnose these problems, and potential solutions (all based on the realistic example)
- Case studies from the planning literature that utilize OLS regression

While textbooks on regression analysis are ubiquitous, the goal of this chapter is to make the method especially relevant and vivid for urban planners. Readers requiring more background detail should see the Works Cited at the end of this chapter.

Purpose

Linear regression is at the core of social statistics and is the inferential method researchers often look to first for describing and analyzing patterns in empirical data. The objective is to identify the straight-line (hence linear) equation that best fits the data in question (see Figure 12.0 to determine when to use regression in comparison to other inferential statistical methods). Valid application of linear regression depends on a main assumption: that the relationship between the dependent variable and independent variable(s) is linear. Other assumptions are listed, and dealt with, in the Step by Step section of this chapter.

Regression models can be used for explanation (to better understand what is happening in a relationship), prediction (to estimate the outcome of one event in relation to another), and testing hypotheses. Often regression models accomplish all three purposes. These findings can, in turn, help inform and influence planning and policy decisions. Before turning to the details of how to perform regression analysis, let us consider some examples of research that utilized linear regression for each of these purposes.

Explanation

Regression helps researchers explain the factors behind observed patterns by modeling the relationship between dependent and independent variables with a linear equation. If the model is explanatory, each independent variable is assessed by the degree to which its variation can account for the variation in the dependent variable's values.

In California, researchers were interested in discovering if the presence of particulates from pollution on urban sidewalks (the dependent variable) was related to traffic and land use factors (the independent variables) (Boarnet et al., 2011). Their model was not trying to predict concentrations but simply to explore the relationships among the variables, and found meaningful associations between the dependent variable and the independent variables of interest after accounting for meteorological factors.

Prediction

Regression also allows the modeling of a dependent variable in order to predict values in other places and times, consistently and accurately. If the model is predictive in nature, the regression equation is describing how well each of the independent variables perform as predictors of the dependent variable.

In Minnesota, data on residential proximity to a landfill was used to *predict* the negative effect on housing value. The researchers found that houses within two miles of a landfill lost value because of the landfill; beyond two miles the effect was not present. Their findings suggested implications for the siting of new landfills (Nelson, Genereux, & Genereux, 1992).

Hypothesis Testing

Linear regression allows for the evaluation of hypotheses regarding functional or causal relationships. A classic example, the "Broken Window" theory, asserts that there is a positive relationship between vandalism and other crimes (the more broken windows a neighborhood has, the more other crimes will occur there). A regression analysis can indicate whether or not this association really exists. If the theory is correct, a linear regression would indicate a positively sloped line, where crime (the dependent/outcome variable on the y-axis) increases as the number of broken windows (the independent/predictor variable on the x-axis) increases. And the *fit* of the line to the data would be strong.

In the San Francisco Bay Area, data on residential traffic speeds was evaluated for a relationship with street width (Daisa & Peers, 1997). The researchers were interested in determining if wider streets led to higher speeds. The outcome of their regression model indicated that wider residential streets do experience higher speeds (about 0.8 mph for each five-foot increase). These findings have been used by cities as they consider design standards for new residential streets and traffic calming measures for existing ones (Sacramento Transportation & Air Quality Collaborative, 2005). Later in this chapter, we use a hypothetical dataset based on this example to introduce the mathematics of linear regression.

Wise Use of Regression

Authors of textbooks on regression have noted that students often know how to run a regression model on a computer, but they don't understand what it is they are doing (Draper & Smith, 1998). The use of statistical computer programs has made linear regression, and many other techniques, accessible to nearly everyone. However, this accessibility often leads to misuse or misinterpretation, especially when the researcher is not familiar with the concepts and theory behind the model. This chapter will fill that gap. While linear regression is a simple and elegant tool, it depends upon assumptions and details that require close attention. The successful application of regression analysis requires a balance of theoretical results, empirical rules, and subjective judgment (Chatterjee & Price, 2000).

History

Linear regression has a twofold conceptual and mathematical history. The concept behind regression is commonly traced to Sir Francis Galton and his studies of heredity. Galton's interest focused on how strongly the characteristics of one generation influenced the characteristics of the next generation. Using data he collected on sweet pea plants as well as the heights of fathers and sons, Galton plotted two-dimensional diagrams that illustrated the basic ideas of linear regression (see text box below on the term "regression"). Yet his perceptions were focused on the biological aspects of regression, rather than the mathematics, and others were left to expand it into the robust statistical technique we know today.

The mathematical proofs behind correlation and regression are usually attributed to Karl Pearson, who developed what is known as the Pearson Product Moment Correlation (PPMC). This is commonly referred to as the Pearson correlation coefficient r, and is used to describe the strength of the relationship between two variables without inferring causality (see Chapter 9). The values of r range from –1 to +1.

The square of this correlation coefficient R^2, known as the *coefficient of determination* (which you will learn more about in this chapter), has a more intuitive meaning. It represents the portion of the variation in a dependent variable that can be explained by an independent variable or variables in a regression equation. Since r is squared, R^2 values range from 0 to 1.

The term "regression," in the statistical sense, comes from Sir Francis Galton's work on genetics, where he compared the heights of fathers and their sons. He found that extremely tall fathers had tall sons but usually not as tall as they (the fathers) were. Similarly, extremely short fathers had short sons but usually not as short as they were. In other words, the sons' heights **regressed** or returned towards the mean or average height.

Mechanics

Ordinary least squares (OLS) is the most basic tool of linear regression. OLS can be applied as simple linear regression (with just one independent variable) or as multiple linear regression (with two or more independent variables).

Simple Linear Regression

In its most simple form, OLS regression evaluates the relationship between two variables: a continuous dependent variable and one (usually continuous) independent variable, with the dependent variable expressed as a linear function of the independent variable. In other words, a change in the independent variable affects a constant change in the dependent variable. When this is the case, the relationship can be expressed using the equation:

$$Y = a + bX$$

where
a = intercept with the Y-axis when X = 0
b = the slope of the line ($\Delta Y/\Delta X$)
X = value of the independent variable
Y = value of the dependent variable

For example, if a = 8 and b = 0.75, then the equation for your line is:

$$Y = (8) + 0.75(X)$$

and some corresponding (X, Y) values that fit directly on this line would be:

(0, 8); (1, 8.75); (2, 9.5); (3, 10.25), etc.

As you can see, the relationship is constant. For every one-unit increase in X, Y increases by 0.75.

Plotted, the line Y = (8) + 0.75(X) looks the one shown in Figure 12.1.

In research, your data will never fall exactly on a straight line. For this reason, the standard regression equation describing the relationship between variables for a *population* also contains an error term ε.

$$Y = \alpha + \beta X + \varepsilon$$

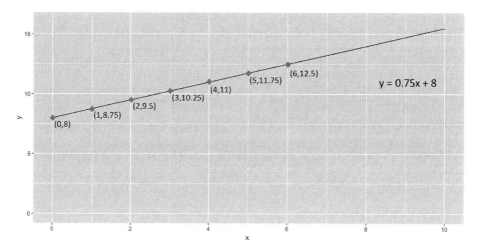

Figure 12.1 A Simple Regression Line

The error term is also known as the disturbance or remainder term. It plays a very important role in regression analysis.

With regression, you can determine an equation for the line that best represents (or *fits*) the relationships between the variables in your dataset. These are sometimes described as best-fit equations. Such equations are defined by the form and values of their *parameters*—α (the intercept) and β (the slope). These, again, apply to a population.

Like Daisa and Peers (1997), let's say you want to explore the theory that traffic speeds increase with street width in residential areas. As a city planner, you have collected data on the traffic speed for five streets in your city, and you know the width of each street. Using this data, you can estimate the relationship between street width and traffic speed using linear regression. You will then be able to predict how a change in the built environment (street width) will impact human behavior (traffic speed) and to use this information for policy decisions about residential street standards in your city. (Note: We start with this simple hypothetical dataset to introduce the mathematics of linear regression. Following the multiple regression in the Step by Step section, we use a large dataset to illustrate realistic regression modeling in SPSS and R.)

The data you have collected is shown in Table 12.1.

Table 12.1 Hypothetical Data of Street Width and Traffic Speed

Street Width (X)	Traffic Speed (Y)
20	25
25	26
30	28
35	35
40	39

Using simple linear regression, we will determine the straight-line equation that provides the best fit to the data:

Y (traffic speed) = a + bX (street width) + e

Best fit means that our goal is to minimize the *estimated error* e—the difference between the true value of Y for each observation (each actual data point) and the estimated or predicted value of Y based on the linear equation. The constant a and coefficient b apply to a *sample*. The estimated error e is also known as the residual.

The square of the estimated errors for each data point, added all together, is called the sum of squared errors (SSE). The line with the lowest possible SSE best describes the relationship between the independent and dependent variables (hence the term *least squares*). Note that the errors must be squared because some will be positive (where the observed data point falls above the regression line), while others will be negative (where the observed data point falls below the line). Large errors on both sides could cancel out, suggesting a good fit to the data when the actual fit is very poor. Squaring the errors eliminates the negatives, thus avoiding this problem.

Linear regression is the only form of regression where the best-fit equation can be computed directly. The other regression methods rely on numerical methods, iterating to best-fit values. In linear regression, we use two equations to determine the

226   *Keunhyun Park et al.*

best-fit line for a dataset. First, we calculate the value of b (the slope), which can be represented as:

$$b = \sum[(Xi - \overline{X})(Yi - \overline{Y})] / \sum[(Xi - \overline{X})^2$$

where
$\overline{X}$ = sample mean of X
$\overline{Y}$ = sample mean of Y
i = Xi, Yi value for each observation, and
$\sum$ = the sum for every case (X, Y)

Second, we calculate the value of a (the intercept), which can be represented as:

$$a = \overline{Y} - b(\overline{X})$$

For our hypothetical example, therefore, we can calculate the best-fit line as follows:

Mean of X ($\overline{X}$) = 30
Mean of Y ($\overline{Y}$) = 30.6

As shown in Table 12.2, thus,

$$b = [(-10) * (-5.6) + (-5) * (-4.6) + (0) * (-2.6) + (5) * (4.4) + (10)1 * (8.4)] / [(-10$$
$$(-5)^2 + (0)^2 + (5)^2 + (10)^2].$$
$$= 0.74$$

and

$$a = 30.6 - 0.74(30) = 8.4$$

So, the best fit regression line is:

$$Y = 8.4 + 0.74X$$

By plugging in different values of X (street width), you can now predict different values of Y (traffic speed). You know that the predicted value of Y will increase by 0.74 for each one-unit increase in X. That is, traffic speed is predicted to increase by 0.74

Table 12.2 Calculating Deviance

Street Width (X)	Traffic Speed (Y)	$X - \overline{X}$	$Y - \overline{Y}$
20	25	−10	−5.6
25	26	−5	−4.6
30	28	0	−2.6
35	35	5	4.4
40	39	10	8.4

mph for each one-foot increase in street width. You must also understand, however, that your predicted values will be different from the actual values. There is a degree of error incorporated in the regression model, which becomes clear when we plot the estimated line along with the observed data (Figure 12.2).

It is important to emphasize that the regression model is not reality, it is a model of the world as we see it. Importantly, the model applies to the range of our experience, or maybe slightly beyond it. Notice in this picture, the model seems to imply that if the street width were zero, the traffic speed would be 8 mph. The problem is that the model is only meant to apply to street widths from 20 or so to 40 or so.

In regression equations, the notations for the parameters a and b are often switched out for b's, such that

$$Y = b_0 + b_1 X_1 + e$$

where
Y = dependent variable
X = independent variable
b = parameters (b_0 is the constant, b_1 the coefficient)
e = random error term—the difference between the observed value of Y and the predicted value of Y

We will use this notation for the remainder of the chapter.

Interpreting Simple Linear Regression Results

Once you've created a regression model with your data, the next step is to assess how good the estimations actually are. In our simple linear regression example, we want to know if the relationship between street width and traffic speed is merely due to

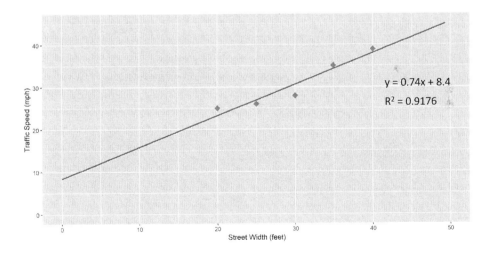

Figure 12.2 A Regression Line Between Street Width and Traffic Speed

228 *Keunhyun Park et al.*

chance, or if it can be generalized as a relationship for all residential streets and thus used as a planning tool.

The basic fit of the model is evaluated using three statistics: R-squared, F-statistic, and t-statistic(s). These evaluate the performance of the overall model (R-squared and F-statistic) and the parameters within the model (t-statistic). When you read research articles that employ regression analysis, R-squared, F-statistic, and t-statistic(s) are the values you usually see reported. We explain each statistic here, in general terms, before illustrating with specific calculations from our hypothetical dataset. Note that whatever statistical software package you use for conducting regression analysis will calculate these for you (as we show using SPSS or R later), but it is important to know where these values actually come from.

R-squared: Goodness of Fit

The R-squared statistic measures the proportion of the variation in the dependent variable explained by the independent variable(s). It is equal to one minus the ratio of the SSE to the sum of squared deviations about the mean of the dependent variable (this is the measure of the total variation of the dependent variable):

$R^2 = 1 -$ (SSE from the regression line/sum of squared deviations from the mean of all Y values)

A high value of R-squared suggests that the model explains the variation in the dependent variable well. This is very important when using a model for predictive or forecasting purposes but is less important when searching for evidence that one variable influences another (hypothesis testing).

Regressions with low R-squared values will often, but not always, yield parameter estimates with small t-statistics for any null hypothesis (see below t-Statistic(s) section). A low R-squared value may indicate that important factors have been omitted from the regression model, which raises the concern of omitted variable bias (see data-related problems later in the chapter).

F-statistic

The F-statistic, or F-ratio, tells you the significance of the model as a whole. The F-statistic evaluates all of the coefficients in the model jointly, indicating whether they collectively are different from zero. Along with the R-squared value, this is a way to tell how well the regression equation fits the data.

$\text{F-statistic} = [R^2 / (1 - R^2)] * [(n - p) / (p - 1)]$

where
$R^2 =$ the model's R-squared value
n = the number of observations
p = the number of parameters in the regression equation (number of coefficients plus the constant)

Intuitively, the F-statistic formula compares the accuracy of the model R^2 to the inaccuracy $(1-R^2)$, adjusting for the degrees of freedom (df). For the numerator of the preceding equation, R^2, df equals p–1. For the denominator of the preceding equation, $(1-R^2)$, df equals n–p.

The F-statistic relies on the F distribution, a probability distribution with a table of critical values (see Figure 12.3). The critical value at any significance level depends upon the degrees of freedom of the model (df_1, df_2). If the computed F-statistic is greater than the critical value from the F table for the appropriate degrees of freedom, then you can reject the null hypothesis that the combination of your regression coefficients is zero, or equivalently reject the null hypothesis that the model with its independent variable(s) is no better than the null model with a constant term only.

t-Statistic(s)

The t-statistic, also called the t-ratio, is defined by the following equation:

$$t = b_1 / SE_{b1}$$

where b_1 is the slope of the regression line and SE_{b1} is the standard error of the slope. This value tells you the significance of the coefficient estimate b_1.

The significance of the t-statistic is based on the probability distribution known as the Student's t distribution (see Chapter 10 and Figure 12.4). The value against which the t-statistic is compared comes from a t table and depends upon degrees of freedom, n–p. If the t-statistic calculated from your model is greater than the critical t value for the appropriate degrees of freedom, then you can reject the null hypothesis that the coefficient b_1 is equal to zero, which is equivalent to saying that there is no relationship between the independent variable and the dependent variable.

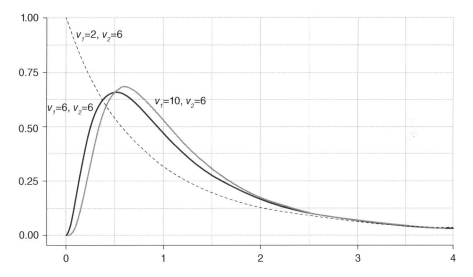

Figure 12.3 Probability Distribution Curves for F-Statistic With Different Degrees of Freedom

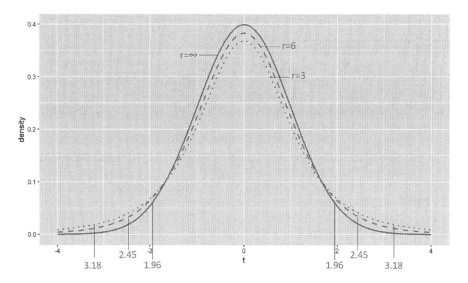

Figure 12.4 Probability Distribution Curves for t-Statistic With Different Degrees of Freedom

It is standard convention to adopt the 95 percent confidence level, or 0.05 significance level, in such comparisons. At the 0.05 significance level, only 5 percent of the area under the probability distribution curve exceeds that particular value of F or t. Thus, while it is possible to obtain a value of F or t larger than this critical value by chance, it is unlikely. In other words, at the 0.05 significance level, you can be 95 percent certain that the value of F or t is different from zero, or equivalently that the observed relationship between X_1 and Y is due not to chance but to a real association between the variables.

For our hypothetical dataset, expanded with values of the error term, we can calculate these three statistics (Table 12.3).

$$R^2 = 1 - \left[\sum(Y - \check{Y})^2 / \sum(Y - \bar{Y})^2\right]$$
$$= 1 - [(1.8)^2 + (-0.9)^2 + (-2.6)^2 + (0.7)^2 + (1)^2] /$$
$$[(-5.6)^2 + (-4.6)^2 + (-2.6)^2 + (4.4)^2 + (8.4)^2]$$
$$= 1 - (12.3 / 149.2)$$
$$= 1 - 0.0824$$
$$= 0.9176$$

Our equation explains almost 92 percent of the variation in Y, or equivalently, street width explains almost 92 percent of the variation in traffic speed.

Linear Regression 231

Table 12.3 Calculating Error Terms

Street Width (X)	$X - \bar{X}$	Traffic Speed (Y)	Predicted Value of Y ($\hat{Y}$)	Residual ($Y - \hat{Y}$)	$Y - \bar{Y}$
20	−10	25	23.2	1.8	−5.6
25	−5	26	26.9	−0.9	−4.6
30	0	28	30.6	−2.6	−2.6
35	5	35	34.3	0.7	4.4
40	10	39	38	1	8.4

$$\text{F-statistic} = [R^2 / (1 - R^2)] * [(n - p)/(p - 1)]$$
$$= (.9176/.0824) * ((5 - 2)/(2 - 1))$$
$$= 11.136 * 3$$
$$= 33.41$$

The critical F-statistic for 1 and 3 degrees of freedom is 34.116 at the 0.01 significance level. Since our F-ratio is slightly smaller than this, but close, we look for the 0.05 significance level. The critical value for 1 and 3 degrees of freedom at the 0.05 significance level is 17.443, much below the F-statistic of the model. We therefore conclude that our model as a whole is significant at approximately the p = 0.01 level.

$$\text{t-statistic} = b_1 / SE_{b1}$$

where

$$SE_{b1} = \sqrt{[1/(n - p) * \left(\sum (Y_i - \check{Y})^2\right]} / \sqrt{\left(\sum (X_i - \bar{X})^2\right)}$$
$$= \sqrt{\left[(1/3) * \left[(1.8)^2 + (-0.9)^2 + (-2.6)^2 + (0.7)^2 + (1)^2\right]\right]} /$$
$$\sqrt{\left[(-10)^2 + (-5)^2 + (0)^2 + (5)^2 + (10)^2\right]}$$
$$= \sqrt{(4.1)} / \sqrt{(250)}$$
$$= 2.0248/15.8114$$
$$= 0.12806$$

The symbol $\sqrt{}$ represent the square root; thus

$$\text{t-statistic} = 0.74/0.12806 = 5.7785$$

The critical t-value for 3 degrees of freedom (five observations minus two parameters) at the 0.01 significance level is 4.5407. Since our t-statistic is larger than the critical value at this significance level, we can conclude that the coefficient estimate b_1 is significant at the 0.01 level or beyond. There is only one chance in 100 that this strong association between X_1 and Y is due to chance.

Multiple Linear Regression

Whereas simple linear regression uses only two variables—one dependent and one independent—multiple regression involves multiple independent variables. Planners primarily use multiple regression rather than simple regression. The world is usually not so simple as to have the variance in one single variable completely explain the variance in another. Thus, if researchers do not include multiple variables in their models, they run the risk of under-specifying their regression equation, which may produce biased regression coefficients.

In Chapter 5, you were introduced to several types of variables: determinants, correlates, confounders, moderators, and mediators. All may find their way into multiple regression analyses (and more sophisticated models we consider subsequently). In multiple regression, we particularly want to control for confounding variables. These variables, as you may recall, are correlated with determinants and causally related to outcome variables. A failure to control for them, through multiple regression, will cause researchers to attribute some of the effects of confounding variables to other determinants. We momentarily return to our example of street width versus traffic speed to illustrate this phenomenon.

With multiple variables, we must think in terms of multiple dimensions. With three variables, for example—one dependent variable (Y) and two independent variables (X_1 and X_2)—we would be estimating a best-fit plane (see Figure 12.5). Just as with

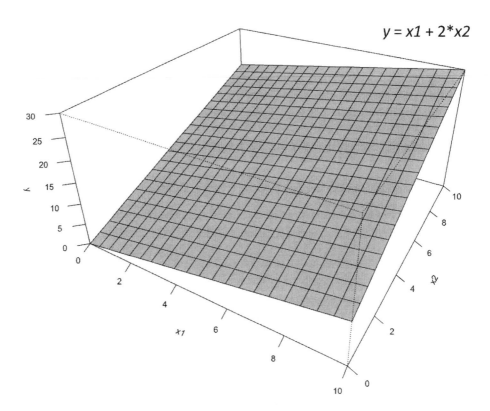

Figure 12.5 A Best-Fit Plane of a Regression With Two Independent Variables

Linear Regression 233

the best-fit line, the best-fit plane minimizes the distance between the actual values of Y and the predicted values of Y. The constant is the intercept of the plane with the Y-axis when both X variables equal zero.

For example, in our hypothetical study, factors other than street width likely affect traffic speed. One possibility could be that the average setback of buildings from the street edge affects traffic speed. It has long been speculated that small building setbacks reduce the perceived width of streets, thus calming traffic. If you wanted to evaluate both setbacks and street widths together, you would use a multiple regression equation with these two independent variables. The Y-axis/dependent variable would still be traffic speed, but now you would have two X-axes—one for street width and one for average setback.

A data table for our new example might look like Table 12.4.

The generic regression equation for this example would be:

$$Y = b_0 + b_1 X_1 + b_2 X_2$$

If you perform calculations like those shown in the preceding simple regression section, you would find that the best-fit regression equation is:

$$Y = 8.3 + 0.56X_1 + 0.35X_2$$

Multiple regression estimates the marginal effect of each independent variable, holding the other independent variables constant. This equation suggests that controlling for the average building setback, a one-foot increase in street width is associated with a 0.56 mph increase in traffic speed. This is less than the 0.74 mph marginal increase we estimated using simple linear regression with only one independent variable, average street width. This means that the average building setback confounds the relationship between average street width and traffic speed, being correlated with average street width and accounting for some of the effect of average street width when average setback is not controlled.

The statistics for interpreting multiple regression models are the same as for simple linear regression, except that each independent variable in the multiple regression model has its own t-statistic. Each t-statistic evaluates whether or not a particular variable's coefficient (b_n) is significantly different from zero.

Again, if you perform calculations like those shown in the preceding simple regression section, you should find the following values:

$R^2 = 0.935$
F-statistic $= 14.341$

Table 12.4 Hypothetical Data of Street Width, Average Setback, and Traffic Speed

Street Width (X_1)	Average Setback (X_2)	Traffic Speed (Y)
20	10	25
25	15	26
30	12	28
35	20	35
40	20	39

234   *Keunhyun Park et al.*

t-statistic for $b_1 = 2.016$
t-statistic for $b_2 = 0.728$

A helpful way to understand these results is to compare them to the simple linear regression. The R^2 is higher, as it must be with one additional independent variable, so the line is a *better fit* to the data. However, the t-statistics for both coefficient estimates are lower in the multiple regression model, as is the F-statistic.

First, consider the F-statistic. Recall that the degrees of freedom are, respectively, p-1 for the numerator, or 2, and n-p for the denominator, or 2. For the F-statistic, as the first value increases with more independent variables, the second value decreases. The critical F-value at the 0.05 significance level for the indicated degrees of freedom is 19.0. Thus, since our F-statistic is less than the critical value, we conclude that our model as a whole is not significant at 0.05 level. The probability that our results are due to chance is greater than 5 percent, but just a little bit (6.5 percent). If we adopt the 0.10 significance level instead, the F-statistic becomes significant.

Now consider the t-statistics. Since we've added a variable to the equation, we now have one fewer degrees of freedom (n-p = 2). For 2 degrees of freedom, at the 0.05 significance level, the minimum t value is 2.92. Since our t-statistics (2.016 and 0.728, respectively) are both smaller than this critical value, we cannot conclude that either coefficient is significantly different from zero.

Three things are going on here that distinguish this case from the single-independent-variable case, where we established statistical significance. Recall that:

$$t = b_1 / SE_{b1}$$

Controlling for average building setback has reduced the apparent strength of the relationship between average street width and traffic speed, reducing the value of b_1. At the same time, losing a degree of freedom has increased the value of SE_{b1} (see preceding formula) and increased the critical t-values for statistical significance. The critical values for t and F fall dramatically when df gets past 4 or so. It was only for the calculation in the simple regression section that we kept the sample size so small. With seven or eight street segments, the results could have been very different.

This book does not cover Bayesian statistics, but they are relevant at this point. It is not that street width is unrelated to traffic speed. There is ample evidence that the two are related. It is just that we cannot be confident (at a conventional level) of a relationship based on such a small sample of streets. Given a larger sample, the same value of b_1 might have been statistically significant and we could have asserted a relationship between the two variables with some confidence. Also, reviewing previous studies of street width versus traffic speed, we would not have given too much weight to the negative finding in this case (Ewing, 2012).

Overall, we would conclude that while the model as a whole performs fairly well, the independent variables do not perform well and are not easily interpreted.

As you might imagine, multiple regression generally involves more than two independent variables. In generic terms, we want to estimate an equation with n independent variables that minimizes the sum of squared errors between observed values of Y and the predicted values of Y on a *hyperplane* in k dimensions. The equation for a regression model with k variables is:

$$Y = b_0 + b_1X_1 + b_2X_2 + \cdots b_kX_k + e$$

where
Y = dependent variable
X = 1 to k independent variables
b = associated parameters
e = random error term

The Y-intercept is still the constant term (the value of Y when all independent variables are zero), and the coefficient b_k for each variable X_k still represents the slope of Y with respect to X_k, holding other independent variables constant. The R-squared value still represents how much variation in Y is explained by the independent variables collectively. The F-statistic still determines whether or not the model as a whole is significant, and the t-statistic for each independent variable still determines whether or not that variable's coefficient can be considered significantly different from zero.

Step by Step

The examples so far have been purposefully simplified to illustrate the mathematics of OLS regression. We now turn to a more sophisticated example to illustrate realistic multiple regression in planning research. We use this example to highlight the assumptions and challenges inherent in OLS regression.

In this example, we begin to test the theory of induced traffic. This theory, referenced in Chapters 1 and 3, states that increases in highway capacity lead to increases in total traffic volume. The reason is simple: supply and demand (see Figures 3.1 and 3.2). An increase in highway capacity reduces congestion, at least in the short run, and this in turn reduces travel times and the generalized cost of travel. This leads to an increase in the quantity of travel demanded. In the short run, a variety of sources contribute to increased traffic. These include changes in route, mode, time of travel, and destination. In addition, there is the possibility of new trips that would not have occurred without the new infrastructure capacity. In a meta-analysis, Cervero (2002) computes a short-run elasticity of VMT with respect to highway capacity of between 0 and 0.40.

In the long run, increases in highway capacity may improve accessibility to developable lands and lower travel times to the point where residences and businesses are drawn to locate near the expanded highway capacity, often in sprawling patterns (Ewing, 2008). This causes an upward shift in the travel demand curve, and the quantity of travel increases further. In a meta-analysis, Cervero (2002) computes a long-run elasticity of VMT with respect to highway capacity of between 0.63 and 0.73.

In this Step by Step section, we use the UZA dataset (UZA.sav). Highway supply is operationalized as lane miles of highway capacity; highway demand is operationalized as vehicle miles traveled (VMT). To draw a scatter plot, go to "Graphs" menu, select "Legacy Dialogs," and select "Scatter/Dot." When the Scatter/Dot menu screen appears, select "Simple Scatter" and click "Define" button (Figures 12.6 and 12.7).

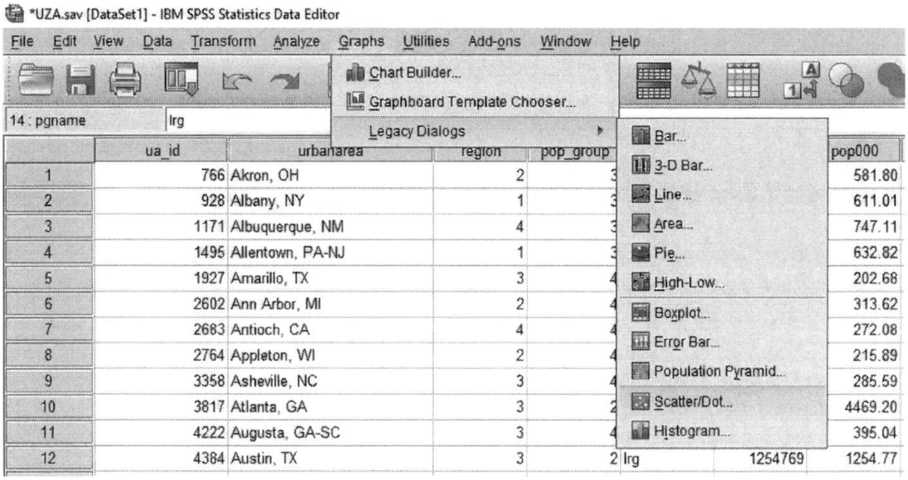

Figure 12.6 Finding "Scatter/Dot" Menu

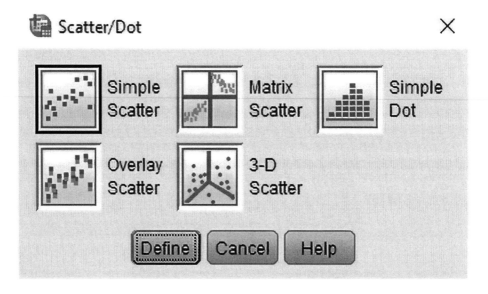

Figure 12.7 "Scatter/Dot" Window

In the Simple Scatterplot window (Figure 12.8), enter the dependent variable (*vmttotal*) on the Y-axis and an independent variable (*lmtotal*) on the X-axis by selecting from the list and clicking the left-to-right arrow buttons. Then click "OK."

As you can see in the scatterplot in Figure 12.9, total lane miles (*lmtotal*; independent variable) has a strongly positive linear relationship to total VMT (*vmttotal*; dependent variable). One might see this as evidence of the theory of induced demand. But not so fast.

Linear Regression 237

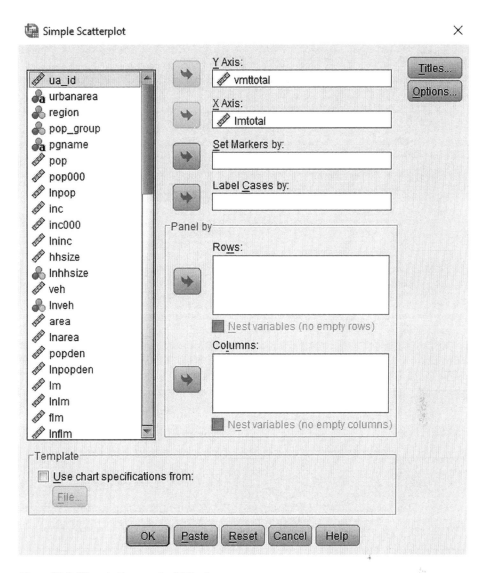

Figure 12.8 "Simple Scatterplot" Window

Contrary to induced demand theory, if we switch two variables with each other (*vmttotal* variable to X-axis and *lmtotal* variable to Y-axis), total VMT (independent variable) shows the same linear relationship with total lane miles (dependent variable) (Figure 12.10). In this case, would you call it the theory of induced road building (i.e., more vehicle use promotes more road building)? A theory cannot be developed from a simple correlation.

Let's look at another scatter plot (Figure 12.11). The total VMT is also related to total population. It is obvious that larger urban areas have more VMT. Big areas have

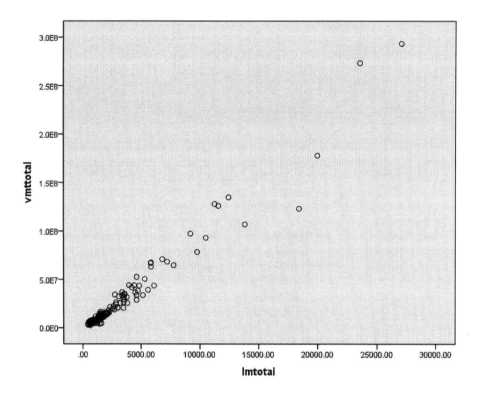

Figure 12.9 Scatter Plot Between Total Lane Miles and Total VMT

more of everything than small areas, including coffee houses and pigeons and VMT and lane miles. Unless you control somehow for area size, or population in our case, area size will confound other relationships. Therefore, in this Step by Step section, the variables are represented on a per capita basis to partially control for the effect of population size.

Simple Regression

Let's begin with a simple regression—one dependent variable (VMT per capita) and one independent variable (lane miles per 1000 population).

First, click the "Analyze" tab, scroll down to the "Regression" menu, and select the "Linear" option (Figure 12.12).

Then, we specify the appropriate data fields. Under "Dependent," we insert *vmt* (VMT per capita) by selecting from the variable list on the left-hand side and then clicking the left-to-right arrow button. Using the same process, under "Independent(s)," we insert *lm* (lane miles per 1000 population) (Figure 12.13).

Now, we can run a simple regression by clicking "OK." The results will appear in the SPSS Output Viewer (Figure 12.14).

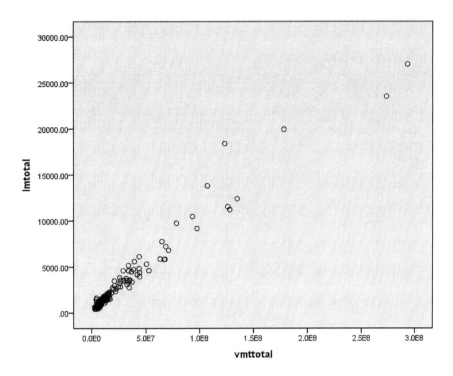

Figure 12.10 Scatter Plot Between Total VMT and Total Lane Miles

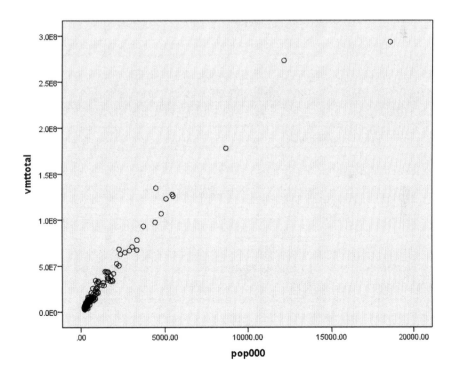

Figure 12.11 Scatter Plot Between Population Size and Total VMT

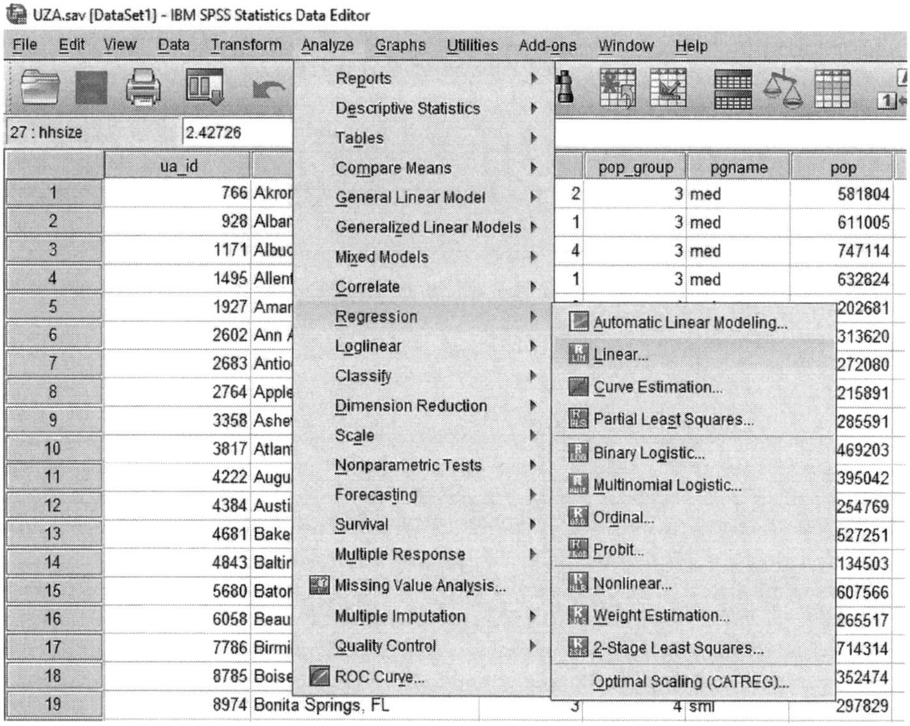

240   *Keunhyun Park et al.*

Figure 12.12 Linear Regression Menu

The first "Model Summary" table shows an R-squared of 0.253, meaning that lane miles explains 25.3 percent of the variance in VMT in our data. The second "ANOVA" table shows an F statistic of 52.418 at a significance level of $p < .001$, meaning that the model as a whole is significant and that there is less than a one chance in a thousand that our results are due to chance. The last "Coefficients" table contains two important pieces of information: the estimated values of the coefficients in our regression equation (shown as "B"), and the significance of each independent variable (shown as "t" and a corresponding "Sig." level).

The intercept is 13.586, meaning that when the independent variable has a zero value (i.e., there are no roads at all), the estimated VMT per capita is 13.586. That does not make sense for sure; it is just a mathematically hypothetical situation, as discussed previously. Regression results are roughly limited to the range of values in the dataset.

The *lm* variable has an estimated coefficient of 3.326; the positive sign indicates that as lane miles per 1000 population increase, VMT per capita also increases. To be specific, a one-mile increase in lane miles per 1000 population is associated with about a 3.3 mile increase in VMT per capita. For example, if an urban area has just one lane mile per 1000 population, the expected VMT per capita is 13.586 (Y-intercept) plus 3.326, which is 16.912. This finding is logical and confirms earlier research.

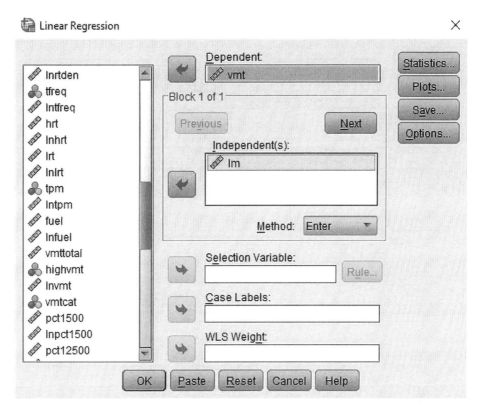

Figure 12.13 Adding Two Variables in the Linear Regression Window

Along with an estimated coefficient, the independent variable, *lm* in the model, has a t-statistic and a corresponding significance level. The *lm* variable has a significance level of 0.001 or beyond (t = 7.240), meaning we can be more than 99.9 percent confident that our high coefficient estimate for this variable is not due to chance.

Multiple Regression

Following the literature, let's add more independent variables. Prior research has shown that VMT is also affected by total population size, population density, transit ridership, and fuel price.

In the Linear Regression menu ("Analyze" → "Regression" → "Linear"), you can add four additional variables: *pop000* (population in thousands), *popden* (population density), *tpm* (annual transit passenger miles per capita), and *fuel* (fuel price) under "Independent(s)" box (Figure 12.15).

Figure 12.16 illustrates the result of multiple regression with five independent variables. Note that while the SPSS output presents very small numbers as zero (".000"), this actually does not mean zero but rather "less than 0.001 (< .001)."

242 *Keunhyun Park et al.*

Model Summary

Model	R	R Square	Adjusted R Square	Std. Error of the Estimate
1	.503[a]	.253	.248	4.57750

a. Predictors: (Constant), lm

ANOVA[b]

Model		Sum of Squares	df	Mean Square	F	Sig.
1	Regression	1098.340	1	1098.340	52.418	.000[a]
	Residual	3247.794	155	20.954		
	Total	4346.133	156			

a. Predictors: (Constant), lm

b. Dependent Variable: vmt

Coefficients[a]

Model		Unstandardized Coefficients		Standardized Coefficients	t	Sig.
		B	Std. Error	Beta		
1	(Constant)	13.586	1.469		9.250	.000
	lm	3.326	.459	.503	7.240	.000

a. Dependent Variable: vmt

Figure 12.14 Regression Model Summary of VMT Per Capita Regressed on Lane Miles per 1000 Population

Among the independent variables, *popden, tpm,* and *fuel* have negative signs on the estimated coefficients. This implies that, for example, as population density and fuel price increase (i.e., the region is more compact and gas is more expensive), VMT decreases. Again, this finding is logical and consistent with earlier work. The *lm* and *pop000* show expected positive relationships with VMT per capita. Areas with more highway capacity per 1000 population and more population (a proxy for area size) would be expected to generate more VMT per capita.

Along with an estimated coefficient, each independent variable in the model has a t-statistic and a corresponding significance level. Only *lm* variable has a significance level of 0.001 while fuel price is marginally significant at the $p < .1$ level ($p = .083$). Since our ultimate interest is in the theory of induced travel, the positive and significant coefficient on *lm* provides preliminary support for the theory. *pop000, popden,* and *tpm* are not statistically significant (with p values of .211, .251, .982, respectively), meaning that our coefficient estimates for these variables are not statistically different from zero. Why, for example, wouldn't transit passenger miles per capita have a

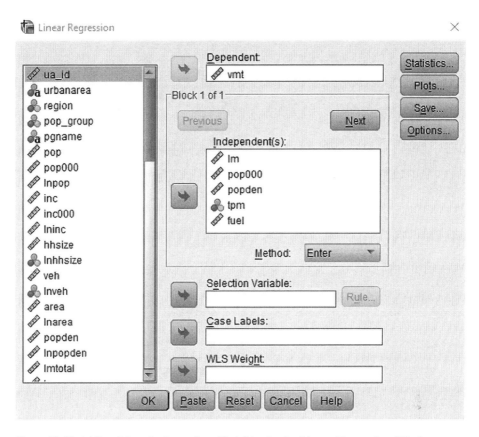

Figure 12.15 Adding More Independent Variables in the Linear Regression Window

significant relationship with VMT per capita? We might speculate that transit mode shares are so small in most urbanized areas that a variable operationalizing transit ridership doesn't rise to a level of significance.

Model fit is slightly better than the previous model (R-squared = 0.294, F-statistic = 12.581). However, with a moderate-to-low R-squared of 0.294 and with parameter estimates that are not statistically significant, we would conclude that our current OLS regression model of VMT performs rather poorly. To explore why this might be, we now turn to the assumptions behind OLS and to various potential diagnostics.

Assumption Behind the Model

The estimated parameters for an OLS regression model should exhibit two key properties: they must be *efficient*, with minimal variance around the estimator, and they must be *unbiased*, or close to the true values. Figure 12.17 illustrates both properties graphically.

Model Summary

Model	R	R Square	Adjusted R Square	Std. Error of the Estimate
1	.542[a]	.294	.271	4.50757

a. Predictors: (Constant), fuel, pop000, lm, tpm, popden

ANOVA[b]

Model		Sum of Squares	df	Mean Square	F	Sig.
1	Regression	1278.084	5	255.617	12.581	.000[a]
	Residual	3068.049	151	20.318		
	Total	4346.133	156			

a. Predictors: (Constant), fuel, pop000, lm, tpm, popden

b. Dependent Variable: vmt

Coefficients[a]

Model		Unstandardized Coefficients		Standardized Coefficients	t	Sig.
		B	Std. Error	Beta		
1	(Constant)	31.542	8.396		3.757	.000
	lm	2.511	.641	.380	3.915	.000
	pop000	.000	.000	.134	1.256	.211
	popden	-.001	.001	-.134	-1.153	.251
	tpm	-9.094E-5	.004	-.002	-.023	.982
	fuel	-5.142	2.947	-.157	-1.744	.083

a. Dependent Variable: vmt

Figure 12.16 Regression Model Summary With Four Additional Independent Variables

A large number of potential problems can introduce inefficiency or bias into a linear regression model. Each of these problems violates one or more of the basic assumptions of OLS regression, which must hold true for a model to produce valid and reliable results:

- The relationship between the dependent variable and each independent variable must be linear.
- The model must be specified properly—that is, the relevant independent variables must be included.
- The independent variables must be linearly independent of each other.

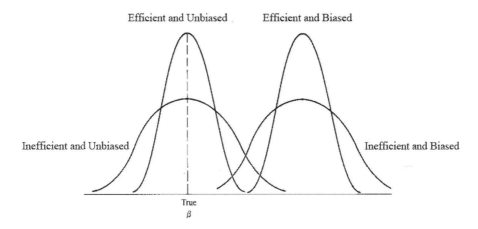

Figure 12.17 Efficiency and Bias in Sample Distributions

- The error term for the model must be randomly distributed.
- The variance in the error term must be constant for all values of the independent variables.
- The error term and the independent variables must be independent of one another.
- Successive values of the error term must be uncorrelated with each other.

Problems that might violate these assumptions pertain either to the data used in the model or to the error term. We explore both issues next.

Data-Related Problems

If a researcher's raw data has flaws, her linear regression model will inherit those flaws. Thus, she must understand the assumptions behind OLS and learn to diagnose when those assumptions have been violated. Data-related problems for OLS regression can take many forms: omitted variables, irrelevant variables, incorrect functional form, multicollinearity, measurement error, outliers, selection bias, dependence of observations, etc.

Omitted variables are independent variables that could explain a significant amount of variance in the dependent variable but are missing from the regression equation. What is missing in our VMT model? After reviewing the list of variables in Table 1.2, we might expect that VMT will increase with income, as higher income households consume more of almost everything than do lower income households, including travel (and automobiles). If we add an income measure (*inc000*) as an additional independent variable, the results change as shown in Figure 12.18.

Note that the addition of income causes the R-squared and F-statistic to increase, and the significance levels of nearly all independent variables to improve. Per capita income is statistically significant, and when we control for income, other

246   *Keunhyun Park et al.*

Model Summary

Model	R	R Square	Adjusted R Square	Std. Error of the Estimate
1	.606[a]	.367	.341	4.28375

a. Predictors: (Constant), inc000, lm, pop000, fuel, tpm, popden

ANOVA[b]

Model		Sum of Squares	df	Mean Square	F	Sig.
1	Regression	1593.560	6	265.593	14.473	.000[a]
	Residual	2752.574	150	18.350		
	Total	4346.133	156			

a. Predictors: (Constant), inc000, lm, pop000, fuel, tpm, popden

b. Dependent Variable: vmt

Coefficients[a]

Model		Unstandardized Coefficients		Standardized Coefficients	t	Sig.
		B	Std. Error	Beta		
1	(Constant)	28.145	8.021		3.509	.001
	lm	2.178	.615	.329	3.542	.001
	pop000	.000	.000	.163	1.603	.111
	popden	-.001	.001	-.160	-1.450	.149
	tpm	-.006	.004	-.160	-1.510	.133
	fuel	-6.328	2.816	-.193	-2.247	.026
	inc000	.318	.077	.311	4.146	.000

a. Dependent Variable: vmt

Figure 12.18 Regression Model Summary With an Additional Income Variable

variables come closer to statistical significance due to correlations between these other variables and income. With an R-squared of 0.367, we are still only explaining a little over one-third of the variation in VMT per capita across urbanized areas.

Another source of measurement error in OLS regression is *irrelevant variables*. Inclusion of an irrelevant independent variable does not bias coefficient estimates; however, if an irrelevant predictor is correlated with a relevant predictor, the irrelevant variable will compromise the significance of the relevant variable by increasing its standard error. In our example, we may conclude that population size and transit passenger miles themselves are not important in explaining VMT per capita.

Indeed, if we remove these two variables from the regression equation, the standard errors of the coefficients of the remaining variables decrease, and the overall fit of the model remains about the same (R-squared = 0.354) (Figure 12.19).

Other data-related problems of OLS regression involve *measurement procedures*. Sometimes a variable cannot be measured accurately, or does not accurately represent an underlying construct (see Chapter 6). In our example, we might conclude that the population density variable poorly represents the construct compact development, since gross density calculations over entire urban areas frequently misrepresent the actual density at finer-grained scales. Also, density is only one dimension of compactness. Being aware of this problem, we might decide to replace *popden* with a

Model Summary

Model	R	R Square	Adjusted R Square	Std. Error of the Estimate
1	.595[a]	.354	.337	4.29814

a. Predictors: (Constant), inc000, lm, fuel, popden

ANOVA[b]

Model		Sum of Squares	df	Mean Square	F	Sig.
1	Regression	1538.078	4	384.519	20.814	.000[a]
	Residual	2808.055	152	18.474		
	Total	4346.133	156			

a. Predictors: (Constant), inc000, lm, fuel, popden

b. Dependent Variable: vmt

Coefficients[a]

Model		Unstandardized Coefficients		Standardized Coefficients	t	Sig.
		B	Std. Error	Beta		
1	(Constant)	32.569	7.608		4.281	.000
	lm	2.319	.611	.350	3.797	.000
	popden	-.001	.001	-.101	-1.037	.301
	fuel	-8.076	2.638	-.247	-3.061	.003
	inc000	.289	.070	.282	4.107	.000

a. Dependent Variable: vmt

Figure 12.19 Regression Model Summary After Dropping the Population Size and Transit Passenger Mile Variables

248 *Keunhyun Park et al.*

density factor (*denfac*) derived by Ewing and Hamidi (2017) from five different density variables via principal component analysis, or alternatively replace *popden* with an overall compactness measure (*compact*) developed by Ewing and Hamidi (2017) combining 15 different built environmental variables to form four different factors, and then summing. This also uses principal component analysis; five variables load on a density factor, two variables on a mixed use factor, four variables on a centering factor, and four variables on a street factor. The principal component analysis can also solve the issue of multicollinearity as long as the group of variables are logically related and the linear function among those makes sense (see Chapter 5 of *Advanced Quantitative Research Methods for Urban Planners*).

Substituting *compact* for *popden* in our regression equation, the new variable is highly significant where the gross density variable was not. Indeed, all four independent variables are now highly significant. As important, with the new variable, the R-squared of the regression equation jumps from 0.354 to 0.411 (Figure 12.20).

Model Summary

Model	R	R Square	Adjusted R Square	Std. Error of the Estimate
1	.641[a]	.411	.396	4.10340

a. Predictors: (Constant), compact, inc000, lm, fuel

ANOVA[b]

Model		Sum of Squares	df	Mean Square	F	Sig.
1	Regression	1786.770	4	446.692	26.529	.000[a]
	Residual	2559.364	152	16.838		
	Total	4346.133	156			

a. Predictors: (Constant), compact, inc000, lm, fuel

b. Dependent Variable: vmt

Coefficients[a]

Model		Unstandardized Coefficients		Standardized Coefficients	t	Sig.
		B	Std. Error	Beta		
1	(Constant)	35.770	7.293		4.905	.000
	lm	2.120	.490	.320	4.331	.000
	fuel	-7.365	2.429	-.225	-3.032	.003
	inc000	.295	.067	.289	4.435	.000
	compact	-.059	.015	-.277	-3.994	.000

a. Dependent Variable: vmt

Figure 12.20 Regression Model Summary After Replacing *popden* With *compact* Variable

Nonlinearity and Outliers

We return to a fully specified model, including *pop000* and *tpm*. We retain *compact*, however, as a better measure of urban form than *popden*.

To establish linearity between the dependent and independent variables and outliers, we first investigate the relationship between the dependent variable and the independent variables using scatterplots. Go to "Graphs" → "Legacy Dialogs" → "Scatter/Dot" (Figure 12.21). We will begin with lane miles per 1000 population as an independent variable and VMT per capita as a dependent variable (Figure 12.22).

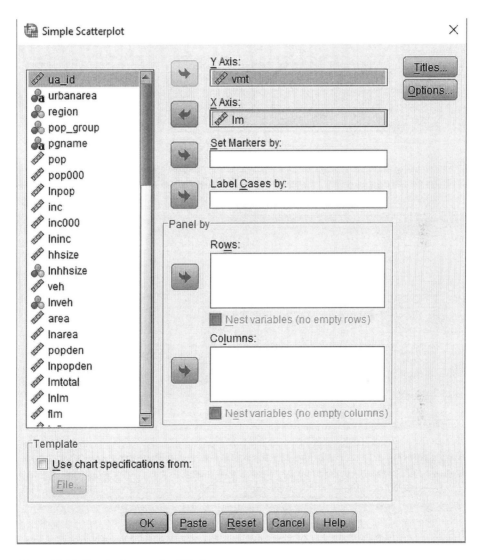

Figure 12.21 Simple Scatterplot Window

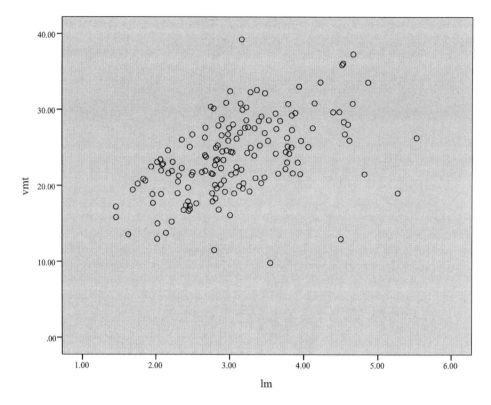

Figure 12.22 Scatterplot Between Lane Miles per 1000 Population and VMT Per Capita

The relationship looks roughly linear, though the slope may be leveling off a bit at high *lm* values. There may also be slight nonlinearity between compactness and VMT per capita. Nonlinearity can bias linear regression coefficients.

The scatterplot between population in 1000s and VMT per capita (Figure 12.23) shows that there may be outliers with extremely large values, particularly New York and Los Angeles. Outliers can bias regression coefficients. The plot also suggests the possibility of something called heteroscedasticity. The same is true of the relationship between transit passenger miles per capita and VMT per capita. Put simply, heteroscedasticity (also spelled heteroskedasticity) refers to the circumstance in which the variability of a variable is unequal across the range of values of a second variable that predicts it. We will come back to these issues later.

We now introduce a common test for outliers, using something called leverage values to identify them. Click on the Save button in the Linear Regression window, and check "Leverage values." Run a regression using *lm, pop000, tpm, fuel, inc000*, and *compact* as independent variables, and of course *vmt* as the dependent variable. You now have a new final column in your dataset labeled LEV_1. By convention, leverage values of more than approximately 0.20 signify outliers. By this convention, Los Angeles and New York are outliers. We could delete these two cases from the dataset,

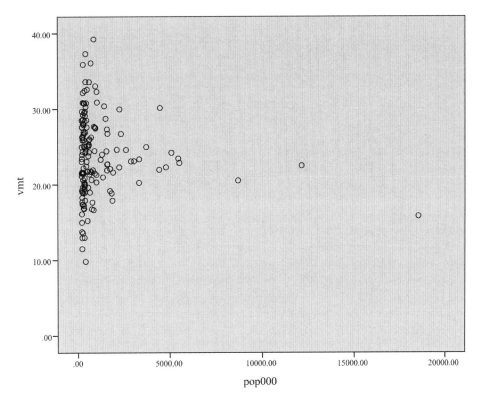

Figure 12.23 Scatterplot Between Population in 1000s and VMT Per Capita

but with only 157 cases, we hate to lose two. Moreover, these two UZAs are unique and important cases from a planning standpoint. Fortunately, there is another way to handle outliers that allows them to be retained in this example.

Log-transformation

Incorrect functional form refers to the relationship between dependent and independent variables being modeled incorrectly (e.g., linear form when it is non-linear). In order to handle outliers and nonlinearity—both violating the assumptions of OLS regression, we may need to transform the data. The most common method of transforming data is to take the natural logarithms of one or more variables. A very useful feature of linear regression is that the model results remain valid if one or even both sides of the equation change form through logarithm, polynomial expansion, etc.

The use of logarithms often gives the dependent variable a more normal distribution, while making relationships among our variables more nearly linear, and reducing the influence of outliers (such as New York and Los Angeles).

Please note that in the dataset, all variables are already presented both in linear and logged forms. Thus, the following steps for log-transformation are optional.

252 *Keunhyun Park et al.*

To create a new log-transformed variable, click the "Transform" menu and select "Compute Variable" (Figure 12.24).

In the Compute Variable window (Figure 12.25), type the name of your new variable in the "Target Variable" field, for example: lnvmtcap. Then, in the "Numeric Expression" field, type the equation for the new variable, in this case *ln(vmt)*. When you click "OK," SPSS will add the new variable's column with the transformed values of the corresponding variable. Repeat these steps for any variable you wish to compute. Note that this step is optional as your data already have a log-transformed version for most variables.

By taking the natural logarithms of VMT per capita and population in 1000s, and creating a scatterplot as just described, we find a relatively linear relationship between the variables. Note that this relationship is not perfectly linear and is still heteroscedastic—in fact, there may still be concerns about inefficient estimates—but it is nonetheless an improvement over the previous scatterplot.

Also, the scatterplot (Figure 12.26) shows that outliers become less obvious.

When performing logarithmic transformations, researchers can take the natural log of the left-hand (dependent variable) side of the equation, the right-hand (independent variable) side of the equation, or both. Logging just one side produces a *semi-log* model (log linear or linear log), while logging both sides produces a *double-log* (log-log) model. This latter option offers a major advantage, because the coefficient estimates of a double-log regression model can be interpreted as elasticities.

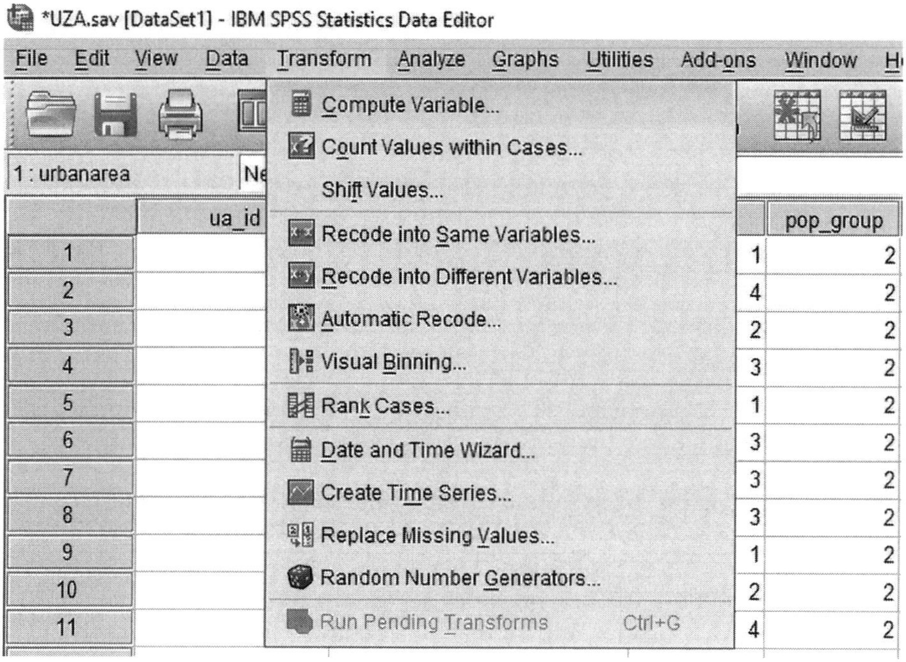

Figure 12.24 Finding "Compute Variable" Option

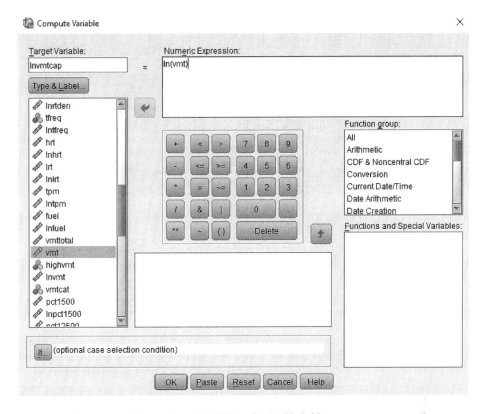

Figure 12.25 Log-Transformation of VMT Per Capita Variable

Elasticity, or *effect size*, describes the proportional change in the dependent variable given a 1 percent shift in the independent variable. An estimated coefficient of –2, for instance, would indicate that every 1 percent increase in the independent variable corresponds to a 2 percent decrease in the dependent variable.

We estimated a double-log model using our sample dataset, *lnvmt* as our dependent variable, and *lnlm, lnpop000, lntmp, lnfuel, lninc000*, and *lncompact* as independent variables. Doing so, we obtained the results shown in Figure 12.27.

Note that the model as a whole has remained significant, and that the coefficient of population size approaches significance at the 0.10 level. Knowing that the coefficients represent elasticities, we can conclude that a 10 percent increase in lane miles per 1000 population is associated with a 2.93 percent increase in VMT per capita. Likewise, a 10 percent increase in compactness index is associated with a 2.06 percent decrease in VMT per capita, respectively. Note that New York and Los Angeles are no longer outliers, according to the leverage values. Overall, we conclude that the double-log transformation has improved the performance of our model and has produced more interesting results. However, the R-squared (and overall explanatory power) of the model is still lower than we would ideally like it to be.

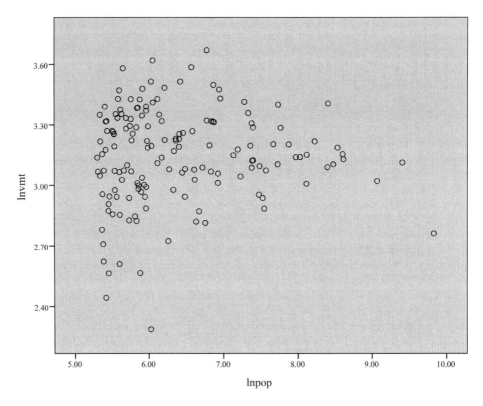

Figure 12.26 Scatterplot Between Log-Transformed Population Size and Log-Transformed VMT Per Capita

Multicollinearity

Another common issue in linear regression is *multicollinearity*, which arises when two or more independent variables are highly correlated with one another. Multicollinearity presents a challenge because OLS regression cannot distinguish the independent impact of highly correlated predictor variables. Much as with irrelevant variables, multicollinearity produces inefficient estimates by inflating the standard errors and depressing the t-statistics of the correlated variables.

Multicollinearity exists, to one degree or another, in virtually all regression models. The predictor variables that explain an outcome variable are likely to have some relationship with one another, rather than showing complete independence. For this reason, multicollinearity is not a black/white distinction but a matter of degree, and researchers use *tolerance* levels or *variance inflation factors* (VIFs) to create cutoff points.

Tolerance represents how much the variance in one independent variable can be explained by the other independent variables in the model. A tolerance of 0.9 means that only 10 percent of the variance in one predictor can be explained by the other predictors. A tolerance of 0.1 means that 90 percent of the variance in one predictor can be explained by the others. Generally, a tolerance greater than 0.1 or 0.2 is

Model Summary

Model	R	R Square	Adjusted R Square	Std. Error of the Estimate
1	.640[a]	.410	.386	.18288

a. Predictors: (Constant), lncompact, lnpop, lnfuel, lninc, lntpm, lnlm

ANOVA[b]

Model		Sum of Squares	df	Mean Square	F	Sig.
1	Regression	3.484	6	.581	17.362	.000[a]
	Residual	5.017	150	.033		
	Total	8.501	156			

a. Predictors: (Constant), lncompact, lnpop, lnfuel, lninc, lntpm, lnlm

b. Dependent Variable: lnvmt

Coefficients[a]

Model		Unstandardized Coefficients		Standardized Coefficients	t	Sig.
		B	Std. Error	Beta		
1	(Constant)	3.100	.538		5.767	.000
	lnlm	.293	.080	.330	3.674	.000
	lnpop	.032	.021	.131	1.523	.130
	lntpm	-.024	.018	-.118	-1.338	.183
	lnfuel	-.695	.336	-.168	-2.072	.040
	lninc	.389	.094	.316	4.140	.000
	lncompact	-.206	.070	-.219	-2.951	.004

a. Dependent Variable: lnvmt

Figure 12.27 Regression Model Summary With Log-Transformed Variables

considered acceptable, while a tolerance less than 0.1 or 0.2 indicates unacceptable multicollinearity. VIF values are just the reciprocals of tolerance values, with corresponding cutoff values of 5.0 or 10.0.

SPSS can compute collinearity diagnostics, including tolerance. In the Linear Regression window, after entering your variables but before running the model, click the "Statistics" button. In the following menu, check the box labeled "Collinearity diagnostics" and click "Continue." Then click "OK" to run the model. See Figure 12.28.

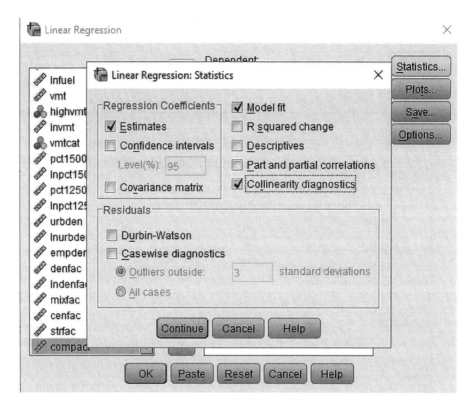

Figure 12.28 Checking "Collinearity diagnostics" in "Linear Regression: Statistics" Window

Now, in the Output Viewer, you will find two new columns labeled "Tolerance" and "VIF" at the end of the Coefficients table (Figure 12.29). Running collinearity diagnostics on our sample dataset, we obtained the following results. Tolerance values for all variables are greater than 0.2, indicating that multicollinearity is not an issue in the current model. If you tried to model total VMT (*vmttotal*), total lane miles (*lmtotal*), and total population (*pop000*) of UZAs instead of per capita versions of these variables, as we did initially, you would have problematic multicollinearity due to the high degree of correlation between *lmtotal* and the confounding variable *pop000*.

When multicollinearity does pose a problem (when tolerance is unacceptably low), researchers have two potential solutions. First, we can drop the variable with the lowest tolerance and least theoretical significance. Collinear variables are often sufficiently similar so that dropping one variable does not severely impact model fit or theoretical utility. Sometimes, however, several collinear variables are important to the theoretical framework behind an OLS regression model. In these circumstances, the planning researcher may want to use factor analysis to create a new independent variable that is the weighted linear sum of the original variables. But only when the variables represent the same underlying construct (see Chapter 5 of *Advanced Quantitative Research Methods for Urban Planners*).

Coefficients[a]

		Unstandardized Coefficients		Standardized Coefficients			Collinearity Statistics	
Model		B	Std. Error	Beta	t	Sig.	Tolerance	VIF
1	(Constant)	3.100	.538		5.767	.000		
	lnlm	.293	.080	.330	3.674	.000	.489	2.047
	lnpop	.032	.021	.131	1.523	.130	.535	1.871
	lntpm	-.024	.018	-.118	-1.338	.183	.506	1.975
	lnfuel	-.695	.336	-.168	-2.072	.040	.596	1.676
	lninc	.389	.094	.316	4.140	.000	.676	1.480
	lncompact	-.206	.070	-.219	-2.951	.004	.712	1.405

a. Dependent Variable: lnvmt

Figure 12.29 Regression Model Summary With Collinearity Statistics

Residual Error-Related Problems

In addition to issues with the raw data, problems with the error term can introduce bias into a regression model. These problems include autocorrelation, heteroscedasticity, and endogeneity.

Also known as serial correlation, *autocorrelation* means that the residual errors from adjacent observations are correlated with one another. If the errors are correlated, then least-squares regression can underestimate or overestimate the standard errors of the coefficients. Underestimated standard errors can make your predictors seem to be significant when they are not. Positive autocorrelation will suppress the standard error of a model's coefficient estimates, thus inflating the t-statistic and possibly causing coefficients to appear significant when they actually are not. Negative autocorrelation will inflate standard errors and suppress t-statistics, meaning that significant coefficients may appear insignificant when they actually are significant (as with irrelevant variables and multicollinearity).

Autocorrelation is most common when the data is part of a time series analysis. In these cases, the problem usually involves error terms associated with successive time periods: dependent variables may act in a cyclical manner, and effects may endure over time. Other sources of autocorrelation can include omission of an important explanatory variable or incorrect use of a functional form (e.g., a linear model applied to data that have a parabolic or asymptotic relationship) (Nerlove & Wallis, 1966). Spatial autocorrelation is also common in cross-sectional data, where values of variables for nearby cases, subjects, or observations are correlated (see Chapter 9 of *Advanced Quantitative Research Methods for Urban Planners*).

Diagnostics for autocorrelation include visual inspection of the residuals for different periods in time series data, and more generally the Durbin-Watson test. The Durbin-Watson statistic ranges from 0 to 4, with a value of 2 indicating no autocorrelation, a value of 0 indicating strong positive autocorrelation, and a value of 4 indicating strong negative autocorrelation.

SPSS can calculate the Durbin-Watson statistic (Figure 12.30). First sort the cases by an independent variable of interest, like *lnlm*. In the Linear Regression window, after entering your variables but before running the model, click the "Statistics" button and check the box labeled "Durbin-Watson."

In the Output Viewer, the Durbin-Watson statistic will appear as a new column in the Model Summary table (Figure 12.31). As you can see, our sample dataset has a Durbin-Watson statistic of 1.898. Since this value is in the rule-of-thumb range of 1.5 to 2.5, we conclude that our model does not suffer from autocorrelation.

When autocorrelation does present a problem, researchers can often correct for it by adding important but missing independent variables.

Another source of residual error bias in OLS regression models is *heteroscedasticity*. OLS assumes that the error term in the regression equation is homoscedastic. In other words, the error term, or residuals, of a regression model should be randomly distributed across all values of the predicted value of the dependent variable. When this is not the case—when a specific non-random pattern is found on the spread in residual errors, heteroscedasticity becomes an issue. Heteroscedasticity makes simple least square coefficient estimates inefficient.

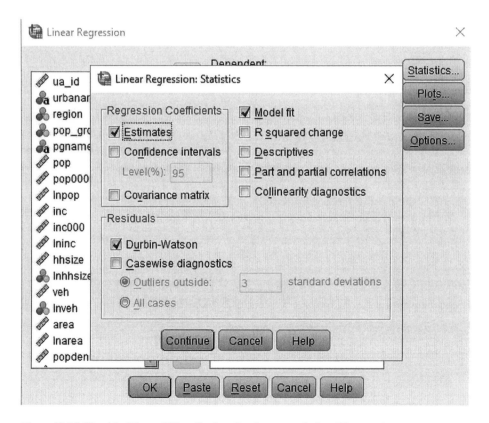

Figure 12.30 "Durbin-Watson" Test Option for Autocorrelation Diagnostics

Model Summary[b]

Model	R	R Square	Adjusted R Square	Std. Error of the Estimate	Durbin-Watson
1	.640[a]	.410	.386	.18288	1.898

a. Predictors: (Constant), lncompact, lnpop, lnfuel, lninc, lntpm, lnlm

b. Dependent Variable: lnvmt

Figure 12.31 Model Summary Table With Durbin-Watson Autocorrelation Diagnostics

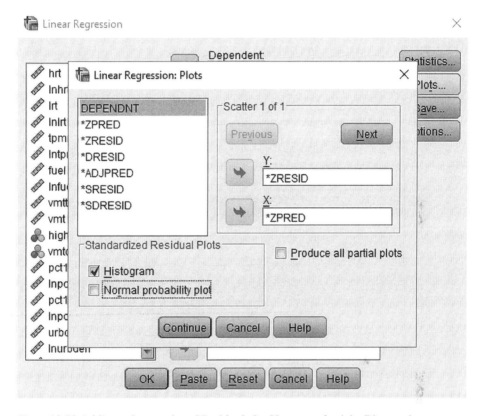

Figure 12.32 Adding a Scatterplot of Residuals for Heteroscedasticity Diagnostics

Researchers can search for heteroscedasticity using scatterplots in SPSS (Figure 12.32). In the Linear Regression window, after entering your variables but before running the model, click the "Plots" button. In the following menu, add "*ZRESID" to the Y-axis and "*ZPRED" to the X-axis. Check on "Histogram" box and click "Continue."

At the end of the regression results, you will see two charts (Figure 12.33). The first chart is a histogram of residuals, which should be normally distributed. The second one is a scatterplot of residuals for predicted values of the dependent variable, which should be randomly distributed. The current results seem to meet both assumptions.

Planning researchers usually assume the dependent variable to be normally distributed. This is, however, a common misconception. Statistically, it is residuals, or errors, that should have a normal distribution. As seen earlier, this assumption can be explored through a histogram of residuals.

Moreover, by the law of large numbers and the central limit theorem, the residuals in a linear regression model still will be approximately normally distributed (Li, Wong, Lamoureux, & Wong, 2012). Thus, in a large sample, the use of a linear regression technique, even if the dependent variable violates the *normality assumption*, remains valid.

If heteroscedasticity is found, a natural logarithm transformation can sometimes correct for it. Another solution for heteroscedasticity is weighted least squares regression (WLS). WLS assigns differential weights to each observation, with the weight inversely proportional to the variance in residual error, thus producing a homogenously distributed spread.

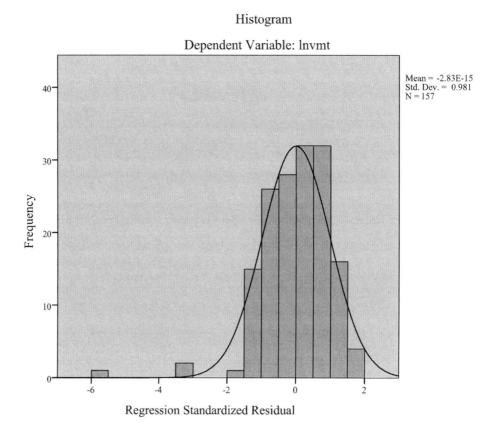

Figure 12.33 Two Graphs of Model Residuals for Heteroscedasticity Diagnostics

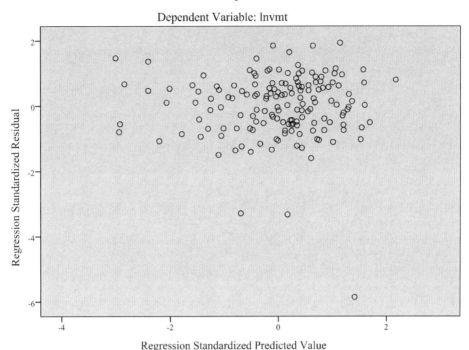

Figure 12.33 Continued

In R

Figures 12.34 through 12.36 show an R script to replicate our Step-by-Step section for linear regression models in SPSS. We first start with a scatter plot between *vmt* (VMT per capita) and *lm* (road lane miles per 1000 population) for all urbanized areas. Then, figure 12.35 shows a result of the final regression model for *lnvmt* with six independent variables. Figure 12.36 presents R scripts for the Durbin-Watson autocorrelation test result as well as a histogram and a scatter plot of model residuals.

Planning Examples

Role of the Arts in Neighborhood Change

The arts are widely credited with sparking neighborhood change resulting in both positive—neighborhood revitalization that benefits existing residents—and negative outcomes—gentrification and displacement of lower-income residents. While most studies about the impact of the arts on communities are based on case study methods, Carl Grodach, Nicole Foster, and James Murdoch III (2014) conducted a statistical test using linear regression for 100 large metropolitan areas in the United States.

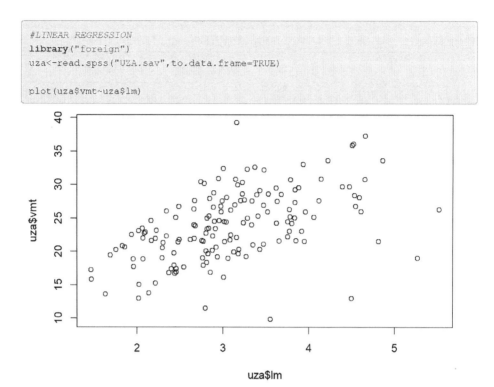

Figure 12.34 Reading SPSS Data and Drawing a Scatterplot: R Script and Outputs

To be specific, they tested how two different types of arts activities—the fine arts and commercial arts industries—are associated with conditions indicative of urban revitalization and gentrification. The study areas were neighborhoods (zip-code-level) within ten miles of the central business district (CBD) in each metropolitan area.

The dependent variables measuring neighborhood change were based on a set of ten variables found in the literature (e.g., changes in income, workers, educational attainment, the White population, housing value, population density, etc.). To reduce the number of dependent variables to be modeled, they conducted an exploratory factor analysis (see Chapter 5 of *Advanced Quantitative Research Methods for Urban Planners*) and found three factors that capture different dimensions of neighborhood change: "neighborhood revitalization," "neighborhood upscaling," and "neighborhood build-out." The latter two categories represent gentrification and potential displacement.

Then the authors estimated linear regression models for each of three factors, meaning three different linear regression models (Table 12.5). The key independent variables are two different sets of arts industries—fine arts (e.g., visual and performing arts and museums) and commercial arts (e.g., film, music, design)—and other control variables are a range of social, economic, and housing variables.

```
lm1<-lm(lnvmt~lnlm+lnpop000+lntpm+lnfuel+lninc000+lncompact,data=uza)
summary(lm1)
```

```
##
## Call:
## lm(formula = lnvmt ~ lnlm + lnpop000 + lntpm + lnfuel + lninc000 +
##     lncompact, data = uza)
##
## Residuals:
##      Min       1Q   Median       3Q      Max
## -1.07092 -0.10096  0.01914  0.11534  0.35382
##
## Coefficients:
##             Estimate Std. Error t value Pr(>|t|)
## (Intercept)  3.10011    0.53760   5.767 4.46e-08 ***
## lnlm         0.29325    0.07982   3.674 0.000332 ***
## lnpop000     0.03180    0.02088   1.523 0.129849
## lntpm       -0.02387    0.01784  -1.338 0.182917
## lnfuel      -0.69541    0.33558  -2.072 0.039953 *
## lninc000     0.38851    0.09385   4.140 5.78e-05 ***
## lncompact   -0.20609    0.06985  -2.951 0.003682 **
## ---
## Signif. codes:  0 '***' 0.001 '**' 0.01 '*' 0.05 '.' 0.1 ' ' 1
##
## Residual standard error: 0.1829 on 150 degrees of freedom
## Multiple R-squared:  0.4099, Adjusted R-squared:  0.3862
## F-statistic: 17.36 on 6 and 150 DF,  p-value: 3.389e-15
```

Figure 12.35 Running a Linear Regression: R Script and Outputs

The commercial arts have a significant association with both of the gentrification factors, but show no relationship to neighborhood revitalization. Conversely, the fine arts have a positive association with neighborhood revitalization, but correlate negatively with gentrifying neighborhoods. These findings support the claim of the role of the arts in revitalizing central city neighborhoods, but also clarify their role in the gentrification processes, especially by commercial arts industries.

The linear regression was not the only test used in this paper. Because neighborhoods that experience different levels of change may have varying associations with arts activity, they use quintile regression. It divides the dependent variable into five levels of change.

Their findings show that the arts are not necessarily connected with either gentrification or revitalization. Also, the fine arts and commercial arts have different impacts on communities. While fine arts are more associated with revitalization, commercial arts seem to be inducing gentrification (and hence displacement).

```
library(lmtest)
dwtest(lm1)
```

```
##
##  Durbin-Watson test
##
## data:  lm1
## DW = 1.8978, p-value = 0.2651
## alternative hypothesis: true autocorrelation is greater than 0
```

```
hist(lm1$residuals,freq=F)
lines(density(lm1$residuals,adjust=2))
```

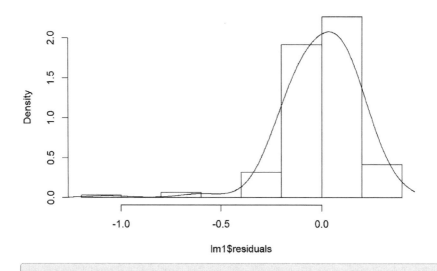

```
plot(lm1$residuals~lm1$fitted.values)
```

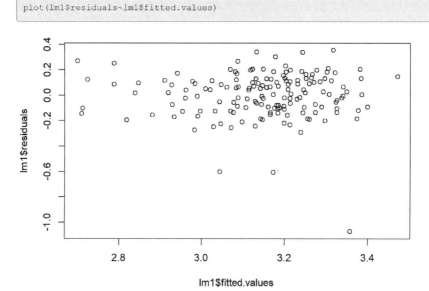

Figure 12.36 Durbin-Watson Test and Residual Plots: R Script and Outputs

Linear Regression 265

Table 12.5 OLS Regression Results: The Relationship Between the Arts and Neighborhood Change

Variables	Revitalization	Upscaling	Build-Out
Commercial arts	0.014	0.092***	0.404***
Fine arts	0.050***	–0.024*	–0.055***
Amenities	–0.036***	–0.109***	0.167***
Population density	0.092***	0.024	–0.048***
Employment	–0.230***	–0.368***	–0.090***
. . .	. . .	. . .	. . .
Adjusted R^2	0.360	0.460	0.430
N	4,284	4,284	4,284

*p < .1; **p < .05; ***p < .01
Source: Grodach et al., 2014

Residential Yard Management and Crime

When it comes to crime, vegetation is a debatable element. It can afford criminals concealment and a place to stash stolen goods or weapons. On the other hand, well-designed trees and lawns can make spending time outdoors more appealing, leading to more "eyes on the street," informal surveillance networks (Jacobs, 1961). Also, vegetation might discourage crime, as it can be seen as a *territorial marker* or a *cue to care* (the inverse of the "broken window" hypothesis) signaling that the residents are actively involved with their surroundings.

Troy, Nunery, and Grove (2016) examined the relationship between residential yard management and neighborhood crime in Baltimore City and County. The researchers surveyed more than 1,000 front yards and collected multiple indicators of yard management vegetation maintenance. Crime data were summarized for a 150-meter buffer around each parcel.

The crime counts were modeled as a function of yard characteristics and surrounding tree canopy, after controlling for socio-economic or housing-related variables. Three statistical approaches—ordinary least squares (linear regression), spatial error regression (see Chapter 9 of *Advanced Quantitative Research Methods for Urban Planners*), and Poisson regression (see Chapter 4 of *Advanced Quantitative Research Methods for Urban Planners*)—were used comparatively to evaluate the stability and consistency of results. OLS was used for its simplicity and ease of interpretation, and this section will focus on the OLS regression results.

The OLS results show that indicators of yard management, from cut lawns to presence of yard trees, are inversely associated with crime, while indicators of neglect, such as litter or desiccation, are positively associated with crime (Figure 12.37). R-squared was 0.58 in the OLS. The results were similar to those in other two advanced models.

The authors admitted that the regression results do not imply causality but the possibility of mechanisms by which environment design may reduce crime. Their theories are *cues to care* and *eyes on the street* drawn by active involvement of neighbors and appealing landscape features, which in turn deter criminals.

Parameter	Linear Regression	
	B	T-test
(Intercept)	178.290	8.853[***]
Avg.treecover	−0.582	−6.759[***]
Dess	3.833	2.217[**]
DetHousePct	−15.271	−4.835[***]
Garden.hose.sprinklers	−4.727	−3.204[***]
Lawn	−23.880	−4.224[***]
Lawn.uncut	3.807	2.677[***]
Litter	7.808	4.181[***]
Lnlnc	−7.863	−3.958[***]
Num.street.sm	17.020	4.994[***]
Popdens	0.002	5.416[***]
SFH	−11.861	−6.145[***]
Shrubs	−3.639	−1.816[*]
Yard.pervious	−0.093	−2.410[**]
Yard.trees	−3.455	−2.265[**]
Lambda		
Model fit	R-squared	0.58

[*] Significant at 90% level.
[**] Significant at 95% level.
[***] Significant at 99% level

Figure 12.37 Regression Results
Source: Troy et al. (2016)

Conclusion

Our exploration of linear regression closes by considering causality, conceptual frameworks, and circumstances when other statistical models are more appropriate.

Causality

Like correlation, linear regression evaluates the strength of the relationship between variables. However, regression can contribute more to the analysis, namely the ability to infer causality. Correlation, as you will recall (from Chapter 9), only measures the degree of association between variables—the extent to which knowing one variable's value enables you to predict the other variable. While one-directional cause and effect could explain the relationship between correlated variables, there are other alternative explanations:

1. The variables may simply be associated by coincidence;
2. The variables may both be influencing one another (the relationship may be two-directional); or
3. An unobserved variable may be creating the appearance of a relationship between the observed variables, when no such relationship actually exists (a confounder).

While correlation results are useful, therefore, they are often insufficient evidence for a researcher to draw causal conclusions.

All things being equal, linear regression will suffer from these same caveats. It is possible, however, to use regression to show causal relationships. Three steps are required. First, the researcher must show statistical association; the proposed cause must be correlated with the proposed effect. Second, the researcher must control for all known confounding factors by including them as independent variables in the regression equation or by employing a quasi-experimental research design (Chapter 14). In other words, rival explanations for the proposed effect must be eliminated. Third, the researcher must show a time sequence in the observed relationship—that is, the proposed cause must always precede the proposed effect. When these three conditions are met, a linear regression model can be considered a causal explanation for the dependent variable. This is a powerful achievement, as causal models allow planners to make much stronger statements about why past events have occurred and what future events will occur.

Conceptual Frameworks

The variables included in a linear regression model should be justified by a conceptual framework. Chapter 5 discusses conceptual framing in detail. Here, we simply observe that planning researchers need an underlying argument in order to decide what might be an interesting or important dependent variable to model, what might be the relevant predictors of that variable, and what might be the necessary controls. Control variables must include variables shown by earlier work to affect the dependent variable, particularly confounders. In addition, a researcher will generally be testing one or more new independent variables that have not previously been shown to influence the dependent variable. To determine what new predictors merit a closer examination, a conceptual framework is desirable.

When Other Models Are More Appropriate

Linear regression models are conceptually appealing and broadly relevant. Nevertheless, the fact that regression can be applied in most quantitative research doesn't mean that it is always the appropriate method. In cases with a categorical dependent variable, logistic regression is required (see Chapter 13). In cases with nested data structures, multilevel modeling is the proper tool (see Chapter 7 of *Advanced Quantitative Research Methods for Urban Planners*). In cases with important mediating

268 *Keunhyun Park et al.*

variables or complex bi-directional causality, structural equation modeling should be employed (see Chapter 8 of *Advanced Research Methods for Urban Planners*). This list goes on; see *Advanced Research Methods for Urban Planners* book for those and other advanced tools.

Nevertheless, linear regression models are useful and appropriate in countless research applications. There will always be a balance between finding the best possible model to explain data, minimizing unnecessary complexity, and producing findings that are interesting to other researchers while remaining useful to planning practitioners. For this reason, linear regression remains a very powerful and widely applicable research tool.

Works Cited

Allen, M. (1997). *Understanding regression analysis.* New York, NY: Plenum Press.

Boarnet, M. G., Houston, D., Edwards, R., Princevac, M., Ferguson, G., Pan, H., & Bartolome, C. (2011). Fine particulate concentrations on sidewalks in five Southern California cities. *Atmospheric Environment, 45*(24), 4025–4033.

Cervero, R. (2002). Induced travel demand: Research design, empirical evidence, and normative policies. *Journal of Planning Literature, 17*(1), 3–20.

Chatterjee, S., & Price, B. (2000). *Regression analysis by example.* Wiley Series in Probability and Mathematical Statistics (3rd ed.). New York, NY: John Wiley & Sons.

Daisa, J., & Peers, J. (1997). Narrow residential streets: Do they really slow down speeds? *ITE Annual Meeting Compendium, 1997,* 546–551.

Draper, N., & Smith, H. (1998). *Applied regression analysis.* Wiley Series in Probability and Mathematical Statistics (3rd ed.). New York, NY: John Wiley & Sons.

Ewing, R. (2008). Highway-induced development: Research results for metropolitan areas. *Transportation Research Record, 2067*(1), 101–109.

Ewing, R. (2012, December). A "new" (250-year-old) way of thinking about statistics. *Planning,* 45.

Ewing, R., & Hamidi, S. (2017). *Costs of sprawl.* New York, NY: Taylor & Francis.

Field, A. (2009). *Discovering statistics using SPSS* (3rd ed.). London: Sage Publications.

Greene, W. H. (2012). *Econometric analysis.* New York, NY: Prentice Hall.

Grodach, C., Foster, N., & Murdoch III, J. (2014). Gentrification and the artistic dividend: The role of the arts in neighborhood change. *Journal of the American Planning Association, 80*(1), 21–35.

Jacobs, J. (1961). *The death and life of great American cities.* New York, NY: Random House.

Li, X., Wong, W., Lamoureux, E. L., & Wong, T. Y. (2012). Are linear regression techniques appropriate for analysis when the dependent (outcome) variable is not normally distributed? *Investigative Ophthalmology & Visual Science, 53*(6), 3082–3083.

Linear Regression. (2008). International encyclopedia of the social sciences. *Encyclopedia.com.* Retrieved May 8, 2012, from www.encyclopedia.com/doc/1G2-3045301360.html

Meijers, E. J., & Burger, M. J. (2010). Spatial structure and productivity in US metropolitan areas. *Environment and Planning A, 42,* 1383–1402.

Nelson, A. C., Burby, R. J., Feser, E., Dawkins, C. J., Malizia, E. E., & Quercia, R. (2004, Autumn). Urban containment and central-city revitalization. *Journal of the American Planning Association, 70*(4), 411–425.

Nelson, A. C., Genereux, J., & Genereux, M. (1992). House price effects of landfills. *Land Economics, 68*(4), 359–365.

Nerlove, M., & Wallis, K. F. (1966). Use of the Durbin-Watson statistic in inappropriate situations. *Econometrica: Journal of the Econometric Society,* 235–238.

Sacramento Transportation & Air Quality Collaborative. (2005). *Best practices for complete streets*. Retrieved May 12, 2012, from www.completestreets.org/webdocs/resources/cs-bestpractices-sacramento.pdf

Schroeder, L., Sjoquist, D., & Stephan, P. (1986). *Understanding regression analysis: An introductory guide*. Series: Quantitative Application in the Social Sciences. Sage University Paper. Beverly Hills: Sage Publications.

Stanton, J. (2001). Galton, Pearson, and the peas: A brief history of linear regression for statistics instructors. *Journal of Statistics Education, 9,* 3.

Sykes, A. (2005). Introduction to regression analysis. *The inaugural coase lecture*. Retrieved from www.law.uchicago.edu/files/files/20.Sykes_.Regress8ion.pdf?utm_source=twitterfeed&utm_medium=twitter

Troy, A., Nunery, A., & Grove, J. M. (2016). The relationship between residential yard management and neighborhood crime: An analysis from Baltimore City and county. *Landscape and Urban Planning, 147,* 78–87.

13 Logistic Regression

Sadegh Sabouri, Amir Hajrasouliha, Yu Song, and William H. Greene

Method	Dependent Variable	Independent Variables	Test Statistics
Chi-Square	Categorical	Categorical	chi-square statistic
Difference of Means	Continuous	Categorical (two categories)	t-statistic
ANOVA	Continuous	Categorical (multiple categories)	F-statistic
Linear Regression	Continuous	Continuous (though can represent categorical)	t-statistic R2 statistic
Logistic Regression	Categorical (Dichtomous)	Continuous (though can represent categorical)	asymptotic t-statistic pseudo-R2 statistic
Poisson/Negative Binomial Regression	Count	Continuous (though can represent categorical)	Wald statistic pseudo-R2 statistic

Figure 13.0 Logistic Regression

Overview

A common objective of planning research is to model the probability of a categorical outcome based on predictors. Logistic regression is a statistical technique used to achieve this goal. In the realm of urban planning, logistic regression has been used to investigate the effects of urban form on travel mode choice (Johnson & Parker, 2006; Krizek & Johnson, 2006), the importance of walkable green spaces (Takano, Nakamura, & Watanabe, 2002), the effects of urban form on physical activity (Frank, Schmid, Sallis, Chapman, & Saelens, 2005), the factors influencing walking and total physical activity (Forsyth, Hearst, Oakes, & Schmitz, 2008), the growth of urban areas (Hu & Lo, 2007; Cheng & Masser, 2003), the dynamics of urban sprawl (Fang, Gertner, Sun, & Anderson, 2005), the dynamics of rural land-use change (Theobald & Hobbs, 1998), the impact of business improvement districts on retailers (Sutton, 2014), and many other discrete phenomena. A review of JAPA and JPER issues for the decade between 2004 and 2014 indicates that logistic regression is now used as frequently as linear regression—the universal standard until the early 1970s. With the growing preference in quantitative research for disaggregate analysis over aggregate analysis, the popularity of logistic regression is assured.

Logistic regression has other names and applications, such as binomial regression, binary logistic regression, binomial logit modeling, and the parallel terms for multinomial modeling. Binary or binominal logistic regression is a multiple regression technique for a dichotomous categorical variable i.e., "move/don't move," "chosen/not chosen," "true/false," or "yes/no." Multinomial applies when the dependent variable is nominal or ordinal with more than two levels, such as mode of transportation (nominal: walk, bike, transit, and auto) or level of physical activity (ordinal: high-, medium-, and low-level of physical activity). The last case—multinomial regression with ordinal (or ordered) variable—is also called ordinal logistic regression (O'Connell, 2006).

This chapter describes the conditions required to use logistic regression followed by a demonstration of how to estimate a logistic regression model. This chapter also presents two case studies from the field of planning that use binomial and multinomial logistic regression, respectively.

Purpose

The purpose of logistic regression is to model the probability of a categorical outcome based upon a set of independent or predictor variables. Figure 13.1 suggests the advantage of logistic regression models compared to linear regression models for predicting probabilities of an event occurring. Logistic regression imposes the constraint of probability value, which always varies from zero to one. A value close to 0 indicates that the event is very unlikely to occur, and a value close to 1 means that it is very likely to occur. Also, just like linear regression, each independent variable X in the logistic

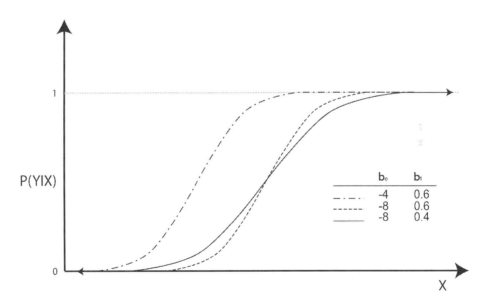

Figure 13.1 Shape of Logistic Probability Function (Depends on b_0 and b_1)

regression equation has its own coefficient. In Figure 13.1, b_1 is the coefficient of X in a binary logistic regression; b_0 is an intercept.

The main goal of the analysis is to estimate and use the values of these coefficients. For that we need to estimate the model. Coefficients are estimated by fitting models, based on the available data. The values of the coefficients are estimated using maximum-likelihood estimation. This technique calculates coefficients that make the observed values of dependent variable most likely to have occurred (Field, 2009).

History

The logistic function originated in the early 19th century for the study of the growth of populations and the course of autocatalytic chemical reactions (Cramer, 2002). Since then, the further application of this technique is due to the individual actions of a few scholars (i.e., Pearl and Reed from 1920 to 1940) to apply the logistic growth curve to living populations from fruit flies to the human population of the French colonies in North Africa as well as to the growth of cantaloupes. The simplicity and elegance of the logistic growth curve made it popular in economics, in epidemiology, and in the social sciences. In 1973, while working as a consultant on a California public transportation project, Daniel McFadden linked the multinomial logit model to the theory of discrete choice from mathematical psychology, work that earned him a Nobel Prize in 2000 (Cramer, 2002).

Historically, researchers fit binary outcome data using what is called a linear probability model. In a linear probability model, a 1/0 outcome is modeled using simple linear regression (see Figure 13.2—straight line). There are problems with the linear probability model, as illustrated by Figure 13.2 and the following example.

In the previous chapter, we learned that vehicle miles traveled per household (VMT) is non-normally distributed, positively skewed to the right. To use linear regression, we took the natural logarithm of VMT, which became our dependent variable. But there was one problem with that approach. VMT has a large number of zero values for households that generate no VMT. These households use only alternative modes such as transit or walking. Eleven percent of households in the sample fall into

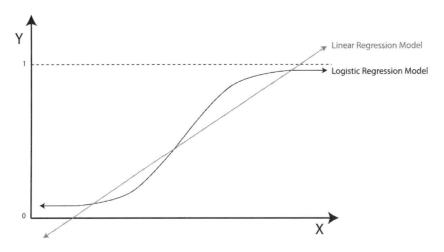

Figure 13.2 Linear Probability Versus Logistic Model

Logistic Regression 273

this category. When VMT is log transformed, these households have undefined values of the dependent variable. In this chapter, we convert the continuous dependent variable into a categorical variable as either households generating VMT or not.

The combination of a logistic model to predict households with and without VMT, and a linear model to predict the amount of VMT for households with VMT, is known as a two-stage hurdle model, and is one way of dealing with excess zero values in the dataset (Ewing et al., 2015). In the planning literature, the problem of zero values is often handled by adding a very small value (e.g., 1.0) to the value of a dependent variable and then log transforming the variable. The 1 becomes a 0 when transformed. This is not econometrically correct, however, if households with zero values are qualitatively different than those with positive values.

> In some settings, the zero outcome of the data-generating process is qualitatively different from the positive ones. The zero or nonzero values of the outcome is the result of a separate decision whether or not to *participate* in the activity. On deciding to participate, the individual decides separately how much to, that is, how intensively [to participate].
>
> (Greene, 2012, p. 824)

Plotting histograms of *lnvmt* and *anyvmt* in our household dataset (HTS. household.10regions.sav), the *lnvmt* follows a normal distribution, while the distribution of *anyvmt* is dichotomous (Figures 13.3 and 13.4). Linear regression is appropriate for continuous variables, but not generally for discrete variables. This is the case when the dependent variable is *lnvmt*, but not when it is *anyvmt*.

Mechanics

A few similarities and differences between logistic regression and linear regression will be discussed to facilitate the understanding of this method.

The main similarity between logistic and linear regression is that in both cases, we specify linear relationships between the dependent variable and the independent variables. Also, we try to include all relevant variables and exclude irrelevant variables.

The main difference between linear and logistic regression is that instead of predicting the value of a dependent variable with one or several independent variables, logistic regression predicts the log odds of the outcome, and from that, the *probability* of the outcome, with one or several independent variables. The transformation from log odds to probability means that the probability is a nonlinear function of the independent variables.

For example, we can calculate the *probability* of a randomly selected household having *any* VMT. As you remember from Chapter 12, the Linear Regression chapter, in its simplest form, the dependent variable Y is predicted from the following equation in the case of two independent variables.

$$Y = b_0 + b_1 X_1 + b_2 X_2 + \varepsilon \tag{1}$$

where
Y: predicted value of the dependent variable
b_0: Y intercept

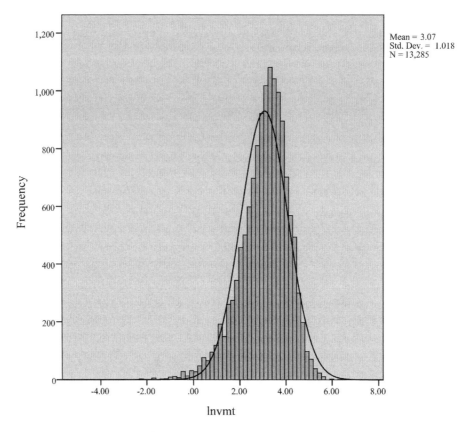

Figure 13.3 Frequency Distribution of *lnvmt* Variable (Excluding Zero Values of VMT)

b_i: the regression coefficients
X_i: the value of the independent variables
ε: error term

The logistic regression equation is very similar to the preceding linear regression equation. Only, instead of using linear regression to model the *probability* of an outcome, we use logistic regression to model the *log odds* of the outcome and then back into the *probability*.

$$\ln \text{odds}(Y \mid X) = b_0 + b_1 X_1 + b_2 X_{2...} \qquad (2)$$

Terminology and Transformations

At this point, you need to become familiar with four terms: probability, odds, log odds, and odds ratio. Probability is the likelihood that an outcome will occur. The term *outcome* is synonymous with *event* and *occurrence*, terms used in the literature on

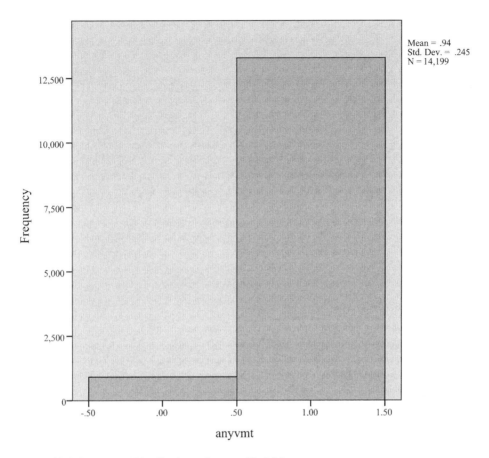

Figure 13.4 Frequency Distribution of *anyvmt* Variable

logistic regression. It is an outcome, an event, or an occurrence when a commuter chooses to use transit rather than another mode, or a parcel of land is developed while others are not, or a family moves out of a gentrifying neighborhood while others remain, or one city adopts a growth management measure and other cities do not.

The *odds* of an outcome occurring are defined as the probability of an outcome occurring divided by the probability of that outcome not occurring. *Odds* should not be confused with the more colloquial usage of the word to refer to probability.

$$odds\,(outcome) = \frac{probability\,(outcome)}{probability\,(different\,outcome)} \tag{3}$$

As an example, if we flip a fair coin, the *probability* of getting heads is 0.5, while the *odds* of getting heads are 50:50 or 0.5/0.5, which equals 1. Likewise, if we say the odds are 2 to 1 that our horse will win the race, there are three chances in total. For two of them, the desired outcome will occur. For one, it will not. The *odds* are thus 2/1 or 2, while the *probability* of winning is 2/3 or 0.67.

276 *Sadegh Sabouri et al.*

In our earlier example, the odds of having any VMT for any given household equals the probability of having any VMT divided by the probability of not having any VMT. Let's say, a given suburban household has a probability of 90 percent of having any VMT. The probability of the same household not having VMT is, then, 10 percent. The odds of having any VMT are thus nine to one, or 9.0 (0.9/0.1).

The log odds is just the natural logarithm of the odds. In the suburban household example, the log odds is equal to ln (9), or 2.197. If we consider other values of the probability, we find that through these transformations, a probability between 0 and 1 translates into an odds between 0 and $+\infty$ and a log (odds) between $-\infty$ and $+\infty$ (see Table 13.1). That is, the transformations have converted a bounded variable into a continuous variable equivalent to Y in linear regression. This transformed variable could then be used as the dependent variable in a linear equation.

Exponentiation of equation (2) (taking the anti-log of both sides) gives the following expression for odds of Y.

$$\left[\mathrm{odds}(Y|X) = e^{b_0 + b_1 X_1 + b_2 X_2 \cdots} \right]$$

The probability of Y can thus be computed as:

$$\left[p(Y|X) = \left(e^{b_0 + b_1 X_1} \right) / \left(1 + e^{b_0 + b_1 X_1} \right) \right]$$

$$p(Y|X) = \frac{1}{1 + e^{-(b_0 + b_1 X_1 \cdots)}}$$

where

$p(Y|X)$: The probability of outcome Y as a function of the Xs.
Since *probability, odds,* and *log odds* can easily be transformed into each other, we can calculate the probability of an outcome from the log odds, and the log odds from a linear equation. Probability is clearly a nonlinear function of the Xs.

One more term requires our attention. The odds ratio (OR) is the proportionate change in odds when the independent variable increases by one unit.

$$\mathrm{odds\ ratio} = \frac{\mathrm{odds\ after\ a\ unit\ increase\ in\ X}}{\mathrm{original\ odds}}$$

If the OR is greater than 1, it indicates that as the value of the independent variable increases, the odds of the outcome occurring increase. Conversely, an OR less

Table 13.1 Transformation of Random Numbers Between Probability, Odds, and Log Odds

Probability	Odds	ln (Odds)
1	$+\infty$	$+\infty$
0.999999	999999	13.81551
0.99	99	4.59512
0.5	1	0
0.01	0.010101	−4.59512
0.000001	0.000001	−13.81551
0	0	$-\infty$

Logistic Regression 277

than 1 indicates that as the independent variable increases, the odds of the outcome decrease. In other words, ORs reveal the sign of the independent variable's contribution to the probability of the outcome. The relationship between the OR and the independent variable i's estimated regression coefficient is expressed as $OR_i = e^{bi}$. It is noteworthy that this odds ratio is constant over all values of X_i. Thus the OR_i is often reported along with (or instead of) the regression coefficient b_i.

Goodness of Fit

Using maximum likelihood estimation, we can create a model for the outcome variable based on the independent variables. The likelihood function is used to select parameters in the logistic regression model. Rather than choosing parameters to minimize a sum of squared errors as in linear regression, the logistic regression procedure chooses parameters that maximize the predicted probability of observing the sample values (the likelihood of the sample).

Loose parallels to the F statistic and R-squared values in the linear model can be constructed for the logistic regression. A test for "overall model fit," based on the null hypothesis that none of the independent variables are *significant*, can be based on the log of the likelihood function (compared to the likelihood for a model with only a constant term, which must be inferior) or the multivariate counterpart to *t*-tests for the coefficients, such as the Wald statistic. Measures of the fit of the model to the observed data are based either on the likelihood function or on the correspondence between model predictions of the outcomes and the actual data. Other fit measures based on predicted probabilities and the actual data, such as the *deviance* and various R-squared like statistics, have also been proposed.

In computing the likelihood ratio, the fitted model is compared to a null model, with only a constant term. The likelihood L is a small positive number, so the log likelihood is a large negative number, larger for the null model than the fitted model. Since both likelihoods are logged, the log of the likelihood ratio is just the difference between the two (null minus fitted).

By multiplying the log likelihood ratio by –2, the resulting statistic is positive and follows a chi-square distribution. Larger values suggest better prediction of the dependent variable (Menard, 2010).

Planners are used to reporting R^2 statistics for linear regression, and therefore often report *pseudo-R squareds* for logistic regression, even though the interpretation of the statistic is very different. Two pseudo R squareds are computed automatically by SPSS—Cox and Snell and Nagelkerke's R squared. Nagelkerke's R^2 is more similar to R^2 used in linear regression, because it can reach to a theoretical maximum of 1 unlike Cox and Snell's R^2. However, there is no interpretation under which the pseudo R squared represents a proportion of explained variation as in linear regression.

Another common pseudo R squared is the McFadden statistic, which is just one minus the ratio of the log likelihood of the fitted model divided by the log likelihood of the null model (a model with only a constant term). Oddly enough, SPSS does not compute the McFadden R^2. Other software packages do. But you can compute it easily enough yourself from the SPSS output (see Step by Step section later in the chapter).

An urban planning example of binary logistic regression is the modeling of vehicle ownership ("1 = owns a vehicle, 0 = does not own a vehicle") in terms of some

278 *Sadegh Sabouri et al.*

household attributes variables such as household size, income, and location (Jun, 2008). Another example is Frank et al. (2005) where they used binary logistic regression to investigate whether the probability of walking is associated with community design. The binary outcome was whether or not an indivdual gets 30 minutes and more of moderate physical activity per day. While controlling for socio-demographic covariates, they assessed how physical activity is related to the physical environment around each participant's home. The result showed that individuals in the highest walkability quartile were 2.4 times more likely than individuals in the lowest walkability quartile to meet the recommended ≥30 minutes of moderate physical activity per day.

A common (but not necessarily correct) example of multinomial logistic regression is the modeling of how many vehicles a household owns (0 = no vehicle, 1 = one vehicle, 2 = two vehicles, 3 = three or more vehicles). What makes this application suspect is that vehicle ownership is a count variable rather than a categorical variable. A better example is the modeling of mode choice, either choice of auto, transit, or walk/bike. Clearly, this variable is categorical. When the outcome variable has more than two categories, multinomial logistic regression can be used.

Step by Step

In this section, we are going to use a sample dataset (HTS.household.10regions.sav) and use SPSS and R to generate a logistic regression model. In our dataset, we have a sample of 14,212 households in ten regions of the United States with a selection of built environment and demographic related variables.

We are going to test the significance of selected independent variables for predicting which households use vehicles for travel instead of just relying on walking and transit or not traveling at all. The dependent variable is *anyvmt* with a binary outcome of whether a certain household generates any automobile travel or not. Independent variables include household size, number of workers in a household, household income, and 5D built environment variables. The 5Ds are development density, land use diversity, street design, destination accessibility, and distance to transit (Ewing et al., 2015).

To open the Logistic Regression window in SPSS, select "Analyze" > "Regression" > "Binary Logistic" (Figure 13.5). Insert *anyvmt* into the "Dependent" box and six independent variables—*hhsize, hhworker, lnhhincome, entropy, pct4way,* and *stopden*—into the "Covariates" box. These variables respectively represent household size, number of workers in the household, the natural logarithm of household income, land use entropy (a measure of land use diversity), percentage of four-way intersections (a measure of street design), and transit stop density (a measure of distance to transit).

In this example, we do not have any categorical independent variable. Otherwise, we need to click on the "Categorical" box on the top right side of the window, add categorical variables to the "Categorical Covariates" box, and select the reference group.

Optionally, it is possible to save predicted values, residuals, and outlier-related statistics from the "Save" box (Figure 13.6). The predicted probabilities are the probabilities of *anyvmt* occurring given the values of each predictor for a given household, with values ranging from 0 to 1. Group membership is based on this probability, with

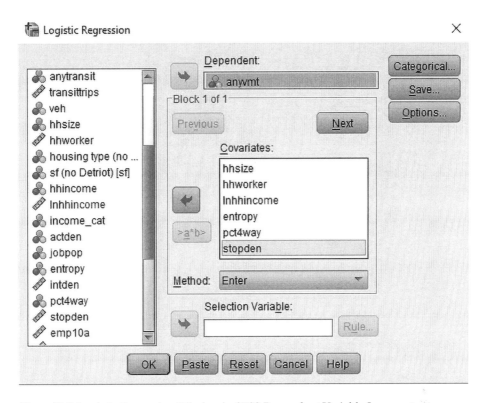

Figure 13.5 Logistic Regression Window in SPSS-Dependent Variable Is *anyvmt*

values greater than or equal to 0.5 predicted to have some VMT and values less than 0.5 predicted to have no VMT. You may check the boxes for probabilities and group membership.

Go back to the Logistic Regression window and click "OK" to run the model. You can see the output in the output window. First, take a look at the "Classification Table" at "Block 0: Beginning Block" (Figure 13.7). This tells us about the model when only the constant is included (i.e., all independent variables are omitted). The base model assigns every participant to a single category of the outcome variable. In this example, there were 12,341 households with any VMT, and only 822 without any VMT. Therefore, SPSS predicts that every household has some VMT, which makes it correct 93.8 percent (12,341 out of 13,163).

Then, look at the classification at "Block 1: Method = Enter" (Figure 13.8). Here, SPSS adds all predictors to the model and produces another classification table that compares observed outcomes with predicted outcomes. The table shows that out of 822 households that have zero VMT, our model was able to make a correct prediction for 48 cases (i.e., 5.8 percent approx.). Likewise, out of 12,341 households with some VMT, 12,301 were correctly classified, for a correct rate of 99.8 percent. There are more false positives than false negatives. The overall percentage of correct predictions is 93.8 percent, which shows no improvement from the base model.

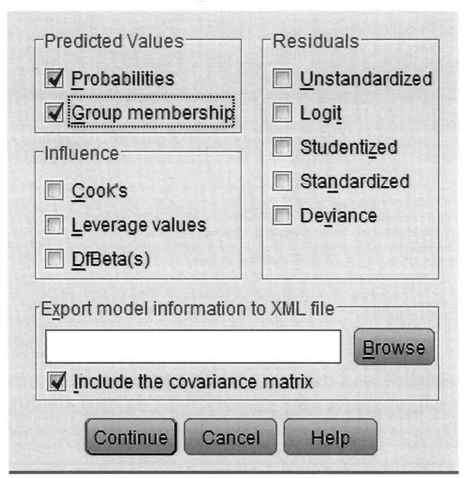

Figure 13.6 Saving Predicted Values, Residuals, and Influence

Classification Table[a,b]

			Predicted		
			anyvmt		Percentage
	Observed		.00	1.00	Correct
Step 0	anyvmt	.00	0	822	.0
		1.00	0	12341	100.0
	Overall Percentage				93.8

a. Constant is included in the model.

b. The cut value is .500

Figure 13.7 Classification Table—Block 0

Classification Table^a

			Predicted		
			anyvmt		Percentage
Observed			.00	1.00	Correct
Step 1	anyvmt	.00	48	774	5.8
		1.00	40	12301	99.7
	Overall Percentage				93.8

a. The cut value is .500

Figure 13.8 Classification Table—Block 1

Model Summary

Step	-2 Log likelihood	Cox & Snell R Square	Nagelkerke R Square
1	5023.433^a	.082	.220

a. Estimation terminated at iteration number 6 because parameter estimates changed by less than .001.

Figure 13.9 Model Summary Statistics

The SPSS Output also tells us the values of −2 Log likelihood, Cox and Snell's R^2, and Nagelkerke's R^2. Cox and Snell's measure is 0.082, and Nagelkerke's R^2 value is 0.220. The first statistic is highly significant when compared to a chi-square distribution. A higher value is better. The next two statistics are measures of relative model fit, which while not analogous to a R^2 value in linear regression, can be used to compare one model to another. Again, higher values are better. We would report all three values in an academic planning paper.

We might also report the McFadden R^2. The SPPS output gives you −2 log likelihood of the fitted model, 5023 in this case (Figure 13.9). If you check "Iteration history" in the Options window, the output displays −2 log likelihood of the null model at the end of Iteration History table for Block 0. The value is 6151. Hence the McFadden R^2 is 1−(5023/6151) or 0.183.

The final table ("Variables in the Equation"), shown in Figure 13.10, provides the coefficients of the predictors included in the model. The coefficient, or the B-value, tells us how the log odds varies with one-unit change in the predictor variable. The table shows that all independent variables have significant p-values and expected signs. Household size, number of workers, and income are positively associated with the log odds, odds, and probability of any VMT, while the three D variables are negatively associated with the log odds, odds, and probability of any VMT. These results are consistent with theory and prior empirical studies.

282 *Sadegh Sabouri et al.*

Variables in the Equation

		B	S.E.	Wald	df	Sig.	Exp(B)
Step 1[a]	hhsize	.211	.039	28.627	1	.000	1.235
	hhworker	.419	.062	46.336	1	.000	1.521
	lnhhincome	.624	.046	181.875	1	.000	1.867
	entropy	-1.269	.160	63.013	1	.000	.281
	pct4way	-.016	.002	81.922	1	.000	.984
	stopden	-.007	.001	55.627	1	.000	.993
	Constant	.900	.200	20.181	1	.000	2.459

a. Variable(s) entered on step 1: hhsize, hhworker, lnhhincome, entropy, pct4way, stopden.

Figure 13.10 Logistic Regression Model Result

A crucial statistic that we haven't yet introduced is the Wald statistic, which follows a chi-square distribution and tells us whether the B coefficient for the predictor is significantly different from zero. A higher Wald value indicates that a particular predictor contributes to the overall estimation. In this example, natural log of household income has the highest Wald value and it is significant at the $p < .001$ level. This means that there is less than one chance in a thousand that you will get a value this large by chance, in other words that the coefficient of that variable is almost certainly greater than zero.

Using the B value, we can calculate the odds ratio, which is already presented in the far right "Exp(B)" column. The odds ratio is a measure of effect size, like elasticity in linear regression. In this example, the odds ratio of pct4way is 0.984. It means that when the percentage of four-way intersections increases by 1 unit (e.g., 30 percent to 31 percent), with all other factors held constant, then the odds of having any VMT will decrease by 1.6 percent. Likewise, the odds of having any VMT increase by almost 52 percent (1.521 minus 1) for one more worker in a household (*hhworker* variable).

If you saved probabilities and group membership, you will find these in the final columns of your dataset. The probability that the first case (household 60002001) will have any VMT is 0.95219, so this household is predicted to have VMT (predicted to be a member of group 1). Interestingly, it is one of the relatively few households without any VMT. It did not make any trips at all on its travel day.

Multinomial Logistic Regression

When the outcome has more than two categories, the multinomial logit model is appropriate. An example of a three-categorical outcome is in a soccer match, when teams can either win, lose, or tie. Multinomial logistic regression can be viewed similarly to binomial logistic regression because it is basically a series of comparisons between pairs of categories. One of the categories may be designated as a baseline or reference category. Then, pairwise comparisons to the base case reveal the alternative with the highest probability (in the binary case, either the base case or the other case has the higher probability).

Logistic Regression 283

SPSS's capabilities for studying multinomial outcomes are rather limited. Researchers typically use a more specialized package such as Stata, R, or NLOGIT for this purpose. The following analysis is done first with SPSS to better understand the similarities and differences between the two logistic regression types and then, with Stata to show how to overcome the shortcomings of SPSS calculations.

The example is again based on the "HTS.household.10regions.sav" file. We are going to build a model for the choice of housing type by households with different socio-demographic characteristics in different built environments. For practice estimating a multinomial model, the dependent variable will be housing type with three categories, i.e., 1 = single family detached (sfd), 2 = single family attached (sfa), 3 = multi-family (mf). Another related trip database is available upon request for the households in the "HTS.household.10regions.sav" file. This supplemental file provides data for every trip made by members of each household, including their mode of travel, a categorical variable best analyzed with multinomial logistic regression.

Independent variables in the model include *hhsize, hhworker, lnhhincome, actden, entropy,* and *jobpop.* Before doing the analysis, let's exclude all the observations (households) that have the value of "others" in the housing type variable and make the computation just based on three categories. For doing so, go to "<u>D</u>ata" → "<u>S</u>elect Cases . . ." (Figure 13.11).

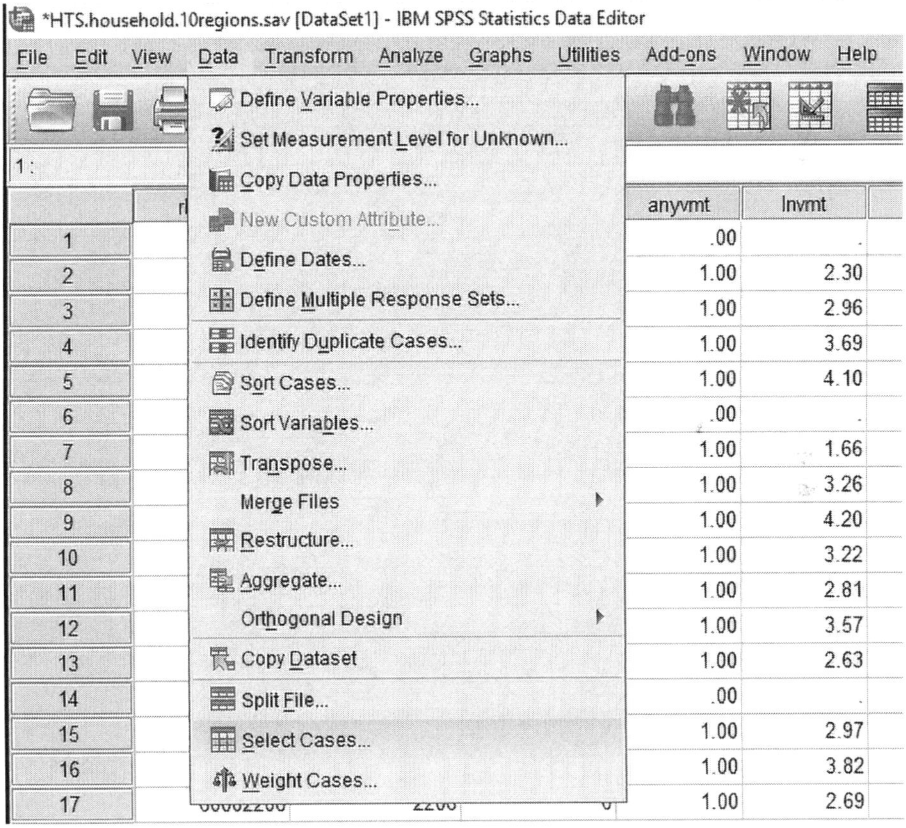

Figure 13.11 Select Cases From Top Menu

Now, choose the second option which is "If condition is satisfied" and then, click on "If . . . " to write a new statement.

You may be now familiar with this window (see Figure 13.12). Now, you want to tell SPSS to select cases that are not equal to 0 (others). Write this expression: htype <> 0.

This "<>" sign means not equal to in SPSS. Click on Continue and then OK to go back to your dataset. Now you can see that some of the observations are crossed out. This means that SPSS will not use these cases in any computation. Note that when you are done with your analysis and want to work on your original dataset, you should go to Select Cases and click on the first option, which is "All cases."

Now we are ready to estimate a multinomial regression model. To run this model in SPSS, go to "Analyze" menu → "Regression" → "Multinomial Logistic" (Figure 13.13).

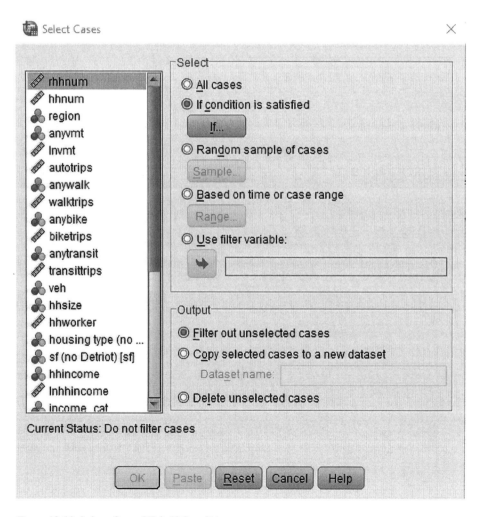

Figure 13.12 Select Cases With If Condition

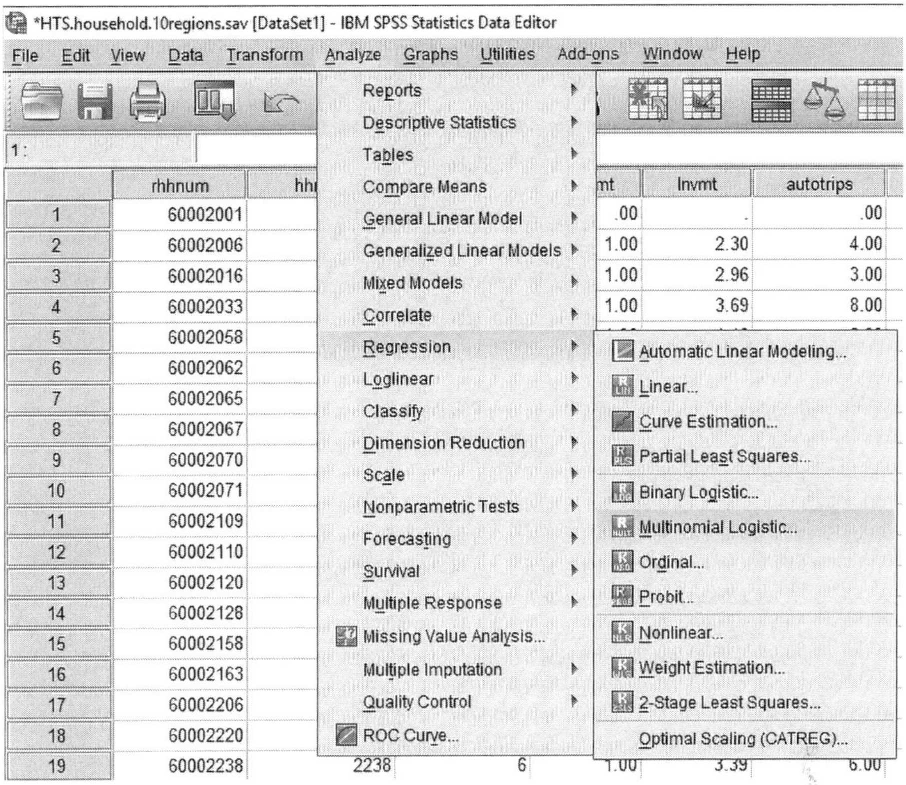

Logistic Regression 285

Figure 13.13 Multinomial Logistic Regression Menu

Add *htype* as the dependent variable and *hhsize, hhworker, lnhhincome, actden, entrop, pct4way,* and *stopden* to "Covariate(s)" box. If there is any categorical independent variable, it should go to "Factor(s)" box (Figure 13.14).

We also have to specify a reference category against which we want to compare other categories (Figure 13.15). The default is the last category and we will change it to the first category. In our example, it makes more sense to select single-family detached as the baseline.

By clicking on "Statistics . . ." we can obtain certain statistics (Figure 13.16). We are going to add "Classification table" and "Goodness of Fit" options. Then, run the analysis.

Overall summary of data is given in the first table—"Case Processing Summary" (Figure 13.17). Out of 12,067 valid cases, 82.1 percent of households live in single-family detached houses, while only 7.1 percent and 10.9 percent of households live in single-family attached and multi-family housing types, respectively.

The next table is about model fit (Figure 13.18). The log-likelihood is a measure of how much unexplained variability there is in the data; therefore, the difference in log-likelihood indicates how much new variance has been explained by the model. The chi-square test shows that the decrease in unexplained variance from the baseline

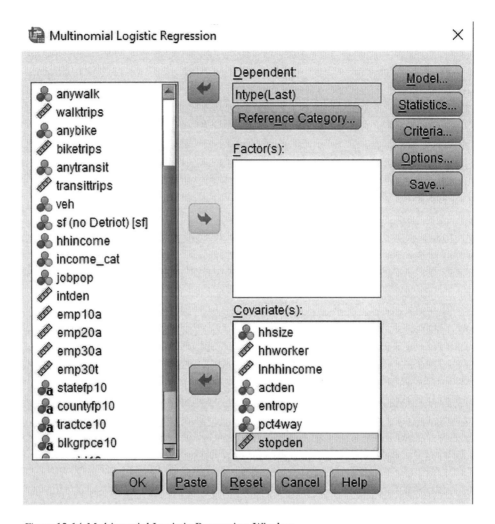

Figure 13.14 Multinomial Logistic Regression Window

model (14256.7) to the final model (11346.1) is significant at $p < .001$ level. So, our model has a better fit than does the null model.

The next part of the output also relates to the fit of the model to the data (Figure 13.19). We know that the model is significantly better than the null model, but is it a good fit of the data? Both the Pearson and deviance statistics test goodness-of-fit, whether the predicted values from the model differ significantly from the observed values. If these statistics are not significant, the model is a good fit. Here we have contrasting results between the two measures. The output also shows us the three other measures of pseudo-R-squared. Notice that unlike binomial logit model, here we also have the McFadden pseudo-R-squared. These

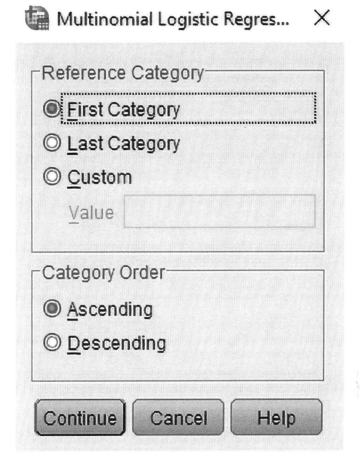

Figure 13.15 Set the First Category as a Reference Category

pseudo-R-squared are difficult to interpret since it can be only used to compare models fit between different models. In principle, higher pseudo-R-squared means a better model.

The "Parameter Estimates" table (Figure 13.20) shows the individual coefficient estimates. Note that the table is split into two parts because the parameters compare pairs of outcome categories (with the reference group of single family detached). Let's look at the effects one by one. For the purpose of legibility, the right two columns—confidence interval—are removed.

Briefly, almost all variables are statistically significant in all two categories. They also have expected signs; household size and household income are negatively associated with the probability of selecting more compact housing (i.e., single-family attached and multi-family) and D variables are positively associated. In other words, as the

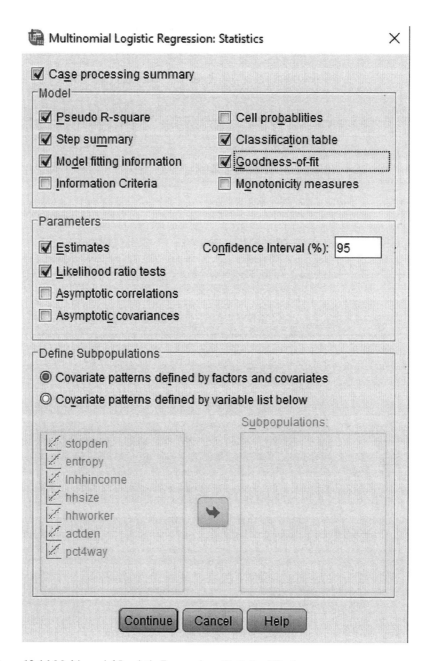

Figure 13.16 Multinomial Logistic Regression: Statistics Window

household size or income increases, it is more likely for a household to choose to live in a single-family detached house. On the other hand, households living in mixed and dense areas are more likely to choose multi-family houses over single-family attached and detached houses. The insignificant variables in the model are number

Logistic Regression   289

Case Processing Summary

		N	Marginal Percentage
housing type (no Detroit)	single family detached	9902	82.1%
	single family attached	851	7.1%
	multi-family	1314	10.9%
Valid		12067	100.0%
Missing		989	
Total		13056	
Subpopulation		12057a	

a. The dependent variable has only one value observed in 12057 (100.0%)
subpopulations.

Figure 13.17 Case Processing Summary Table

Model Fitting Information

	Model Fitting Criteria	Likelihood Ratio Tests		
Model	-2 Log Likelihood	Chi-Square	df	Sig.
Intercept Only	14256.714			
Final	11346.069	2910.646	14	.000

Figure 13.18 Model Fitting Information

of workers in household and job-population balance in single-family attached (versus single-family detached). The odds ratio in "Exp(B)" column shows the odds of living in single family attached or multi-family houses compared with living in single-family detached houses in response to one-unit change in the predictor variable.

Lastly, the classification says 84.1 percent of households are accurately classified (Figure 13.21). The accuracy is particularly low for single-family attached category (0 percent).

Goodness-of-Fit

	Chi-Square	df	Sig.
Pearson	23157.515	24098	1.000
Deviance	11346.069	24098	1.000

Pseudo R-Square

Cox and Snell	.214
Nagelkerke	.309
McFadden	.204

Figure 13.19 Model Fit Outputs

Parameter Estimates

housing type (no Detroit)[a]		B	Std. Error	Wald	df	Sig.	Exp(B)
single family attached	Intercept	.234	.203	1.330	1	.249	
	hhsize	-.283	.038	56.639	1	.000	.753
	hhworker	.009	.054	.027	1	.870	1.009
	lnhhincome	-.695	.049	199.472	1	.000	.499
	actden	.069	.011	42.019	1	.000	1.071
	entropy	1.639	.151	118.300	1	.000	5.150
	pct4way	-.007	.002	11.466	1	.001	.993
	stopden	-.003	.001	3.936	1	.047	.997
multi-family	Intercept	.932	.190	24.098	1	.000	
	hhsize	-.631	.042	220.688	1	.000	.532
	hhworker	.162	.053	9.147	1	.002	1.175
	lnhhincome	-.878	.046	356.440	1	.000	.416
	actden	.143	.009	278.539	1	.000	1.154
	entropy	2.605	.144	325.555	1	.000	13.537
	pct4way	-.014	.002	54.410	1	.000	.986
	stopden	-.001	.001	.466	1	.495	.999

a. The reference category is: single family detached.

Figure 13.20 Parameter Estimates Table

Classification

	Predicted			
Observed	single family detached	single family attached	multi-family	Percent Correct
single family detached	9741	0	161	98.4%
single family attached	759	0	92	.0%
multi-family	904	0	410	31.2%
Overall Percentage	94.5%	.0%	5.5%	84.1%

Figure 13.21 Classification Table From the Multinomial Logistic Regression

As it was described earlier, SPSS's capabilities for this model are rather limited. First, the multinomial logistic regression in SPSS includes a fixed set of independent variables in all pairwise models. In reality, however, some predictors may not have an impact on a certain group in the outcome variable. If the outcome variable is mode of transportation (e.g., walk, bike, transit, auto), the relevant built environment variables might vary by mode. For example, the provision of sidewalk might matter only in the walk model. But in SPSS, you cannot include that specific variable only in the walk model; you should either include it in all models or throw it away. In our current housing type example, you cannot drop the insignificant *hhworker* in the single-family attached housing model and *stopden* only in multi-family housing type.

Other software such as Stata can handle this issue. Here we will briefly show you how to run a multinomial regression in Stata. Stata is a powerful statistical package equipped with many advanced modeling tools. It is both menu-driven and command-driven. For the latter one, you have two options; either use the *Command* box at the bottom of the Stata or use a Do-file. For the sake of simplicity, we will use the *Command* window. We used Stata 14.0, but other versions of Stata work similarly.

To read the data in Stata, we first need to export it from SPSS. Go back to your file in SPSS and select "File" → "Save As" and save your file in csv format (dat or xls format also works). Now, as you can see in Figure 13.22, open Stata and select "File" → "Import" → "Text data (delimited, *. csv, . . .)."

A new window will pop up and you can select your file by clicking on the "Browse" button. After you select the data file, Stata will show the preview of the variables in the "Preview" box. You might see that some of the continuous variables are in red. This means that Stata treats them as string variables. Hold the Ctrl key (on Windows PC) on your keyboard and select all variables that you believe shouldn't be strings. Here, we know that all variables should be numeric. So, you can select these variables and then, right click on one of them and choose "Force selected columns to use numeric types" as shown in Figure 13.23.

When you are done with selection, click on "Ok." Now, you can see your variables on the right side of the program. And also, Stata tells you that you have 39 variables and 14,212 observations. It is better to save your file by clicking on "File" → "Save as." Notice that the type of file that Stata uses is ".dta."

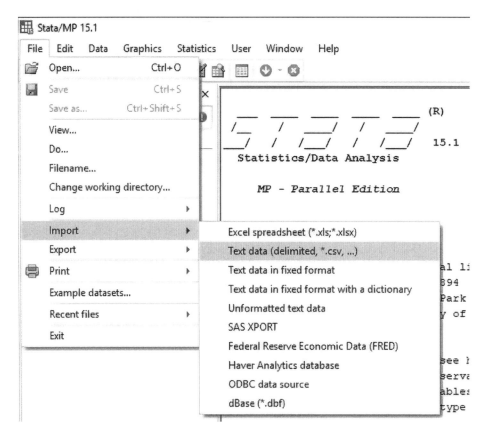

Figure 13.22 Importing the Household Dataset to Stata

The *htype* variable might be read as a categorical (string) variable. In case you did not choose "Force selected columns to use numeric types" when you imported the data into Stata, in the Command window type this syntax to convert it to a numeric variable.

destring htype, replace

The next step is defining the variables that we do not want to be selected for all of our categories for Stata. More specifically, we want to tell Stata not to use *hhworker* for category 2 (single-family attached housing type) and *stopden* for category 3 (multi-family housing type). For doing this, you need to use the Command window. Type this syntax.

constraint 1 [2]hhworker = 0

"1" is the name of the constraint and "2" within a bracket is the category 2 ("households who live in single-family attached houses"). This constraint forces Stata to pretend that there are no workers in households of this housing type. Then Stata actually

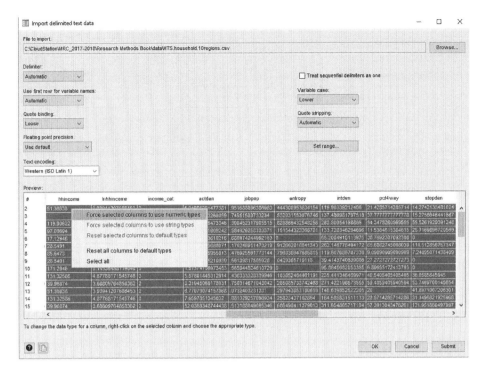

Figure 13.23 Converting String Variables to Numeric Variables

omits this variable for that specific category. Next, type this line of command and then press enter:

constraint 2 [3]stopden = 0

It tells Stata to define the second constraint to omit transit-stop density for category 3. Now, we have two constraints and are ready to run multinomial logistic regression using *mlogit* command. Type this syntax in one line and press enter:

mlogit htype hhsize hhworker lnhhincome actden entropy pct4way stopden if htype!=0, b(1) constraints(1,2)

Stata treats the very first variable that you type after *mlogit* as your dependent variable and the rest of the them as predictor variables. After typing the last variable which is *stopden*, we use a comma to add our optional commands. Before that, for this example, we write an if statement about housing type of 0 ("others"). Remember that the housing data has four housing types, i.e., others = 0, sfd = 1, sfa = 2, mf = 3. We only want to include categories 1 to 3. That "!=" sign means "not equal" in Stata. Notice the different expressions between SPSS and Stata. In SPSS (or Excel), we use "<>" as a not equal sign, but in Stata (or R), we use "!=." After this statement, we define two

294 *Sadegh Sabouri et al.*

options (remember to put a comma before that). First, making category one our reference group by typing *b(1)* and then telling Stata to include two constraints that we previously defined by typing *constraints(1,2)*. Learning such syntaxes takes time, but after you get used to it, it can save you time because you can simply type it instead of clicking multiple menus and can easily modify your previous commands.

You can see the modeling result. The table looks similar to the "Parameter Estimates" table in SPSS output; it has a set of variables for two categories, coefficients, standard errors, z values, p values, and 95 percent confidence intervals (Figure 13.24). Then, you will notice that both *hhworker* in the single-family attached model and *stopden* in multi-family housing model are omitted. Like the results in SPSS, all variables are significant. Note that you see a message about completely determined observations and questionable standard errors at the end. You can ignore this message in this example since we do not have any duplicated observation or a collinearity issue.

Missing is the odds ratio (Exp(B)). To get it, type "rrr" after the previous syntax. "rrr" is relative risk ratios. These are basically the same as odds ratios (Figure 13.25).

mlogit htype hhsize hhworker lnhhincome actden entropy jobpop if htype!=0, b(1) constraints(1,2) rrr

```
Multinomial logistic regression                    Number of obs    =      12,056
                                                   Wald chi2(10)    =     1731.05
Log likelihood = -5694.2885                        Prob > chi2      =      0.0000

 ( 1)  [2]o.hhworker = 0
 ( 2)  [2]o.jobpop = 0
```

htype	Coef.	Std. Err.	z	P>|z|	[95% Conf. Interval]	
1	(base outcome)					
2						
hhsize	-.2798676	.0341311	-8.20	0.000	-.3467632	-.2129719
hhworker	0	(omitted)				
lnhhincome	-.6697617	.0453246	-14.78	0.000	-.7585963	-.5809271
actden	.042381	.0086251	4.91	0.000	.0254762	.0592858
entropy	1.501625	.1464023	10.26	0.000	1.214682	1.788568
jobpop	0	(omitted)				
_cons	.0466514	.1914004	0.24	0.807	-.3284865	.4217892
3						
hhsize	-.6134192	.0418943	-14.64	0.000	-.6955305	-.531308
hhworker	.1278059	.0526638	2.43	0.015	.0245868	.2310251
lnhhincome	-.8317904	.0457612	-18.18	0.000	-.9214807	-.7421002
actden	.1163407	.0067501	17.24	0.000	.1031108	.1295706
entropy	2.502979	.1417854	17.65	0.000	2.225084	2.780873
jobpop	.3101685	.1357924	2.28	0.022	.0440204	.5763167
_cons	.3084895	.2076841	1.49	0.137	-.0985638	.7155429

```
Note: 3 observations completely determined.  Standard errors questionable.
```

Figure 13.24 Multinomial Logit Regression Output in Stata

```
Multinomial logistic regression          Number of obs   =    12,056
                                          Wald chi2(10)   =   1731.05
Log likelihood = -5694.2885               Prob > chi2     =    0.0000

 ( 1)  [2]o.hhworker = 0
 ( 2)  [2]o.jobpop = 0
```

htype	RRR	Std. Err.	z	P>|z|	[95% Conf. Interval]	
1	(base outcome)					
2						
hhsize	.7558838	.0257991	-8.20	0.000	.7069727	.8081788
hhworker	1	(omitted)				
lnhhincome	.5118305	.0231985	-14.78	0.000	.4683234	.5593795
actden	1.043292	.0089985	4.91	0.000	1.025803	1.061078
entropy	4.488977	.6571965	10.26	0.000	3.369221	5.980882
jobpop	1	(omitted)				
_cons	1.047757	.200541	0.24	0.807	.7200127	1.524687
3						
hhsize	.5414962	.0226856	-14.64	0.000	.4988098	.5878356
hhworker	1.136332	.0598436	2.43	0.015	1.024892	1.259891
lnhhincome	.4352693	.0199184	-18.18	0.000	.3979294	.4761129
actden	1.123379	.0075829	17.24	0.000	1.108614	1.13834
entropy	12.21884	1.732453	17.65	0.000	9.254263	16.1331
jobpop	1.363655	.1851739	2.28	0.022	1.045004	1.779472
_cons	1.361367	.2827343	1.49	0.137	.9061379	2.045297

```
Note:  _cons estimates baseline relative risk for each outcome.
Note: 3 observations completely determined.  Standard errors questionable.
```

Figure 13.25 Multinomial Logit Regression Output in Stata (Showing Odds Ratio)

In R

Figures 13.26 and 13.27 show an R script example of binary and multinomial logistic regression models. In Figure 13.26, a logistic regression model for *anyvmt* variable is run using *glm* function (which you can run diverse types of generalized linear models such as Poisson regression). Then Figure 13.27 uses the *mlogit* function (*mlogit* package) to build a multinomial logistic regression model for the housing type variable (*htype*). The model result replicates the SPSS outputs (see Figures 13.17 through 13.20).

Planning Examples

Smart Growth Policies and Automobile Dependence

Portland is well known for its smart growth policies. One of the policy objectives of smart growth is the reduction of automobile dependence. Jun (2008) examined

296 *Sadegh Sabouri et al.*

```
# LOGISTIC REGRESSION
library(foreign)
hts<-read.spss("HTS.household.10regions.sav",to.data.frame=TRUE)

glm1<-
glm(anyvmt~hhsize+hhworker+lnhhincome+entropy+stopden+pct4way,data=hts,family
=binomial())
summary(glm1)

##
## Call:
## glm(formula = anyvmt ~ hhsize + hhworker + lnhhincome + entropy +
##       stopden + pct4way, family = binomial(), data = hts)
##
## Deviance Residuals:
##     Min       1Q   Median       3Q      Max
## -3.3178   0.1513   0.2311   0.3540   3.9722
##
## Coefficients:
##               Estimate Std. Error z value Pr(>|z|)
## (Intercept)  0.8997143  0.2002743   4.492 7.04e-06 ***
## hhsize       0.2112821  0.0394867   5.351 8.76e-08 ***
## hhworker     0.4194136  0.0616116   6.807 9.94e-12 ***
## lnhhincome   0.6243676  0.0462961  13.486 < 2e-16  ***
## entropy     -1.2686861  0.1598188  -7.938 2.05e-15 ***
## stopden     -0.0066923  0.0008973  -7.458 8.76e-14 ***
## pct4way     -0.0158301  0.0017489  -9.051 < 2e-16  ***
## ---
## Signif. codes:  0 '***' 0.001 '**' 0.01 '*' 0.05 '.' 0.1 ' ' 1
##
## (Dispersion parameter for binomial family taken to be 1)
##
##     Null deviance: 6151.1  on 13162  degrees of freedom
## Residual deviance: 5023.4  on 13156  degrees of freedom
##   (1049 observations deleted due to missingness)
## AIC: 5037.4
##
## Number of Fisher Scoring iterations: 6
```

Figure 13.26 Reading SPSS Data and Running a Logistic Regression: R Script and Outputs

whether or not smart growth policies are effective in reducing automobile dependence. This study modelled the effects of smart growth policies on commuters' choice to drive alone with emphasis on four types of smart growth policies implemented in Portland: the urban growth boundary (UGB), public transit such as the MAX light rail system and bus service, mixed land use, and transit-oriented development (TOD).

Figure 13.28 shows changes in density and mode share within Portland's UGB over the 1990–2000 period. Preliminary results from inter-metropolitan comparisons and analysis of density and mode share changes within Portland's UGB might support the smart growth proponents' argument that smart growth policies contributed to a reduction in automobile use and encouraged a mode shift to alternatives to automobile travel. However, such a conclusion would be premature because there is no control over other factors that might affect commuter mode choice, such as

```
library(mlogit)
hts2<-subset(hts,htype!="other");hts2$htype<-factor(hts2$htype)
mlogit1 <- mlogit(htype ~
1|hhsize+hhworker+lnhhincome+actden+entropy+pct4way+stopden, data = hts2,
                shape="wide", reflevel = "single family detached")
summary(mlogit1)

##
## Call:
## mlogit(formula = htype ~ 1 | hhsize + hhworker + lnhhincome +
##        actden + entropy + pct4way + stopden, data = hts2, reflevel = "single family
detached",
##        shape = "wide", method = "nr")
##
## Frequencies of alternatives:
## single family detached        multi-family single family attached
##                 0.820585           0.108892                 0.070523
##
## nr method
## 6 iterations, 0h:0m:1s
## g'(-H)^-1g = 0.00224
## successive function values within tolerance limits
##
## Coefficients :
##                                    Estimate Std. Error  z-value  Pr(>|z|)
## multi-family:(intercept)          0.9319137  0.1898399   4.9089 9.157e-07 ***
## single family attached:(intercept) 0.2343539  0.2031734   1.1535 0.2487184
## multi-family:hhsize              -0.6310389  0.0424783 -14.8555 < 2.2e-16 ***
## single family attached:hhsize    -0.2834179  0.0376589  -7.5259 5.240e-14 ***
## multi-family:hhworker             0.1615244  0.0534070   3.0244 0.0024912 **
## single family attached:hhworker   0.0088323  0.0538384   0.1641 0.8696903
## multi-family:lnhhincome          -0.8778064  0.0464950 -18.8796 < 2.2e-16 ***
## single family attached:lnhhincome -0.6951045  0.0492163 -14.1235 < 2.2e-16 ***
## multi-family:actden               0.1433748  0.0085907  16.6894 < 2.2e-16 ***
## single family attached:actden     0.0685980  0.0105824   6.4822 9.037e-11 ***
## multi-family:entropy              2.6054131  0.1443992  18.0431 < 2.2e-16 ***
## single family attached:entropy    1.6390230  0.1506930  10.8766 < 2.2e-16 ***
## multi-family:pct4way             -0.0138762  0.0018812  -7.3763 1.628e-13 ***
## single family attached:pct4way   -0.0067273  0.0019867  -3.3861 0.0007088 ***
## multi-family:stopden             -0.0007633  0.0011181  -0.6827 0.4948243
## single family attached:stopden   -0.0028991  0.0014613  -1.9839 0.0472723 *
## ---
## Signif. codes:  0 '***' 0.001 '**' 0.01 '*' 0.05 '.' 0.1 ' ' 1
##
## Log-Likelihood: -5673
## McFadden R^2:  0.20416
## Likelihood ratio test : chisq = 2910.6 (p.value = < 2.22e-16)
```

Figure 13.27 Running a Multinomial Logistic Regression: R Script and Outputs

socio-demographic, location, and transportation-related variables. All of these factors have been considered in the model of this study.

The effect of Portland's smart growth strategies on the reduction of commuter auto dependence was then assessed using logistic regression. The model was based on the probability that a commuter chooses to drive alone. The outcome is a binary variable of "driving alone" and "any other travel mode except driving alone." The dependent variable was presented as Log $(P_i/[1 - P_i])$, which is just the log odds. P_i refers to the probability of driving alone for zone i, while $(1 - P_i)$ refers to the

	1990 (A)	2000 (B)	Difference (B − A)
Density			
Housing (housing units/km^2)	457.6	569.3	111.7
Jobs (jobs/ km^2)	844.0	1068.1	225.1
Commuter Mode Choice			
Automobile	87.9%	85.5%	−2.4%
Drive alone	75.2%	73.5%	−1.7%
Carpool	12.7%	12.0%	−0.7%
Public transit	7.2%	9.0%	1.8%
Others	4.8%	5.4%	0.6%

Source: Computed by author using U.S. Bureau of Census (1990, 2000) and U.S. Department of Transportation (1990, 2000).

Figure 13.28 Gross Housing Density and Commuter Mode Share Within the Urban Growth Boundary, 1990–2000

Source: Jun (2008)

probability of choosing alternative modes to driving alone. The logit transformation of the observed probability was used as the dependent variable.

Socioeconomic, land use, location, and transportation-related variables were selected as independent variables. For residential analyses, logistic regression models were built with nine predictor variables for 1990 and 13 variables for 2000. For workplace analyses, models were estimated with seven predictor variables for 1990 and 11 variables for 2000.

Figures 13.29 and 13.30 show the results. Diversified land use in neighborhoods, more extensive provision of public transit service, and decreasing accessibility to freeway interchanges are associated with lower probability of driving alone, while making settlements compact via an urban growth boundary and transit-oriented development had no clear relationship to the probability of driving alone. The analyses also suggest that provision of public transit service and mixed land use implemented in residential zones (origins) were more effective in reducing automobile dependence than those implemented in places of work (destinations).

Mobility Disability and the Urban Built Environment

The second example explores the effects of the built environment in the pathway from impairment to disability (Clarke, Alishire, Bader, Morenoff, & House, 2008). This research examined the effects of built environment characteristics on mobility

	1990		2000	
Variable	β	t	β	t
Intercept	−7.6617	−14.59[**]	−6.5868	−9.44[**]
Log (median household income)	0.7540	15.10[**]	0.6166	10.24[**]
Share of blacks and Hispanics in population	−0.5407	−4.59[**]	−0.8612	−7.01[**]
Share of families with children under 18 years	0.1122	0.65	0.1841	0.95
Share of resident workers employed in the central city	−0.1301	−1.14	−0.1782	−2.75[**]
Log (distance from the CBD: miles)	0.2513	8.00[**]	0.2543	6.27[**]
Log (housing density: housing units/km^2)	0.0284	1.72	0.0082	0.44
Vehicles available per resident worker	0.2883	6.10[**]	0.4877	7.66[**]
Log (distance from the nearest MAX station)	0.0627	2.90[**]	0.0642	3.43[**]
TOD (MAX dummy*log[housing density])	0.0092	0.55	0.0098	0.77
Log (distance from the nearest freeway interchange: miles)	—	—	−0.0357	−2.64[**]
Number of bus stops	—	—	−0.0025	−3.79[**]
Share of mixed land use in zoning	—	—	−0.3045	−2.50[*]
Share of single family residential land in zoning	—	—	0.1408	2.26[*]
	$N = 808$		$N = 851$	
	$R^2 = .681$		$R^2 = .731$	

Note: CBD = central business district; MAX = Portland's light-rail system; TOD = transit-oriented development.
*$p < .05$. **$p < .01$.

Figure 13.29 Mode Choice by Residence Block Group (Origin)

Source: Jun (2008)

disability—i.e., using a wheelchair, walker, or cane—among adults aged 45 or more years (n = 1,195) according to their level of lower extremity physical impairment. The authors used multinomial logistic regression as their method.

The data source for this research was face-to-face interviews with a sample of 1,195 adults aged 45 or more years, and stratified into 343 neighborhood clusters in the city of Chicago. To measure built environment characteristics, trained survey raters collected observational data for each block surrounding the respondent's residential address under the premise that "broken curbs and streets in disrepair are likely to be associated with more obstacles (e.g., rubble, uneven pavement) for pedestrians navigating along sidewalks and crossing streets" (Clarke et al., 2008, pp. 507–508).

A set of control variables for the neighborhood effect was added to this analysis to better isolate the effects of street quality on mobility disability. Neighborhood "social and physical disorder" and "residential security" were two constructs operationalized in the analysis. To control for individual characteristics, key socio-demographic and health factors were added to the models, including age, gender, marital status, race/ethnicity, and socioeconomic position.

The outcome variable in this study was a nominal variable which includes three levels of outdoor mobility disability: no difficulty, some difficulty, severe difficulty walking two to three blocks. You can now see why multinomial logistic regression was used

300 *Sadegh Sabouri et al.*

	1990		2000	
Variable	β	t	β	T
Intercept	–1.9211	–3.76**	–8.8476	–8.58**
Log (median income for workers)	0.2235	4.53**	0.8881	8.49**
Share of professional jobs	1.3942	4.32**	0.8362	3.75**
Share of sales jobs	1.1328	2.48*	1.4408	3.77**
Log (distance from the CBD: miles)	0.2312	4.67**	0.2726	7.27**
Log (employment density: jobs/km²)	0.0049	0.20	0.0125	0.50
Log (distance from the nearest MAX station: miles)	0.0129	0.39	0.0146	0.54
TOD (MAX dummy* log[employment density])	–0.0051	–0.40	–0.0025	–0.23
Log (distance from the nearest freeway interchange: miles)	—	—	–0.0196	–1.16
Number of bus stops	—	—	0.0004	0.61
Share of mixed land use in zoning	—	—	–0.2680	–1.33
Share of commercial and industrial land in zoning	—	—	0.0760	0.56
	$N= 244$		$N= 293$	
	$R^2= .345$		$R^2= .428$	

Note: CBD = central business district; MAX = Portland's light-rail system; TOD = transit-oriented development.
*$p < .05$. **$p < .01$.

Figure 13.30 Mode Choice by Workplace Tract (Destination)
Source: Jun (2008)

to examine the effects of individual and built environment characteristics on these three categories of outcomes.

Figures 13.31 and 13.32 report the results of the multinomial logistic regression analyses (no disability is the reference group). The tables present the logistic regression coefficients and odds ratios for the independent variables. Figure 13.31 relates to the outcome of "some difficulty walking two to three blocks" and Figure 13.32 relates to the outcome of "severe difficulty walking two to three blocks." The results show that older individuals with a greater number of health problems, and cigarette smoking, are more likely to experience problems of mobility. Being male and African American increase the odds of mobility disability compared with females and Caucasians. Look at the Figures 13.31 and 13.32 to try to find other independent variables that have a significant effect on each outcome.

In this study, authors were specifically interested in the effects of the built environment on mobility disability. As you can see from the resulting tables, the presence of any street in not-so-good (fair or very poor) condition increases the odds of mobility disability, all else being equal.

Conclusion

Logistic regression is the go-to model for categorical response data, being commonly used for a wide variety of planning applications. It is distinguishable from

Parameter	Model A		
	Estimate	Odds ratio	95% confidence interval
Intercept	−5.101***		
Sociodemographics			
Age, years			
60–69	0.738*	2.09	1.15, 3.81
≥70	1.496***	4.46	2.39, 8.32
Gender			
Male	0.531*	1.70	1.05, 2.77
Race/ethnicity			
Black	0.539‡	1.71	0.99, 2.95
Hispanic/other	0.223	1.25	0.54, 2.89
Marital status			
Separated/divorced	−0.382	0.68	0.35, 1.31
Widowed	−0.392	0.68	0.31, 1.46
Never married	0.246	1.28	0.56, 2.90
Lives alone	−0.208	0.81	0.44, 1.50
Socioeconomic position			
Less than high school education	−0.271	0.76	0.38, 1.54
High school education	−0.331	0.72	0.38, 1.35
Economic hardship	0.504*	1.66	1.03, 2.66
Health status			
Health conditions	0.378***	1.46	1.27, 1.68
Cognitive impairment	−0.042	0.96	0.75, 1.22
Current smoker	0.850**	2.34	1.37, 4.01
Body mass index	0.002	1.00	0.97, 1.04
Lower body impairment	2.308***	10.06	5.81, 17.41
Built environment			
Neighborhood disorder	0.082	1.09	0.93, 1.27
Neighborhood security	−0.170	0.84	0.63, 1.13
Any street in fair/poor condition	0.542*	1.72	1.02, 2.91
Fair/poor streets × lower body impairment			

* $p < 0.05$; **$p < 0.01$; ***$p < 0.001$.
† No disability is the reference group.
‡ $p < 0.10$.

Figure 13.31 Multinomial Logistic Regression Models for Mobility Disability Category 2 (Some Disability), 2001–2003

Source: Clarke et al. (2008)

| | Model A | | |
Parameter	Estimate	Odds ratio	95% confidence interval
Intercept	−9.294***		
Sociodemographics			
Age, years			
60–69	0.758‡	2.13	0.96, 4.75
≥70	2.304***	10.02	4.40, 22.81
Gender			
Male	0.574‡	1.78	0.95, 3.33
Race/ethnicity			
Black	1.520***	4.57	2.26, 9.25
Hispanic/other	0.441	1.55	0.50, 4.86
Marital status			
Separated/divorced	−0.837‡	0.43	0.18, 1.05
Widowed	0.017	1.02	0.42, 2.46
Never married	0.459	1.58	0.53, 4.70
Lives alone	0.174	1.19	0.58, 2.44
Socioeconomic position			
Less than high school education	0.617	1.85	0.69, 5.00
High school education	0.024	1.02	0.39, 2.67
Economic hardship	1.210***	3.35	1.81, 6.20
Health status			
Health conditions	0.608***	1.84	1.54, 2.19
Cognitive impairment	0.009	1.01	0.76, 1.34
Current smoker	0.653‡	1.92	0.93, 3.96
Body mass index	−0.010	0.99	0.95, 1.03
Lower body impairment	3.862***	47.55	23.43, 96.52
Built environment			
Neighborhood disorder	−0.157	0.85	0.70, 1.04
Neighborhood security	−0.071	0.93	0.65, 1.33
Any street in fair/poor condition	0.786*	2.20	1.15, 4.19
Fair/poor streets × lower body impairment			

* $p < 0.05$; **$p < 0.01$; ***$p < 0.001$.
† No disability is the reference group.
‡ $p < 0.10$.

Figure 13.32 Multinomial Logistic Regression Models for Mobility Disability Category 3 (Severe Disability), 2001–2003

Source: Clarke et al. (2008)

linear regressions in that (1) the dependent variable is categorical in nature and (2) the model assumes a nonlinear relationship between the outcome and explanatory variables.

As with linear regression, researchers can use logistic regression in order to achieve one of two main objectives: explanation or prediction. In many studies, the focus is on the independent variables, with the goal being to identify the extent to which each one explains the outcome variable. In other studies, the focus is primarily on the outcome and how to predict one of the categories of that outcome variable.

In recent years, there is an increasing number of applied and methodological studies discussing the extension of (or alternative to) the logistic regression models. They include multilevel logistic regression (when the data has a nested structure), classification tree or random forest (when you are more interested in the classification process and/or outcome rather than probability or hypothesis testing), and support vector machines (when you have too many independent variables). As these advanced methods are beyond the scope of this book (except the multilevel modeling in Chapter 7 in *Advanced Quantitative Research Methods for Urban Planners*), see Agresti (2012); Hastie, Tibshirani, and Friedman (2009); and Izenman (2008) if you want more information.

Works Cited

Agresti, A. (2012). *Categorical data analysis* (3rd ed.). New York, NY: John Wiley & Sons.

Cheng, J., & Masser, I. (2003). Urban growth pattern modeling: A case study of Wuhan city, PR China. *Landscape and Urban Planning, 62*(4), 199–217.

Clarke, P., Alishire, J., Bader, M., Morenoff, J., & House, J. (2008). Mobility disability and the urban built environment. *American Journal of Epidemiology, 168*(5), 506–513.

Cramer, J. (2002). *The origins of logistic regression.* Tinbergen Institute discussion Paper. Retrieved from http://dare.uva.nl/document/204

Ewing, R., Tian, G., Goates, J., Zhang, M., Greenwald, M. J., Joyce, A., . . . Greene, W. (2015). Varying influences of the built environment on household travel in 15 diverse regions of the United States. *Urban Studies, 52*(13), 2330–2348.

Fang, S., Gertner, G., Sun, Z., & Anderson, A. (2005). The impact of interactions in spatial simulation of the dynamics of urban sprawl. *Landscape and Urban Planning, 73*(4), 294–306.

Field, A. (2009). *Discovering statistics using SPSS* (3rd ed.). London: Sage Publications.

Forsyth, A., Hearst, M., Oakes, J., & Schmitz, H. (2008). Design and destinations: Factors influencing walking and total physical activity. *Urban Studies, 45*, 1973–1996.

Frank, L., Schmid, T., Sallis, J., Chapman, J., & Saelens, B. (2005). Linking objectively measured physical activity with objectively measured urban form. *American Journal of Preventive Medicine, 28*(2), 117–125.

Greene, W. H. (2012). *Econometric analysis.* New York, NY: Prentice Hall.

Hastie, T., Tibshirani, R., & Friedman, J. (2009). *The elements of statistical learning: Data mining, inference, and prediction* (2nd ed.). New York, NY: Springer Series in Statistics.

Hosmer, D., Hosmer, T., Le Cessie, S., & Lemeshow, S. (1997). A comparison of goodness-of-fit tests for the logistic regression model. *Statistics in Medicine, 16*, 965–980.

Hosmer, D., & Lemeshow, S. (1989). *Applied logistic regression.* New York, NY: John Wiley & Sons.

Hu, Z., & Lo, C. (2007). Modeling urban growth in Atlanta using logistic regression. *Computers, Environment and Urban Systems, 31*(6), 667–688.

Izenman, A. J. (2008). *Modern multivariate statistical techniques: Regression, classification, and manifold learning.* New York, NY: Springer.

Johnson, B., & Parker, B. (2006). School trips: Effects of urban form and distance on travel mode. *Journal of the American Planning Association, 72*(3), 337–346.

Jun, M. (2008). Are Portland's smart growth policies related to reduced automobile dependence? *Journal of Planning Education and Research, 28*, 100–107.

Krizek, K., & Johnson, P. (2006). Proximity to trails and retail: Effects on urban cycling and walking. *Journal of the American Planning Association, 72*(1), 33–42.

Menard, S. (2010). *Logistic regression, from introductory to advanced concepts and applications.* Thousand Oaks, CA: Sage Publications.

O'Connell, A. (2006). *Logistic regression models for ordinal response variables.* London: Sage Publications.

Stoltzfus, J. (2011). Logistic regression: A brief primer. *Academic Emergency Medicine, 18*, 1099–1104.

Sutton, S.A. (2014). Are BIDs good for business? The impact of BIDs on neighborhood retailers in New York City. *Journal of Planning Education and Research, 34*(3), 309–324.

Takano, T., Nakamura, K., & Watanabe, W. (2002). Urban residential environments and senior citizens' longevity in megacity areas: The importance of walkable green spaces. *Journal of Epidemiol Community Health, 56*, 913–918.

Theobald, D., & Hobbs, T. (1998). Forecasting rural land-use change: A comparison of regression- and spatial transition-based models. *Geographical & Environmental Modeling, 2*(1), 65–82.

14 Quasi-Experimental Research

Keunhyun Park, Katherine Kittrell, and Reid Ewing

Overview

Quantitative studies typically use one of three research designs:

1. A randomized, controlled experiment
2. A quasi-experiment
3. A non-experiment with statistical controls

Randomized, controlled experiments are the gold standard for research because causality can be established. However, when randomized selection of an experimental group before and after a treatment is not feasible, a quasi-experiment is the next best thing. The quasi-experiment, if well designed, can provide valid causal inferences, comparable to a randomized experiment (Campbell & Stanley, 1963).

Experimental innovations frequently start in physical sciences and are later applied to social sciences—the study of society and relationships among individuals within society. Quantitative social research, at a minimum, determines whether an action creates more or less of a given behavior, and by what order of magnitude, like twice as much or three times as much. The examples from planning research in this chapter illustrate how quasi-experiments have been used in planning research, and how quasi-experimental design can improve the design of studies without random assignment.

Purpose

To understand the quasi-experimental design, we need to first know what the randomized, controlled experiment is and how it works. Controlled experiments separate research subjects into a control group and an experimental group. Both groups are identical at the beginning of the study and no treatment is given to the control group. Changes are made to the experimental group to test a theory, typically by manipulating one key variable, but keeping the remaining conditions constant. The control group is important to eliminate alternative explanations of experimental results.

Random assignment is used in a controlled experiment to ensure that the treated and control groups are equivalent at the outset. The researcher assigns a treatment to the test group and a placebo (or nothing) to the control group. Or dosage can vary when one group receives more treatment and another group receives less. Group attributes should be reasonably equivalent between the treated and control groups.

306   *Keunhyun Park et al.*

Randomized, controlled experiments are rare in planning. Fixed controls and random assignments can introduce ethical or practical problems in a study. We cannot, for example, randomly assign households to neighborhoods to see how neighborhood design affects travel behavior.

One of the rare examples of a true experiment in planning is the federally funded Experimental Housing Allowance Program. Researchers randomly assigned eligible households to multiple treatment groups and one control group to measure demand for different housing allowances (Olsen, 2003). The study found that housing vouchers are more cost effective than subsidized construction programs. Though the study results guided national housing policy for the next decade, a critical reader can say that the same conclusions could have been obtained with predictive time-series or cross-sectional regression studies using available data. She could also find fault with the study's fixed controls and narrow focus. The cost was almost $200 million, in the 1970s. Because of excessive costs, ethical issues, and inflexible study design, true experiments are rarely conducted in planning.

But occasionally, it is possible to design a simple, controlled experiment to answer a planning question. In 2011, Zhan Guo, Asha Weinstein Agrawal, and Jennifer Dill performed a controlled experiment for a pilot mileage fee. The behavior of a small number of drivers was studied to explain how congestion pricing might work. Drivers were randomly assigned to two groups. In the first group, drivers paid a set fee for each mile traveled. In the second group, drivers paid a variable fee for each mile, with a varying rate that was based on the amount of road congestion at the time that they drove. The researchers used regression models to show how mileage differed between the two groups, controlling for differences in drivers and routes. The study showed that demand pricing is more effective in high-density, mixed-use neighborhoods with travel alternatives, like walking and transit, and less effective in low-density suburban neighborhoods (Guo, Agrawal, & Dill, 2011).

Compared to the randomized, controlled experiment, quasi-experiments lack the random assignment, because of ethical or practical constraints. The assignments are not directly controlled by the researcher, although good design ensures that the control and experimental groups are as similar as possible at the beginning of the experiment. If the differences in the groups are random, and the sample size is large, then the groups can be treated as though they are equivalent.

Like the controlled experiment, quasi-experiments also measure the treated and control groups after a treatment. The difference between two groups after the intervention is the effect of the treatment. Although causation is impossible to prove, the quasi-experimental design provides moderately strong evidence that the intervention *might cause* the differences.

Sometimes a quasi-experiment can be equated with a *natural experiment* in terms that the assignments occur naturally. Natural experiments are quasi-experimental in design if measurements are taken before and after an intervention. Some authors distinguish between the two because in a quasi-experiment, the criterion for assignment is selected by the researcher, while in a natural experiment, the assignment occurs naturally, without the researcher's intervention (Shadish, Cook, & Campbell, 2002). An example of a natural experiment could be studies done on cities that have experienced a natural disaster and those that have not, because the disaster cannot be assigned.

Figure 14.1 helps illustrate the differences in different designs. A true, controlled experiment uses random assignment to separate cases between the control group and the experimental group. If random assignment cannot be used, then there is a chance to create a quasi-experiment, which can be nearly as good as a true experiment. As long as the control group and the experimental group both have the same attributes, and measurements are taken after the treatment, the study can be designed as a quasi-experiment (see Figure 14.1).

History

In the 16th and 17th centuries, modern experimental science was founded by scientists such as Francis Bacon, Leonardo da Vinci, and Galileo Galilei (Hacking, 1983; Jones, 1969). Scientific experiments improved upon earlier philosophical theory by using observation instead of reasoning and religion. By the time of Galileo's death, the method of using observation to correct theoretical and religious first principles was accepted (Harre, 1981). The earth was round.

The scientific revolution of the 16th and 17th centuries gave birth to the experiment: a deliberate action designed to test a theory, followed by systematic observations. Controls were needed to isolate extraneous influences that might limit or bias the observations. In the early 20th century, random assignment (Fisher, 1925) and adding control groups (Coover & Angell, 1907) were introduced. The resulting studies indicated a causation between the action and the observed changes following the action. Although causal inference is inherently qualitative, quantitative causal models were developed using Rubin's Causal Model (RCM), founded on the problem of nonrandom assignment-to-treatment levels (Holland, 1986; Rubin, 1974, 1977, 1978, 1986). The RCM turns the random assignment mechanism into a formal

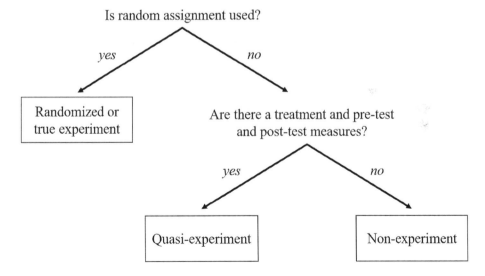

Figure 14.1 Experiments, Quasi-Experiments, and Non-Experiments

308   *Keunhyun Park et al.*

mathematical framework for assessing causation in observational data, based on the idea of potential outcomes and the assignment mechanism: every unit has different potential outcomes depending on their *assignment* to a condition (Barringer, Eliason, & Leahey, 2013). As a result, a researcher can obtain the average treatment effect (ATE), the expected value of the difference between the treated and non-treated outcome random variables. Quasi-experiments are derived from Rubin's work and refinements that are being developed to this day.

Mechanics

Because quasi-experiments lack random assignment between conditions, alternative explanations are difficult to rule out. As explained in the Chapter 6 of this book, the term *validity* refers to the relation between the conclusion of an inference and its supporting evidence. Especially, the *internal validity* of a study refers to whether the intervention has a causal relationship with the outcome. Of particular relevance to quasi-experimental designs are threats to internal validity as they increase the likelihood that a plausible alternative explanation for the experimental outcome exists, leading to false positives or false negatives.

For example, let's think about a study on the relationship between a road diet and pedestrian satisfaction. Even in a hypothetical experiment that compares pedestrian satisfaction between a narrowed street and another conventional wide street, it is still not a true experiment unless the pedestrians are randomly assigned and the street environments other than the street width are identical between two streets. Thus, a researcher cannot eliminate all plausible alternative explanations—for example, people might be different between two cases or existing street qualities other than road width might have an impact on pedestrian satisfaction.

Because threats to internal validity are prominent in quasi-experiments, care must be taken to ensure that the influence of these threats to validity is minimized. Shadish et al. (2002) discuss three principles useful in this respect: identification and study of plausible threats to internal validity, design controls that limit threats to internal validity (e.g., control groups, pretest/posttest designs), and specific hypotheses that limit the number of viable alternative explanations. Three types of quasi-experimental designs applicable in planning research are discussed, each of which has its own advantages and disadvantages concerning threats to internal validity.

Two-Group Pretest-Posttest Design

The two-group pretest-posttest design, also called nonequivalent-groups design, is the most common, basic form of a quasi-experiment. It involves the comparison of a treatment group and a similar, but not randomly selected, control group before and after the intervention is implemented. Because confounding variables are assumed randomly present in both groups, the effect of the treatment is the difference in outcomes between the test and the control groups. The researcher collects data before

Quasi-Experimental Research 309

and after the intervention for both groups. The notation for two-group pretest-posttest is as follows:

$$NR \ O_1 \ X \ O_2$$
$$------------$$
$$NR \ O_1 \quad O_2$$

NR and the dashed line mean that the treatment group (above) and the control group (below) were not randomly assigned. O_1 refers to observations before the intervention for each group. O_2 refers to observations after the intervention. X indicates the intervention.

Among many examples of this type of quasi-experiment in planning, three are presented here, borrowed from the *Research You Can Use* columns written by the third author of this chapter.

1. For a well-done study using the pretest–posttest design with a comparison group, we refer readers to the winter 2011 issue of *Journal of the American Planning Association* (JAPA), in which Rebecca Lewis and Gerrit Knaap evaluated Maryland's Rural Legacy Program. These two researchers had previously shown that the state's Priority Funding Program, which directs urban infrastructure investments to existing communities, had been marginally effective. For the current study, the two conducted a statistical analysis of development in and near the legacy areas both before and after they were designated. While mixed, their findings nevertheless add to the growing evidence of the limitations of targeted spending as a smart growth strategy.
2. Another example appears in a 2010 New York City study lead by Jeanette Sadik-Khan (New York City Department of Transportation, 2010). The study tested travel speeds and safety for two sides of town: one with the treatment and one without the treatment. In the treatment neighborhood, West Midtown, a pedestrian mall, was created by closing a major street, Broadway, to vehicular traffic. Streets in the control neighborhood, East Midtown, were not changed. Any differences in northbound, southbound, eastbound, and westbound trip speeds and accident rates between the treated and the control group were assumed to be caused by the intervention, the pedestrian mall. The study is a natural experiment because the streets within the neighborhoods studied were not precisely equivalent before the treatment. The neighborhood similarities before the intervention are enough to infer that the pedestrian mall caused the differences observed after its construction.
3. A last example appeared in the JAPA's Winter 2006 issue. Using a survey of California cities, John Landis (2006) evaluated the effects of five growth management techniques. What Landis did is to carefully match a group of cities with growth management programs to cities without such programs. In that way, differences in growth rates could reasonably be attributed to the programs themselves. With matching peer groups, Landis could infer how five different growth control and management techniques affected the balance between housing demand and supply for a ten-year period. As a result, Landis discovered that three techniques— residential caps, annexation controls, and requirements for a supermajority

310   *Keunhyun Park et al.*

rezoning approval—significantly limit growth in the cities that adopt them. The other two techniques—adequate public facilities ordinances (APFOs) and urban growth boundaries (UGBs)—apparently do not.

Regression to the Mean

A particular threat to causal inference with this study design is regression toward (or to) the mean. This common phenomenon suggests that if a variable value for a case is extreme on its first measurement, it will tend to be closer to the average on its second measurement. Regression to the mean is why it is so important to have matching treatment and control groups before the treatment. In the example of traffic calming in New York City, presented in Chapter 10, streets selected for traffic calming treatment are likely to have higher crash rates than average before the treatment, and thus they would likely regress to mean in any event in a second measurement, with or without traffic calming.

Propensity Score Matching

Propensity score matching (PSM) is a type of pretest-posttest design with a control group (i.e., two group pretest-posttest design). PSM has been widely used to overcome non-random assignment of treatment in the evaluation of social programs (Oakes & Johnson, 2006). In evaluation studies, individuals in the treatment group are likely to differ systematically from those in the control group. For example, households living in suburban regions could be more affluent than their counterparts in downtown, a result of residential self-selection. Therefore, the observed difference in behavioral outcomes between the groups is confounded by residential self-selection. Statistically, it generates a biased estimate of the treatment effect.

The propensity score is defined as the conditional probability of assignment to a particular treatment given a set of observed covariates (Rosenbaum & Rubin, 1983). The propensity score for matching purpose can be best calculated when we include as many variables as possible that serve as confounders for the causal path between independent and dependent variables.

The first step is to develop a binary logit model to estimate a propensity score using the subsample of treatment group and control group. Then you can match each subject in the treatment group with those in the control group based on their propensity scores. Nearest neighbor matching is the most common match approach and Caliper length of 0.03 is often used for matching, meaning that for a treatment observation, you search matching control observations whose propensity scores are within 0.03 of the score of the treatment observation (Austin, 2009). The choice of caliper width is a trade-off between bias and variance, because a too wide width will select control cases too different from treated ones and a narrower width will reduce sample size, leading to more variance in the treatment effect (Austin, 2011). Third, to check the quality of the matching, you can evaluate whether the matched subjects in the treatment group are systematically different from those in the control group, using a t-test.

The final goal of PSM is to compute the *true* impact of treatment on an outcome variable. Once the matching is complete, you can compute the average treatment effect (ATE), which is computed as a difference in the outcome variable between treatment and control groups (see Figure 14.2). Sometimes, the ratio of ATE over the observed influence is calculated as the proportion of the observed difference that can be attributed to treatment itself. A planning example of propensity score matching is presented in the next section.

The validity of propensity score matching relies on the assumption that unobserved characteristics do not influence treatment participation. The propensity scores are only as unbiased as the predictors included in their calculation (Beal & Kupzyk, 2014). As a result, failing to include an important confounder in the calculation of a propensity score will lead to biased results (Stürmer, Schneeweiss, Avorn, & Glynn, 2005). Another assumption is that when properly modeled, the distributions of propensity scores are close to equal between two groups. When this assumption is not met, propensity scores will also lead to biased results (Rosenbaum & Rubin, 1983).

Regression Discontinuity (RD)

Regression discontinuity (RD) has been rarely used in planning research, but has potential for evaluation research of a specific public program. Assignment to the treatment or the control group is made based on a cutoff value, or threshold (e.g., test score, income, density). Although assignment is not random, assignment to, and differences between, the control and treatment group near the cutoff value are assumed to be random. Trochim and Donnelly (2008, p. 216) define RD as "a pretest-posttest program-comparison group quasi-experimental design in which a cutoff criterion on the preprogram measure is the method of assignment to group."

An advantage of RD design is that it is appropriate when a researcher wants to target a program to those who most need or deserve it (Trochim & Donnelly, 2008). For example, school children who obtain scores that fall below a cutoff value on an achievement test can be assigned to remedial training and compared to those who

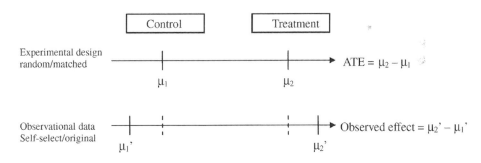

μ_1 and μ_1' are means of controls; μ_2 and μ_2' are means of treatments.

Figure 14.2 The Relationship Between Observed Effect and Treatment Effect
Source: Cao, Xu, & Fan (2010)

312   *Keunhyun Park et al.*

obtain higher scores. Because of the cutoff criterion, treated and control groups are deliberately and maximally different on pre-program characteristics in RD designs. Contradictory to the assumption in experimental or other quasi-experimental designs that two groups are equivalent prior to the program, the RD design assumes that in the absence of the program, the pre-post relationship would be equivalent for the two groups (Trochim & Donnelly, 2008).

In RD designs, you draw a regression line for each group, cut at the cutoff value. A discontinuity in regression lines indicates a program effect. In other words, a program effect in the RD design is not calculated as a difference between the posttest measures of two groups, but by a change in the pre-post relationship at the cutoff point. Trochim and Donnelly (2008) point out that while the RD design is strong in internal validity, it needs as much as 2.75 times the participants as a randomized experiment, to achieve the same level of statistical accuracy.

Take a hypothetical example used by Lan Deng and Lance Freeman in the Summer 2011 edition of JPER (Deng & Freeman, 2011). In their example, neighborhoods with 15 percent or less homeownership rates are offered a public program to increase their homeownership rate. If the intervention has an impact, then neighborhoods barely qualifying for the program should be significantly different than neighborhoods barely missing the qualification after the intervention. Figure 14.3 demonstrates two possible research results. In the first regression, the public program has no impact. The regression line is exactly the same for both the treatment group and the control group. The homeownership rate increases at the same rate for both the treatment group and the control group. In contrast, the second regression clearly shows an interruption caused by the treatment; homeownership rises from 15 percent to 60 percent in the treatment group after the intervention. Neighborhoods just missing the cutoff see no change after the policy is implemented. The authors argue that the RD design can be especially useful in evaluating targeted place-based programs.

Planning Examples

Light Rail Transit Expansion

In a 2014 *Journal of the American Planning Association* study, changes in household vehicle miles traveled are analyzed before and after the implementation of Portland's Westside Max light rail transit (LRT) line. The study compares the travel characteristics of the *treated* corridor, households near station areas before and after the operation of new station areas, and the *control* corridor, households near highway intersections. The purpose of the research is to identify the transit multiplier: one mile traveled on transit corresponds with a disproportionately higher reduction in driving. The transit multiplier found in the study, about 3, is similar to that found by their literature review.

Reid Ewing and Shima Hamidi began by selecting households within one and a quarter mile buffers around 17 stations on the Westside Max LRT line as their experimental group. Households within these buffers in 1994 represent the pretest group. Households within these buffers in 2011 represent the posttest group. For each group, various travel characteristics were quantified. The total VMT per household was the

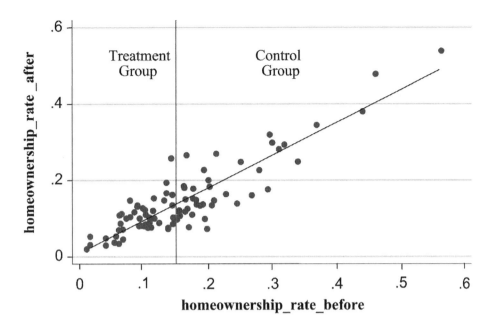

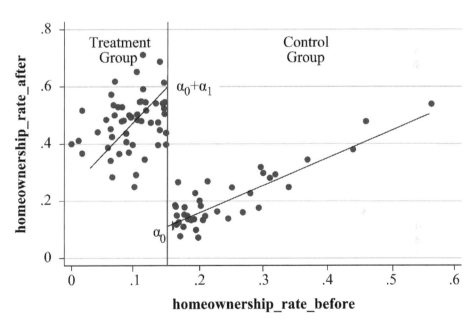

Figure 14.3 Program for Neighborhood With 15 Percent or Less Homeownership Rate; No Impacts (Above) and Impacts (Below)

Source: Deng & Freeman (2011)

variable of ultimate interest. However, to explain variations in VMT, the researchers also computed number of transit trips and number of walk trips. As another independent variable, the authors measured the density of development in quarter mile buffers around each household, and as controls they measured socio-demographics of households living within buffers.

Selecting a control group was tricky. Three highway corridors serving the west side of Portland were considered as controls (Figure 14.4). The SW Pacific highway corridor was ultimately selected as the control, because it most closely matched the experimental corridor in terms of socio-demographic, land use, and travel characteristics before LRT was built.

The researchers found that transit use increased more dramatically in the transit corridor than in the highway corridor, but that walking and density also increased more in the transit corridor.

Furthermore, modeling household VMT in terms of these variables plus socio-demographic variables allowed the researchers to parse out the direct effect of transit use on VMT versus the indirect effect of transit-oriented development on VMT through higher walk trip frequencies and higher densities. The direct effect occurs through increases in transit ridership and associated reductions in household VMT.

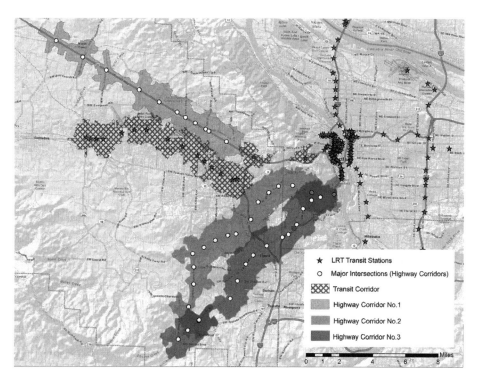

Figure 14.4 Transit Corridor Versus Three Comparative Highway Corridors
Source: Ewing & Hamidi (2014)

Quasi-Experimental Research 315

The indirect effect is achieved through increased walking and increased densities around stations.

Assessing Bids

In January 2015, the third author of this chapter wrote a *Research You Can Use* column for *Planning* magazine on propensity score matching. We borrow from that column now.

In the September 2014 issue of the *JPER*, Stacey Sutton of Columbia University applied the PSM technique to the assessment of business improvement districts (BIDs) in New York City.

During the 1970s a handful of cities, starting with Toronto, then New Orleans and New York City, adopted the BID model as "a novel mechanism for financing and managing the revitalization of forlorn commercial corridors and downtown shopping districts" (p. 309), Sutton's study says. By 2009, more than 1,500 BIDs had been established in hundreds of urban and suburban municipalities across the United States and internationally. BIDs proliferated in New York under Mayor Michael Bloomberg, who actively promoted them.

BIDs provide a variety of place-based services—such as street cleaning, security, streetscape enhancement, and façade improvement—to enhance overall commercial life. BID operating expenses are largely covered by a compulsory tax assessment on businesses. Since the self-financing mechanism of BIDs becomes a tax on retail tenants, Sutton's study examined whether the BID model improves retail performance relative to comparable areas of the city that never adopted BIDs. She is one of the first to systematically examine the utility of the BID model.

How to select *comparable areas* for purposes of such an assessment? In the New York case, not all BIDs have obvious comparables, and that is where propensity score matching comes in. Sutton matched BIDs to non-BID census tracts based on observed pre-BID attributes known to affect BID adoption (retail density, assessed property value, and many other variables). This exercise produced a credible control group of non-BID census tracts that had a high probability of BID adoption but had not done so.

The most common matching approach, known as nearest neighbor matching, matches each case in the treated group to the case in the control group that has the most similar propensity score. In Sutton's case, each BID tract was matched with the two *nearest neighbor* non-BID tracts with the closest propensity scores to create a matched trio (Figure 14.5).

Sutton's primary finding was that both sales and employment declined for existing independent neighborhood retailers within BIDs relative to comparable non-BID areas. She noted that BID functions and capacities were highly variable and tended to be correlated with BID size. Commercial vibrancy observable in large corporate BIDs such as the Times Square BID may not be obtainable by much smaller, community BIDs.

The use of propensity score matching reduces potential bias in selecting treatment and control cases, here by building those cases "up from the data." In Sutton's paper, the use of propensity score matching led to a different conclusion than a simpler research design might have.

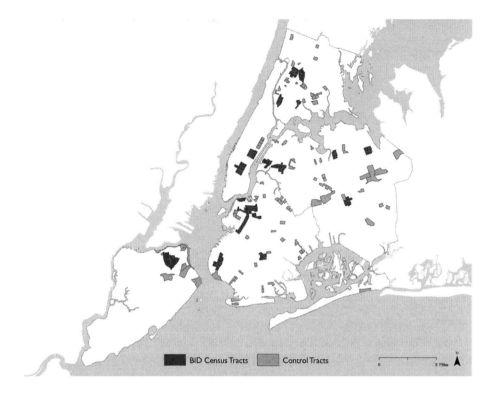

Figure 14.5 Propensity Score Matched BID and Non-BID Tracts
Source: Sutton (2014)

Conclusion

Quasi-experimental designs look like randomized, true experimental designs, but they lack random assignment to treated and control groups. Three types of quasi-experimental designs, particularly applicable to planning research, were discussed: two-group pretest-posttest design, propensity score matching, and regression discontinuity. All three are pre-post, two-group designs, and they differ primarily in the way they are used to assign the groups. To conclude, when properly designed, quasi-experiments may provide a mechanism with which to infer causality in situations where randomized controlled trials are not possible.

Works Cited

Austin, P. C. (2011). An introduction to propensity score methods for reducing the effects of confounding in observational studies. *Multivariate Behavioral Research, 46,* 399–424. doi:10.1080/00273171.2011.568786

Austin, P. C. (2009). Some methods of propensity-score matching had superior performance to others: Results of an empirical investigation and Monte Carlo simulations. *Biometrical Journal: Journal of Mathematical Methods in Biosciences, 51*(1), 171–184.

Barringer, S. N., Eliason, S. R., & Leahey, E. (2013). A history of causal analysis in the social sciences. In S. L. Morgan (Ed.), *Handbook of causal analysis for social research* (pp. 9–26). Dordrecht: Springer.

Beal, S. J., & Kupzyk, K. A. (2014). An introduction to propensity scores: What, when, and how. *The Journal of Early Adolescence, 34*(1), 66–92. https://doi.org/10.1177/0272431613503215

Campbell, D. T., & Stanley, J. C. (1963). *Experimental and quasi-experimental designs for research.* Chicago, IL: Rand McNally.

Cao, X. J., Xu, Z., & Fan, Y. (2010). Exploring the connections among residential location, self-selection, and driving: Propensity score matching with multiple treatments. *Transportation Research Part A: Policy and Practice, 44*(10), 797–805. https://doi.org/10.1016/j.tra.2010.07.010

Coover, J. E., & Angell, F. (1907). General practice effect of special exercise. *The American Journal of Psychology, 18*(3), 328–340. https://doi.org/10.2307/1412596

Deng, L., & Freeman, L. (2011). Planning for evaluation: Using regression discontinuity to evaluate targeted place-based programs. *Journal of Planning Education and Research, 31*(3), 308–318. https://doi.org/10.1177%2F0739456X11412784

Ewing, R., & Hamidi, S. (2014). Longitudinal analysis of transit's land use multiplier in Portland (OR). *Journal of the American Planning Association, 80*(2), 123–137. https://doi.org/10.1080/01944363.2014.949506

Fisher, R. A. (1925). *Statistical methods for research workers.* Edinburgh: Oliver & Boyd.

Guo, Z., Agrawal, A. W., & Dill, J. (2011). Are land use planning and congestion pricing mutually supportive? Evidence from a pilot mileage fee program in Portland, OR. *Journal of the American Planning Association, 77*(3), 232–250. https://doi.org/10.1080/01944363.2011.592129

Hacking, I. (1983). *Representing and intervening: Introductory topics in the philosophy of natural science.* Cambridge: Cambridge University Press.

Harre, R. (1981). The positivist-empiricist approach and its alternative. *Human Inquiry: A Sourcebook of New Paradigm Research*, 3–17.

Holland, P. W. (1986). Statistics and causal inference. *Journal of the American Statistical Association, 81*(396), 945–960.

Jones, W. T. (1969). *A history of Western philosophy: Vol. 3. Hobbes to Hume* (2nd ed.). New York, NY: Harcourt, Brace and World.

Landis, J. D. (2006). Growth management revisited: Efficacy, price effects, and displacement. *Journal of the American Planning Association, 72*(4), 411–430. https://doi.org/10.1080/01944360608976763

Lewis, R., & Knaap, G. J. (2012). Targeting spending for land conservation: An evaluation of Maryland's rural legacy program. *Journal of the American Planning Association, 78*(1), 34–52.

New York City Department of Transportation. (2010, January). *Green light for midtown evaluation report.* Retrieved from www.nyc.gov/html/dot/downloads/pdf/broadway_report_final2010_web.pdf

Oakes, M. J., & Johnson, P. J. (2006). Propensity score matching for social epidemiology. In M. J. Oakes & J. S. Kaufman (Eds.), *Methods in epidemiology.* New York, NY: John Wiley & Sons.

Olsen, E. O. (2003). Housing programs for low-income households. In R. Moffitt (Ed.), *Means-tested transfer programs in the U.S.* (pp. 365–442). Chicago, IL: University of Chicago Press.

Rosenbaum, P. R., & Rubin, D. B. (1983). The central role of the propensity score in observational studies for causal effects. *Biometrika, 70*(1), 41–55. doi:10.1093/biomet/70.1.41

Rubin, D. B. (1974). Estimating causal effects of treatments in randomized and nonrandomized studies. *Journal of Educational Psychology, 66*(5), 688–701. http://dx.doi.org/10.1037/h0037350

Rubin, D. B. (1977). Assignment to treatment group on the basis of a covariate. *Journal of Educational Statistics, 2*(1), 1–26.

Rubin, D. B. (1978). Bayesian inference for causal effects: The role of randomization. *Annals of Statistics*, 34–58.

Rubin, D. B. (1986). Comment: Which ifs have causal answers. *Journal of the American Statistical Association, 81*(396), 961–962.

Shadish, W. R., Cook, T. D., & Campbell, D. T. (2002). *Experimental and quasi-experimental designs for generalized causal inference.* Boston, MA: Houghton Mifflin.

Stürmer, T., Schneeweiss, S., Avorn, J., & Glynn, R. J. (2005). Adjusting effect estimates for unmeasured confounding with validation data using propensity score calibration. *American Journal of Epidemiology, 162*(3), 279–289. doi:10.1093/aje/kwi192

Sutton, S. A. (2014). Are bids good for business? The impact of bids on neighborhood retailers in New York city. *Journal of Planning Education and Research, 34*(3), 309–324.

Trochim, W. M. K., & Donnelly, J. P. (2008). *The research methods knowledge base* (3rd ed.). Mason, OH: Cengage Learning.

Contributors

Florence Buaku (Chapter 12) is a Ph.D. student in the Department of City and Metropolitan Planning at the University of Utah.

Dong-ah Choi (Chapter 7) is a Ph.D. student in the Department of City and Metropolitan Planning at the University of Utah.

Carl Duke, J.D. (Chapters 6 and 8), is Vice President at Property Reserve Inc.

Reid Ewing, Ph.D. (editor; Chapters 1–3, 5–9, 12, and 14), is Distinguished Professor of City and Metropolitan Planning and Distinguished Chair for Resilient Places at the University of Utah and an associate editor of the *Journal of the American Planning Association.*

James B. Grace, Ph.D. (Chapter 5), is a senior research scientist at the Wetland and Aquatic Research Center of the United States Geological Survey (USGS).

William H. Greene, Ph.D. (Chapters 12 and 13), is Emeritus Professor in the Department of Economics at New York University Stern School of Business.

Amir Hajrasouliha, Ph.D. (Chapter 13), is an assistant professor in the City and Regional Planning Department at California Polytechnic State University, San Luis Obispo.

Shima Hamidi, Ph.D. (Chapter 6), is Bloomberg Assistant Professor of Public Health in the Bloomberg School of Public Health at Johns Hopkins University.

Ja Young Kim (Chapter 11) is a Ph.D. student in the Department of City and Metropolitan Planning at the University of Utah.

Junsik Kim (Chapter 4) is a Ph.D. student in the Department of City and Metropolitan Planning at the University of Utah.

Katherine Kittrell (Chapter 14) is President of Micro Villas and a Ph.D. student in the Department of City and Metropolitan Planning at the University of Utah.

Anusha Musunuru, Ph.D. (Chapter 9), is an engineering associate at Kittelson & Associates, Inc.

Keunhyun Park, Ph.D. (editor; Chapters 1, 4, 5, 7, 8, 12, and 14), is an assistant professor in the Department of Landscape Architecture and Environmental Planning at Utah State University.

320   *Contributors*

Susan Petheram (Chapter 12) is an associate at FFKR Architects and a Ph.D. candidate in the Department of City and Metropolitan Planning at the University of Utah.

David Proffitt (Chapter 10) is a Ph.D. candidate in the Department of City and Metropolitan Planning at the University of Utah.

Robin Rothfeder, Ph.D. (Chapters 2 and 12), is an assistant professor in the Department of Human Dimensions of Natural Resource Management at the University of Wisconsin-Stevens Point and a land use specialist with the University of Wisconsin-Madison Division of Extension.

Sadegh Sabouri (Chapters 4 and 13) is a Ph.D. student in the Department of City and Metropolitan Planning at the University of Utah.

Thomas W. Sanchez, Ph.D. (Chapter 4), is Professor of Urban Affairs and Planning at Virginia Tech.

Fariba Siddiq (Chapter 7) is a Ph.D. student in the Department of Urban Planning at UCLA Luskin School of Public Affairs.

Yu Song (Chapter 13) is a former Ph.D. student in the Department of Civil and Environmental Engineering at the University of Utah.

Philip Stoker (Chapter 11) is an assistant professor of Planning and Landscape Architecture in the College of Architecture, Planning and Landscape Architecture at the University of Arizona.

Pratiti Tagore (Chapter 7) is a Ph.D. candidate in the Department of City and Metropolitan Planning at the University of Utah.

Guang Tian, Ph.D. (Chapters 9 and 11 and contributed to the collection of two datasets used throughout the book), is an assistant professor in the Department of Planning and Urban Studies at the University of New Orleans.

Robert A. Young, Ph.D. (Chapter 3), is Professor Emeritus in the School of Architecture and a former director of the Historic Preservation Program at the University of Utah.

Index

Note: Page numbers in *italics* indicate figures and in **bold** indicate tables on the corresponding pages.

AARP Public Policy Institute 69
Addams, J. 47
Advanced Quantitative Research Methods for Urban Planners 23, 44, 50, 52, 54, 57, 78, 101, 171, 220, 248, 256, 257, 262, 265, 267, 303
aggregate data 5
Agrawal, A. W. 306
alternative hypothesis 8, 175
American Community Survey (ACS) 67, 194–195
American FactFinder 67
American Housing Survey 67
American Planning Association (APA) 19
American Public Transportation Association (APTA) 68
AMOS 57
analysis of contingency tables 134
analysis of variance (ANOVA) 54, 128; history of 198–199; interpreting results of 200; mechanics of *199*, 199–200; overview of 197, *197*; planning examples 210–219, *212–216*, *218*; post-hoc tests 209–210, **211**; purpose of 198; in R 210; in SPSS 200–210, *201–208*, **209**; step by step procedure for 200–210, *201–208*, **209**
arts role in neighborhood change 261–264, *262–264*, **265**
Association of Collegiate Schools of Planning (ACSP) 15
attitudes toward growth management 146–148, **148**
autocorrelation 257–258
average treatment effect (ATE) 310–311, *311*

Bacon, F. 307
bar charts 115, *116*
Behavioral Risk Factor Surveillance System (BRFSS) 69, 107–108
Bem, D. 22, 28
best-fit model 8; equation 225–226

bias and sampling 63
big data 69–71
Bing 93, *93–94*
Bolboacă, S. D. 135
Booth, C. 47
boxplots 201–203, *201–203*
Bracken, I. 4
Brown, B. B. 175
Brownson, R. C. 89
Budinski, K. G. 26
Bureau of Economic Analysis (BEA) 67
Bureau of Labor Statistics (BLS) 67
business improvement districts (BIDs) 315, *316*

case studies 54
categorical data 133, 135–136
categorical variables 6
causal models 82–83
causation 7, 49, 151; linear regression and 266–267
Census Bureau 67, *68*, 71
Center for Disease Control (CDC) 107
central tendency 111–112, 120, *120–121*, **121**
Cervero, R. 32–33, 52, 235
Chapin, T. 146
checking of data 66
Chen, C. 180
Chen, L. 180
Chiesura, A. 127
chi-square 54, 115, 148; assumptions in 135–136, **136**; calculating the test statistic in **137**, 137–138; history of 134–135; hypothesis in 136; mechanics of 135–139, **136–137**, *138*; overview of *133*, 133–134; planning examples 144–148, *145–146*, **147–148**; purpose of 134; step by step procedure for 139–142, *140–143*, **143–144**; strength test for 139; types of data in 135
citations in writing 36
Clark, J. J. 4

322 *Index*

clean data 66
Clemente, O. 89, 92
cluster analysis 54
coefficient of determination 223
Cohen's Kappa 92
computer software *15*, 14–15, **10–11**, **13–15**
conceptual framework 6–7, 86–87;
    limitations of 84; linear regression and
    267; mechanics of 80–85, *81–85*; overview
    of 76–79, *77–78*; purpose of 79–80; step by
    step procedure for 86
conceptual plausibility 100
confounders *77*, *82*, 83
Connerly, C. 146
construct validity 97–98, *98–99*
Consumer Expenditure Survey 67
contingency table 136, **136**, **143**
continuous variables 6
correlation 7, 49, 54, 171; history of 151–152;
    intraclass correlation coefficient (ICC)
    92, 152, 154–156, *155–156*, 162–165, *164*,
    165, 170–171, **170–171**; mechanics of
    152–156, *153*, *155–156*; overview of 150;
    Pearson correlation coefficient 151–152,
    153, 156–158, *157–158*, **159**, **161**; planning
    examples 166–171, **170–171**; purpose of
    150–151; in R 165, *166–169*; Spearman
    correlation coefficient 151, 153–154,
    160–162, *161–162*; in SPSS 156–158,
    157–158, **159**, 162–165, *164*, **165**; step by
    step procedures for 156–165, *157–158*,
    159, *160–162*, **161**, **163**, *164*, **165**
correlation coefficients 92
County Business Patterns 67
Cramer's V 139, 141
Cronbach's alpha 93, 94–95
cross-sectional data 5; repeated 5
cross tabulation 115, 120, 122, *122–123*, **123**,
    129, *140–142*

Daisa, J. 225
data 4–6; aggregate 5; big 69–71; categorical
    133, 135–136; checking of 66; in chi-
    square 135; clean 66; cross-sectional 5;
    demographic 67, *68*; disaggregate 5;
    economic 67; environmental 69; housing
    67; longitudinal 5, 50; machine learning
    and mining of 71–74; nominal 133;
    observable 4; open 71; ordinal 134; panel
    5; primary 4, 62–63; problems in linear
    regression related to 245–251, *246–251*;
    public health 69; qualitative 64; repeated
    cross-sectional 5; sampling and bias in
    63; scale of measurement of 6; secondary
    4, 62–63; sources of 66–69; spatial *65*,
    65–66; structured and unstructured 64–65;
    tabular 63, *64*; time series 5; transportation

68–69; triangulation of 51–52; types of
    47–48, 61–63; visualization of 114–115,
    114–117; *see also* research
data analysis 66; using descriptive statistics
    128
data matrix 114, **114**
data mining 71–74
datasets 9–14, **10–11**, **13–15**
data visualization 114–115, **114–117**
da Vinci, L. 307
Decennial Census 67
deductive logic 48
degrees of freedom 135, 138–139, 199, *199*
demographic data 67, *68*
Deng, L. 312
dependent samples *t*-test 175, 180–181
dependent variables 7, 100, 221
descriptive statistics 7, 54; data analysis
    using 128; data visualization in 114–115,
    114–117; history of 108–109, **109–110**;
    mechanics of 110–114; overview of 107;
    planning examples 125–128, *126–131*,
    130; purpose of 107–108; in R 125, *129*; in
    SPSS 118–124, *118–125*, **119**, **121**, **123**
Dickey, J. W. 2
difference of means *See* t-tests
Dill, J. 306
disaggregate data 5
dispersion 112–114, 120, *120–121*, **121**
distribution free test 135
Donnelly, J. P. 311
Doyle, S. 154
Durbin-Watson statistic 258, *258–259*

economic data 67
editing 35–37
Ellin, N. 22, 31, 32
EnviroAtlas 69
Envirofacts 69
environmental data 69
Environment and Behavior 84
Environment and Planning 39
environment equity 166–170, *169*
equivalency reliability 92–93, *93–94*
ethnographic research *53*, 53–54
Everyscape 93, *93–94*
Ewing, R. 6, 52, 57, 73, 89, 92, 95, 97–98,
    162, 180, 193, 248, 312
Excel 14
Experimental Housing Allowance Program
    306
exploratory data analysis (EDA) 128
external validity 100–101

face validity 95–97, *96*
factor analysis 54
Fang, K. 73

Federal Highway Administration (FHWA) 9, 56–57, 69, 162–165, *164*, **165**
Fisher, R. A. 134–135, 152, 198
Fisher's exact test 135
fitted model 8
Flyvbjerg, B. 20–21, 26, 27–28, 30, 32
focus groups 54
Forrester, J. 32
Foster, N. 261
Frank, L. 278
Freeman, L. 312
frequency distribution 111; chi-square 138, *138*
frequency table 114, **115**, *118–119*, 118–120, **119**
F-statistic 199, *199*, 209, 228–231, *229*, **231**, 233–234, 277–278

Gaber, J. 4
Gaber, S. 4
Galilei, G. 307
Galton, F. 223
Garrick, N. 76–79, *77–78*
Gehl, J. 46
geographic information systems (GIS) 56–57, 67, 71
Gober, P. 125
goodness-of-fit test 134, 228, 277–278
Good Urbanism 22, 31
Google Scholar 14, 38
Google Street View 93, *93–94*
Gosset, W. S. 175
Grace, J. 55, 57
Grace, J. B. 97–98
graphs, informative 115, *116–117*
Graunt, J. 108–109
Greene, B. 55
Greene, W. H. 273
Grodach, C. 261
grounded theory 48, *53*, 53–54
Grove, J. M. 265
growth management, attitudes toward 146–148, **148**
Guhathakurta, S. 125
Guo, Z. 306

Haenszel, W. 135
Hamidi, S. 6, 97–98, 193, 248, 312
Handy, S. 89, 92, 217
Hess, C. 79
heteroscedasticity 258–260, *260–261*
Hibbing, M. V. 84
Highway Statistics 56
histograms 115, *117*, 124, *125*, *129*
Hollander, J. B. 194–195
Household Dataset 12–14, **13–14**, 56; multinomial logistic regression with

282–294, *283–295*; research design and 50–51; step by step procedure for chi-square with 139–142, *140–143*, **143–144**; triangulation of data in 52
housing data 67
Huberman, M. A. 76
human-environment interactions 166–170, *169*
Hussain, M. 210
hypothesis 6; in chi-square test 136; linear regression for testing 222

independence test 134
independent samples *t*-test 175, 176–177, 185, *187–189*
independent variables 7, 100, 221
inductive logic 48
inferential statistics 7–8, **109**
informative graphs 115, *116–117*, 122, 124, *124–125*
internal consistency 93, 95
internal validity 99–100, 308
inter-rater reliability 91–92, 154
interval measurement 6
interviews 54
intraclass correlation coefficient (ICC) 92, 152, 154–156, *155–156*; step by step procedure for 162–165, *164*, **165**; urban design qualities case study 170–171, **170–171**

Jackson, J. B. 46
Jacobs, J. 46, 101
Jäntschi, L. 135
Jepson, E. J., Jr. 144
Jick, T. 55
joint probability of agreement 91–92
Journal of Environmental Management 102
Journal of Planning Education and Research (JPER) 21, 26–27, 39, 55, 73, 144, 270, 312; chi-square in 144; Donald Shoup and 39–40
Journal of Planning Literature 37, 73
Journal of the American Planning Association (JAPA) 20, 23, 73, 76, 85, 101, 103, 312; active voice writing in 28; chi-square in 146; descriptive statistics in 125; Dowell Myers and SungHo Ryu and 40–43, *41–42*; machine learning and data mining and 71; paragraphs in articles in 32; tone and voice in 33; two-group pretest-posttest design in 308
Journal of Urban Economics 55

Kalman, M. 28
Katz, M. J. 35, 37
Kelly-Schwartz, A. C. 154
Knaap, G. 309

324 *Index*

Ko, Y. 37
Koch, G. G. 163
Kuder-Richardson test 94–95

Landis, J. 163, 309–310
Landscape and Urban Planning 127
Lekwa, V. L. 84
Leven's *F*-test 177
Lewis, R. 309
light rail transit expansion 312–315, *314*
linear regression 54; alternatives to
    267–268; causality and 266–267;
    conceptual frameworks and 267; data-
    related problems in 245–251, *246–251*;
    explanation using 221–222; F-statistic 199,
    199, 209, 228–231, *229*, **231**, 233–234;
    history of 223; hypothesis testing using
    222; log-transformation in 251–253,
    252–254; mechanics of 223–235;
    multicollinearity in 254–256, *255–257*;
    multiple *232*, 232–235, **233**, 241–243;
    nonlinearity in 249–251, *249–251*;
    overview of *220*, 220–221; planning
    examples 261–265, *262–264*, **265**, *266*;
    prediction using 222; purpose of 221–223;
    in R 261; residual error-related problems
    in 257–260, *258–261*; R-squared 134, 228,
    234; simple 223–227, *224*, **225–226**, *227*,
    238–241; in SPSS 235–261, *236–261*; step
    by step procedure for 235–261; T-statistic
    228, 229–231, *230*, **231**, 233–234; wise use
    of 222–223
line graphs 115, *117*
literature reviews 37–39
logic, deductive versus inductive 48
logistic regression 54, 300, 303; history of
    272, 272–273; mechanics of 273–278,
    274–275, **276**; multinomial 282–294,
    283–295; overview of *270*, 270–271;
    planning examples 295–300, *296–302*,
    299–300; purpose of *271*, 271–272; in
    R 295; in SPSS 278–294, *279–295*; step by
    step procedure for 278–295, *279–295*
log-transformation 251–253, *252–254*
longitudinal data 5, 50
Longitudinal Employer-Household Dynamics
    (LEHD) 67
Loukaitou-Sideris, A. 85
Lund, H. 52
Lynch, K. 29–30, 31, 32, 46, 101

machine learning (ML) methods 65, 71–74
Mantel, N. 135
mathematical models 7
mediators 83, *83*
meta-analysis 52, 54
meta-regression 52, 54

Miles, M. B. 76
Millard-Ball, A. 55
mixed methods research 46, 54–55, *56*
mobility disability and urban built
    environment 298–300, *301–302*
models 7–8
moderators 83, *83*
Muenchen, R. 14
multicollinearity in linear regression
    254–256, *255–257*
multilevel modeling 54
multinomial logistic regression 282–294,
    283–295
multiple linear regression *232*, 232–235, **233**,
    241–243
Murdoch, J., III 261
Myers, D. 20, 40–43

narrative research *53*, 53–54
National Crime Victimization Survey
    (NCVS) 5
National Health and Nutrition Examination
    Survey (NHANES) 69
National Health Interview Survey (NHIS) 69
National Household Travel Survey 69
National Land Cover Database (NLCD)
    162–163
National TOD database 68
National Transit Database 56
natural experiments 50–51, 306
Németh, J. 101
Newton, R. R. 52
nominal measurement 6; data 133
non-experiments 50–51
nonlinearity in linear regression 249–251,
    249–251
non-technical writing 21–22
null hypothesis 8, 139, 163, 165, 175,
    184–185, 203
null model 8
Nunery, A. 265

observational methods 54
Occam's Razor 8
Oil Price Information Service 57
one-way analysis of variance (ANOVA)
    200–210, *201–208*, **209**
open data 71
ordinal measurement 6; data 134
ordinary least squares (OLS) 223–227,
    224, **225–226**, *227*, 243–245; data-related
    problems in 245–251, *246–251*
organization of writing 33–35, *34*
over-specified model 8

Pamfil, D. C. 135
panel data 5

paragraphs 30–31; cohesion within and between 31–32
Pascal, J. B. 108–109
Patton, C. V. 4
Pearson, K. 134, 151–152, 223
Pearson correlation coefficient 92, 151–152, *153*, **161**; ICC and 154–156, *155–156*; step by step procedure for 156–158, *157–158*, **159**
Pearson Product Moment Correlation (PPMC) 223
Pearson's chi-square test 134–135, 141
Peers, J. 225
Pellegrino, V. C. 19, 30, 31
Petty, W. 108
phenomenology *53*, 53–54
pie charts 115, *116*
planning: conceptual framework of 6–7; importance of data use in 61; *JAPA* and 23; textbooks on qualitative methods in 1–2; use of machine learning in 71–74; writing as essential tool for 18
Planning (magazine) 23–24, 76, 315
Planning Accreditation Board (PAB) 2
Poisson and negative binomial regression 54
polishing of writing 35–37
population 7
post-hoc tests 209–210, **211**
practical significance *179*, 179–180
primary data 4, 62–63
probability 275–276
propensity score matching (PSM) 310–311, *311*
psychological ties to community 85
public health data 69
public scholarship 20–21
public spaces security 101–102, *102*
Public Transportation Ridership Report 5
Python 15

qualitative data 64
qualitative research 1; history of 46–47; methods in *53*, 53–54
quantitative research: history of 46–47; methods in 54; textbooks on 2–4, **3**
quasi-experiments 50–51, 54, 316; history of 307–308; mechanics of 308–312, *311*; overview of 305; planning examples 312–315, *314*, *316*; propensity score matching 310–311, *311*; purpose of 305–307, *307*; regression discontinuity (RD) 311–312, *313*; regression to the mean 310; two-group pretest-posttest design 308–310

R 14, **15**, 15; analysis of variance (ANOVA) in 210; chi-square in 142; correlation

procedure in 165, *166–169*; descriptive statistics in 125, *129*; linear regression in 261; logistic regression in 295; *t*-tests in 189, *191–192*
random assignments 305
randomized experiments 50–51, 306
range 113–114
raster data *65*, 66
rational planning model 61, *62*
regression discontinuity (RD) 311–312, *313*
regression to the mean 310
relational data structures 63, *64*
reliability 89–91, *90*, 103–104; equivalency 92–93, *93–94*; internal consistency and 93, 95; inter-rater 91–92; overview of 88–89, *89*; planning examples 101–103, *102*, *104*
repeated cross-sectional data 5
research: choosing which method to use in 55–57; data types in 47–48; deductive versus inductive logic in 48; design types in 50–51; general concepts in 47–52; history of 46–47; mixed methods (*See* mixed methods research); overview of 46; qualitative (*See* qualitative research); quantitative (*See* quantitative research); timeframe of 48–50, *49*; for writing 23–24, *25*, 26; *see also* data
residential water use 125–126, *126–127*, **130**
residential yard management and crime 265, *266*
residual error-related problems in linear regression 257–260, *258–261*
rewriting 35–37
Rice, T. W. 84
Rinner, C. 210
rival explanations for relationships 100
Ross-Larsen, B. 28–29
R-squared 134, 228, 234, 277–278
Rubin's Causal Model (RCM) 307
Rudestam, K. E. 52
Ryu, S. 20, 40–43

Sadik-Khan, J. 309
sample 7
sampling 63
SAS **15**
saturated model 8
Sawicki, D. S. 4
scales of measurement 6
Schlossberg, M. 154
Schmidt, S. 101
scope of writing 24, 38
secondary data 4, 62–63
sentences 28–30
serial correlation 257
Sestraș, A. F. 135
Sestraș, R. E. 135

326 *Index*

Shadish, W. R. 308
Shoup, D. 39–40
Sideris, A. 85
significance, determining *179*, 179–180
Silva, E. A. 4
simple linear regression 223–227, *224*, **225–226**, *227–228*, 238–241; interpreting results of 227–228; *see also* linear regression
smart growth policies and automobile dependence 295–298, *298*, *299–300*
spatial data *65*, 65–66
spatial econometrics 54
Spearman, C. 151–152
Spearman correlation coefficient 151, 153–154; step by step procedure for 160–162, *161–162*
Spearman's rank correlation 92
split-halves test 94
SPSS 14, **15**, 15; descriptive statistics in 118–124, *118–125*, **119**, **121**, **123**; intraclass correlation coefficient (ICC) in 162–165, *164*, **165**; linear regression in 235–261, *236–261*; logistic regression in 278–294, *279–295*; one-way analysis of variance (ANOVA) in 200–210, *201–208*, **209**; Pearson correlation coefficient in 156–158, *157–158*, **159**; *t*-tests in 181–189, *182–189*, **189–190**
standard deviation 113
standard error 177–178, *178*
Stata **15**
statistical significance *179*, 179–180
statistics 7–8
Stockard, J. 154
Stone, B. 102–103, *104*
storytelling 21–22; narrative research *53*, 53–54
strength test for chi-square 139
structural equation modeling (SEM) 54, 57
structured data 64–65
Strunk, W. 28
sum of squared errors (SSE) 225
supervised learning 72
survey research 54
sustainable development policies 144–146, *145–146*, **147**

tabular data 63, *64*
technical writing 19–20; versus non-technical writing 21–22
Texas Transportation Institute 98
theoretical explanation *53*, 53–54
theory 6
timeframe, research 48–50, *49*
time sequence 100
time series data 5
tone and voice in writing 32–33, 37

Tooke, T. R. 166
TransitFeeds 68
transportation data 68–69
triangulation 51–52
Trochim, W. M. K. 311
Troy, A. 265
T-statistic 228, 229–231, *230*, **231**, 233–234
t-tests 54, 195; dependent samples 175, 180–181; determining significance with *179*, 179–180; history of 175; independent samples 175, 176–177, 185, *187–189*; mechanics of 175–181, *176*, *178–179*; overview of *174*, 174–175; planning examples 193–195, **194**; purpose of 175; standard error and 177–178, *178*; step by step procedure for 181–189, *182–192*, **189–190**
two-group pretest-posttest design 308–310
Type I error 198

under-specified model 8
unit of analysis 5
unit of observation 5
unstructured data 64–65
unsupervised learning 72
urban design qualities 170–171, **170–171**
urban form and travel behavior 217–219, *218*
urban heat islands (UHI) effect 210–214, *212–216*
urban parks 127–128, *128*, *130–131*
urban sprawl and air quality 102–103, *104*
U.S. Economic Census 67
U.S. Environmental Protection Agency (EPA) 69
U.S. Geological Survey 162–163
UZA (Urbanized Area) dataset 9, **10–11**, **13–14**, 48, 56; linear regression using 235; one-way ANOVA test using 200–210, *201–208*, **209**; triangulation of data in 52

validity 103–104; construct 97–98, *98–99*; defined 95; external 100–101; face 95–97, *96*; internal 99–100, 308; overview of 88–89, *89*; planning examples 101–103, *102*, *104*
variables 6; causal 82–83; dependent 7, 100, 221; independent 7, 100, 221; in linear regression (*See* linear regression)
vector data 65, *65*
visualization, data 114–115, **114–117**
VMT (Vehicle Miles Traveled) dataset 6, 9–12, 48, 56–57; correlation and causation in 49–50, 151, 156–158, *157–158*, **159**, 165; independent samples *t*-test 181–189, *182–192*, **189–190**; linear regression using 235–261, *236–261*; logistic regression using 272–273; quasi-experiments 314–315; triangulation of data in 52; *t*-tests on 193–195, **194**

Wald statistic 282
WalkScore 69
Wasatch Front Regional Council (WFRC) 5
Watts, T. M. 2
Weber, M. 47
Wei, Y. D. 97–98
weighted least squares regression (WLS) 260
Werner, C. M. 175
White, E. B. 28
Whyte, W. H. 18, 46, 101
Willemain, T. R. 2
Winston, E. 89
words used in writing 27–28
writing: accuracy of 38; analysis of 38;
    connection to planning 38–39; examples
    of planning 39–43; literature reviews and
    37–39; mechanics of 27–35; organization
of 33–35, *34*; overview of 18–19;
paragraphs in 30–32; preliminaries in
24–27; public scholarship 20–21; purpose
and types of 19–24; research for 23–24,
25, *26*; rewriting, editing, and polishing
in 35–37; scope of 24, 38; sentences
in 28–30; style of 37–38; systematic
instruction and practice in 43; technical
19–20; technical versus non-technical
21–22; tone and voice in 32–33, 37; words
used in 27–28
Wundt, W. 47

Yates, F. 135
Yates' correction for continuity 135

Zinsser, W. 28, 32, 33, 35, 43

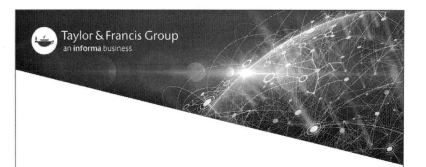